Green Finance, Sustainable Development and the Belt and Road Initiative

Can China's Belt and Road Initiative (BRI) promote sustainable development, alongside its primary aims of increasing commercial connectivity with China's partners?

In discussions of the BRI the focus has tended to be on the implications for infrastructure construction, connectivity, and economic diplomacy. Rather less attention has been paid to its potential impact on sustainability. The initiative has not only set principles to prevent climate change and promote sustainable development, but also pledged to align with the UN's environmental objectives. The contributors to this volume describe and evaluate the consequent policy coordination in the areas of green finance, green energy, and sustainable development in the Belt and Road regions. They examine both the challenges and opportunities of these projects, and the role that Hong Kong can play in supporting their assessment, finance, and implementation. With contributions from authors based in mainland China, Hong Kong, Australia, Qatar, the UK, and the US – with experience in corporate social responsibility, international finance, environmental policy, and international relations – this book presents a thorough and rigorous analysis of the green side of the BRI.

This is a valuable resource for scholars of the BRI and its many implications for China, its partners, and the development of sustainable infrastructure.

Fanny M. Cheung is former Pro-Vice-Chancellor and Choh-Ming Li Professor of Psychology at the Chinese University of Hong Kong. She is currently Senior Advisor of Hong Kong Institute of Asia-Pacific Studies and Co-Convenor of the Global China Research Programme at the Chinese University of Hong Kong.

Ying-yi Hong is the Choh-Ming Li Professor of Management at the Faculty of Business, Associate Director of Hong Kong Institute of Asia-Pacific Studies and Co-Convenor of the Global China Research Programme at the Chinese University of Hong Kong.

Routledge Studies on Asia in the World

Routledge Studies on Asia in the World will be an authoritative source of knowledge on Asia studying a variety of cultural, economic, environmental, legal, political, religious, security and social questions, addressed from an Asian perspective. We aim to foster a deeper understanding of the domestic and regional complexities which accompany the dynamic shifts in the global economic, political and security landscape towards Asia and their repercussions for the world at large. We're looking for scholars and practitioners – Asian and Western alike – from various social science disciplines and fields to engage in testing existing models which explain such dramatic transformation and to formulate new theories that can accommodate the specific political, cultural and developmental context of Asia's diverse societies. We welcome both monographs and collective volumes which explore the new roles, rights and responsibilities of Asian nations in shaping today's interconnected and globalized world in their own right.

The Series is advised and edited by Matthias Vanhullebusch and Ji Weidong of Shanghai Jiao Tong University.

Interpreting the Chinese Diaspora
Identity, Socialisation, and Resilience According to Pierre Bourdieu
Guanglun Michael Mu and Bonnie Pang

Chinese Peace in Africa
From Peacekeeper to Peacemaker
Steven C.Y. Kuo

The Quest for Legitimacy in Chinese Politics
A New Interpretation
Lanxin Xiang

Indian Migrants in Tokyo
A Study of Socio-Cultural, Religious and Working Worlds
Megha Wadhwa

Green Finance, Sustainable Development and the Belt and Road Initiative
Edited by Fanny M. Cheung and Ying-yi Hong

Find the full list of books in the series here: https://www.routledge.com/Routledge-Studies-on-Asia-in-the-World/book-series/RSOAW

Green Finance, Sustainable Development and the Belt and Road Initiative

Edited by
Fanny M. Cheung and Ying-yi Hong

Routledge
Taylor & Francis Group

LONDON AND NEW YORK

First published in English 2021
by Routledge
2 Park Square, Milton Park, Abingdon, Oxon OX14 4RN

and by Routledge
52 Vanderbilt Avenue, New York, NY 10017

Routledge is an imprint of the Taylor & Francis Group, an informa business

© 2021 selection and editorial matter, Fanny M. Cheung and Ying-yi Hong;
individual chapters, the contributors

The right of Fanny M. Cheung and Ying-yi Hong to be identified as the authors
of the editorial material, and of the authors for their individual chapters,
has been asserted in accordance with sections 77 and 78 of the Copyright,
Designs and Patents Act 1988.

British Library Cataloguing-in-Publication Data
A catalogue record for this book is available from the British Library

Library of Congress Cataloging-in-Publication Data
A catalog record has been requested for this book

ISBN: 978-0-367-89880-9 (hbk)
ISBN: 978-1-003-02166-7 (ebk)

Typeset in Galliard
by Newgen Publishing UK

Contents

Figures

Tables

Contributors

David C. Broadstock Assistant Professor of Economics, School of Accounting and Finance, Hong Kong Polytechnic University.

Jianghui Chen Macro Analyst, Guangfa Securities, China.

Louis T.W. Cheng Professor of Finance, School of Accounting and Finance, Hong Kong Polytechnic University.

Gordon C.K. Cheung Associate Professor in the International Relations of China, School of Government & International Affairs, Durham University, UK.

Kathinka Furst Associate Director, Environmental Research Center, Duke Kunshan University, China.

Hua Guo Research Associate, Hong Kong Institute of Asia-Pacific Studies, The Chinese University of Hong Kong.

Guoping Hu Research Fellow, Department of Chemical Engineering, the University of Melbourne, Australia.

Kai Jiang PhD candidate, School of Chemical Engineering, the University of Queensland, Australia.

Johnson C. S. Kong Assistant Researcher, Our Hong Kong Foundation.

Natalie H. T. Lau Assistant Researcher, Our Hong Kong Foundation.

Cheung-kwok Law Honorary Senior Research Fellow, Hong Kong Institute of Asia-Pacific Studies, The Chinese University of Hong Kong.

Kevin Gang Li Senior Lecturer, Department of Chemical Engineering, the University of Melbourne, Australia.

Pansy Hon Ying Li Teaching Fellow, Department of Management and Marketing, The Hong Kong Polytechnic University.

Ning Liu Assistant Professor, Department of Public Policy, The City University of Hong Kong.

Carlos Wing-Hung Lo Head and Professor, Department of Government and Public Administration, The Chinese University of Hong Kong.

Gloria W. T. Luo Assistant Researcher, Our Hong Kong Foundation.

Minggao Shen Chief Economist, Guangfa Securities, China.

Rui Wang Director Assistant of EOR Division, SINOPEC E&P Research Institute, China.

Tiantian Wang Doctoral candidate, Research Institute of Economics and Management, Southwestern University of Finance and Economics.

Wen Wang Executive Dean of Chongyang Institute for Financial Studies, Vice President of Silk Road School, Renmin University of China.

Stephen Y. S. Wong Deputy Executive Director and Head of Public Policy Institute, Our Hong Kong Foundation.

Steven Wright Associate Professor of International Relations; Associate Dean for Academic Affairs and Research, College of Humanities and Social Sciences, Hamad bin Khalifa University, Qatar.

Fanxin Yang Research Fellow, Chongyang Institute for Financial Studies, Rnemin University of China.

Victor Zheng Associate Director (Executive), Hong Kong Institute of Asia-Pacific Studies and Co-Convenor of the Global China Research Programme at the Chinese University of Hong Kong.

Introduction

The Belt and Road Initiative and sustainability

The Belt and Road Initiative (BRI) was announced by Chinese president Xi Jinping in 2013. Following President Xi's proposal, in 2015 Beijing introduced an action plan for the BRI, *Vision and Actions on Jointly Building Silk Road Economic Belt and 21st-Century Maritime Silk Road*. The main purpose of this initiative is to promote regional connectivity, economic cooperation, cultural exchanges, and mutual learning of China with economies along the Silk Road Economic Belt and the 21st-Century Maritime Silk Road. The initiative aims to establish a number of multilateral mechanisms and multilevel platforms to promote facilities connectivity, unimpeded trade, financial integration, people-to-people bonds, and policy coordination. As a financial foundation, in 2014 Beijing established the Silk Road Fund to foster investment in Belt and Road (B&R) partner economies. The initiative also established the Asian Infrastructure Investment Bank (AIIB) in 2016. As a multilateral policy bank, AIIB has quickly attracted the attention of economies within and outside the initiative. As of 2019, AIIB had approved members of 100 countries or economies (AIIB 2019). Other multilateral platforms for cooperation of educational institutes, NGOs, and businesses have sprouted quickly under the initiative. Beijing also organized the Belt and Road Forum for International Cooperation in 2017 and 2019. By the end of August 2019, China had signed cooperation agreements with 136 economies and 30 international organizations (Belt and Road Portal 2019).

Construction of infrastructure for connectivity in B&R economies is a fundamental goal of the BRI. Environmental degradation and climate change have become a major concern throughout the world. Whether the BRI can be carried out in an environmentally friendly and sustainable way has attracted considerable international attention. In response to this attention, Beijing announced a few official documents and declarations. In 2017, it released the *Guiding Opinions on Promoting the Green Construction of the 'Belt and Road Initiative'* and introduced the concept of 'Green Belt and Road'. As the largest greenhouse gas emitter, China ratified the Paris Agreement in 2016 and pledged to reduce carbon emissions to curb climate change. In addition, the second Belt and Road Forum in 2019 announced *Green Investment Principles for BRI*. China's emphasis on sustainability for the BRI is unprecedented in the narratives of Beijing on development. This indicates a change of circumstance and of understanding of the relationship between sustainability and development. These changes are deeply rooted in the circumstances of China's economic development and reflect the international strategies China has been taking.

Sustainability and economic development in China

China surpassed Japan as the second largest economy by GDP in 2010. Since then, although China can still enjoy an annual growth rate of GDP of 6–7%, the growth rate has been in decline. Seemingly in consideration of the weakening economic dynamism in China and global challenges like international politics and regional integration, Beijing announced the grand initiative of the BRI. Admittedly, although the Chinese economy is still one of the fastest growing, China cannot sustain the former rough model of development it once had. The decline from an almost double-digit growth rate since 2010 is a watershed for China's economy. Since then, the drive from high consumption to high production cannot be sustained. From the opening up of the economy until 2010, China's increasing industrial production has been at the expense of the environment. In 2017, China was the largest emitter of greenhouse gases and was responsible for 27% of global emissions (Friedrich et al. 2017). The emission of sulphur dioxide, nitrogen oxides, and particulates has long been at a high level and has made China one of the most polluted regions in the world (Yang et al. 2018).

Choking smog and terrible air pollution in Beijing and other major metropolises is an alarm signal to the public and the government about the severe cost that China has had to pay for its model of development. Sustainability has become a priority that the Chinese government has highlighted in relation to its national development as well as in its political legitimacy. The Chinese government has been making unprecedented efforts to promote green, circular, and low-carbon development in the systematic, comprehensive, and coordinated reform of China's institutions. China is now a pioneer of investment in renewable energy including wind, solar, and hydro power. It is the largest manufacturer of and market for electric vehicles (Lee 2018). For the first time, the concept of an eco-civilization was written into the ruling party's constitution at the 18th National Congress of the Communist Party of China and has been included in China's national security outlook.

Environmental protection is no longer deemed a sacrifice for economic growth but on the contrary is seen as a fortune to invigorate the economy. As a famous quote by President Xi Jinping goes, 'lucid waters and lush mountains are invaluable assets'. Subnational governments have been taking measures to integrate sustainability into their targets of economic growth (Linster and Yang 2018). Beijing has not only tightened the enforcement of environmental laws but has also taken measures to solve some environmental problems through various means. For example, China has been replacing coal with natural gas for the supply of winter heating in northern China. According to various studies, the air quality of Beijing and some major metropolises has gradually improved (Bloomberg News 2018). Satellite images also show a greener China than that of 20 years ago (Nace 2019). Although environmental problems are still devastating in China, the governments from top to bottom have been moving away from their former attitude of ignorance or avoidance to taking more proactive measures.

The country with its fast-growing middle-class population has to take every means to address environmental issues quickly. This change of attitude to environmental issues will improve the governance of the China in every level. Moreover, a reversion to stressing sustainability is an opportunity for the country to upgrade from processing industries of severe pollution and high energy consumption to innovative industries of low carbon emissions and high added value. This change can help China broaden its horizons for future development. In other words, sustainability has become internally driven in China. Beijing is no longer treating environmental sustainability in a reactive manner but is proactively making it an opportunity to change from the past rough model of development.

Sustainable development as an international strategy

Faced with unprecedented climate change, increasing global consensus on sustainable development has produced urgent requirements for countries to regulate emissions of greenhouse gases. This also threatens the economic interest of developing countries at the early stage of their industrialization. For developed countries, however, it is an opportunity to transfer clean technologies and to acquire soft power, especially through advocating international agreements on global climate change. In global cooperation, Beijing has vowed to provide solutions to global ecological security. Beijing ratified the Paris Agreement in 2016 and promised to reduce China's emission of greenhouse gases. According to one study (Korsbakken et al. 2019), China has been adhering to the agreement and is reducing its carbon emissions. This is in contrast to the attitude of the US, which refused to sign the Kyoto Accord and withdrew from the Paris Agreement. This contrast creates benefits for China's soft power. Sustainability has created an opportunity for China to raise its international profile and to solve its problems in development, rendering China a world leader in battling global climate change (Zheng and Hollingsworth 2017).

As the flagship of China's international ambition, the BRI is indicative of Beijing's intention to leverage its economic power through lending and participating in infrastructure construction along the Silk Road Economic Belt and the 21st-Century Maritime Silk Road. As mentioned, the BRI has been largely associated with the construction of infrastructure and the exchange of resources with collaboration between China and the B&R economies (extended to economies as they have agreed to join). However, limited attention has been given to sustainability and the initiative. The BRI not only sets principles for addressing climate change and promoting sustainable development but also pledges to align the initiative with the environmental objectives of the United Nations. Principles for an ecological civilization were laid out in the *Guidance on Promoting Green Belt and Road*, published in April 2017. The second B&R forum also announced *Green Investment Guidelines*. Beijing pledges to make the green concept the priority of the BRI, take the leading role in green development, ensure observation of laws and regulations and develop holistic integration and orderly advancement.

Unlike traditional models of international aid, the BRI is a market-oriented and market-driven means of international collaboration. Economies joining the initiative can use credit from China to construct their necessary infrastructure and repay the credit through revenues generated from increased productivity. China can transfer its overcapacity of manufacturing and services to participating economies. If properly implemented, these projects could be beneficial to both parties. However, the BRI has been involved in various controversies, calling it as economic colonialization, debt diplomacy, and poor quality of white elephant projects (Balding 2018). These controversies could be associated with competition for regional influence and geopolitics. However, some issues have not been properly addressed in the implementation of the BRI.

One of the major issues is environmental damage due to BRI projects. For example, in 2017, the World Wildlife Federation claimed two motorway projects in Myanmar would have damaging effects on the local population (Zuo 2019). The construction of the Myitsone Dam in Myanmar was also suspended due to environmental concerns. These incidents are wake-up calls for China to ensure higher standards of environmental protection and better risk management when implementing the BRI. However, some environmental controversies raised by the media are more fuelled by distrust of the BRI rather than by solid facts and rigorous analysis of specific projects. For example, during the second Belt and Road forum in 2019, a few media outlets indicated China's funding of a large number of coal-fired power projects in some B&R partner economies like Indonesia, Kenya, and Pakistan. These projects were claimed to export China's carbon emission and surplus labour rather than to encourage the use of renewable energy to curb climate change (Jong 2019; Ullman 2019; Watts 2019; Yu and Shearer 2019). But studies on energy projects under the BRI have revealed a large number of renewable energy projects in B&R economies by both the state and private investors (Chen 2019).

A fairer view of these coal projects should see solutions from the technological advancement and collaborative nature of the projects under the BRI framework. Technically, coal-fired power projects could be very efficient if they implement ultra-supercritical technology and measures of emission control in which China has leading expertise (Myllyvirta 2017; Tang et al. 2019). A coal project in Lamu, Kenya, financed by China, is an example of using ultra-supercritical technology components and air quality control systems (Ullman 2019). Advancement of technology can also offer solutions to capture and store CO_2 to alleviate the impact of coal projects on climate (see the detailed introduction in Chapter 7). In addition, infrastructure investment has to consider endowment of the economy, costs, and benefits of projects, and demand of the economies prior to planning and design. The BRI framework intends to form a multilateral and multilevel platform for policy collaboration. When many developing economies of the BRI have abundant coal reserves, it is not reasonable to abandon their accessible endowment and ignore their current level of development for options whose stability is still being tested and whose cost is out of sight (Feng 2017). The arguments related to the coal projects suggest that a discussion on the environmental sustainability of the BRI has to have more first-hand observation and rigorous analysis, which is also the purpose of the book.

Nonetheless, the BRI has to ensure compliance with the *Green Investment Principles* (GIPs) with professional management to meet high international requirements for environmental protection. Some reviews suggested that Chinese banks follow international codes of best practice for environmental and social (E&S) issues for offshore projects, such as the Equator Principles for green finance. According to a report by PwC (2013), Chinese banks, while having to follow the *Green Credit Guidelines* by the China Banking Regulatory Commission, still lag behind international banks in board leadership, dedicated resources, risk policies on credit screening, training, independent due diligence process, and disclosure on E&S issues. As of October 2019, only three Chinese banks have signed up for the Equator Principles – they are all joint-stock commercial banks. No large state-owned banks and policy banks have signed up for these principles. Given the large number of infrastructure projects financed under the BRI, compliance of Chinese banks with the international code of best practice is essential. However, this issue cannot be reduced to a signature on an environmental initiative. According to past studies on the Equator Principles (Wörsdörfer 2013; UNEP 2016), this voluntary and self-regulatory E&S standard for green banking has many flaws: limited to a small part of banking business; lack of transparency, accountability, and liability; and inadequate monitoring and enforcement of dirty projects. The publicity of ABN-AMRO Bank's large investment in CO_2 emission projects was an alarming case of how a gold standard and international code of best practice could race to the bottom when good governance was absent. A focus on governance of green finance should be the priority instead. The GIPs brought up in the second B&R forum could be seen as an attempt by China to set international standards and a code of best practice on green finance. If well directed, investment under the BRI could bring more opportunities for green finance. The international community should welcome and encourage China's initiative on environmental sustainability. What is more important is to encourage China to guarantee compliance with these principles through good governance and policy coordination of the BRI.

The BRI may also increase public understanding through inclusion of the private sector in the investment and construction of infrastructure projects. China has been actively promoting public–private partnerships (PPP) in financing BRI projects since 2017 (Xinhua 2017). This measure can alleviate the budget burden of the governments involved and motivate participation of the private sector to finance suitable infrastructure projects (Sugden 2017; PBOC and the City of London 2018; Deloitte 2018). Some projects have been implemented in this arrangement (HKTDC 2019). Similar to the issue of green finance, it is still more important to make PPP project compliance with the international code of best practice a priority under the BRI. For example, the World Bank, the European Bank for Reconstruction and Development, the Asian Development Bank, and the International Federation of Consulting Engineers all have mature toolboxes to facilitate offshore PPP projects. They could be good starting points for projects financed under the BRI (Russel and Berger 2019). In addition, involvement of NGOs to monitor compliance with the principles of green finance and sustainability is becoming more and more important in the management of offshore projects. The BRI can offer unprecedented opportunities to promote Chinese NGOs in expanding and outreach to B&R economies. In the section on PPP, this edited volume has a dedicated chapter (Chapter 9) discussing Chinese NGOs and the BRI.

Hong Kong, as the most open portal to the mainland, has various advantages in professional services for the national agenda on sustainable development and international cooperation in the BRI. The Chief Executive of Hong Kong, Mrs. Carrie Lam, in her remarks at the Belt and Road Summit in September 2017 in Hong Kong, announced that Hong Kong's aim is 'to foster green finance, establishing a green bond market, formulating green credit guidelines, setting standards and assessments for green financing' (Lam 2017). On the one hand, Hong Kong raised US$1 billion in the oversubscribed first green bond in 2019 (Fioretti 2019). In addition to the ability to promote green finance, Hong Kong has world-class institutions of tertiary education and renowned research facilities and talents. This will make Hong Kong an ideal place to promote green BRI. But on the other hand, although Hong Kong has a longer history of culture exchange with developed economies in North America and Western Europe than mainland China, the experience of Hong Kong in B&R economies is very limited. Most of the B&R countries are emerging economies with institutions and cultures very different from those of western economies. Hong Kong may have to increase its know-how and skill set through dedicated training and research. Though backed by mainland China to participate in the BRI, Hong Kong's different political and economic institutions may need to adapt to the specialty of BRI. For example, the 'small government' of Hong Kong has limited influence on the overwhelming private sector. Moreover, the private sector in Hong Kong is not used to investmenting in long-term offshore projects with low short-term return. Hong Kong could either elevate its capacity in services or create more opportunities for PPP projects under the BRI. For example, Hong Kong is striving to build an international centre for dispute resolution. The strength of Hong Kong in professional services related to E&S could accommodate the demand that may increase with more investment under the BRI. The green bond successfully issued could also be seen as an attempt by the Hong Kong government to engage more in directing the economy to sustainability. Notwithstanding, Hong Kong still has to make efforts to keep social stability and to find effective means to curb social unrest which could be a strike against the confidence of Beijing or international investors. This edited book has an in-depth analysis of the role of Hong Kong in greening the BRI.

Main content of the book

Although several years have passed since the launching of the BRI, little is known about the goal of sustainability being achieved in its implementation. The main aim of this edited volume is to examine and evaluate the extent to which sustainable development has been accomplished. This book is a combination of current in-depth observations and analyses of the topic of environmental sustainability of the BRI in relation to Hong Kong, China, and selected B&R economies. Some specialized reports have been published to conceptualize green finance (ADB 2017), introduce the BRI and sustainability in general (OECD 2018), map the BRI's potential impact on sustainability (Hong and Johnson 2018), and set guidelines for green financing of the BRI (PBOC and City of London 2018). Unlike these specialized reports about specific issues on green finance, sustainability, or the BRI, this edited book intends to enrich existing discussions through frontline academic research and first-hand observations in B&R partner economies. This volume on greening the BRI was contributed to by experts in several related fields. Some are researchers from thinktanks specialized in the BRI and regional studies; some are renowned researchers on finance, renminbi (RMB), and China's economy; some are specialized in green technologies, energy, and manufacturing; and some have made first-hand observations of the working of the BRI. The book can be a solid foundation of knowledge for academia, policymakers, experts of regional studies, investors, business analysts, researchers, and students in this growing area of the B&R economy and development. In particular, the material covered in the book could be handy for practitioners. Environmental requirements and responsibilities used to be seen as burdens to business, but they could become new opportunities when the old exploitative model of development is losing support. A new horizon has been set when green technologies create more business opportunities. The section on green development and PPP includes studies on business opportunities and entrepreneurship.

As stated, the main aim of this book is to examine and evaluate the extent to which sustainable development is accomplished. It could be seen as a trailblazer in this field of study on the BRI. Specifically, discussions are to understand the environmental potentials of economic and financial cooperation in the B&R economies; to study the opportunities and challenges in connection with sustainable projects in the B&R economies; and to reveal the capacity of Hong Kong to help competitive firms to assess, finance, and implement green projects to international standards. More importantly, the book not only brings sustainability to the forefront of discussions on the BRI but also looks into measures that Beijing has been taking to leverage sustainability for internal political legitimacy and international ambition. They are not limited to governance, finance, technology and international relations.

The first section of the book looks into the BRI and national competitiveness. Starting from a retrospective evaluation of what the BRI has accomplished in the first five-year period (2013–18), the first chapter looks into the change of competitiveness in B&R economies. Using the Global Competitiveness Index (GCI), the chapter compares B&R and non-B&R economies in different sub-indices that reflect the various aspects of development. The chapter suggests that the BRI can bring business and investment opportunities in a highly turbulent and fragile global economic environment.

Moving on from a review of the BRI's impact on competitiveness of participating economies, Section 2 of the book focuses on RMB internationalization and green finance. One of the opportunities can be green foreign direct investment (FDI) from China to B&R economies. Chapter 2 sees green finance as a new model of growth for Chinese corporates to transform, upgrade, and restructure. The authors chart the green process of China's FDI and propose possible policy assistance that the Chinese government could use to support green investment under the framework of the BRI.

Coupled with China's green FDI, increased use of RMB in B&R economies can be seen as a way to hedge the risks of depending on a single currency in international trade not only for China but also for B&R economies. China has experimented with yuan-denominated oil future contracts. As the author of Chapter 3 suggests, the use of the petro-yuan could promote other commodities to trade in RMB, especially in neighbouring countries in the Asia-Pacific region. The author acknowledges that there is a long way to go for RMB internationalization but it is a necessary attempt to achieve a better international financial order of stability. Chapter 4 looks into RMB internationalization from a more internal perspective of sustainable development. The authors discuss rising consumerism in China and the possible contribution of consumption to upgrade China's manufacturing sector. The authors believe the internationalization of RMB could not only save China from falling into the middle-income trap but also ease the current trade tensions between China and the US.

In addition to a perspective on monetary policies, the financial market could provide investment vehicles for certified green projects of the BRI. The green bond is a solution to problems of financing sustainable projects. The authors of Chapter 5 argue that friction in market efficiency and obstacles to evaluate performance in environment, social, and governance investment have to be addressed before a sophisticated green bond market can be formed.

As well as discussion of financial vehicles for sustainability in the BRI, Section 3 looks into innovations of clean energy, technology, and manufacturing for sustainability of the BRI. Chapter 6 sees liquefied natural gas (LNG) from Qatar as an answer to China's environmental sustainability and a solution to its high carbon emissions. The global energy geopolitics and regional insecurity in the Gulf region has increased Qatar's involvement with China and active interest in joining the BRI. In other words, the BRI can be seen as an alternative for Gulf countries to stabilize their economic future when the petro-dollar is in decline. Though China could reduce pollution through adopting clean energy, the issue of carbon emissions must be urgently addressed in the face of rapid climate change.

As the largest carbon emitter, China may use innovative means to capture and store carbon, as suggested in Chapter 7. The authors, from a perspective of engineering, introduce the mechanism and future prospects of the breakthroughs to trap CO_2 and reveal implications to a whole value chain for carbon capture and storage. Chapter 8 assesses the way Hong Kong manufacturers could green their operations in their traditional stronghold of the Pearl River Delta and seek the green opportunities brought by the BRI. Based on data collected from surveys of Hong Kong manufacturers in Guangdong, the authors found changes in corporate environmental management under growing pollution regulatory pressure. They urge Hong Kong manufacturers to realign corporate strategies and operations when managing the environmental footprint in industrial investment in B&R economies.

A green BRI calls for involvement of different stakeholders to join the construction. Section 4 looks into ways public and private sectors could be complementary partners in the implementation of the BRI. Chapters 9, 10, 11 see the BRI from the perspectives of NGOs and corporates. NGOs have been growing rapidly in China and have started to 'go global', especially on E&S issues. The author of Chapter 9 looks into the efforts of Chinese environmental NGOs on green BRI. The author found four trajectories of Chinese environmental NGOs' global engagement and cites cases to illustrate the major factors enabling or impeding Chinese environmental NGOs in their global engagement. Chapter 10 goes a step further, to see sustainability through entrepreneurship. The grand objectives of the BRI and the implementation of the BRI, as suggested by the author, cannot be achieved without the participation and contribution of entrepreneurship. A successful partnership between the public and private sector cannot exist without a code of best practice. An integrated green standard for infrastructure projects could serve the demand in the partnership. The final chapter (Chapter 11) focuses on the making of green standards for implementation of infrastructure projects in BRI. It not only gives an overview of the key existing standards, but also proposes an integrated approach to the making of them. Moreover, the special role that Hong Kong can contribute to the green standards is highlighted in the chapter.

In conclusion, this book aims to give a first-hand description, in-depth examination, and rigorous evaluation of policy coordination in green finance, green energy, and green development in B&R economies. The role Hong Kong could play in greening the initiative is specially underlined. Notwithstanding its strength, this edited book may not be able to offer a comprehensive view on the topic of sustainability and the BRI, because the study of the BRI is still at the beginning stages of research. But this selection could set a horizon for future studies on greening the BRI. It could serve as a stepping stone for further studies on green finance, green energy, and green development under the framework of the BRI. Moreover, at a time when globalization and sustainability are facing severe challenges and increasing doubt, a book dedicated to sustainability and the BRI may lend support to those who still believe in a better world.

References

ADB (Asian Development Bank) 2017, 'Catalyzing green finance: a concept for leveraging blended finance for green development'. Asian Development Bank. Available from: www.adb.org/sites/default/files/publication/357156/catalyzing-green-finance.pdf [23 October 2019].

AIIB (Asian Infrastructure Investment Bank) 2019, 'Members and prospective members of the bank'. Asian Infrastructure Investment Bank. Available from: www.aiib.org/en/about-aiib/governance/members-of-bank/index.html. [23 October 2019]

Albert, E & Xu, B 2016, 'China's environmental crisis', *Council on Foreign Relations*, 18 January. Available from: www.cfr.org/backgrounder/chinas-environmental-crisis [15 July 2019].

Balding, C 2018, 'Why democracies are turning against Belt and Road', *Foreign Affairs*, 24 October. Available from: www.foreignaffairs.com/articles/china/2018-10-24/why-democracies-are-turning-against-belt-and-road [15 July 2019].

Belt and Road Portal 2019, 'A list of countries that had signed BRI cooperation agreements with the Chinese government'. Available from: www.yidaiyilu.gov.cn/gbjg/gbgk/77073.htm (in Chinese) [23 October 2019].

Bloomberg News 2018, '"Airpocalypse" over? Beijing breathes easier as clean air drive pays off, US embassy smog readings suggest', *South China Morning Post*, 20 August. Available from: www.scmp.com/news/china/policies-politics/article/2160444/beijings-clean-air-drive-paying-swift-recovery [15 July 2019].

Chen, H 2019, 'Greener power projects for the Belt & Road Initiative (BRI)', *NRDC*, 22 April. Available from: www.nrdc.org/experts/han-chen/greener-power-projects-belt-road-initiative-bri [28 October 2019].

Deloitte 2018, 'Embracing the BRI ecosystem in 2018: navigating pitfalls and seizing opportunities', *Deloitte*. Available from: www2.deloitte.com/us/en/ insights/economy/asia-pacific/china-belt-and-road-initiative.html [23 October 2019].

Economy, E C 2007, 'The Great Leap backward? The costs of China's environmental crisis', *Foreign Affairs*, vol. 86, no. 5, pp. 38–59.

Feng, H 2017, China's Belt and Road Initiative still pushing coal', *China Dialogue*, 12 May. Available from: www.chinadialogue.net/article/show/single/en/9785-China-s-Belt-and-Road-Initiative-still-pushing-coal [28 October 2019].

Fioretti, J 2019, 'Hong Kong raises $1 billion in oversubscribed first green bond', *Reuters*, 21 May. Available from: www.reuters.com/article/us-hongkong-green-bond/hong-kong-looks-to-raise-up-to-1-billion-in-green-bonds-idUSKCN1SR0AS [15 July 2019].

Friedrich, J, Ge, M & Pickens, A 2017, 'This interactive chart explains world's top 10 emitters, and how they've changed', *World Resources Institute*, 11 April. Available from: www.wri.org/blog/2017/04/interactive-chart-explains-worlds-top-10-emitters-and-how-theyve-changed [15 July 2019].

HKTDC 2019, 'Bangladesh's first PPP project set to be delivered via BRI backing', *HKTDC Research*, 18 January. Available from: http://economists-pick-research.hktdc.com/business-news/article/International-Market-News/Bangladesh-s-First-PPP-Project-Set-to-Be-Delivered-Via-BRI-Backing/imn/en/1/1X000000/1X0AGAPH.htm [31 October 2019].

Hong, C-s & Johnson, O 2018, 'Mapping potential climate and development impacts of China's Belt and Road Initiative: a participatory approach'. Stockholm Environment Institute. Available from: www.sei.org/wp-content/uploads/2018/10/china-belt-and-road-initiative-hong-johnson.pdf [23 October 2019].

Jong, HN 2019, 'Survey: less coal, more solar, say citizens of Belt & Road countries', *Mongabay*, 25 April. Available from: https://news.mongabay.com/2019/04/survey-less-coal-more-solar-say-citizens-of-belt-road-countries/ [28 October 2019].

Korsbakken, JI, Andrew, R & Peters, G 2019, 'China's CO2 emissions grew slower than expected in 2018', *CarbonBrief*, 5 March. Available from: www.carbonbrief.org/guest-post-chinas-co2-emissions-grew-slower-than-expected-in-2018 [15 July 2019].

Lam, C 2017, 'Speech by the chief executive, Mrs Carrie Lam, at the Belt and Road summit today', The government of HKSAR press release, 11 September. Available from: www.info.gov.hk/gia/general/201709/11/P2017091100442.htm [15 July 2019].

Lee, A 2018, 'China's electric car market is growing twice as fast as the US. Here's why', *South China Morning Post*, 27 April. Available from: www.scmp.com/business/companies/article/2143646/chinas-ev-market-growing-twice-fast-us-heres-why [15 July 2019]

Linster, M & Yang, C 2018, 'China's progress towards green growth: an international perspective', OECD Green Growth Papers, no. 2018/05. Paris: OECD Publishing.

Myllyvirta, L 2017, 'How much do ultra-supercritical coal plants really reduce air pollution?', *Renew Economy*, 22 June. Available from: https://reneweconomy.com.au/how-much-do-ultra-supercritical-coal-plants-really-reduce-air-pollution-70678/ [28 October 2019].

Nace, T 2019, 'NASA says earth is greener today than 20 years ago thanks To China, India', *Forbes*, 28 February. Available from: www.forbes.com/sites/trevornace/2019/02/28/nasa-says-earth-is-greener-today-than-20-years-ago-thanks-to-china-india/#25c7341e6e13 [28 October 2019].

Ng, E 2019, 'Chinese firms to build more coal power plants in Asia despite Beijing's pledge for greener Belt and Road Initiative projects', *South China Morning Post*, 18 September. Available from: www.scmp.com/business/article/3027792/chinese-firms-build-more-coal-power-plants-asia-despite-beijings-pledge [28 October 2019].

OECD (The Organization for Economic Co-operation and Development). 2018. *The Belt and Road Initiative in the global trade, investment and finance landscape*. OECD Publishing, Paris. Available from: https://doi.org/10.1787/bus_fin_out-2018-6-en [23 October 2019].

PBOC (The People's Bank of China) and the City of London Corporation 2018, *Building an investment and financing system for the Belt and Road Initiative: how London and other global financial centres can support*. Available from: www.cityoflondon.gov.uk/business/asia-programme/greater-china/Documents/building-an-investment-and-financing-system-for-the-bri.pdf. [23 October 2019].

PwC 2013, 'Exploring green finance incentives in China'. PwC. Available from: www.pwchk.com/en/migration/pdf/green-finance-incentives-oct2013-eng.pdf [30 Oct 2019].

Russel, D & Berger, B 2019, 'Navigating the Belt and Road Initiative', Asia Society Policy Institute. Available from: https://asiasociety.org/sites/default/files/2019-06/Navigating%20the%20Belt%20and%20Road%20Initiative_2.pdf [23 October 2019].

Sugden, C 2017, 'Belt and Road PPPs: opportunities and pitfalls', *The Interpreter*, 13 June. Available from: www.lowyinstitute.org/the-interpreter/belt-and-road-PPPs-opportunities-pitfalls [23 October 2019].

Tang, L, Qu, Z, Mi, J, Bo, X, Chang, X, Anadon, LD, Wang, S, Xue, X, Li, S, Wang, X & Zhao, X 2019, 'Substantial emission reductions from Chinese power plants after the introduction of ultra-low emissions standards', *Nature Energy*, 7 October. Available from: www.nature.com/articles/s41560-019-0468-1 [28 October 2019].

Ullman, D 2019, 'When coal comes to paradise', *Foreign Policy*, 9 June. Available from: https://foreignpolicy.com/2019/06/09/when-coal-came-to-paradise-china-coal-kenya-lamu-pollution-africa-chinese-industry-bri/.

UNEP 2016, *The Equator Principles: do they make banks more sustainable?* UNDP. Available from: http://unepinquiry.org/wp-content/uploads/2016/02/ The_Equator_Principles_Do_They_Make_Banks_More_Sustainable.pdf [23 October 2019].

Watts, J 2019, 'Belt and Road summit puts spotlight on Chinese coal funding', *The Guardian*, 25 April. Available from: www.theguardian.com/world/2019/apr/25/belt-and-road-summit-puts-spotlight-on-chinese-coal-funding [28 October 2019].

Wörsdörfer, M 2013, '10 years Equator Principles: a critical appraisal', in K Wendt (ed) *Responsible investment banking. Risk Management Frameworks, Sustainable Financial Innovations and Softlaw Standards*. Springer 475–503. Available from: https://papers.ssrn.com/sol3/papers.cfm?abstract_id=2355962 or http://dx.doi.org/10.2139/ssrn.2355962 [23 October 2019].

Xinhua 2017, 'China to promote PPP model in Belt and Road Initiative', *the Xinhua Net*, 15 Jan. Available from: www.xinhuanet.com//english/2017-01/15/c_135983879.htm [23 October 2019].

Yang, N, Zhang, Z, Xue, B, Ma, J, Chen, X & Lu, C 2018, 'Economic growth and pollution emission in China: structural path analysis', *Sustainability*, vol. 10, no. 7, pp. 1–15.

Yu, A & Shearer, C 2019, 'Time for China to stop bankrolling coal', *the Diplomat*, 29 April. Available from: https://thediplomat.com/2019/04/time-for-china-to-stop-bankrolling-coal/ [28 October 2019]

Zheng, S & Hollingsworth, J 2017, 'How China overtook the US in leading the battle against climate change', *South China Morning Post*, 1 June. Available from: www.scmp.com/news/china/diplomacy-defence/article/2096545/how-china-overtook-us-leading-battle-against-climate [15 July 2019].

Zuo, M 2019, 'UN's environment chief urges China to keep Belt and Road projects green and clean', *South China Morning Post*, 8 June. Available from: www.scmp.com/news/china/politics/article/3013470/uns-environment-chief-urges-china-keep-belt-and-road-projects [15 July 2019].

Section 1

BRI and national competitiveness

1 Development in the Belt and Road Regions from a competitiveness perspective

The first lustrum review

Victor Zheng and Hua Guo

Introduction

Initiated by Chinese President Xi Jinping in 2013, the Belt and Road Initiative (BRI) – a grand strategy to promote regional and international cooperation, interaction, and development in different dimensions – celebrated its fifth anniversary in 2018. From the first day that the BRI was proposed until this moment, there has been a mixture of views, optimism, pessimism, or even observationism in different parts of the world. Some regard it as carrying economic-political-cultural threats and challenges ('One belt, one road and many questions' 14 May 2017; Mardell 2017); some see it as offering multidimensional development opportunities for common or mutual prosperity ('Countries welcomed to join in mutual benefits of Belt, Road' 4 September 2018; Liu and Dunford 2016). Although there is no dearth of reports and analyses from different views and perspectives to address the background, strategic consideration, and even China's calculation (Cai 2017; 'Embracing the BRI ecosystem in 2018' 2018), little objective evaluation has been made of outcomes achieved, impacts brought, problems that have arisen, or better ways for seizing opportunities and reducing risks (Li and Schmerer 2017; Hillman 2018).

This chapter attempts to use the Global Competitiveness Index (GCI) to examine the first lustrum of overall development in the Belt and Road regions, especially to compare them with non-Belt and Road regions. Research light is also shed on exploring different sub-indices that reflect the various aspects of development and on explaining how economies or firms can best position themselves to tap various business and investment opportunities in a highly turbulent and fragile economic environment. It is hoped that some insightful policy implications or recommendations can be drawn from this research to further enhance economic development in the Belt and Road regions in the next lustrum.

Competitiveness as elixir of economic growth

Enter the 20th century; the search for sustainable growth has become an important topic not only in academia but also for policymakers, especially after two devastating world wars, the Great Depression, and the fight for independence of many former Western colonies. From Smith (1776) to Keynes (1936), and to so many scholars and policymakers, all hope to create wealth for their nations or to find the elixir for their country's economic growth. Perfect competition, profit maximization, free market, investment and capital accumulation, regional integration, and international trade are considered key principles or theories that lay the foundation for energizing economic activities, productivities, and efficiencies (Rostow 1960; Barro and Sala-i-Martin 1995; Krugman 1995; Solow 2000; Armstrong and Taylor 2000; Siudek and Zawojska 2014).

With tremendous technological advancement and the end of the Cold War, the process of globalization has accelerated since the 1990s. Living in a highly globalized village, not only people but also economies or countries are getting closer and more interdependent. There is no individual person, firm, or economy that is like an island isolated from others and able to survive without interacting or trading with the rest of the world (Friedman 2006). A profound economic phenomenon is that whenever there is trade, basic theories such as comparative competitiveness or economy of scale are applied.

If one takes a country or economy as a basic unit, its level of competitiveness clearly determines its capability for generating income to its people. We may ask: 'What is competitiveness?' Porter (2005, xi) elaborated as follows:

> Competitiveness is defined as the set of institutions, policies, and factors that determine the level of productivity. The level of productivity in turn, sets the sustainable level of prosperity that can be earned by an economy (and) a more competitive economy is one that is likely to grow at larger rates over the medium to long run.

Clearly, competitiveness is synonymous with productivity. If an economy has higher productivity, competitiveness is greater. A follow-up question is: 'In what way can an economy raise its productivity?' In his seminal work on this topic, Porter (1979, 1985, 1990) suggested that key elements such as 'factor conditions', 'demand conditions', 'related and supporting industries', and 'firm strategy, structure, and rivalry' are important in affecting an economy's competitiveness. Later, he further elaborated each category of factors to include more detailed elements. For instance, for 'factor conditions', he pointed out that 'human resources', 'physical resources', 'knowledge resource', 'capital resources', and 'infrastructure resources' are basic. As such, one can see that competitiveness or productivity is a function of various factors like institutions, markets, and policies.

Therefore, if a country or economy improves its economic factors, it can inject development momentum. Then, its productivity can be raised. On the basis of Porter's seminal idea, scholars around the globe have tried to use different formulas to calculate the competitiveness of an economy to better inform policymakers on how to enhance its strengths and avoid weaknesses. In 2004, because of the long-term involvement in the World Economic Forum's research, Xavier Sala-i-Martin and Elsa Artadi developed an important index called the Global Competitiveness Index (GCI) by absorbing McArthur and Sachs's (2001)

Growth Competitiveness Index and Porter's Business Competitiveness Index. They also included the World Economic Forum's Executive Opinion Survey data (of leading business executives and entrepreneurs from over 100 countries) to balance the over-emphasizing of objective indicators but mostly neglecting subjective indicators, to make it more inclusive and comprehensive (McArthur and Sachs 2001; Porter 2001, 2005; Sala-i-Martin and Artadi 2004). Because this index can largely capture the overall performance of an economy, it has become highly influential since it started to be used in 2004.

Although some people are still sceptical about the development of the BRI, an irrefutable fact is that it promotes 'five-connectivity': policy coordination, facilities connectivity, unimpeded trade, financial integration, and people-to-people bond. These are the bases for the strengthening of the economic growth of the countries/economies involved. Hence, one can reasonably argue that the BRI can enhance the competitiveness of the whole region. As this initiative is pushed forward, construction of infrastructure, free flow of economic factors, allocation of resources, and integration of markets are enhanced, so one can expect multi-dimensional potentials will be gradually released. In this chapter, we use the GCI to evaluate the economic performance in the past five years in the Belt and Road regions in comparison to the non-Belt and Road regions. We will see which part in the Belt and Road regions is doing better and will assess in which fields.

Methodology and data source

Before detailed discussion, it is necessary to sketch the methodology and data source for comparison and analyses. As mentioned, the World Economic Forum has published the GCI annually since 2004, by incorporating both MacArthur and Sachs's (2001) and Porter's (2001, 2005) indices under the expounding of Sala-i-Martin and Artadi (2004). As this index can reflect the growing need to take into account a more comprehensive set of factors that significantly influence an economy's growth performance, it quickly became internationally renowned and influential.

Specifically, the GCI is calculated by a set of 12 pillars: institutions, infrastructure, macroeconomic environment, health and primary education, higher education and training, goods market efficiency, labour market efficiency, financial market development, technological readiness, market size, business sophistication, and innovation.[1] These 12 pillars are grouped into three domains according to their nature or functions: Basic Requirements, Efficiency Enhancers, and Innovation and Sophistication Factors. Basic Requirements are regarded as 'factor-driven economies' because they are for supporting basic economic development. They include institutions, infrastructure, macroeconomic environment, health, and primary education. Efficiency Enhancers are factors for improving economic performance. They comprise higher education and training, goods market efficiency, labour market efficiency, financial market development, technological readiness, and market size. Innovation and Sophistication Factors are key forces for an 'innovation-driven economy' because they can generate new sources of development momentum for further economic expansion and competitiveness. They consist of business sophistication and innovation.[2]

When the GCI started in 2005, 104 countries or economies were included in the list for evaluation. In the subsequent years, the number kept changing but on the whole gradually increased. For instance, in 2006 and 2008, the numbers went up to 117 and then 128. Then, in 2010 and 2012, the numbers were 139 and 142. In 2014, 2016 and 2018, the numbers further changed to 148, 149, and 137. Several features can be summarized from the GCI: (1) If counted according to GDP, in 2018, the selected 137 countries or economies had over 98% of the world economy (Schwab 2018, 12). (2) As expected, developed economies mostly top the list, and developing economies rank at the bottom. (3) In recent decades, the growth momentum in European and North American economies has been weakening while in developing economies in Asia, Africa, and Latin America it has been strengthening (*The Global Competitiveness Report* various years). More importantly, longitudinal data on each selected economy since 2007 is available for public access. Therefore, we can use this dataset for in-depth analyses.

As indicated in the *Vision and Actions on Jointly Building Silk Road Economic Belt and 21st-Century Maritime Silk Road* (National Development and Reform Commission 2015), the BRI is 'an ambitious economic vision of the opening-up of and cooperation among the countries along the Belt and Road'. A follow-up research question is: 'Which countries or economies are included in the Belt and Road'? Although in a broader sense there is no strict geographical limit on the coverage and it can extend to the whole world, in a narrower scope, it only includes two parts: The Silk Road Economic Belt and the 21st-Century Maritime Silk Road. The Silk Road Economic Belt covers Central Asia, West Asia, the Middle East, and Europe. The Maritime Silk Road includes the South China Sea, the South Pacific Ocean, and the Indian Ocean. Since most of the countries or economies in the Belt and Road regions are included in the GCI, it is a highly useful source for longitudinal evaluation and examination.

In the first five years, because mainly only countries or economies in the Silk Road Economic Belt and the 21st-Century Maritime Silk Road joined, our analysis focuses on these narrower scopes of coverage. However, apart from China, 11 countries in South East Asia, 11 in Central and West Asia, 7 in South Asia, 15 in the Middle East and North Africa, and 20 in Central and Eastern Europe are included (Table 1.1). Some countries/economies are well developed, while many others are not. The countries/economies vary greatly, a fact that presents both huge challenges and opportunities for promoting international interaction and cooperation.

In the following sections, research attention will firstly be given to evaluating the overall economic performance between the economies in the Belt and Road regions and non-Belt and Road regions from the perspective of the GCI. Special focus will be given to comparing the situation before and after the commencement of the BRI, particularly reviewing the past five years' development. In order to give a fair view, Greater China of Mainland China, Taiwan, and Hong Kong are considered 'host' economies and thus not included for comparison. Afterwards, analyses will review the performance in the three domains of Basic Requirements, Efficiency Enhancers, and Innovation and Sophistication

Table 1.1 Belt and Road Economies and Regions in the Analysis

Southeast Asia	South Asia	Central and West Asia	Middle East and North Africa	Central and Eastern Europe
Brunei Darussalam	Bangladesh	Afghanistan	Bahrain	Albania
Cambodia	Bhutan	Armenia	Egypt	Belarus
Indonesia	India	Azerbaijan	Iraq	Bosnia and Herzegovina
Lao PDR	Maldives	Georgia	Israel	Bulgaria
Malaysia	Nepal	Iran	Jordan	Croatia
Myanmar	Pakistan	Kazakhstan	Kuwait	Czech Republic
Philippines	Sri Lanka	Kyrgyzstan	Lebanon	Estonia
Singapore		Mongolia	Oman	Hungary
Thailand		Tajikistan	Palestine	Latvia
Timor-Leste		Turkmenistan	Qatar	Lithuania
Viet Nam		Uzbekistan	Saudi Arabia	Macedonia
			Syria	Moldova
			Turkey	Montenegro
			United Arab Emirates	Poland
			Yemen	Romania
				Russian Federation
				Serbia
				Slovakia
				Slovenia
				Ukraine

Factors. Then, examination will be extended to different geographical sub-regions in the Belt and Road regions: (1) South East Asia, (2) Central and West Asia, (3) South Asia, (4) Middle East and North Africa, and (5) Central and Eastern Europe. Through multidimensional review, one can better understand the economic development between the Belt and Road regions and non-Belt and Road regions, and before and after the commencement of the BRI.

Overall competitiveness comparison

Because the historical background and stages of development are different, although European and North American economies are near the top of the GCI, since the development of the BRI, developmental momentum in the Belt and Road regions and the world has marked gradual and intricate changes. However, to what extent has the BRI promoted economic development in the Belt and Road regions in the past five years? There have been few objective analyses so far. The change in the GCI can give us a brief and authoritative answer to this question.

Figure 1.1 shows the changes in the GCI from 2007 to 2018 in the Belt and Road regions and the non-Belt and Road regions.[3] One can see clearly that before 2010, the average GCI in non-Belt and Road regions was higher than in

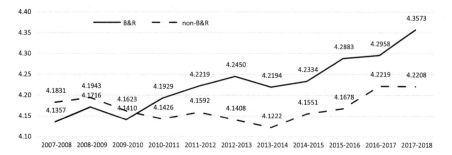

Figure 1.1 The average scores of GCI in Belt and Road and non-Belt and Road economies: 2007–2018

Source: *The Global Competitiveness Report* 2007–2018.

the Belt and Road regions. However, after 2010, the average GCI in the Belt and Road regions surpassed that of the non-Belt and Road regions and kept rising, whereas the average GCI in the non-Belt and Road regions remained almost stagnant.

Specifically, in 2007, the average GCI score in non-Belt and Road regions was 4.1831 while in the Belt and Road regions it was 4.1357. In 2010, the figure in the non-Belt and Road regions was 4.1592 and in Belt and Road regions it was 4.1929. Then, in 2013 when the BRI was first spelt out, the average score of the GCI in the Belt and Road regions was 4.2194, while in the non-Belt and Road regions it was 4.1222. Since that year, the average score of the GCI in both the Belt and Road regions and the non-Belt and Road regions has risen gradually, but the Belt and Road regions have showed greater dynamism. Therefore, one can see that in the Belt and Road regions, the average GCI score increased to 4.2883 in 2016 and 4.3573 in 2018, but in the non-Belt and Road regions, the average score rose to 4.1678 and 4.2208 respectively. If we simply calculate the change in the average score of the GCI in the past 11 years, we can see that in the Belt and Road regions, it increased 0.2216 (4.3573–4.1357), or 5.09%. In the non-Belt and Road regions, it increased 0.0377 (4.2208–4.1831), or 0.01%.

Interpreting from this perspective, one can confidently say that since the implementation of the BRI, the economies in the Belt and Road regions clearly show more significant improvement. However, it seems clear that the better performance of the Belt and Road economies started earlier than the commencement of the BRI, while the critical factor that drove the competitiveness to decline in the non-Belt and Road economies since 2008 was clearly the 'financial tsunami' that erupted in the United States. From that year onwards, the competitiveness in the Belt and Road regions kept improving but in non-Belt and Road regions it kept dropping until 2013 – the year BRI was announced. Since 2013, the competitiveness in both the Belt and Road regions and the non-Belt and Road regions has increased gradually, but the former made slightly more improvement.

Based on this change of competitiveness between the Belt and Road regions and the non-Belt and Road regions in the past decade, one can reasonably conclude that the better performance of the Belt and Road economies can be traced to 2008. Of course, the BRI also added development momentum which further drove the competitiveness between the Belt and Road regions and the non-Belt and Road regions apart. As argued by McArthur and Sachs (2001), Porter (2001, 2005), and Sala-i-Martin and Artadi (2004) that competitiveness determines the overall performance of economy and therefore serves as primary impetus for economic growth. The higher competitiveness score in the Belt and Road regions clearly implies that their economies can maintain better improvement than can the non-Belt and Road regions in the year to come.

Domain-specific comparison

As argued by Rostow (1960) and Porter (1990), each country is at a different stage of development, so its pace, strategic focus, and comparative competitiveness are also different. Simply put, the cost of production in poor countries is usually very low. Therefore, they should compete through price, i.e. make thing less expensive. Richer countries that have reached a higher level of development should compete in quality, i.e. make better things rather than less expensive. In the richest and most developed countries, the most distinctive competitiveness is innovation, so they should invest more in innovation. Therefore, Snowdon (2006, 117) made the following comment:

> This means that the factors that determine how cheap you can produce should be given more weight in countries that are poor than in richer countries. The factors that determine efficiency should be given more weight in intermediate countries, and the factors that drive innovation need to be given more weight in rich developed countries.

Based on these principles or arguments, in this section, we examine the variation among three domains: Basic Requirements, Efficiency Enhancers, and Innovation and Sophistication Factors.

First, let's compare the average score of Basic Requirements in the Belt and Road regions and the non-Belt and Road regions in the past decade (Figure 1.2). In 2007, we can see that the average score of Basic Requirements in the Belt and Road regions is slightly lower than that of the non-Belt and Road regions. As mentioned, the 2008 financial tsunami seemed to bring tremendous impact to the non-Belt and Road economies because the average score dropped in 2009, and in subsequent years it was nearly stagnant. In the Belt and Road regions, although the average score of Basic Requirements also decreased in 2009, it bounced back continuously in subsequent years, and after the commencement of the BRI it rose further.

Specifically, in 2007 the average scores of Basic Requirements in the Belt and Road regions and the non-Belt and Road regions were 4.4377 and 4.4933. The non-Belt and Road regions' score was higher than that of the Belt and Road

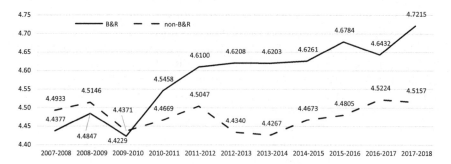

Figure 1.2 The average scores of Basic Requirements in Belt and Road and non-Belt and Road economies: 2007–2018

Source: *The Global Competitiveness Report* 2007–2018.

regions, but the difference was very small. After 2010, the score in the Belt and Road regions surpassed that of the non-Belt and Road regions. From 2011 to 2014, the score in the Belt and Road regions was stagnant while in the non-Belt and Road regions it dropped. From 2014 to 2018, the score in the Belt and Road regions rose further while in the non-Belt and Road regions, although there was improvement, it was less significant.

In the past decade, the average score of Basic Requirements in the Belt and Road regions increased 0.2838 (4.7215–4.4377) or 6.40%, while in the non-Belt and Road regions, it increased 0.0224 (4.5157–4.4933), or 0.05%. In other words, the Belt and Road regions made more improvement in Basic Requirements than did the non-Belt and Road regions in the past decade. After the commencement of the BRI, significant contribution in economic dynamism is seen.

Secondly, we compare the average score of Efficiency Enhancers in the Belt and Road regions and the non-Belt and Road regions (Figure 1.3). In 2007, the average score of Efficiency Enhancers in the Belt and Road regions was 3.9614 while in the non-Belt and Road regions it was 4.0417. The latter had a far better score than did the former. In 2009, the score in the Belt and Road regions surpassed that of the non-Belt and Road regions. From that year to 2014, the score in the Belt and Road regions kept increasing while in the non-Belt and Road regions it remained almost stagnant. From 2014 to 2018, both scores in the Belt and Road regions and the non-Belt and Road regions rose, but the former seemed to make more improvement.

Calculated by the score and percentage changes in the past decade, in the Belt and Road regions, the change was 0.2712 (4.2326–3.9614) or 6.85%. In the non-Belt and Road regions, the change was 0.0836 (4.1253–4.0417) or 2.07%. Again, the economies in the Belt and Road regions showed more improvement of Efficiency Enhancers than did the economies in the non-Belt and Road regions in the past decade while the effect of the BRI was still clear.

Thirdly, let us contrast the average scores of Innovation and Sophistication Factors in the Belt and Road regions and the non-Belt and Road regions

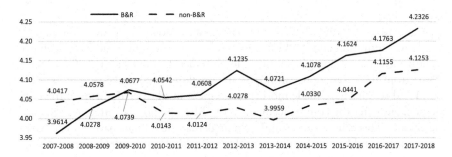

Figure 1.3 The average scores of Efficiency Enhancers in Belt and Road and non-Belt and Road economies: 2007–2018

Source: *The Global Competitiveness Report* 2007–2018.

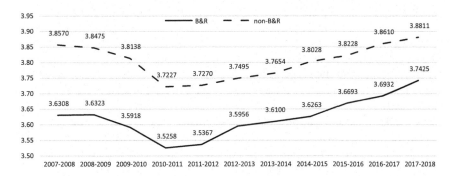

Figure 1.4 The average scores of Innovation and Sophistication Factors in Belt and Road and non-Belt and Road economies: 2007–2018

Source: *The Global Competitiveness Report* 2007–2018.

(Figure 1.4). As mentioned, many countries in the non-Belt and Road regions are developed economies, so they have far higher scores in this domain. In 2007, the average score of Innovation and Sophistication Factors in the Belt and Road regions was 3.6308, and in the non-Belt and Road regions it was 3.8570. The gap in scores between them was big. From 2007 to 2010, the average scores in both regions decreased. From 2010 to 2018, the scores kept increasing, but the Belt and Road regions made more improvement than did the non-Belt and Road regions.

In 2018, the average score in the Belt and Road regions was 3.7425, and in the non-Belt and Road regions it was 3.8811. In the past decade, the average score in the Belt and Road regions increased 0.1117 (3.7425–3.6308), or 3.08%. In the non-Belt and Road regions, it increased 0.0241 (3.8811–3.8570), or 0.62%. Clearly, even in innovation, although the non-Belt and Road regions had far higher average scores, the Belt and Road regions made more progress. The commencement of the BRI brought obvious effects.

One has to bear in mind that countries at different stages of development are equipped with various institutional set-ups and face different constraints. Non-Belt and Road regions, particularly developed economies, clearly enjoy higher scores in Innovation and Sophistication Factors, whereas Belt and Road regions indicate greater advantages in Basic Requirements and Efficiency Enhancers. Apart from these variations, an important developmental signal is that the Belt and Road regions have made more improvement in all three domains in the past decade, and after the commencement of the BRI, the positive effect was equally significant. This echoes other similar findings that the regions have shown dynamism in the world economy in recent decades (PricewaterhouseCoopers 2017).

Geographical differences and evaluation

Geography has an important impact on economic performance. Being endowed with rich natural resources such as precious minerals, oil, and nature gas, or favourable climate and topology is considered positive, whereas an extremely hot or cold climate that prohibits living or experiences disasters or diseases is thought to be negative. Whether a country is coastal or landlocked also affects economic development (Bloom and Saches 1988; Gallup et al. 2003).

The geography in the Belt and Road regions varies tremendously. Some countries are very rich in valuable natural resources, whereas others are not. Some are landlocked, and some are in coastal regions and may have deep-sea harbours. Even the latitude and altitude of these countries vary greatly. Some are well developed and have a stable socio-political system. Others are not and are frequently plagued by wars or serious armed conflicts. One can see that the variation presents both huge challenges and opportunities for building infrastructure and promoting international trade to link the haves and the have-nots.

Have there been geographical development variations since the implementation of the BRI? As mentioned, the Belt and Road regions cover three continents (Asia, Africa, and Europe) and include over 60 countries and territories, so there are not only huge geographical variations but also socio-political and religious ones. Therefore, there must be very different paces of development. In order to have a better picture for further analysis, we have divided them into five groups according to their geographical locations: South East Asia, Central and West Asia, South Asia, the Middle East and North Africa, and Central and Eastern Europe (Table 1.1).

Figure 1.5 shows the average scores of the GCI by five geographical subregions in the Belt and Road regions in the past decade. The average score of the GCI in Central and West Asia was the lowest in 2007, but it rose from 3.7287 to 4.0260 in 2012 and then to 4.2139 in 2018, the greatest percentage improvement of 13.01%. Conversely, the average score of the GCI in the Middle East and North Africa was the highest in the Belt and Road regions in 2007, but in the following year, it was almost stagnant. From 2007 to 2018, the GCI score dropped by 0.0088, or −0.02%. In other words, the Middle East and North African regions made the least improvement in the past decade. The BRI brought little effect to these regions.

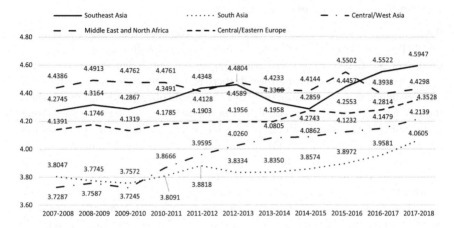

Figure 1.5 The average scores of GCI by geographical regions in the Belt and Road regions: 2007–2018

Source: *The Global Competitiveness Report* 2007–2018.

By average GCI score, South Asia also ranked at the bottom in the Belt and Road regions. In 2007, the average score was 3.8047. In 2008 and 2009, the average scores dropped. From 2010 onward, it rose slowly but steadily to 4.0605. In the past decade, the average score in East Asia rose by 0.2558, or 6.72%. As the score rose from 2013 onward, a positive effect generated by the BRI was speculated to be the reason.

The average scores of South East Asia and Central and Eastern Europe are in the middle. Although their average scores also record a gradual increase, the speed of improvement is relatively slower than that of Central and West Asia. In 2007, the average score in South East Asia was 4.2745; in Central and Eastern Europe it was 4.1391. In subsequent years, the score in Central and Eastern Europe rose steadily to 4.3528 in 2018. In South East Asia, although the overall score was rising, it fluctuated. In 2018, the score went up to 4.5947 and became the highest score in the Belt and Road regions. If measuring by percentage in the past decade, South East Asia made 7.5% improvement, and in Central and Eastern Europe, it made 5.2% improvement (Figure 1.5).

Evaluating the average scores of the GCI, one sees that the differences among the five geographical sub-regions in the Belt and Road regions are clear and significant. These figures support the argument that the potential for promoting trade and interaction between different countries is tremendous (Liu and Dunford 2016; Cai 2017; 'Embracing the BRI' 2018). The continuous improvement in the average GCI in the Belt and Road regions (except the Middle East and North Africa) further implies that the regions show economic dynamism, which may also be the case in the years to come, particularly in Central and West Asia, and South East Asia; this sub-region has made far more progress in the past decade.

Key findings, policy implications and conclusion

Based on the above findings, we can generally conclude that since the start of the BRI in 2013, the economies in the Belt and Road regions have experienced significant positive changes when compared to the non-Belt and Road regions. Therefore, one can argue that although there is still scepticism and pessimism, as more evidence shows that those on board have made obvious advancement when the BRI is progressing, more countries can realize the opportunities or potential and may be more positive or even likely to join. The change of attitude towards the BRI of the Japanese government in October 2018 is one example.

However, one can argue that the better performance of the Belt and Road regions started earlier than the BRI, and the most important turning point was clearly 2008, especially after the financial tsunami. Looking closer, the continuous economic growth of the Chinese economy since the 1980s seems to be the most important force that drove its neighbouring economies (the Belt and Road economies) to grow even after the financial tsunami. In contrast, the financial tsunami brought serious negative impact to the non-Belt and Road regions, especially developed economies.

To a certain extent, the BRI is an extension of the 'China effect'. With further development incentive and policy stimulation from China, and the continuous growth of China's economy, the Belt and Road economies could keep improving after 2013. Conversely, as the financial tsunami further triggered European economic recession, the non-Belt and Road economies fell into the doldrums. That explains why the average score of GCI in the non-Belt and Road economies remained almost stagnant from 2008 to 2014. After 2014, although some improvement was seen, the dynamism of recovery was weak. In short, the continuous economic improvement in Belt and Road region was the 'China effect', i.e. the prolonged economic growth of China, whereas the economic stagnancy in non-Belt and Road was the financial tsunami, i.e. the prolonged decline in productivity.

Looking at the possible effect of the BRI, one can see that since the 'five-connectivity' could strengthen directly some of the pillars, e.g. infrastructure, of an economy, taking part in the BRI is clearly beneficial (Zheng and Luk 2019). Since most economies in the Belt and Road regions are emerging, their infrastructure, macroeconomic environment, and financial market are by no means sound and well established. Through the building of big infrastructure projects such as hydro power plants, high-speed railways, and port and container terminals, not only can transportation capability and natural resources usage be hugely improved, but productivity and efficiency can be greatly increased.

In recent decades, in many developed economies, there has been a wave of post-materialism, which toned down the importance of economic development. Undoubtedly, economic development that may cause serious hazards to the environment should be suppressed. However, one needs to bear in mind that without economic development, the materialistic base for improving people's livelihood is just an empty promise; as Schwab (2018, 1) argued 'although (economic) growth does not guarantee human improvement, there are no examples of coun-tries (economies) improving the welfare of their populations without growth'. As such, not only in the developed economies but in the developing economies does enhancing economic growth top the government's policy priority.

Narrowing the focus to the Belt and Road regions, as there are big variations economically, politically, culturally, and geographically, promoting socio-economic interaction and cooperation could generate far more synergy. Given that some sub-regions are currently affected by wars or serious armed conflicts and some are plagued by political instability, cooperation can start from and accelerate in the stable and favourable regions, for instance South East Asia and South Asia. As more solid progress is achieved, the world can see that the model works. Again, more countries will be interested in joining.

Last but not least, GCI is calculated by using various reliable data sources, so it is no doubt more objective and authoritative for reviewing economic per-formance. However, there are some shortcomings to bear in mind. First, not all countries or economies in the Belt and Road regions are included in the GCI, so the picture sketched is by no mean complete. Secondly, GCI only focuses on economic and financial aspects, so non-economic aspects such as policy coord-ination and people-to-people bonds are not available for closer evaluation, and their impact may be underestimated. Thirdly, the standard or criteria for calcula-tion for CGI are from the Western Christian culture or values, but many Belt and Road countries are under Islamic, Buddhist, or Confucian influence; hence, the index may be tinged with cultural prejudice.

Without doubt, the effect of an ambitious, tremendous regional cooperation and integrated strategy like this will not be easily seen in the short term. More time for development and incubating is needed. Judging from the above initial research findings, one can see that although the challenges are numerous, poten-tial or opportunities are equally large. A succinct description made by the inter-nationally renowned accounting firm Deloitte can provide a footnote to the first lustrum development and an end to this chapter.

If we were to draw an analogy, it would be this: BRI is a journey, one with opportunities and risks, and one that – four years in – is still closer to its start than its end. That means that investors need to take a longer view on projects than they are accustomed to doing. And while we do not downplay the risks, we believe they are less severe than many assume ('Embracing the BRI' 2018, 2).

Notes

1 The twelve pillars combine 114 indicators that 'capture the concepts that matter for productivity and long term prosperity' (Schwab 2018, 11). In other words, it is a highly inclusive and comprehensive index.

2 For a detailed methodology of obtaining data and calculation of the index, please refer to the methodology section in the *Global Competitiveness Report* (Schwab 2018).

3 The 2018 report marks a big change in the calculation of the GCI index to address the issue of 'the Fourth Industrial Revolution'. However, this change of constituents of the index makes pre-2018 longitudinal comparison very difficult.

References

Armstrong, H & Taylor, J 2000, *Regional economics and policy*. Blackwell, Oxford.

Barro, RJ & Sala-i-Martin, X 1995, *Economic growth*. McGraw-Hill, Boston, MA.

Bloom, DE & Saches, JD 1988, 'Geography, demography and economic growth in Africa', *Brookings Papers on Economic Activity*, No. 2.

Cai, P 2017, *Understanding China's Belt and Road Initiative*. Lowy Institute, Vienna. Available from: http://hdl.handle.net/11540/6810.

'Countries welcomed to join in mutual benefits of Belt, Road' 2018, *China Daily*, 4 September.

'Embracing the BRI ecosystem in 2018', *Deloitte Insights*. Deloitte, Hong Kong.

Friedman, TL 2006, *The world is flat: the globalized world in the twenty-first century*. Penguin Books, London.

Gallup, JL, Gaviria, A, & Lora, E 2003, *Is geography destiny? Lessons from South America*. The World Bank, Washington, DC.

Hillman, J E 2018, 'China's Belt and Road Initiative: five years later'. Centre for Strategic & International Studies. Available from: www.csis.org/analysis/chinas-belt-and-road-initiative-five-years-later-0.

Keynes, JM 1936, *The general theory of employment, interest, and money*. Macmillan, London.

Krugman, P 1995, *Development, geography and economic theory*. MIT, Cambridge, MA.

Li, Y & Schmerer, HJ 2017, 'Trade and the New Silk Road: opportunities, challenges, and solutions', *Journal of Chinese Economic and Business Studies*, vol. 15, no. 3, pp. 205–213.

Liu, WD & Dunford, M 2016, 'Inclusive globalization: unpacking China's Belt and Road Initiative', *Journal of Area Development and Policy*, vol. 1, no. 3, pp. 323–340.

Mardell, J 2017, 'One Belt, One Road, and one big competition', *The Diplomat*, 15 December.

McArthur, JW & Sachs, JD 2001, 'The Growth Competitiveness Index: measuring technological advancement and stages of development'. *The Global Competitiveness Report: 2001–02*. Oxford University Press, New York.

National Development and Reform Commission, Ministry of Foreign Affairs, and Ministry of Commerce of the People's Republic of China, with State Council authorization 2015, *Vision and actions on jointly building Silk Road Economic Belt and 21st-Century Maritime Silk Road*. Available from: http://en.ndrc.gov.cn/newsrelease/201503/t20150330_669367.html.

'One belt, one road and many questions' 2017, *Financial Times*, 14 May.

Porter, M 1979, 'How competitive forces shape strategy', *Harvard Business Review*, vol. 57, no. 2, pp. 137–145.

Porter, M 1985, *Competitive advantage*. The Free Press, New York.

Porter, M 1990, 'The competitive advantage of nations', *Harvard Business Review*, vol. 68, no. 2, pp. 73–93.

Porter, ME 2001, 'Enhancing the microeconomic foundations of prosperity: the current competitiveness index', in ME Porter (ed), *The Global Competitiveness Report: 2004–2005*. Oxford University Press, New York.

Porter, ME 2005, 'Building the microeconomic foundations of prosperity: findings from the Business Competitiveness Index', in ME Porter, K Schwab, & A López-Claros (eds), *The Global Competitiveness Report: 2005–2006*. World Economic Forum, Geneva.

PricewaterhouseCoopers 2017, *The long view: how will the global economic order change by 2050?* Available from: www.pwc.com/gx/en/world-2050/assets/pwc-the-world-in-2050-full-report-feb-2017.pdf

Rostow, W 1960, *The stages of economic growth*. Cambridge University Press, Cambridge.

Sala-i-Martin, X & Artadi, E 2004, 'The Global Competitiveness Index', in ME Porter (ed), *The Global Competitiveness Report: 2004–05*. Oxford University Press, Oxford.

Schwab, K (ed) 2018, *The Global Competitiveness Report: 2017–2018*. World Economic Forum, Geneva.

Smith, A 1776, *An inquiry into the nature and causes of the wealth of nations,* in RH Campbell & AS Skinner (eds). Clarendon, Oxford.

Snowdon, B 2006, 'The enduring elixir of economic growth: Xavier Sala-i-Martin on the wealth and poverty of nations', *World Economics,* vol. 7, no. 1, pp. 73–130.

Solow, R 2000, *Growth theory: an exposition*. Oxford University Press, Oxford.

Suidek, T & Zawojska, A 2014 'Competitiveness in the economic concepts, theories and empirical research'. *Oeconomia,* vol. 13, no. 1, pp. 91–108.

Zheng, V & Luk, R 2019, 'A bounty of benefits, thanks to "BRI factor"', *China Daily,* global version, 20 February 2019, pp. 1 & 3.

Section 2

Renminbi internationalization and green finance

2 The Belt and Road Initiative and China's green foreign direct investment[1]

Wen Wang and Fanxin Yang

Preface

The "13th Five-Year" Plan clearly proposed that China should "develop green finance" and make the construction of a green financial system a national strategy. China has established a relatively complete policy framework for developing green finance, marked by the *Guiding Opinions on Building the Green Financial System* statement issued by seven ministries and commissions, including the People's Bank of China, in August 2016. Promoting green development through green finance has become a new method to promote growth in the current period of national transformation, upgrading, and structural adjustment.

Since the "Belt and Road Initiative" was proposed, the concept of green development has run through it. Chinese enterprises "going global" have actively practised green construction of the "Belt and Road Initiative". This has greatly stimulated a huge green investment and financing space and provided a broader market for a new generation of green products and technologies. At present, this potential has not been fully developed, as there are still limitations on Chinese green finance impacting globally. In this context, it is necessary to explore the possible methods for supporting China's green FDI.

Research on China's green FDI and significance

From the worldwide perspective, the green economy has become a new engine of economic growth, and the development of green finance and green investment has become a trend. Currently, China is in a critical period of economic structural adjustment and transformation of developmental mode. China's demand for green finance supporting the sustainable development of green industry, economy, and society in domestic China, and international green FDI, has continuously expanded. Promoting green investment and developing green finance has conformed to the requirements of green development and promoting ecological civilization construction, and are also a profound reflection of practising sustainable and green development.

The "Belt and Road" green investment is an important part of building an ecological system

China is promoting green FDI through a top-down method. In 2015 the Chinese Government released the *General Scheme for Reform of the Ecological Civilization System*, proposing to accelerate the promotion of ecological civilization construction and promote the formation of a new pattern of modernization construction, characterized by resource utilization efficiency and the harmonious development of humanity and nature. In 2017, the Ministry of Ecology and Environment, Ministry of Foreign Affairs, National Development and Reform Commission, and Ministry of Commerce of the People's Republic of China jointly released the *Guiding Opinions on Promoting the Green Construction of the "Belt and Road Initiative"*, proposing to highlight the concept of ecological civilization, promote green development, strengthen the ecological environmental protection and jointly build the "Green Belt and Road" (MEE 2017).

In 2017 President Xi Jinping proposed to construct the "Green Belt and Road", practice the concept of green development, make green the "bottom colour", and construct the ecological civilization to realize the sustainable development target by 2030 (Liu 2017). In the earlier First and Second Belt and Road Forum for International Cooperation (BRF), the joint communiqués of the leaders' roundtable meeting underlined the importance of promoting green development and addressing the challenges of environmental protection and climate change. This included enhancing cooperation to implement the Paris Agreement, promote sustainable and low-carbon development, foster green development towards ecological sustainability, encourage the development of green finance, including the issuance of green bonds as well as development of green technology, encourage exchange of good practices on ecological and environmental policies towards a high level of environmental protection, and build the platforms of International Coalition for Green Development on the Belt and Road. On 25 April, *Green Investment Principles (GIP) for the Belt and Road Initiative* was included in the list of the 2nd BRF proceedings, and 27 global institutions signed up to the GIP to promote green investment in the Belt & Road region.

Green finance is developing rapidly in China

In practice, China has achieved a good result in developing green finance. The Green Finance Committee of China Society for Finance and Banking (hereafter referred to as the "Green Finance Committee"), founded in April 2015, is China's first industry guidance institution with green finance as the theme (Ma 2018). The *General Scheme for Reform of the Ecological Civilization System* clearly proposed the strategy of building a green financial system for the first time, indicating that China has determined a top-down design to guide the development of green finance. In August 2016, seven ministries and commissions, including People's Bank of China, jointly issued the *Guiding Opinions on Building the*

Green Finance System, expounding the overall thinking to guide developing green finance in China. In 2017, China launched five "green finance" pilot zones including Zhejiang, Jiangxi, Guangdong, Guizhou, and Xinjiang, to explore experiences that could be replicated and promoted in the system and mechanism.

Research on green investment needs to be further improved

The research on green investment in all circles in China needs to be further promoted. Even the green investment projects at the Green Finance Committee level lack in-depth research. This includes the green finance series, such as *Analysis on the Environmental Risks, ESG Sustainable Investing, Research on the Development of Green Funds at Home and Abroad,* and *Green Bonds.* Furthermore, book and report series have been compiled by Chongyang Institute for Financial Studies, Renmin University of China, such as *"Belt and Road Initiative" and Green Finance, Report on Development of Green Development in China in 2017, Research Report on Development of Green Development in China in 2018, Accounting of Costs and Benefits of the "Belt and Road Initiative" Green Investment,* and *Standards of the "Belt and Road Initiative" Green Investment.* Also, books and research reports have been edited by Greenovation Hub, Industrial and Commercial Bank of China Urban Financial Research Institute, and SGS-CSTC Standards Technical Services Co. Ltd., such as *Reference Manual for Management of Environmental Risks of China's Foreign Direct Investment.* In this context, we explore the supporting conditions required for green investment, by discussing the process of China's FDI.

China's FDI process and characteristics

To investigate China's shift to green investment, we first need to understand the development process of China's FDI. China began sending FDI at the end of 1970s, when the reform and opening-up policy was carried out. In 1979, China proposed the policy of, "allowing enterprises to go abroad" (Hua 1979) and thus opened the curtain of China's FDI.

China's FDI has gradually increased since the reform and opening-up

From 1979 to 2012, the development of China's FDI has generally gone through the following phases:

Slow, start phase (1979–1991). During this period, China's FDI flows were always less than US$1 billion a year, amid fluctuations. The scale of foreign direct investment was small, the level was low, and the growth was slow.

Stable development phase (1992–2001). From 1992 to 1994, China's FDI flows saw two small peaks, respectively reaching US$4 billion in 1992 and US$4.4 billion in 1994 (CEPII 2000). From 1994 to 2000, China's FDI flows were at a low level again, and they shrank for two consecutive fiscal years, 1998 and 2000.

Significant change phase (2001–2008). After joining the World Trade Organization (WTO), China's FDI steadily expanded, and both flows and foreign holdings grew significantly. During this period, China established a statistical reporting system for FDI. Since 2003, the former Ministry of Foreign Trade and Economic Cooperation (now the Ministry of Commerce), the National Bureau of Statistics, and other government units began jointly issuing the "Statistical Bulletin on China's Foreign Direct Investment" to be an authoritative, clear, and intuitive annual report on the status of FDI to the public.

Continued growth phase (2008–2012). In the context of the 2008 global financial crisis and the spread of the European debt crisis, the growth rate of China's FDI accelerated markedly. At the end of 2012, China's FDI flows reached an annualized US$87.8 billion, holding a stock of US$531.94 billion, accounting for 6.3% and 2.3% of global current flows and stocks respectively. The flow ranked third in terms of global countries and regions, and the stock ranked 13th, the total assets of Chinese companies outside the country exceeded US$2.3 trillion (MOFCOM OFDI 2013).

China's FDI continuous to grow rapidly after the "Belt and Road Initiative" was launched

Since the "Belt and Road Initiative" was launched in 2013, China's FDI flows have grown year on year, setting new records. From 2013 to 2018, Chinese companies directly invested more than US$90 billion in countries along the Belt and Road routes, with an average annual growth rate of 5.2%. The turnover of China's overseas contracted projects that were signed in the countries along the route exceeded US$600 billion, with an average annual growth rate of 11.9%. Chinese enterprises have built a number of overseas economic and trade cooperation zones along the "Belt and Road" countries. By the end of October 2017, Chinese enterprises had promoted 75 overseas economic and trade cooperation zones in 24 countries along the routes, with 3412 enterprises entering the zones, the accumulative investment is more than US$30 billion. The economic and trade cooperation zones have become an important platform for local economic growth and industrial agglomeration, driving host countries to employ nearly 300,000 people (MOFCOM 2017).

Investment scale continues to expand, and flow of foreign investment continues to grow rapidly

Since China established the FDI statistics system in 2003, China's FDI flow has achieved rapid growth for 14 consecutive years to 2016, with an average annual growth rate of 35.8% (MOFCOM 2017). In 2013, China's FDI exceeded US$100 million for the first time (see Figure 2.1). In 2015, China's FDI achieved a historic breakthrough, the flow rate jumping from the 26th in the world in 2002 to the second place in the world. The amount of China's FDI exceeded the amount of foreign investment in China for the first time. In 2016, China's FDI

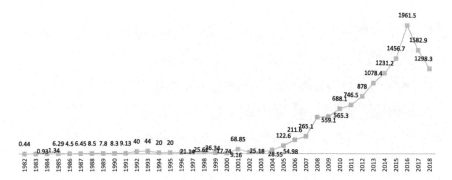

Figure 2.1 China's FDI flow (in USD100 million)
Source: UNCTAD, MOFCOM

broke through double digits for the first time, setting a new record of US$196.15 billion. The flow scale continued to rank second in the world, accounting for 13.5% of the global total. Although China's FDI showed negative growth in 2017, it still ranked third in the world with US$158.29 billion, and continued to be first in developing countries.

Investment area continues to expand, and investment along the Belt and Road routes has increased significantly

According to the Ministry of Commerce, as of the end of 2017, a total of 25,500 Chinese enterprises had established 39,200 FDI enterprises outside the country, distributed in 189 countries and regions around the world, and the total assets of overseas enterprises reached US$6 trillion. The stock of China's foreign direct investment reached US$1809.04 billion (MOFCOM 2018). Among them, China's investment flows to Asia accounted for the largest proportion, followed by Latin America, Europe, North America, Africa, and Oceania (see Figure 2.2). In 2017, China's FDI in Europe and Africa grew rapidly, up 72.7% and 71.1% respectively year-on-year. Affected by protectionist policies adopted by the Trump administration, China's FDI in North America, Latin America, Asia, and Oceania all declined year-on-year, down 68.1%, 48.3.%, 15.5%, and 2.1% respectively, and Chinese companies' direct investment in the United States plummeted by 62.2%.

Diversified investment industries and gradually optimized investment structure

China has seen a further optimized structure of foreign investment industries. The investment in the tertiary sector has been an important part of China's FDI. From 2013 to 2017, the proportion of the mining industry in China's FDI gradually declined from more than 20% to around 1% (see Figure 2.3). In 2017, China's FDI involved 18 industries of national economic significance, US$126.27 billion

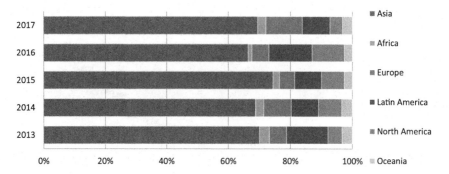

Figure 2.2 Regional distribution of China's FDI 2013–2017 (in USD100 million)
Source: *Statistical Bulletin Regarding China's Foreign Direct Investment*, MOFCOM (2013–2017)

flowed to the tertiary sector, accounting for 79.8% of the total amount of China's FDI in that year; US$29.51 billion flowed to the secondary sector, and US$2.51 billion flowed to the primary sector (agriculture, forestry, animal husbandry, and fishery), respectively accounting for 18.6% and 1.6% of total FDI. In this period, FCI exceeded US$10 billion a year in four key industries: leasing and commercial service, manufacturing, wholesale and retail, and the financial industry. Dampened by factors such as stricter supervision and restrictions on foreign investment and mergers, implemented in developed countries, the flow of FDI in information transmission, software, and information technology services was US$4.43 billion, a sharp decline of 76.3% on a year-on-year basis (MOFOM OFDI 2017).

Increasingly strengthened interconnection and cooperation in infrastructure

The cooperation between China and the countries along the "Belt and Road" has been increasingly growing around infrastructure. The interconnected framework of "six corridors, six ways, multiple countries, and multiple ports" has been basic-ally formed, and a large number of cooperation projects have been implemented, such as major projects including, Mombasa–Nairobi Railway, Jakarta–Bandung High-Speed Railway, China–Laos Railway, Ethiopia–Djibouti Railway, Hungary–Serbia Railway, Gwadar Port, and Piraeus Port. Such major projects have achieved significant progress, which is of positive significance in improving the infrastruc-ture in the countries along the route, improving the level of industrialization and urban development, increasing employment and taxes, and promoting mutual benefit and win-win cooperation between China and the relevant countries.

According to the data released by the Ministry of Commerce, from January to July 2018, the new contracts on China's foreign contracted projects were mainly concentrated on traffic and transportation, power engineering, and construction industries, in total accounting for 68.2% of new contracts. There were 418 new

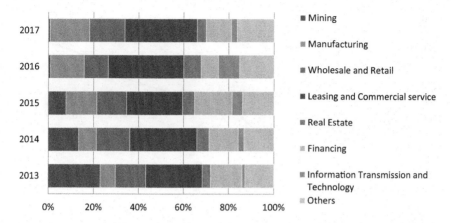

Figure 2.3 Industrial distribution of China's FDI Flow 2013–2017 (in USD100 million)
Source: *Statistical Bulletin Regarding China's Foreign Direct Investment,* MOFCOM (2013–2017)

projects whose contract amount was individually more than US$50 million, the total amount being US$106.74 billion, accounting for 85.2% of new contracts (Belt and Road Portal 2018).

China's new foreign contracted projects have increased over consecutive years from 2012, in which large and medium-scale projects have increased (see Figure 2.4). The foreign project contracting has been mainly concentrated on infrastructure such as traffic and transformation, e.g. high-speed rail, common house building, power and water conservation, while some industries such as environmental protection, manufacturing and processing, and electronic communications are relatively weak.

China's foreign investment needs to be green

The driving factors and trends of the international "green economy" proposal, global environmental problems, environmental knowledge and media reports, environmental awareness and public opinions, as well as environmental regulations and legislation have promoted the transformation and upgrading of investment to green investment. This is to meet the new requirements for the development of a green economy, such as the increasingly severe environmental and climate changes in the world.

Environmental laws and regulations and the international "green economy" proposal have strengthened the feasibility of green investment

Environmental legislation and supervision actions can stimulate various stakeholders' demands for "green" investment and services. After the outburst

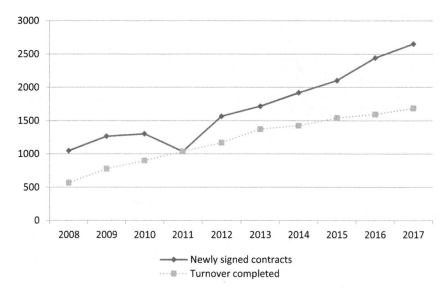

Figure 2.4 China's foreign contracting projects (in USD100 million)
Source: *Statistical Bulletin Regarding China's Foreign Direct Investment,* MOFCOM
(2013–2016)

of the global financial crisis in 2008, the UN proposed the "green economy"
and "green new policy" worldwide (UNEP 2016), and the concept of "green
economy" formally entered the view of countries, rapidly setting off a new wave
of transformation to the green economy. In Europe, active government policies such as the European Carbon Dioxide Trading System, German Renewable
Energy Feed-in Law, and the Dutch Green Fund raised the environmental protection requirements for foreign investment. Some ASEAN countries have set a
goal of keeping up with environmental laws of developed countries, and since
2010, Indonesia has formulated a legal system for recycling and waste treatment.
Vietnam requires that entities investing there should submit documents such as an
Environmental Impact Assessment Report (EIA Report) and an Environmental
Protection Undertaking (EPU). One of the targets stipulated in *The Charter of
the Association of Southeast Asian Nations* is:

> To strengthen the sustainable development to ensure that the regional environ-
> ment is protected, natural resources can be maintained, the cultural heritage
> can be preserved and citizens can have the high-quality life.

(ASEAN 2008)

The vision of the ASEAN Community by 2020 is, "to be clean and green and to
comprehensively establish the sustainable development mechanism".

The "Agenda for Sustainable Development by 2030" and the *Paris Climate Agreement* indicate that policies related to the environment and climate change have now shifted from a narrow environmental focus to a broader focus on the new order of the world, and that the transformation to a low-carbon economy has already begun in the economy, society, and culture. The United Nations Conference on Sustainable Development has generated a direct and important influence on the development process of China's environmental laws, and has encouraged China to develop toward a green economy.

Global environmental laws and regulations require green investment

There have been more than 500 international environmental treaties ratified, including multiple trade-related environmental protection regulations, and international environmental treaties involving cross-border environmental pollution aimed to prevent cross-border pollution transfer problems, such as; *Basel Convention on the Control of Transboundary Movements of Hazardous Wastes and Their Disposal, Convention on International Trade in Endangered Species of Wild Fauna and Flora, Convention on Biological Diversity* and *Cartagena Protocol on Biosafety, The United Nations Framework Convention on Climate Change, OILPOL, Vienna Convention for the Protection of the Ozone Layer* (1985), *Montreal Protocol on Substances that Deplete the Ozone Layer* (1987), *International Convention for the Regulation of Whaling and OILPOL.*

In many important bilateral and multilateral trade rules, environmental rules and issues have become inevitable points, and in many bilateral and multilateral investment agreements, environmental protection has also become a standard rule that must be discussed. For example, under the cooperation framework of China and ASEAN, Shanghai Cooperation Organization, Asia-Pacific and Lancangjiang-Meigonghe, there have been environmental cooperation plans and action plans; regional, pan-regional, and sub-regional environmental cooperation has been implemented; relevant research has begun on the regional cross-border environmental problems, environmental management of foreign investment; and a green supply chain policy and practice have been carried out. The *Action Plan for the Joint Declaration of China-ASEAN Strategic Partnership for Peace and Prosperity* (2016–2020) has emphasized promoting environmental cooperation. The negotiations of the *Regional Comprehensive Economic Partnership Agreement* (RCEP) have also covered environmental standards and environmental protection.

Environmental protection awareness of the international public has promoted the demand for green investment

Issues in politics and the environment, receiving attention from countries around the world, have increased and been gradually popularized. This includes issues such as environmental pollution, desertification, population growth, species extinction, scarcity of natural resources, global warming, and sustainable development. Environmental protection has gradually become one of the central factors in decision making in social policy, politics, and the economy.

According to the global education test report, environmental knowledge has been increasingly included in formal school curriculums. According to the analysis of school curriculums in the 78 countries of the report, 55% use the term "ecology" and 47% of them use "environmental education" to popularize environmental knowledge (UNESCO 2017).

The information era enables countries around the world to rapidly gain unprecedented awareness of the seriousness, sources, and implications of all kinds of environmental problems, such as air quality, water shortage, and soil erosion. The media plays an extremely important role in promoting the green and sustainable development process of environmental protection by carrying out extensive social mobilization, building people's identification with environmental risks, realizing information exchange, and improving the public awareness of active participation in environmental protection.

The importance of environmental problems has risen to an extremely high level in the opinions of the international public, reflecting the fact that more international consumers want greener products and are willing to spend money in using new technologies helpful for reducing greenhouse gas emissions. Governments and enterprises are required to be responsible for taking actions for environmental problems, and being green needs to be included in the scope of investment.

Industrial transfer and technological upgrading completed in developed countries has driven investment in green industries

More and more developed countries have taken multilateral issues, such as climate change and low-carbon development, as their main approach and means of seeking an effective market-led initiative based on basically having completed traditional industrial transfer and technological upgrading. The green economy in the UK is mainly reflected in aspects such as green energy, green lifestyle, and green manufacturing. The focus in Germany on developing a green economy is to develop ecological industries. France focuses on developing nuclear and renewable energy and researching and developing clean electric or low-carbon automobiles. The USA is taking the development of new energy and a green economy as the main driving force to revive the economy after the 2008 global financial crisis. Japan has promoted energy conservation and emission reduction plans and has proposed building a low-carbon society. South Korea has proposed to revive its economy through low-carbon and green growth.

With the transfer and technological upgrading of traditional low-end manufacturing and polluting industries, developed countries have utilized their advantage as international system founders, advanced internet technology, and the "reindustrialization" process to promote new transfers to the green economy and green technology and to establish the international green development market. The American strategic plan for an advanced manufacturing country, the British industry 2050 strategy, and German manufacturing 4.0 contain strong requirements for green economic development as well as green standards of environmental upgrading.

The trend of investment centralization in six corridors has had higher requirements for green

There is an obvious agglomeration trend in the industries in which China has invested along the "Belt and Road". According to data from Mergermarket, for which China has carried out transboundary mergers and acquisitions in the countries along the "Belt and Road", the top five industries are energy (55.6%), metal mining and smelting (11.6%), traffic manufacturing (8.2%) and property (6.8%), which shows clear resource seeking characteristics, the merger and acquisition of resources accounting for 67.2% (MOFCOM 2017) of investment. In a sense, such an industrial structure is a double-edged sword; for example, the Sino-Arab "1+2+3" cooperation pattern needs to be more rapidly green.

In the Sino-Arab "1+2+3" cooperation pattern, green is the main axis of cooperation: "1" refers to promoting green development with energy; "2" refers to strengthening the green and low-carbon construction of infrastructure and the ecologicalization of investment and trade (Zhang 2017); and "3" refers to the greening of three tertiary sector fields, including nuclear energy, aerospace, and new energy.

Enlightenments of foreign investment project failure caused by environmental risk

Environmental risk is the one risk that Chinese enterprises need to pay the most attention to when they go global (ICBC 2018). The risks faced by co-construction of the "Belt and Road" not only include traditional financial risks, but also extend to the environmental and social. During the investment and production process, Chinese enterprises often get protests from local residents because of environmental issues, which causes losses. Examples of this include issues such as the Aral Sea crisis over the New Eurasian Land Bridge, or the Myitsone Dam event in Myanmar.

In September 2011, President Thein Sein of Myanmar announced that they would shelve the Sino-Burmese Myitsone Dam project. The reason was that this project might have a significant negative impact on the local environment and local people's livelihood; these are environmental and social risks.

There is no denying that the reasons for halting the Sino-Burmese Myitsone Dam project included the complicated political situation in Myanmar, propaganda from western media and powers, and the complexity of overseas investment. However, ecological environmental problems were the target of the public voice. In the Kachin language, Myitsone means the "convergence of rivers", which is highly respected by local residents. This led to local residents protesting against the dam location. They thought the Myitsone Dam might damage the habitat of animals living in the catchment basin, and they were concerned that the dam lake would submerge a large forests and fertile farmland. Meanwhile, the ecological environment downstream may have been affected. Also, being located on a geologic fault line, the dam might break if an earthquake took place. To some extent, this reflected the opinion of opposing voices that enterprises did not pay enough attention to environmental concerns.

The Myitsone Dam event is a profound warning that as Chinese enterprises and financial institutions intend to "go global" and conduct investment and construction overseas, the identification of overseas investment environmental and social risks must not be ignored. The green requirement in foreign investment has been lifted to a strategic level.

Progress in China's green foreign investment

Since the 18th National Congress of the CPC, the Chinese government has begun to prioritize ecological civilization construction in the overall strategy of reform, development, and modernization construction. China has proposed that by 2025, the concept of ecological civilization and green development will be integrated into the construction of the "Belt and Road Initiative". China will build a foundation and form a good structure for ecological and environmental cooperation. China now promotes the co-construction of the "Green Belt and Road". In the ecological and environmental field, China actively deepens multilateral dialogues, communication, and cooperation with countries along the route. China enhances the information supporting services for ecological environment and advances cooperation on environmental standards, technologies, and industries, as well as promoting China's green foreign investment.

China explores building the green financial policy system of the "Two Mountains" collaborative development

With the continuous deepening of the "green development concept", China has gradually developed a new economic pattern of higher efficiency, harmony, and sustainability. It has formed the social economy led by the *General Scheme for Reform of the Ecological Civilization System* and the scientific policy system of collaborative development of "green hills and clear waters" and "mountains of gold and silver", helping to improve social and economic development and ecological environment quality (see Table 2.1). This supports the implementation of the UN *Sustainable Development Goals in 2030*, and provides "Chinese approaches" for global ecological security and sustainable development (Wang and Cao 2018).

Financial institutions actively guide the green foreign investment for social capital.

A new round of global industrial revolution brings new opportunities for promoting green development. Chinese financial institutions actively participate in

Table 2.1 Overview of relevant policies of green finance

Year	Relevant Policy	Main Contents
2012	Green Credit Guidance	Promote and guide banking financial institutions to develop green credit
2013	Statistical System of Green Credit	Reflect the implementation achievements of green credit of banking financial institutions
2013	Guidance on Pilot Work of Compulsory Liability Insurance for Environmental Pollution	Advance the pilot work of compulsory liability insurance for environmental pollution
2014	Revised Environmental Protection Law	Promote ecological civilization construction and advanced economic and social sustainable development
2015	Established the Green Finance Committee of China Society for Finance and Banking	The first industry guidance institution with a green finance theme in Chinese history
2015	Vision and Action on Promoting the Construction of Silk Road Economic Belt and the 21st Century Maritime Silk Road	Co-construction of the "Green Belt and Road" became the important content of the top-level design of the "Belt and Road Initiative"
2015	Opinions of the Central Committee of the Communist Party of China and the State Council on Accelerating the Construction of Ecological Civilization	Green development was included in the institutional system of ecological civilization
2015	General Scheme for Reform of the Ecological Civilization System	Clearly proposes to "build China's green financial system" for the first time
2015	Contents of Green Bond Project Supporting (2015)	Provide system guidance to financial institutions for issuing green bonds
2015	Pilot Proposal for Reform of Compensation System for Eco-environmental Damage	Clarifies the compensation system was strictly implemented for the person responsible for eco-environmental damage
2016	Guidance on Issuing Green Bond	Define the project scope and key supports for green corporate bonds
2016	The 13th Five-Year Plan for National Economic and Social Development of the People's Republic of China	"Green Finance" was brought into China's Five-Year Plan for the first time
2016	Notice on Pilot Project of Green Corporate Bonds	Put green corporate bonds into the exchange bond market
2016	Guiding Opinions on Building the Green Financial System	China became the first economic entity in the world building a framework system for green financial policy
2016	Green Development Planning of Industry (2016–2020)	Speed up the construction of a green manufacturing system
2016	Guidelines on Implementation of Green Manufacturing Engineering (2016–2020)	Accelerate the green production mode and the construction of the green manufacturing system

(*continued*)

Table 2.1 Cont.

Year	Relevant Policy	Main Contents
2017	Guidance on Supporting the Development of Green Bonds	Guide the bond market to serve green industries
2017	Guiding Opinions on Promoting the Construction of the "Belt and Road Initiative"	Build the green "Belt and Road" in an all-round way and help countries along the route to achieve the UN 2030 sustainable development goals
2017	Guiding Opinions on Accelerating the Development of Environmental Protection Equipment Manufacturing Industry	Fully implement green manufacturing
2017	Cooperative Planning for Eco-environmental Protection of the "Belt and Road Initiative"	Apply green financial tools to investment and trade projects
2017	Built innovation pilot zones of green financial reform in Guangdong, Guizhou, Jiangxi, Zhejiang and Xinjiang	Accelerate the innovation mechanism of the green financial system and advanced the green transformation and upgrading of the economy
2017	Measures of Compulsory Liability Insurance for Environmental Pollution (Consultation Draft)	Promote ecological civilization construction and guide the local authority to advance the pilot work for environmental liability insurance
2017	Guiding Opinions of the Construction of the "Belt and Road Initiative" in Insurance Services	Exert the insurance function into all-round services and guarantee the construction of the "Belt and Road Initiative"
2017	Proposal for Reform of Compensation System for Eco-environmental Damage	Tried out the compensation system for environmental damage nationwide
2017	Initiative for Risk Management of China's Foreign Investment Environment	Promote the green trade financing, supply chain financing, and enhanced capacity building in environmental risk management
2017	Development Plan of Standardization System Construction in Financial Industry (2016–2020)	Integrate the green financial standardization project into the standardization plan for the finance industry of the "13th Five-Year Plan".
2018	Notice on Further Perfecting RMB Cross-border Business Policy to Promote Trade and Investment Facilitation	Support foreign investors to join the carbon emission permit trading in China with RMB
2018	Notice on Launching Green Credit Performance Evaluation of Banking Deposit Financial Institutions	Bring green credit into MPA assessment
2018	Principles of Green Investment for the "Belt and Road Initiative"	Integrate the green concept into the whole management process, including project progress, product development, and risk control

Table 2.1 Cont.

Year	Relevant Policy	Main Contents
2018	Notice on Launching Pilot for Supply Chain Innovation and Application	Lists the construction of a green supply chain as a major task
2019	Contents of Green Industrial Guidance (2019)	Further clarifies the industrial borders, guided policies, and capital to promote the development of green industries

Source: Collated by the author based on public data

promoting the co-construction of the "Green Belt and Road", enhancing ecological environment and biodiversity and responding to climate change.

Emission reduction encouraged by green credit gradually demonstrates environmental benefits

Green credit is a major measure for financial institutions to serve the physical economy, drive the sustainable transformation of the economy and support the construction of ecological civilization (see Table 2.2). China has built almost perfect green credit industrial policies. In addition to China Industrial Bank, other banks such as Shanghai Pudong Development Bank and Bank of Beijing, China Development Bank, Export-Import Bank of China, and the Industrial and Commercial Bank of China have entered the green financial market. Twenty-one major banks in China have issued the *Joint Commitment of Banking Green Credit*, increasing the investment to green credit (Ma, Zhou and Wang 2018).

The environmental benefits of green credit have gradually appeared. It is estimated that every year, China's energy conservation and environmental protection project and service loans can save 215 million tons of standard coals, and reduce emissions of 491 million tons of carbon dioxide equivalents, 2.8345 million tons of chemical oxygen demand, 267,600 tons of ammonia nitrogen, 4.6453 million tons of sulphur dioxide, 3.1311 million tons of nitrogen oxide, as well as saving 715 million tons of water. The defective rate of China's green credit is much lower than the whole defective level of all loans. From the end of 2013 to the end of June 2017 the defective rates of energy conservation and environmental protection project and service loans of the 21 major domestic banks were respectively 0.32%, 0.20%, 0.42%, 0.49%, and 0.37% (Xinhua 2018).

Flourishing of green bonds brings capital to green industries

China's green bonds started relatively late, but have made great achievements. In 2016, China became the largest issuing market of green bonds in the world. In 2017, the issuing scale of China's green bonds reached RMB250 billion,

Table 2.2 Green credit of 21 major banks (2013–2017). Overseas projects adopting international practices or international standards (Unit: RMB one hundred million, tonne)

Release Time	Loan Balance	Energy Conservation and Emission Reduction						
		Standard Coal	Carbon Dioxide Equivalent	Chemical Oxygen Demand	Ammonia Nitrogen	Sulphur Dioxide	Nitrogen Oxide	Water Saving
June 30, 2017	371.76	619358.75	1516970.64	244.61	0.05	9285.62	7743.37	0.00
December 31, 2016	230.46	369770.76	983360.29	132.08	0.02	9606.61	6260.56	0.00
December 31, 2015	208.79	2395492.26	6372889.14	54.69	0.01	64042.74	40578.54	0.00
December 31, 2014	181.18	1839566.30	4893849.00	0.00	0.00	52533.00	31141.00	0.00
December 31, 2013	99.82	786543.09	2018978.16	0.00	0.00	15211.30	5077.06	0.00

Source: Collated by the author based on the data released by China Banking Regulatory Commission (CBRC 2018)

accounting for over 20% of the global proportion (CBI 2018). Across the world, the United States ranks first with US$42.4 billion in green bond issuance, closely followed by China and then France.

Compared with the flourishing of green bonds in China, China's overseas green bond issuance still has great potential. During the first half year of 2018, the global green bond issuance increased, reaching a total issuance of US$76.9 billion. The total amount of China's green bonds, which was consistent with the international green bond definition, was US$9.3 billion, accounting for 12% of the global market in the same period, where offshore green bond issuance accounted for 40% of China's total.

The overseas green bonds issued by the leading large-scale enterprises and the large-scale commercial banks accounted for 40% of China's total: ICBC London and ICBC Asia issued green bonds of US$2.3 billion in London Stock Exchange and Hong Kong Stock Exchange, respectively, making Industrial and Commercial Bank of China the biggest issuer of offshore green bonds at the beginning of 2018.

According to the information in Table 2.3, we can see key features of overseas green bonds issued by domestic entities in China: (1) the average period of China's green bonds is still relatively short, less than five years; (2) the standard of China's green bonds is inconsistent with the definition of international green bonds, causing some of China's green bonds not to be counted into the global green bond issuance; and (3) financial industries are still the largest issuing entities. Compared with the number of non-financial enterprises in China, the number of overseas non-financial enterprises has a huge potential for increase. China should strongly focus on the development of the overseas green bond market in future. On one hand, China can look for new business growth for itself, and on the other, China can bring capital into overseas green industries (Ma, Zhou, and Wang 2018).

Preliminary findings of the role of green insurance

Green insurance refers to various insurance plans related to environmental risk management, which is a sustainable financial instrument and an important part of green finance to address problems such as climate change, energy substitution, environmental pollution, and ecological damage. The green insurance system was originated in the industrialized countries in Europe, the United States, and some developing countries have begun to establish it. At present, the green insurance system of major developed countries has entered a relatively mature stage, and has become one of the main ways to solve the problem of liability for environmental damage.

After the national pilot programme of ecological environmental damage compensation in China, the overall market for environmental liability insurance has developed rapidly, and the economic function for insurance has preliminarily slowed. At present, most provinces in China are carrying out pilot programmes for environmental liability insurance, covering industries involving heavy metals,

Table 2.3 Overseas green bonds issued by domestic entities in China

Issuer	Amount	Currency	Issue Date	Expiry Date	Verification Institution	Market
China Construction Bank	500 million	EUR	24/09/2018	24/10/2021	Ernst &Young	Luxembourg Green Stock Exchange
China Everbright Bank	300 million	USD	13/09/2018	19/8/2021	Sustainalytics	Hong Kong Stock Exchange
Capital Environment	250 million	USD	11/09/2018	11/09/2021	Sustainalytics	Hong Kong Stock Exchange
ICBC Asia	200 million	USD	14/06/2018	14/06/2021	HKQAA	Hong Kong Stock Exchange
	300 million	USD	14/06/2018	14/06/2023		
	260 million	HKD	14/06/2018	14/06/2020		
Industrial and Commercial Bank of China	500 million	USD	11/06/2018	11/06/2021	CICERO, International Institute of Green Finance	London Stock Exchange
	500 million	USD	11/06/2018	11/06/2023		
	500 million	EUR	11/06/2018	11/06/2021		
Bank of China	1 billion	USD	31/05/2018	31/05/2023	Ernst &Young	Hong Kong Stock Exchange
Beijing Capital Group	500 million	USD	19/03/2018	19/03/2021	Sustainalytics	Hong Kong Stock Exchange
	630 million	RMB	19/03/2018	19/03/2020		
Tianjin Rail Transit Group	400 million	EUR	13/03/2018	22/06/2022	Sustainalytics	Luxembourg Green Exchange
CGNPC Group Co., Ltd	500 million	EUR	05/12/2017	05/12/2024	Deloitte	Euronext – Paris
Bank of China	500 million	USD	22/11/2017	22/11/2022	Ernst &Young	Euronext – Paris
	1 billion	RMB	22/11/2017	22/11/2020		
	700 million	EUR	22/11/2017	22/11/2020		
China Development Bank	1 billion	EUR	16/11/2017	16/11/2021	Ernst &Young	China Europe International Exchange
Industrial and Commercial Bank of China	500 million	USD	16/11/2017	16/11/2022	CICERO	Hong Kong Stock Exchange
	450 million	USD	12/10/2017	12/10/2020		Luxembourg Stock Exchange (Luxembourg Green Exchange)
	400 million	USD	12/10/2017	12/10/2022	International Institute of Green Finance	
	1.1 billion	EUR	12/10/2017	12/10/2020		
China Three Gorges Corporation	650 million	EUR	21/06/2017	21/06/2024	Ernst &Young	Dublin Exchange

Bank of China	500 million	USD	03/11/2016	03/11/2019	Ernst &Young	London Stock Exchange
Bank of China	750 million	USD	05/07/2016	12/07/2019	Ernst &Young	Luxembourg Stock Exchange
	500 million	USD	05/07/2016	12/07/2019		
	1 billion	USD	05/07/2016	12/07/2021		
	500 million	EUR	05/07/2016	12/07/2021		
	1.5 billion	RMB	05/07/2016	12/07/2018		
GEELY	400 million	USD	26/5/2016	26/5/2021	Deloitte	London Stock Exchange
Agricultural Bank of China	400 million	USD	13/10/2015	24/7/2018	Deloitte	London Stock Exchange
	500 million	USD	13/10/2015	24/7/2020		
	600 million	RMB	13/10/2015	24/7/2017		
Agricultural Bank of China	400 million	USD	13/10/2015	24/7/2018	Deloitte	London Stock Exchange
	500 million	USD	13/10/2015	24/7/2020		
	600 million	RMB	13/10/2015	24/7/2017		
Xinjiang Goldwind Science and Technology	300 million	USD	16/07/2015	24/07/2018	DNV GL	Hong Kong Stock Exchange

Source: Collated by the author based on the statistics of the green financial channel of China's financial information network

petrochemicals, hazardous chemicals, hazardous waste disposal, etc. In 2016, there were 14,400 enterprises insured for environmental liability throughout the country, with the premium of RMB284 million; insurance companies provided a total of RMB26.373 billion risk securities. The number of insurance products participating in the pilot programmes has grown from four at the initial stage to more than 20 now, and all major domestic insurance companies have joined them. In 2017, the annual income from premiums for environmental liability insurance exceeded RMB300 million in China (Qian 2017).

Insurance funds provide financing support for the green transformation of China's economy. According to the statistics of the Insurance Asset Management Association of China, as of the end of April 2018, the total registered size of insurance funds in the form of creditor's investment plans had reached RMB685.425 billion, including some key ecological and environmental protection areas directly invested, such as investing RMB66.6 billion in new energy, RMB50.644 billion in water resources, RMB17.86 billion in municipal service facilities, and RMB5.27 billion in environmental protection (Zhou 2018).

As a financial tool for sharing risk, insurance plays a unique role in supporting the construction of the "Belt and Road Initiative". From 2013 to 2016, People's Insurance Company of China Property and Casualty Company Limited (PICC P&C) participated in underwriting more than 450 engineering and property insurance programmes along the "Belt and Road", covering more than 40 countries and regions along the route, and undertaking risk guarantees amounting to RMB1.076 trillion (Li 2017). From 2013 to October 2017, Sinosure's underwriting amount for Chinese enterprises' export and investment in countries along the "Belt and Road" exceeded US$515 billion, where the investment for Chinese enterprises in countries along the "Belt and Road" exceeded US$135 billion, covering many overseas demonstration investment projects, such as Longjiang Industrial Park in Vietnam, Malaysia Kuantan Industrial Park, and involving many industries such as energy, minerals, electric power, metallurgy, and agriculture (Sinosure 2017).

Insurance has played a unique role in supporting the construction of the "Belt and Road Initiative". However, in order for green insurance to play a risk protection role in building the "Green Belt and Road", it is necessary to establish a corresponding long-term mechanism for green insurance. This commitment includes actively promoting the integration of green insurance as an institutional arrangement into the overall layout of the "Green Belt and Road", coordinating the resources of all parties at home and abroad, and strengthening the exchange and cooperation of international green insurance.

2.4.3 *China and the UK jointly study and promote "Belt and Road Initiative" green investment*

Since 2016, China and the UK have jointly hosted the G20 Green Finance Research Group and launched the China-UK Green Finance Working Group to promote the financial institutions of both countries in strengthening green financial innovation and green bond market interconnection. China and the UK jointly launched the *China-UK Financial Services Strategic Plan*, covering capital markets, asset management, insurance and pensions, banking, green finance, financial technology, the "Belt and Road Initiative" program, and inclusive finance (UK Gov 2017). In 2018, China and the UK launched the China-UK Green Finance Centre, deepened green financial cooperation, and jointly promoted voluntary guidance, measures of green asset securitization, pilots of environmental information disclosure, etc. of the environmental risk management for "Belt and Road Initiative" investment.

Thoughts on promoting China's green foreign investment

The year 2019 was the 70th anniversary of the founding of New China and the key year for the first 100-year goal of building a well-off society. Under the development concept "innovation, coordination, green, openness, and sharing" and economic transformation and upgrading, China's economy has turned to a stage of high-quality development, and green has become the background colour for the co-construction of the "Belt and Road Initiative". Looking into the future, promoting green infrastructure construction, green investment, and green finance will become important tasks in the next stage (Wang, Zhai, and Cao 2018). For this reason, it is suggested to adopt the following measures.

Accelerate the formation of a green investment and financing policy system

Give full play to the leading role of the government, strengthen the top-led strategy in terms of macro-layout, policy interconnection, platform construction, and overall coordination. Guide enterprises that are "going global" to take the green management road and encourage more social forces to participate in green investment and financing projects.

Build international and regional investment and financing cooperation mechanisms to create a green development community

Take advantage of the existing multilateral mechanisms such as China-ASEAN, Shanghai Cooperation Organization, Lancang-Mekong Cooperation, Euro-Asia Economic Forum, FOCAC, and China-Arab States Cooperation Forum to establish an international alliance for green investment and financing, expand international cooperation, and drive more institutions and enterprises in different countries and regions to participate in the creation of the green development community.

2.5.3 Enhance the capacity building of market participants to the role of environmental governance

Encourage market participants such as financial institutions and enterprises to strengthen the capacity of green investment and financing, and strengthen environmental awareness throughout the lifecycle of investment and project operation so as to actively fulfil environmental and social responsibilities.

Actively guide the development of dual multilateral development funds to participate in green investment and financing

Give full play to the synergy effect of complementary advantages of dual multilateral development funds, and lead the AIIB, Silk Road Fund, South-South Cooperation Fund, Asian Development Bank, European Bank for Reconstruction and Development, and other multilateral financial institutions to participate in green investment and financing projects.

2.5.5 Actively explore innovative green investment and financing cooperation

Strengthen the cooperation with governments and regional governments along the "Belt and Road" routes, innovate and develop the private-public partnership (PPP) cooperation model, guide funds and credit support from local governments, promote coordination between local governments and investment entities of green projects, and consolidate environmental risk management of green projects.

Build a green investment and financing information service platform

With the help of "Internet+", big data, satellite remote sensing, and other information technologies, establish a project library of investment destination countries or regions, share information on local ecological environment conditions and environmental policies, regulations, standards, technologies and industrial development, and provide basic information and policy support for green investment and environmental protection of enterprise operation activities to ensure the co-construction of the "Green Belt and Road".

2.5.7 Encourage non-government organizations to participate in green investment and financing activities

Promote thinktanks with international influence to strengthen exchanges in green investment and financing activities with thinktanks of the countries along the "Belt and Road" routes, drive public and social organizations to participate in co-construction green development, vigorously support private environmental protection exchanges and cooperation, carry out various public welfare activities for green investment and financing, and help build the green "Belt and Road".

Establish a green investment and financing supervision mechanism and risk prevention system

Establish a green financial risk prevention mechanism, promote the environmental information disclosure system, improve the green investment and financing supervision mechanism to unify and improve green investment and financing rules and standards, prevent "greenwashing" and "greenwashing" behaviours, and ensure that green financing funds are invested in real green projects to accelerate the process of green investment and financing and contribute to low-carbon green development (Cheng and Ma 2018).

Note

1 A Chinese version was published in the *Journal of Renmin University of China*, Vol. 196, no. 33, pp. 10–22 in 2019.

References

Association of Southeast Asian Nations (ASEAN) 2008, 'Article 1 (9) of the ASEAN Charter 2', *ASEAN Secretariat*, Jakarta, January 2008. Available from: http://asean.org/storage/images/archive/publications/ASEAN-Charter.pdf. [15 February 2019].

Belt and Road Portal 2018, 'China's investment in the countries along the Belt and Road increased by 11.8% in the first seven months', *Yidaiyilu.gov.cn*, 18 August. Available from: www.yidaiyilu.gov.cn/xwzx/roll/63170.htm. [15 February 2019].

Centre d'Etudes Prospectives et d'Informations Internationales (CEPII) 2000, 'FDI and the opening up of China's economy'. Available from: http://cepii.fr/PDF_PUB/wp/2000/wp2000-11.pdf. [12 January 2019].

China Banking Regulatory Commission (CBRC) 2018, 'Green credit data of 21 major banks from 2013 to June 2017'. Available from: www.cnfinance.cn/articles/2018-02/11-27842.html. [5 March 2019].

China Export & Credit Insurance Corporation (SinoSure) 2017, 'SinoSure released the 2017 Analysis Report on Global Investment Risk', Xinhua Net, 12 October. Available from: www.xinhuanet.com/money/2017-10/12/c_129719506.htm. [20 March 2019].

Cheng, L & Ma, J 2018, 'The latest international development of green finance'. Available from: www.pbcsf.tsinghua.edu.cn/Upload/file/20180606/20180606155858_7726. pdf. [27 March 2019].

Climate Bonds Initiative (CBI) 2018, 'China green bonds market'. Available from: www. climatebonds.net/files/reports/china-sotm_cbi_ccdc_final_en260219.pdf. [5 March 2019].

Hua, GF 1979, 'Chinese Government Report 1979', 18 June 1979. Available from: www. gov.cn/test/2006-02/16/content_200759.htm. [12 December 2019].

Industrial and Commercial Bank of China Limited (ICBC) 2018, 'Leads a number of member units of the Green Finance Commission, environmental risk and case analysis by financial institutions', *Xinhua Net*, 19 January. Available from: http://greenfinance. xinhua08.com/a/20180719/1769892.shtml. [15 February 2019].

Li, M 2017, 'PICC P&C escorts the Belt and Road to help enterprises start their journey with peace in mind', *People's Insurance Company of China*, 29 September. Available from: www.epicc.com.cn/renbao/zixunzhongxin/meitiguanzhu/201709/t20170928_10680.html. [15 March 2019].

Liu, WB 2017, *Understanding the Belt and Road Blueprint*. The Commercial Press, Beijing.

Ma, J 2018, 'Working paper of green finance committee 2017–2018'. Available from: http://finance.sina.com.cn/money/bank/bank_hydt/2018-04-21/doc-ifznefkh0602587.shtml. [12 January 2019].

Ma, Z, Zhou, Y & Wang, WB 2018, *2017 China's Green Finance Development Report*. China Financial Publishing House, Beijing.

Ministry of Commerce of the People's Republic of China (MOFCOM) 2013, '2012 statistical bulletin of China's outward foreign direct investment', *China Statistics Press, Beijing*. Available from: http://images.mofcom.gov.cn/hzs/201409/20140918133802073.pdf. [9 April 2019].

Ministry of Commerce of the People's Republic of China (MOFCOM) 2017, 'Report on development of China's outward investment and economic cooperation'. Available from: http://fec.mofcom.gov.cn/article/tzhzcj/tzhz/upload/zgdwtzhzfzbg2017.pdf. [20 January 2019].

Ministry of Commerce of the People's Republic of China (MOFCOM) 2017, 'China's current status and causes of direct investment in countries along the Belt and Road', *China One-stop Business Service Platform*, 14 November. Available from: www.12335.gov.cn/article/ydylycjzl/201711/1923400_1.html. [25 February 2019].

Ministry of Commerce of the People's Republic of China (MOFCOM) 2018, 'Report on development of China's outward investment'. Available from: http://images.mofcom.gov.cn/fec/201901/20190128155348158.pdf. [28 January 2019].

Ministry of Commerce of the People's Republic of China (MOFCOM) 2018, '2017 statistical bulletin of China's outward foreign direct investment'. Available from: http://images.mofcom.gov.cn/hzs/201810/20181029160118046.pdf. [9 April 2019].

Ministry of Ecology and Environment (MEE) 2017, 'Ecological and environmental cooperation plan for the Belt and Road'. Available from: www.mee.gov.cn/gkml/hbb/bwj/201705/t20170516_414102.htm. [10 January 2019]

Qian, L 2017, 'With 10 years of pilot programs, environmental liability insurance is still unpopular in the market', *Financialnews.com.cn*, 8 November. Available from: http://greenfinance.xinhua08.com/a/20171108/1734508.shtml. [10 March 2019].

United Kingdom Government (UK) 2017, 'UK-China 8th EFD policy outcomes'. Available from: https://assets.publishing.service.gov.uk/government/uploads/system/uploads/attachment_data/file/567534/UK-China_8th_EFD_policy_outcomes_zh.pdf. [20 March 2019].

United Nations Environment Programme (UNEP) 2016, 'Green economy'. Available from: www.unenvironment.org/explore-topics/green-economy. [17 February 2019].

United Nations Educational, Scientific and Cultural Organization (UNESCO) 2017, 'Partnering for prosperity: Education for green and inclusive growth; Global education monitoring report 2016'. Available from: https://unesdoc.unesco.org/ark:/48223/pf0000246918. [15 February 2019].

Wang, W & Cao, MD 2018, 'Green insurance escorts the construction of the Belt and Road', *China Financialyst*, no. 1, pp. 131–132.

Wang, W, Zhai, Y & Cao, M 2018, *Evaluation Methodology of Green Investment Cost and Benefit on the Belt and Road*. People's Publishing House, Beijing.

Xinhua 2018, '21 major banks' green credit balances increased to 8.22 trillion RMB', *Xinhua Net*, 14 February. Available from: www.xinhuanet.com/money/2018-02/14/c_1122416988.htm. [28 February 2019].

Zhang, Y 2017, 'Work together to build a green Belt and Road and maintain global ecological security'. Available from: http://cpc.people.com.cn/xuexi/n1/2017/0511/c385474-29269558.html. [14 February 2019].

Zhou, Y 2018, 'The scale of green investment with insurance funds in the form of creditor's rights exceeds RMB680 billion', *Sina*, 30 June. Available from: http://finance.sina.com.cn/money/bond/market/2018-06-20/doc-iheauxvz9827426.shtml?cre=tianyi&mod=pcpager_fin&loc=17&r=9&doct=0&rfunc=100&tj=none&tr=9. [10 March 2019].

3 Sustainability of RMB internationalization

Cheung-Kwok Law

Introduction

RMB (renminbi) internationalization had not been explicitly stated as a policy by the Chinese government in any official documents, though the removal of restrictions on RMB trade settlements in 2009 was a clear decision towards RMB internationalization (Zhang and Tao 2014). In fact, the Chinese State Council approved the introduction of personal RMB businesses in Hong Kong as early as 2003, followed by the appointment of a Clearing Bank (Chan 2014). The internationalization of RMB, following the path of other international currencies (Takagi 2012; Brummer 2017; Ma and Villar 2014; Frankel 2012, Yu 2014a; Kawai 1996), can be broadly divided into three stages.

To start with, border trade would commence with the experiment of using RMB as the medium of exchange, under the auspices of the Chinese government, for example, border trade between Vietnam and the Guangxi Province in the early years of 2000. Vietnamese nationals living near the border are allowed to set up RMB banking accounts in the border towns in Guangxi to facilitate the border trade. Over time, small border transactions using the RMB would expand into large transactions across oceans, as a means of invoicing and settlement (Brummer 2017). The RMB trade settlement would also promote the development of RMB trade finance. Eventually, transactions all across the world may use the RMB as a means of exchange, even the transactions that do not directly relate to China. When the Chinese government decided to promote RMB internationalization in the early 2010s, Hong Kong would naturally become the most promising offshore RMB financial centre.

Once RMB is used for cross-border trade, there would be a gradual liberalization of the Chinese capital markets to support the cross-border RMB trade transactions. The next stage is using RMB for inflow of foreign direct investment from the rest of the world and outflow of direct foreign investment from China. Both ways, portfolio investment under capital market liberalization would follow direct foreign investment. A market-determined RMB exchange rate and interest rates would be the key for such developments.

In order to enhance the sustainability of RMB internationalization, the Chinese government needs to provide the RMB infrastructure (both domestic and offshore) and RMB products to support the RMB offshore holders to participate in the Chinese capital markets and to hold RMB financial and real assets. International financial institutions in various financial centres would also develop new financial products to capture the new RMB business opportunities and to control the associated risks created. This would generate a variety of financial institutions, products, and market intermediaries, covering foreign exchange transactions, trade finance, stocks, bonds, and complex derivatives. Subsequently, the RMB would commence its long journey to develop as a reserve currency for foreign countries. This can be termed the 'functional approach' for RMB internationalization (Yu 2014a).

The Chinese government, multinational institutions, academics, and international financial institutions have been showing great interest in tracking the degree of RMB internationalization. Officially, the People's Bank of China started to release its annual RMB Internationalization Report in 2015. The report focused on the policy measures undertaken by the central bank to facilitate RMB internationalization. Additionally, the International Monetary Institute (IMI, the research arm of International Monetary Fund) and Renmin University of China published an annual report on RMB internationalization (Renmin University and IMI 2017, 2018), with an index comprising RMB's denomination in international trade, finance, and official foreign reserves. Some international financial institutions also launched their own indexes of RMB internationalization, including notably the Standard Chartered Bank's Renminbi Globalization Index (Standard Charted Bank 2012, 2018) and Bank of China Cross-border RMB Index (Bank of China 2013).

This chapter is not a comprehensive exposition of the theory, background, challenges, and prospects of RMB Internationalization. There have been many researchers exploring the background of and critical factors for RMB internationalization (Overholt, Ma and Law 2016; Ballantyn, Garner and Wright 2013; Lowe 2014; Frankel 2012; Takagi 2012; Yu 2014a; Eichengreen 2013; Park 2016).

In the following analysis, we will start with an introduction of the balance of payment crisis experienced by China since 2014, which reduced the pace of RMB internationalization significantly. Then, we will examine the major financial parameters reflecting the latest development of RMB internationalization. The development of RMB as an international reserve currency and its relationship with the bond market will be subsequently analyzed. The further liberalization of China's equity market for overseas investment has been an exciting chapter for RMB internationalization. Indeed, there have been many new liberalization measures facilitating and sustaining offshore RMB businesses in recent years. The necessary financial infrastructure and networks have been greatly strengthened despite the volatility of RMB having regenerated some concerns.

Many international financial institutions have been gearing up their RMB business strategies. The BRI will generate additional impetus to RMB internationalization. One recent highlight is the emerging of the petro-yuan, as several major oil suppliers to China have been willing to accept RMB for their oil transactions. Lastly, we will provide policy recommendations for responding to the challenges and enhancing the sustainability of RMB internationalization.

China's recent balance-of-payment crisis and foreign exchange controls

The pace of RMB internationalization gained momentum between 2012 and 2015, mainly owing to sustained government policies promoting RMB internationalization and the expectation of RMB appreciation. There were many optimistic assessments for the rising of RMB as a major international currency in the medium to long term (HSBC 2018; Overholt, Ma and Law 2016; Asian Banker and China Construction Bank 2018; Deutsche Bank 2017; SWIFT 2017). These were also witnessed by increasing offshore RMB deposits, new RMB products and foreign participation in the RMB market.

China has, for a long time, enjoyed both a current account surplus and a net inflow of foreign direct investment (the difference between inflows and outflows of foreign direct investments). China's huge current account surplus has been supplemented by a net inflow of foreign direct investment (Santacreu and Zhu 2017; Yu 2017; Kang and Kang 2017). In recent years, China's overseas foreign direct investment (OFDI) increased very rapidly. Indeed, China's OFDI was US$42 billion more than that of inflows in 2016. As international financial markets gradually stabilized after the global financial crisis in 2008 and international economic conditions have improved significantly in recent years, domestic and foreign investors in China began to explore other investment opportunities overseas. The recent trend of rising interest rates in the US, the deteriorating balance of payment position, and China's capital flight have added pressure to the RMB. The resulting depreciation of the RMB against the US dollar from about 6.15 in early September 2014 to about 6.95 at the end of December 2016 further accelerated the capital flight from China (Gunter 2017; Otero-Iglesias 2018).

China's foreign exchange reserves and the value of RMB peaked in early 2014. From mid-2014 to year-end 2016, foreign exchange reserves fell by about US$1 trillion, amounting to about 10% of China's GDP (Gunter 2017). Concurrently, the RMB lost about 12% of its value against the US dollar. Obviously, the weakening of the balance of payment position, as indicated by the international monetary statistics, could not satisfactorily explain the sharp fall in foreign reserves by US$1 trillion in two years' time.

The sharp and unexpected depletion of US$1000 billion in international reserves prompted the Chinese government to introduce strong capital control measures (Karnfelt 2017; Kahn 2016; Durden 2017; Davis 2017; Chen and Qian 2016). Indeed, the momentum of RMB internationalization and activities of offshore RMB centres weakened markedly after August 2015 (Davis 2017; Bryson 2018; Lau et al. 2018). The turbulence in China's stock market in 2015 also demanded vigilance of the monetary and financial regulatory authorities in the domestic market. The sustainability of RMB internationalization has been under serious threat.

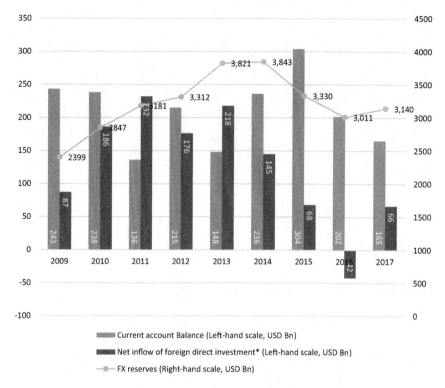

Figure 3.1 China's current account, foreign exchange reserves and net inflow of foreign direct investment

*Note: Net inflow of foreign direct investment = Direct investment liabilities – Direct investment asset (Data provided by IMF)

Source: China SAFE (2018), World Bank (2018), IMF (2018)

In late November 2016, four Chinese government authorities, the National Development and Reform Commission, Ministry of Commerce, State Administration of Foreign Exchange (SAFE) and People's Bank of China, issued a joint directive stating that outbound investments will be subject to strict reviews (McMillan LLP 2017). A strict prohibition shall be applied to the following transactions:

1   any outbound investments of US$10 billion or more;
2   any outbound investments of US$1 billion or more by state-owned enterprises on a single real estate transaction;
3   any outbound investments of US$1 billion or more if they are not included in the Chinese government's core businesses list; and
4   any outbound investments in equity stakes of 10% or less of publicly listed overseas companies.

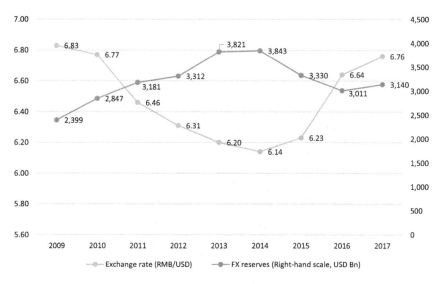

Figure 3.2 RMB/USD exchange rate and foreign reserves of China
Source: China SAFE (2018), World Bank (2018), IMF (2018).

Furthermore, strict scrutiny shall be applied to the following transactions:

1 outbound transfers of foreign currency or RMB equivalent to US$5 million or more;
2 outbound investments by China-domiciled companies with a high asset-to-liability ratio and low return on equity;
3 capital outflows under any investment projects worth US$50 million or more; and
4 outbound investments and profit remittances by foreign investors.

Chinese foreign exchange reserves have since stabilized (US$3,050b in September 2018), the currency appreciating about 4.5% in the first nine months of 2017. Davis (2017) concluded that, based on a review of past balance-of-payment crises experienced by other emerging markets, China's capital control measures could have been the stabilizing factor that averted a full-blown crisis.

The devaluation in the RMB against the US dollar from 6.2 to 6.9 since early 2018 once again has clouded the short-term prospects of RMB internationalization (Setser 2018). Furthermore, if the China-US trade conflict, potential local government and corporate debt problems, the lack of financial and regulatory transparency, and the systemic risk associated with them are not mitigated, the capital account liberalization and full internationalization of the RMB are likely to be impeded.

RMB international transactions

In order to gauge the recent development of RMB internationalization, we resort to the Standard Chartered Index (SCRII) and the Renmin University and IMI Index (RURII) to provide a general understanding of the development and its sustainability. The SCRII is compiled by the Standard Chartered Bank and 2012 was adopted as the base year (Standard Chartered Bank 2012). The index is formulated from four parameters: CNH RMB deposits; trade settlement and other international payments; Dim Sum bonds and certificate of deposit issued; and RMB foreign exchange turnover. The index peaked in September 2015 at 2,476 and declined to the lowest point of 1,730 in June 2017. The index moderately increased to 1,916 in August 2018 (Standard Chartered Bank 2018). Similarly, the RURII started at 0.02 in the first quarter of 2010, peaked at 3.60 in the third quarter of 2015, then declined sharply to 1.49 in the first quarter of 2017. This again rebounded significantly to 3.13 in the fourth quarter of 2017 (Renmin University and IMI 2018).

RMB foreign exchange transactions

According to BIS statistics (Bank of International Settlement 2016), the average daily transactions of RMB foreign exchange were US$202 billion, ranked 8th and accounting for about 2% of global transactions. The Indian rupee's daily foreign exchange transactions were more than that of the RMB in 2010, but the RMB's daily transactions were about four times that of the rupee in 2016. The increase in RMB foreign exchange transactions was the highest of all currencies of the emerging markets between 2013 and 2016.

Of all RMB foreign exchange trading with other currencies in 2017, 97.1% were against the US dollar (SWIFT 2018a). There was no substantial liquidity in any other RMB currency pairs. When reviewing the top foreign exchange trading locations for the RMB, China had the largest share at 30.1%, followed by the UK with 25.7% and Hong Kong with 19.7%.

RMB global cross-border payments

Based on the SWIFT data, consistent with the other RMB parameters, the relative importance of RMB international cross-border payment and settlement declined in 2017 (SWIFT 2018a). The RMB's global payment share for domestic and international payments decreased from 2.31% (ranked 5th) in December 2015 and 1.61% in December 2017 (ranked 5th). If we only estimated international payments excluding intra Eurozone payments, the corresponding share declined from 1.60% (ranked 7th) to 0.98% (ranked 8th). Both shares increased to 2.12% and 1.26% respectively in August 2018 (SWIFT 2018b). Of all cross-border payments in 2017 – of which the ultimate beneficiary was in China or Hong Kong – 80.5% were in US dollars, and RMB transactions only accounted for 5.3%.

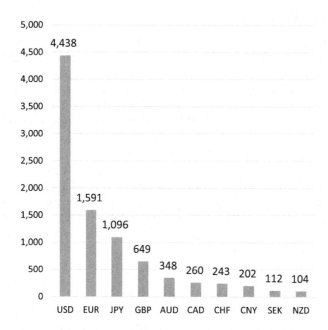

Figure 3.3 Average foreign exchange daily turnover 2016 (USD bn)
Source: BIS, Triennial Central Bank Survey 2016.

There were 101 countries using the RMB for cross-border payments with China and Hong Kong, and 57 of them used the RMB for more than 10% of their total international payments. In 2017, Hong Kong remained the largest RMB clearing centre for cross-border payments with 75.5% activity share (SWIFT 2018a). It was 76.1% in August 2018 (SWIFT 2018b). London remained the largest clearing centre outside Greater China, despite a declining share from 6.5% in 2016 to 5.6% in 2017. This was followed by Singapore, the US and Taiwan. Therefore, Hong Kong is the largest RMB offshore clearing centre, and London is the largest RMB offshore foreign exchange transaction centre.

RMB global cross-border trade settlement

Based on the People's Bank of China and China's Customs Statistics, the value of cross-border RMB trade settlement in 2013 jumped 58%, compared to the same period in 2012. The share of China's trade settlement in RMB peaked at about 31% in the third quarter of 2015 but declined to about 16% in 2017. The sustained increase in the share of China's RMB settlement between early 2012 to the third quarter of 2015 was mainly due to the arbitrage activities under RMB appreciation expectations and the steady growth of China (Yu 2014a). The RMB settlement was over RMB2,000 billion in the third quarter of 2015, then

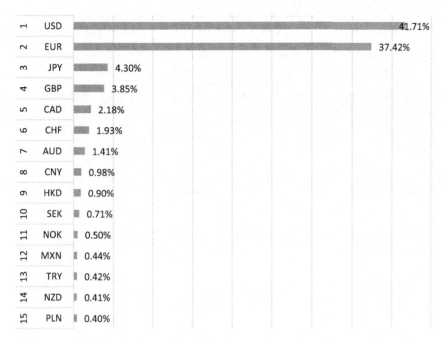

Figure 3.4 SWIFT global payment flow by share: top 15 currencies (March 2018)
Note: Cross-border payments only (excluding intra Eurozone payments).
Source: SWIFT (2018)

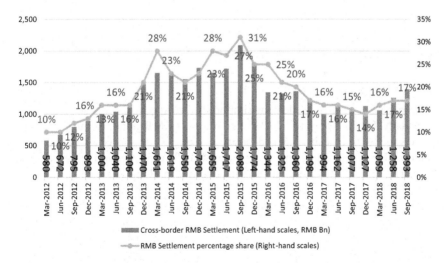

Figure 3.5 Cross-border trade settlements in RMB in China
Source: CEIC (2018).

Table 3.1 RMB cross-border payment (2017)

RMB Transactions	RMB, bn	China Total	RMB, bn	Percent Share
Cross-border RMB trade (goods only)	3270	China total merchandize trade	23,043	14.2%
Cross-border RMB trade (goods and services, other CA items)	4360	China total trade (goods and services, other CA items)	27,743	15.7%
Cross-border RMB trade (goods and services, other CA items) and direct investment	6000	China total trade (goods and services, other CA items) and direct investment	29,697	20.2%

Source: Wind, CEIC.

dropped to about RMB1,000 billion in the second quarter of 2017 and subsequently increased to RMB1,400 billion in the third quarter of 2018.

Because the consensus is that the RMB would fluctuate in two directions in the coming years, the exchange rate and interest rate arbitrages would bear substantial risk. This would result in fewer trade settlements in RMB and a better-balanced import and export trade settlement. Consequentially, there will be less injection of RMB liquidity into offshore financial markets.

Hong Kong still accounted for about 80% of the RMB trade settlement of China. The RMB trade settlement in Hong Kong peaked at RMB6,833 billion in 2015 and then declined to RMB3,927 billion in 2017.

Offshore RMB financial assets and products

RMB offshore deposits

The resulting net RMB settlement (imports over exports) in offshore markets, particularly Hong Kong, would have transferred RMB liquidity into offshore markets in RMB deposits. RMB deposits in Hong Kong surged to RMB1,004 billion in December 2014 and then declined to RMB559 billion in December 2017. The share of RMB deposits to total deposits in Hong Kong declined from about 12% to about 5% in the corresponding period. The major reason is the depreciation of RMB against the US dollar, which substantially reduced the expected rate of return (interest plus expected appreciation) by holding RMB deposits (Liu 2015). RMB deposits gradually increased to RMB600 billion in September 2018.

This development strongly suggested that the holding of RMB deposits in Hong Kong was mainly driven by investment purposes rather than for transaction

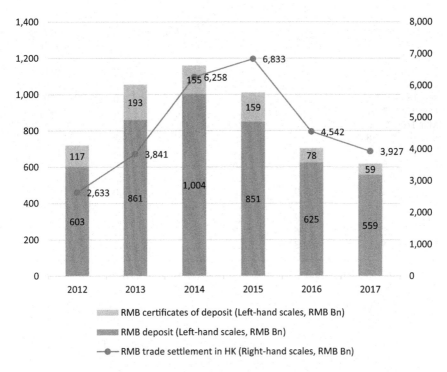

Figure 3.6 RMB deposits and cross-border trade settlements in Hong Kong
Source: HKMA (2018).

purposes. The sharp depreciation of RMB resulted in a negative return for holding RMB deposits, even taking the higher interest offered as compared to Hong Kong dollar deposits (Hong Kong dollar savings deposit interest rate was 0.01% for a very long time).

The recent depreciation of RMB/UD$ from 6.2 in April 2018 to 6.9 in September 2018 would have a similar impact on the RMB as an investment currency (Lau et al. 2018). Indeed, the RMB three-month deposit interest rate in Hong Kong declined from about 3.25% to about 2.25% during the same period. In contrast, the three-month Hong Kong dollar deposit interest rate increased to about 1.5% by the end of 2018. The volatility of the RMB against the US dollar would have weakened the confidence of the people for holding RMB as an investment currency. The overall trend of RMB internationalization has not resulted in the holding of more RMB deposits by individuals and corporations in Hong Kong since 2015.

When we examine RMB deposits vested in other financial centres, Taipei, Singapore, London, etc., we see that a similar trend has been recorded in recent years. The total RMB deposits in these five centres peaked in June 2015 at RMB1,740 billion, then declined to RMB1,030 in March 2017. Of the five

Table 3.2 Shares of RMB deposits in major offshore centres (%)

	Hong Kong	Singapore	Taiwan	South Korea	United Kingdom	Total (RMB bn)
Mar-15	58.0	11.9	19.8	7.0	3.2	1641
Jun-15	57.1	13.4	19.4	6.6	3.5	1740
Sep-15	57.4	14.4	20.7	3.8	3.6	1559
Dec-15	59.1	13.1	22.2	2.1	3.4	1440
Mar-16	57.1	12.3	23.6	2.3	4.7	1330
Jun-16	57.8	11.5	24.9	1.0	4.7	1230
Sep-16	56.3	10.2	26.4	0.9	6.3	1182
Dec-16	52.0	12.0	29.6	0.9	5.5	1052
Mar-17	49.2	12.3	30.0	0.9	7.5	1030
Jun-17	49.3	12.9	29.0	0.8	8.0	1067
Sep-17	50.4	13.1	29.5	0.6	6.4	1062
Dec-17	50.6	13.8	29.2	0.7	5.7	1104
Mar-18	50.4	12.6	29.3	0.6	7.1	1100
Jun-18	52.7	12.3	28.2	0.7	6.2	1109

Source: CEIC, annual reports of central banks of various financial centres, HKMA, MAS, Central Bank of Republic of China (Taiwan), Bank of Korea and Bank of England.

Note: Total is the sum of the five markets.

offshore RMB centres, Hong Kong's share of RMB deposits declined substantially from more about 58% in 2015 to about 50% in 2017, while the share of Taiwan increased from about 20% to 28%. The share of RMB deposits in Singapore stayed at about 12%, while that in London increased from about 3% to 6% during the same period. The significant decline in RMB deposits greatly reduced the need for the development of more RMB products by commercial banks to compete for RMB deposits and curtailed the expansion of RMB loans.

RMB loans and China-related loans in Hong Kong

RMB loans in Hong Kong increased very rapidly in the early 2010s and peaked at RMB297.4 billion by the end of 2014. These loans declined sharply to RMB144.5 billion by the end of 2017, similar to the fluctuation of RMB deposits in Hong Kong.

Nevertheless, under continued economic and financial liberalization in China, banks in Hong Kong sustained a positive growth in their total loans to China-related businesses. Indeed, these loans surged from RMB2,600 billion by the end of 2013 to RMB4,400 billion by the end of June 2018. Thus, banks in Hong Kong have had more China-related businesses in the last five years despite declines in direct RMB loans. In particular, according to the Asian Banker and China Construction Bank Report (2018: 3), total RMB-denominated financial assets (deposits, bonds, equities, etc.) held by foreign institutions and individuals amounted to RMB4.28 trillion (US$630 billion) at the end of 2017, a significant increase of 41.3% compared to 2016.

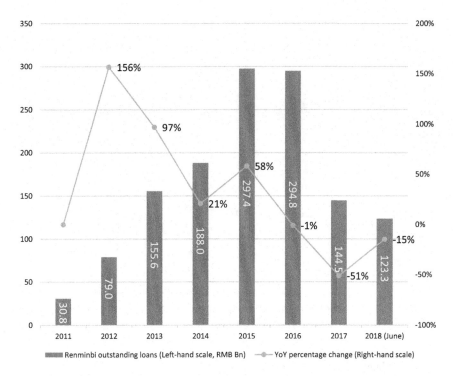

Figure 3.7 Renminbi outstanding loans (RMB bn)
Source: HKMA (2018).

RMB offshore bonds

Hong Kong's outstanding RMB Dim Sum bonds started to decline in 2015, with every major type of issuer, in particular the private mainland issuers. The major reasons are significant higher RMB bond interest rates in Hong Kong as compared to the mainland market. Higher volatility and greater uncertainty in the RMB exchange rates were also contributing factors. The total new issues of Dim Sum bonds peaked at RMB298 billion in 2014, which declined sharply to RMB46 billion in 2017. During the first half of 2018, their new issues rebounded significantly.

The mainland government has also been actively promoting Chinese Panda bonds. A Panda bond is a Chinese RMB-denominated bond from a non-Chinese issuer (including international development institutions, foreign governments, overseas financial institutions, and non-financial companies), sold in mainland China. The first two Panda bonds were issued in October 2005 by the International Finance Corporation and the Asian Development Bank. The Montreal-based National Bank of Canada became the first North American bank to issue debt in China's domestic market. Two bonds totaling RMB4.1

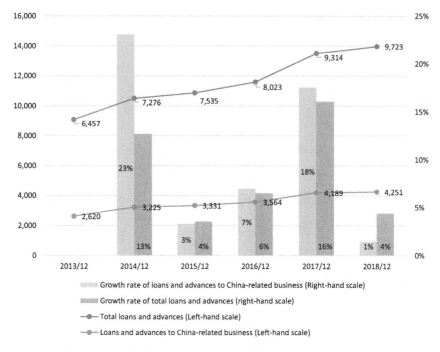

Figure 3.8 China-related loans and advances
Source: HKMA (2018).

billion (US$650 million) have been issued since 2016. The total outstanding Panda bonds stood at RMB160 billion by the end of May 2018 (Reuters 2018a). Uncertain rules regarding issuer qualifications and restrictions on the movement of proceeds onshore and offshore hinder the development of the market. Both Dim Sum bonds and Panda bonds are likely to be interrelated markets. More time is required for more detailed analyses of their specific characteristics and prospects.

RMB as an international reserve currency

On 30 November 2015, the IMF officially announced including RMB as the 5th reserve currency in its SDR basket (an international reserve asset created by the IMF in 1969 to supplement its member countries' official reserves) from 1 October 2016, with a weighting of 10.92%. This would greatly promote the RMB as an international reserve currency. For example, in June 2017, the European Central Bank invested for the first time €500 million of its foreign reserves in RMB assets ('RMB internationalization gets boost from European Central Bank' 2017). Furthermore, the German central bank, Deutsche Bundesbank, announced its including the RMB in its currency reserves in January 2018 (Asian Banker and China Construction Bank 2018). More than 60 countries had included the RMB as a new reserve currency by the end of 2017 (ECNS Wire 2017).

The RMB's development as a reserve currency would be a rather slow process owing to its underdeveloped financial markets (Prasad 2018). Foreign central banks and sovereign funds typically only invest in highly liquid and safe fixed income debt securities. China's government and corporate debt securities markets are relatively small in trading volume and weak in regulatory frameworks. Thus, as at the fourth quarter of 2017, the RMB made up only 1.23% of the world's allocated reserves, compared with 1.07% in the fourth quarter of 2016 and the assigned weighting of 10.92% in the SDR by the IMF. Nevertheless, the RMB share had increased significantly to 1.84% by the end of second quarter of 2018 despite the trade war with the US (Yeung 2018). This respectable increase is encouraging. The possible trend and reasons behind it should be monitored closely.

China's bond market

Government bonds are the major assets for the international reserves holding. China's government and corporate debt securities markets are relatively small in trading volume and weak in regulatory frameworks. The Chinese government's bond market is relatively small, accounting for only 36% of GDP, compared with 194% of GDP in Japan in 2017. Again, the turnover ratio of the public bond market was small, relative to other major markets. Currently, the domestic bond market development has been one of the government's policy priorities for both the mainland capital market development and sustainability of RMB internationalization (McCauley and Ma 2015).

Table 3.3 Currency composition of official foreign exchange reserves (%) (2011–Q2 2018)

	2011	2012	2013	2014	2015	2016	2017	Q2 2018
Shares of US$	62.6	61.5	61.2	65.1	65.7	65.3	62.7	57.1
Shares of euros	24.4	24.1	24.2	21.2	19.1	19.1	20.2	18.6
Shares of Chinese RMB	—	—	—	—	—	1.1	1.2	1.8
Shares of Japanese yen	3.6	4.1	3.8	3.5	3.8	4.0	4.9	4.6
Shares of pounds sterling	3.8	4.0	4.0	3.7	4.7	4.3	4.5	4.1
Shares of A$	—	1.5	1.8	1.6	1.8	1.7	1.8	1.6
Shares of C$	—	1.4	1.8	1.7	1.8	1.9	2.0	1.7
Shares of Swiss francs	0.1	0.2	0.3	0.2	0.3	0.2	0.2	0.1
Shares of other currencies	5.5	3.3	2.8	2.8	2.9	2.4	2.5	2.2

Source: IMF

Table 3.4 Relevant factors for reserve currency consideration (2017)

	Share of Total International FX Reserve Holdings (%)	Central Government Debt (USD bn)	Central Government Debt as % of GDP (%)	FX Reserve as a % of Total Central Government Debt (%)	Share of World Total Trade (%) (2016)
US	62.7	19,190	99.0	0.2	12.6
UK	4.5	2483	94.5	4.9	3.6
Japan	4.9	9488	194.6	12.7	4.3
Australia	1.7	639	46.3	9.2	1.3
China	1.2	2070	16.9	151.7	12.5

Source: IMF, World Bank.

In the first quarter of 2018, only 4% of Chinese government bonds were held by foreign investors, which is much lower than that of Japan and Korea.

In order to promote foreign participation in the bond market, the Chinese government further integrates various trading platforms and foreign participation schemes (QFII, RQFII, etc.). The Bond Connect scheme was jointly announced by the People's Bank of China and Hong Kong Monetary Authority in July 2017 (HKEx 2018). This cross-border Bond Connect platform will offer a well-developed financial infrastructure and market practices in line with international legal and regulatory standards and allow RMB-denominated assets to be more accessible to foreign participants (HKEx 2017).

During the first year's inception of the Bond Connect platform in Hong Kong, the overall international holding in China's bonds, through the interbank bond market, reached RMB1,435 billion at the end of May 2018, an increase of about 70% (HKEx 2018). Also, the number of approved international institutional investors participating in the Bond Connect increased to 356 at the end of June 2018, from 21 jurisdictions. This has been a remarkable achievement to enhance the foreign participation and the liquidity of China's bond market.

China's equity market

Furthermore, a more liberalized equity market in China would promote the awareness of Chinese assets, which would enhance RMB internationalization. In this respect, there have been many important developments in promoting international participation in the Chinese equity markets.

China's A-Share market has been gradually opening up for international investors, who were allowed to participate in the A-Share market in 2003 through the QFII Scheme. Domestic financial institutions in China have also been permitted to invest in foreign financial assets through the QDII Scheme since 2007. In 2014 and 2016, both the Shanghai-Hong Kong Stock Connect and Shenzhen-Hong Kong Stock Connect were open for operation. China also quadrupled the

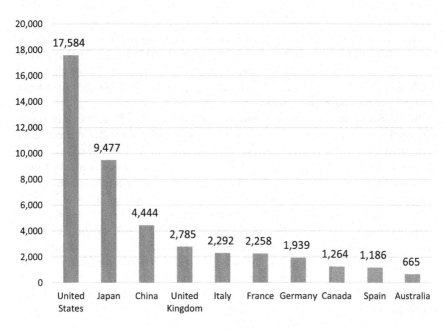

Figure 3.9 Total government debt securities outstanding (USD bn, Q4 2017)
Source: BIS (2018)

Table 3.5 Foreign holding of domestic government bonds (% of the total outstanding, year-end)

	Korea	*Japan*	*Thailand*	*Malaysia*	*Indonesia*	*China*
2013	11.0	8.3	17.5	30.0	32.0	–
2014	10.6	8.5	17.0	29.8	36.3	2.5
2015	10.4	9.6	15.8	31.2	38.5	2.4
2016	10.0	10.3	14.2	33.9	38.6	3.1
2017	11.1	10.9	15.7	27.5	39.4	3.6
Q1 2018	11.6	10.9	15.2	28.9	39.3	4.0

Source: AsianBondsOnline.

daily quota on both Stock Connects from 1 May 2018, an enhancement that could further lead to the integration of its onshore and offshore stock markets in the longer term. Additionally, the London-Shanghai Stock Connect is under the final stage of preparation ('China, Japan agree to bolster economic ties' 2018).

In 2018, A-Shares were selected and incorporated into two major international financial indices (Takungpao 2018a). On 1 June 2018, A-Shares were included for the first time in the MSCI Emerging Markets Index; the weighting was 2.5%

(MSCI 2014; Zhang and Yeung 2018). The weighting may be increased to 20% in early 2019 ('China, Japan agree to bolster economic ties' 2018).

On 27 September 2018, A-Shares were also incorporated into the second-largest followed FTSE Russell Index (FTSE Russell 2017; Lockett 2018; Zhang 2018). The inclusion was gradually implemented in three stages through March 2020, using 25% of the investible market capitalization of RMB A-shares from small to big caps covered by FTSE.

International investment in China's equity market is still at its early stage. The total foreign investment under the QFII Schemes and Stock Connects only accounted for 2.1% of the total market capitalization of A-Shares in circulation at the end of June 2018 (Takungpao 2018a). Even if the potential new investment generated from the inclusion of A-Shares into two major stock indices are in full force, the additional increase in the market share would still be less than 1%. There is still a big gap compared with other emerging markets. Foreign investment accounted for about 30% of the Korean market, 70% of the Taiwanese market, and over 10% of the Indian market (Takungpao 2018a). However, if these indices further increase the A-Shares' weighting towards the relative market capitalization of the Chinese market to the total market capitalization of all emerging markets, there will be a sustained increase in foreign investment into China's equity market in the longer term (Takungpao 2018b).

Other liberalization measures enhancing the sustainability of RMB internationalization

In recent years, despite downturns in some major RMB offshore parameters, the Chinese government has been introducing and deepening many measures to promote RMB internationalization with long-term impacts (see Appendix (1) for the major liberalization measures introduced in 2017). The infrastructure and international network for RMB internationalization have been substantially strengthened. The establishment of a clearing bank in a foreign financial centre is the key infrastructure promoting the utilization of RMB in a foreign country. There were 25 clearing banks by early 2018 and 36 currency swap arrangements totalling over RMB3 trillion (HSBC 2018).

For a long time, the absence of a clearing bank in the US and Japan has been a major obstacle for completing the RMB offshore network. The US Federal Reserves and PBOC signed an agreement in February 2018 to authorize JP Morgan Chase & Co. as the first non-Chinese RMB clearing bank in the US ('China names JPMorgan Chase as yuan clearing bank in U.S.', Reuters 2018a). The US market now has two RMB clearing banks: the Bank of China's New York branch, established in September 2016, and JP Morgan, established in February 2018. The participation of JP Morgan is particularly important, as many US domestic enterprises cover different time zones and do not have support in Asia to facilitate their RMB transactions (Kuo 2018).

In early 2018, China and Japan also indicated the necessity of reviewing the currency swap arrangement and expanding the swap volume, setting up an RMB settlement and clearing centre in Tokyo, and increasing holdings of each other's treasury bonds ('China, Japan agree to bolster economic ties' 2018).

China's central bank announced that overseas RMB clearing banks would be allowed to conduct more business. The Central Bank will grant RMB clearing banks permits for interbank borrowing, cross-border account financing, and bond repurchase business. This will provide additional liquidity support to off-shore RMB markets.

Additionally, the Chinese government took a major step to liberalize the ownership of domestic financial institutions to foreign investors in early 2018 (Leng 2018). In April 2018, China permitted foreign investors to take a maximum of 51% equity in brokerage firms, futures companies and fund management firms. This ceiling will be removed completely within three years. Such liberalization will definitely lead to sustainable and better integration of the RMB onshore and offshore markets and create more business opportunities for international financial firms.

Sustainability of RMB internationalization under Belt and Road Initiative

Trade and investment with BRI

According to an official website (State Information Center & SINOIMEX 2018), there were 71 countries within BRI by March 2018. In the five years between 2013 and 2018, China's total trade with BRI countries amounted to US$5000 billion, and direct foreign investment amounted to US$60 billion ('Xi pledges to bring benefits to people through Belt and Road Initiative' 2018). However, the total trade between China and these BRI countries as a whole did not increase at all between 2013 and 2017, similar to the overall trade performance of the Chinese economy (which declined by about 1% during the period). The total trade between China and BRI countries declined continuously between 2013 and 2016. However, there was a significant rebound of about 17% in 2017.

The performance of these BRI regions varied significantly during the period. There were increases of 32% with South Asia (eight countries), and 11% with Asia and Oceania (fourteen countries) during the period; while the trade with Africa and Latin America (six countries), and Central Asia (five countries) declined by about 30% each.

On the investment side, although the signed contract value with the BRI has increased dramatically since 2014, the completed contract value has only increased moderately. Indeed, the share of accumulated overseas non-financial direct investment in the BRI countries has decreased since early 2014 from about 15% of the total overseas direct foreign investment of China to about 11% in the first half of 2017 (García-Herrero and Xu 2018). Again, China's international investment in BRI countries was not evenly distributed, ASEAN accounting for the bulk of the funding.

Table 3.6 China's trade with BRI countries by region (US$, billion)

BRI Sub-regions	2013	2017	Total Rate of Change	Average Annual Growth Rate
Asia and Oceania (14)	736.3	817.9	11.1%	2.8%
Western Asia (18)	277.1	233.2	−15.8%	−4.0%
Southern Asia (8)	96.3	127.2	32.1%	8.0%
Eastern Europe (20)	157.1	161.2	2.6%	0.6%
Africa and Latin America (6)	93.3	64.9	−30.4%	−7.6%
Central Asia (5)	50.3	36.0	−28.4%	−7.1%
BRI Total (71)	1410.3	1440.3	2.1%	0.5%
China Total	4160.4	4104.7	−1.3%	−0.3%

Source: State Information Center & SINOIMEX 2018 and compiled by the author.

Note: () refers to the number of countries included in the region.

Furthermore, as most of these BRI countries are developing countries and have less-developed financial markets, the utilization and penetration of RMB into the trading and investment transactions are still very much at the rudimentary stage. They still do not have the necessary financial infrastructure to facilitate RMB transactions.

The additional contribution of China's trade and direct investment in BRI has not been obvious to RMB internationalization. The overall RMB trade settlement and the share of cross-border payments has declined in recent years. The initial development of BRI has been very much overshadowed by the balance-of-payment difficulties encountered by China from 2014 to 2016, which demanded the Chinese government implement very stringent foreign exchange controls to stabilize the situation. Furthermore, the high debt position of many developing countries is a constraint for them against accepting more financing from China, particularly for long-term infrastructure projects.

But there have been many reports giving positive assessments regarding the BRI having tremendous potential for promoting RMB internationalization in the longer term, given the improving RMB financial infrastructure and the expanding business network globally (Kuo 2018; Olsson and Fei 2018; The Asian Banker and China Construction Bank 2018; SWIFT 2017). Nevertheless, there has been growing of literature reviewing the challenges encountered by China's infrastructure projects under BRI (McDonald, Bosshard and Brewer 2009; Yu 2014a; Law and Yuen 2019; Johnson 2018; 'China's BRI initiative hits roadblock in countries: report' 2018), and there are many lessons to be learnt.

Development of the petro-yuan

There are many commodity-based economies within BRI, and China has been the major importer for many years. For example, China, the world's second-largest oil consumer, is the largest oil importer now. China's crude oil imports nearly doubled from 4.8 million barrels per day (BPD) in 2010 to 8.4 million BPD in 2017, whereas US imports dropped from 9.2 million BPD to 7.9 million BPD over the same period due to the domestic shale oil boom (Katsomitros 2018). Russia has already settled a part of its oil exports to China in RMB. Pakistan, Iran, Saudi Arabia, and Venezuela, to some extent, also conduct their oil transactions with China in RMB (Katsomitros 2018; Surendran 2018; Lee 2018). A plan to issue loans denominated in RMB was part of the agenda in the China-Saudi Economic Forum in 2017.

If more of China's total oil imports were priced in RMB, that would result in large offshore RMB reserves in oil-exporting countries. They will be: (i) spent on Chinese exports, (ii) recycled into China's financial markets, (iii) invested in other forms of non-financial RMB assets, and (iv) exchanged for other international currencies. This will increase the demand for RMB assets and expand RMB foreign exchange transactions.

As part of the strategy to promote pricing of oil in RMB, China launched an oil futures contract denominated in RMB on 26 March 2018 in the Shanghai International Energy Exchange. Oil trading powerhouses Glencore and Trafigura participated in the first day of the trade (Surendran 2018). The development may rival global oil trading benchmarks such as Brent Crude Futures, traded on the London-based International Exchange, and West Texas Intermediate, traded on the New York Mercantile Exchange. The new oil contract would bring China closer to several big oil suppliers, Russia, Iran, Saudi Arabia, and Venezuela.

In fact, China issued the first domestic oil futures contract in 1993, but the experiment was terminated due to abnormal price fluctuations. The new contract has been introduced under a very different international economic setting. China has transformed into a global manufacturing centre and has become the world's largest oil importer. Its financial sector, although still largely controlled by the government, is much more resilient and liberalized. However, the petro-yuan is still in its infancy, and its possible challenge of the petro-dollar is still very far away (Slav 2018).

The development of the petro-yuan and oil futures contract will provide a valuable experiment for China to promote other major commodities to be traded in RMB. This is a significant breakthrough to draw BRI countries into the RMB family. China can leverage its position as the world's largest commodity consumer and importer (including iron ore, gold, nickel, copper, platinum, tin, etc.) to promote and sustain the use of RMB as the currency of denomination and settlement for China's commodity trades. It is likely that neighbouring countries in the Asia-Pacific region would be more acceptable to consider denominating their commodity and non-commodity trade with China in the RMB in the medium term.

Conclusions and policy recommendations

Conclusions

The development of RMB internationalization gathered momentum in the early 2010s and peaked around the middle of 2015. In recent years, many major RMB offshore parameters have experienced downturns. The sustainability of RMB internationalization has faced some difficulties. However, the Chinese government has been deepening many measures to promote financial liberalization and sustainability of RMB internationalization with long-term impacts. The infrastructure and international networks have been substantially strengthened. There are now more than 1,900 financial institutions participating in RMB international payments (SWIFT 2018a) and they have more opportunities to explore China-related businesses.

Table 3.7 Latest development of RMB internationalization parameters

RMB Internationalization Parameter	Reference Statistics	Latest Statistics
Renmin-IMI RMB Index	1Q 2010: 0.02 3Q 2015: 3.60 1Q 2017: 1.49	4Q 2017: 3.13
Standard Chartered RMB Index	9/2015: 2476 6/2017: 1730	8/2018: 1916
RMB Global FX transactions	2010: 1% (ranked 11th) 2013: 2% (ranked 9th)	2016: 4% (ranked 8th)
RMB domestic and international payments	12/2015: 2.3% (ranked 5th)	12/2017: 1.6% (ranked 5th) 8/2018: 2.1% (ranked 5th)
RMB global cross-border payments (excluding payments within Eurozone)	12/2015: 1.6% (ranked 7th)	12/2017: 1.0% (ranked 8th) 8/2018: 1.3% (ranked 8th)
China's RMB trade settlement	3Q 2015: 32%	2017: 16%
Foreign investment in China's government bonds	4Q 2014: 2.5% 4Q 2016: 3.1%	End-2017: 3.6% 3/2018: 4.0%
Foreign investment in China's equity market	- -	6/2018: 2.1%
Hong Kong RMB deposits (RMB billion)	12/2014: 1,004b 3/2017: 507b	End-2017: 559b 9/2018: 600b
Hong Kong RMB outstanding loans (RMB billion)	End-2014: 297.4b	End-2017: 144.5b 6/2018: 123.3b
Hong Kong outstanding loans to China-related businesses (HK$ billion)	End-2013: 2,600b	6/2018: 4,400b
Hong Kong new issued Dim Sum Bonds (RMB billion)	2014: 298b	2017: 46b 1–5/2018: 54b
HK RMB trade settlement (RMB billion)	2015: 6,833b	2017: 3,927b
RMB share as international reserve currency	End-2016: 1.1% (ranked 7th)	End-2017: 1.2% (ranked 7th) 6/2018: 1.8% (ranked 6th)

Source: Compiled by the author; see details in various sections

In particular, the Chinese government has integrated trading platforms and foreign participation schemes for the bond market. The cross-border Bond Connect platform is offering a well-developed financial infrastructure and market practices in line with international legal and regulatory standards, and allows RMB-denominated assets to be more accessible to foreign participants. Furthermore, a more liberalized equity market in China will promote awareness of Chinese assets, which would greatly enhance RMB internationalization.

In the first half of 2018, we witnessed significant improvements in RMB being used as the international reserve currency and in cross-border payments, and more participation of foreign investments in China's equity and bond markets. Hong Kong's outstanding loans to China-related businesses has also continued to increase. Indeed, according to the Asian Banker and China Construction Bank Report (2018), total RMB-denominated financial assets (e.g. deposits, bonds, equities) held by foreign institutions and individuals amounted to RMB4.28 trillion (US$630 billion) at the end of 2017, a significant increase of 41.3% compared to the amount in 2016. However, the outbreak of the China and US trade conflict, and the subsequent weakening of the RMB, may result in new challenges to RMB internationalization in the medium term.

China's total trade with BRI countries amounted to US$5000 billion and direct foreign investment amounted to US$60 billion in the five years between 2013 and 2018. However, the total trade between China and the BRI countries as a whole remained stagnant between 2013 and 2017. China's trade and direct investment in BRI have not been conducive to RMB internationalization. The initial development of BRI has been very much overshadowed by the balance-of-payment difficulties encountered by China in recent years. RMB internationalization is at its very early stage of development, as witnessed in Table 3.8.

Policy recommendations for sustainability

The sustainability of RMB internationalization would build on the 'trust and confidence' in RMB, the 'value and prospect' of RMB, and the 'scale and liquidity' of RMB. Along these lines, we provide the following policy recommendations to achieve these objectives.

Table 3.8 A comparison of RMB, yen and US$ as an international currency (% Share)

	World GDP (2017)	International Reserves Currency (Q2 2018)	Global Payment Flow (2017)	Turnover of Foreign Exchange (2016)
China	14.9%	1.8% (RMB)	1.0%	2.0%
Japan	6.0%	4.6% (yen)	4.3%	10.9%
US	24.2%	57.1% (US$)	41.7%	43.8%

Source: World Bank, IMF, SWIFT, BIS.

Note: Global payment flow including cross-border payments only (excluding intra-European payments).

Implementing credible monetary policy and financial regulatory regimes

Historically, the US dollar was backed up by the gold standard under the Bretton Woods System (World Gold Council 2018), and the US has run a current account deficit for more than 30 years. The sustained strength of the US economy – in particular its financial sector – and the political leadership projected in the international community have supported the supreme position of the US dollar as the most important international reserve currency and cross-border transaction currency for decades. There is a lot of inertia in the international financial market against shifting out of the US dollar for transaction, investment, and reserves purposes. In particular, the US commands infrastructure superiority.

Because China is a socialist country and does not have gold backing the RMB, the RMB would obviously have been in a relatively disadvantageous position to initiate the internationalization process. The RMB has not been fully convertible, and its 'market' status has been occasionally questioned by some foreign authorities. The strong and discretionary capital control introduced by the Chinese government in recent years has greatly induced uncertainties in the Chinese capital market. Additionally, the non-banking financial sector and local government debts have been generating tremendous anxiety for international observers.

The lack of transparency in the monetary policy and loose financial regulatory regimes have substantially increased the inherent risk associated with the value and prospect of the RMB, as compared with the US dollar and the euro. The recent restructuring of regulatory regimes for different types of financial institution still require time and vigilance for their effective implementation and enforcement. Building trust and confidence in RMB is a long-term process, and sustainable policies and dedicated actions by the Chinese government will be necessary.

Sustaining financial liberalization with a level playing field

All major international financial institutions have a sophisticated and evolving China and RMB business strategy (Bank of China 2013; HSBC 2017; Standard Chartered Bank 2012; Asian Banker and China Construction Bank 2018; Deutsche Bank 2017; JP Morgan Chase & Co 2013, 2018). There will be more China-related offshore financial activities (IPOs, foreign direct investments, trade in goods and services, M&As, international bond connects, stock connects). More RMB products will also be available for overseas investors. International financial institutions now have more opportunities to participate in China-related businesses.

In this respect, further capital account liberalization is necessary. The economic literature provides ample analyses and road maps for guidance (Ishii and Habermeier 2002; Galbis 1994; IBRD, WB and IMF 2005; Johnston 1998; Ma 2012; Yu 2014a; Kawai 1996). The People's Bank of China has taken many steps and implemented pilot schemes to test the operation and impact of various liberalization measures in the past ten years (e.g. exchange rate reform, interest rate reform, foreign ownership liberalization, foreign investment liberalization). Lessons were learnt and enhancements were made. More fundamental changes are likely to be in the pipeline, but the pace and scope very much depend on the stability of the Chinese and global economy.

As China and RMB-related business expands, it is further supported by China's bigger and more liberalized economy. Countries within BRI will be drawing closer into the sphere of influence of RMB. It is vital for China to improve financial regulatory regimes and provide a level playing field for international firms. Despite conscious policies for financial liberalization, there are many restrictions and barriers against the fair competition of international financial institutions in the mainland China market. There was a significant policy breakthrough in early 2018 to permit foreign investors to take a maximum of 51% equity in brokerage firms, futures companies, and fund management firms, which would lead to better integration of the RMB onshore and offshore markets. However, it should be noted that further liberalization of domestic markets may offset some offshore RMB activities.

Creating a vibrant bond market with deep liquidity

Government bonds are the major assets for international reserves. China's government and corporate debt securities markets are relatively small in trading volume and weak in regulatory frameworks. In the second quarter of 2018, only 4% of government bonds were held by foreign investors, which is much lower than that of Malaysia, Thailand, and Indonesia. Hong Kong's Dim Sum bond market is the most important offshore RMB bond market. Yet, new issues of Dim Sum bonds started to decline substantially in 2015.

The IMF announced that RMB accounted for 1.84% of international reserves in the second quarter of 2018, and this was supported by an estimated foreign ownership of about 4% of China's government bonds. Based on the 10.92% assigned weighting of the RMB to the SDR basket, it would require a foreign ownership of China's government bonds of about 24% (this is just a very rough estimate for reference) to achieve this IMF assigned SDR weighting. We could examine the same issue from another dimension. Within the same period, the Japanese yen accounted for about 4.6% of international reserves, and this was supported by an estimated foreign ownership of about 10.9% of Japan's government bonds. If the Japanese yen were given the same SDR weighting of 10.92% as China's RMB, it would require a foreign ownership of Japan's government bonds of about 26% to also achieve the same 10.92% SDR weighting. The two estimates are very similar. There need to be significant structural reforms in the Chinese bond market in order to achieve this magnitude of foreign ownership. It should also be noted that despite China's economy being much larger than that of Japan, the size of the Japanese government bond market is more than twice of that of the Chinese government bond market.

A better-developed corporate RMB bond market, both onshore and offshore, would be necessary for complementing the further expansion of China's bond market. It is essential to raise the corporate governance of Chinese firms up to the international standard in order to sustain the development of the corporate bond market. As for the first-tier Chinese corporations, they may be able to raise US dollar funding in the international market more cost-effectively, compared to issuing RMB bonds. The local government debt market is even more problematic; it has scant transparency and international confidence in the financial accounts of many local governments is weak.

Supplying RMB liquidity

In international transactions, China has enjoyed 'twin surpluses' for a long time. In order to provide RMB liquidity into offshore markets, China began with RMB as an import settlement currency. This was followed by using the RMB in outward foreign direct investment and foreign lending. In order to attract offshore RMB to remain in offshore markets, attractive RMB financial products and other international investment opportunities have to be created offshore. Otherwise, offshore RMB would be recycled back into China, with a corresponding outflow of the US dollar.

Currently, international financial institutions do not access enough RMB to support RMB-denominated bank loans and expand other RMB-related activities offshore. As China is a 'twin surpluses' economy, it is constantly importing foreign currencies and not exporting RMB. China is now moving towards a more consumption-oriented economy, and there is an increasing likelihood that China may sustain a current account deficit in the longer term. This would increase the supply of RMB in the international market.

More sustainable domestic investments would also enlarge the current account deficit, with additional imports of raw materials and capital goods. If China can successfully quote and settle its commodity imports in RMB, it would substantially increase the global supply of RMB liquidity. This would promote RMB internationalization and the possible adoption of RMB in third-parties' transactions in the long term.

Establishing RMB financial infrastructure in developing countries

Of all RMB foreign exchange trading with other currencies in 2017, 97.1% was against the US dollar. RMB direct trading with currencies of developing countries in the foreign exchange market is close to zero. The RMB is also not eligible for the 'payment versus payment' settlement through a global system that would subject RMB trading to counterparty settlement risk and credit limits (Cheng et al. 2018).

Currently, the proportion of China's commodity-trade invoicing in RMB must be very small, other than the recent development in the petro-yuan. If China's commodity imports, mostly from developing countries, were quoted and settled in the RMB, it would substantially increase the global supply of RMB liquidity and provide an incentive for commodity suppliers to hold and use RMB for trade and investment purposes. As China is having much stronger economic interactions with its Asian neighbours, a regional RMB bloc may be the viable medium-term objective (Kwan 2018). This would facilitate RMB internationalization and contribute to international monetary reforms.

The international utilization of RMB is mainly in developed countries and established financial centres. Clearing bank services, stronger swap arrangements, and financial derivatives have been introduced to facilitate RMB cross-border transactions. The promotion of RMB internationalization among developing countries (including most BRI countries) would require China's attention and assistance to develop the necessary settlement system and financial infrastructure in these countries.

Engaging international stakeholders comprehensively

The development of RMB internationalization is not a smooth process, as international financial and economic developments may frequently inflict unaccommodating conditions upon China. A gradualist approach is recommended for its sustainability. It is important for China to maintain domestic financial stability and sustainability as the primary objective. Also, RMB internationalization should not be seen as only benefitting China. China, as a prominent and responsible member of the international community, should have as the objective of RMB internationalization achieving a better international financial order for the benefit of attaining international financial stability and promoting international economic development. The conditions for achieving this objective may not be easily defined. A comprehensive engagement with all international stakeholders, including sovereign states of the developed and developing world, multinational institutions, and international financial institutions, should facilitate the sustainability of RMB internationalization in the right direction.

Appendix 1: Major financial liberalization measures for RMB internationalizaton in 2017

Based on the Renmin and IMI 2018 Report (2018: 43), we present the following financial liberalization measures and developments initiated by the Chinese government for reference.

11 April 2017: The first African offshore RMB bond issued
28 April 2017: Cambodia offered comprehensive RMB banking services
10 May 2017: RMB Clearing Banking in Dubai (UAE) commenced operation
17 May 2017 Bloomberg launched a new platform for RMB bonds
13 June 2017: First RMB investment by EU Central Bank
3 July 2017: Bond Connect online
10 July 2017: HKEx launched gold futures in US$ and RMB
24 August 2017: The first clearing transaction of RMB/Cambodian currency

15 September 2017: Venezuela announced international prices of oil and fuel in RMB

9 October 2017: China's Foreign Exchange Centre launched same-time settlement for RMB/ruble transactions

28 November 2017: Shanghai Clearing Centre and London-based R5RX launched cross-border FX transactions clearing services for emerging markets

4 December 2017: China's Foreign Exchange Centre launched real-time matching services for RMB/US$ FX transactions.

References

Asian Banker and China Construction Bank 2018, *Renminbi internationalization report 2018: optimism towards 'Belt and Road' raised cross-border use of RMB*, June.

Ballantyn, A, Garner, M & Wright, M 2013, 'Development in renminbi internationalization', *RBA Bulletin*, June.

Bank of China 2013, *Bank of China officially launches cross-border RMB index*, 20 September. Available from: www.boc.cn/en/bocinfo/cri/201309/t20130917_2489155.html. [17 August 2018].

Bank of International Settlement 2016, 'Triennial Central Bank Survey of foreign exchange and OTC derivatives markets in 2016', 11 December. Available from: www.bis.org/publ/rpfx16.htm?m=6%7C381%7C677. [30 November 2018].

Brummer, C 2017, 'Renminbi internationalization and systemic risk', IIEL, *Issue Brief*, Georgetown University Law Centre, February.

Bryson, J 2018, 'Internationalization of the RMB: a progress report', *Wells Fargo Securities*, 22 May.

Chan N 2014, *Hong Kong as offshore RMB centre–past and prospects*, HKMA, 18 February. Available from: www.hkma.gov.hk/eng/key-information/insight/20140218.shtml. [19 October 2018].

Chen, J & Qian, X 2016, 'Measuring on-going changes in China's capital controls: a de jure and a hybrid index data set', *China Economic Review*, vol. 38, pp. 167–182.

Cheng, L, Luo, J & Liu, L 2018, 'Is renminbi a (truly) international currency? An evaluation based on offshore foreign exchange market trading patterns', *Munich Personal RePEc Archive*, 8 October. Available from: https://mpra.ub.uni-muenchen.de/id/eprint/89279. [30 November 2018]

'China, Japan agree to bolster economic ties' 2018, *China Daily*, 1–2 September.

'China's BRI initiative hits roadblock in countries: report' 2018, *Economic Times*, 15 April. Available from: https://economic times.indiatimes.com/news/international/world-news/chinas-bri-initiative-hits-roadblock-in-countries-report/articleshow/637715. [16 November 2018].

Davis, JS 2017, 'China's capital controls appear to arrest flight, stabilize currency', *Economic Letter*, Dallas Fed, vol. 12, no. 12, November.

Deutsche Bank 2017, 'Deutsche Bank for renminbi solutions', 15 November.

Durden, T 2017, 'China launches new capital controls: puts $15,000 annual cap on overseas ATM withdrawals', *ZeroHedge*, 30 December. Available from: www.zerohedge.com/news/2017-12-30/china-launches-new-capital-controls-puts-15000-annual-cap-overseas-atm-withdrawals. [18 September 2018].

ECNS Wire 2017, *60 countries and regions use RMB as reserve currency: PBOC report*, 19 October. Available from: www.ecns.cn/cns-wire/2017/10–19/277645.shtml. [10 September 2018].

Eichengreen, B 2013, 'ADB distinguished lecture – renminbi internationalization: tempest in a teapot?', *Asian Development Review*, vol. 30, no. 1, pp. 148–164.

Frankel, J 2012, 'Internationalization of RMB and historical precedents', *Journal of Economic Integration*, vol. 27, no. 3, pp. 329–365.

FTSE Russell 2017, *Preparing for China's inclusion in global benchmarks*, October.

García-Herrero, A & Xu, J 2018, 'Recent developments in trade, investment and finance of China's belt and road', HKUST IEMS Working Paper, no. 2018-50, Hong Kong University of Science and Technology, Hong Kong, January.

Galbis, V 1994, 'Sequencing of financial sector reforms: a review', IMF Working Paper, IMF Office, September.

Gunter, FR 2017, 'Why China lost about $3.8 trillion to capital flight in the last decade', *Forbes Asia*, 22 February. Available from: www.forbes.com/sites/insideasia/2017/02/22/china-capital-flight-migration/#2451f8564a37. [20 October 2018].

HKEx 2017, *Tapping into China's domestic bond market – an international perspective*, May.

HKEx 2018, 'Bond connect celebrates first anniversary', *HKEx*, Press Release, 3 July. Available from: www.hkex.com.hk/News/News-Release/2018/180703news.?sc_lang=en. [20 October 2018].

HSBC 2017, *Renminbi internationalization survey report*, February.

HSBC 2018, *Renminbi internationalization survey report*, February.

International Bank for Reconstruction and Development (IBRD)/World Bank and International Monetary Fund (IMF) 2005, 'Sequencing financial sector reforms', *Financial sector assessment: a handbook*, World Bank, pp. 317–324.

Ishii, S & Habermeier, K 2002, 'Capital account liberalization and financial sector stability', *IMF Occasional Paper* 211, IMF Office.

Johnson, E 2018, 'Deepening China's ties to the world', *Global Finance*, 1 June. www.gfmag.com/magazine/june-2018/deepening-china's-ties-world. [18 October 2018].

Johnston, RB 1998, 'Sequencing capital account liberalization', *Finance and Development*, vol. 25, no. 4, pp. 20–23.

JP Morgan Chase & Co 2013, *Navigate the rising of the global RMB*.

JP Morgan Chase & Co 2018, *JP Morgan Chase takes steps to advance China capabilities*, 14 May.

Kahn, R 2016, 'The case for Chinese capital controls', *Global Economic Monthly*, Council on Foreign Relations, Center for Geoeconomic Studies, February.

Kang, X & Kang, C 2017, 'Chinese balance of payment: disequilibrium and the influences', *Advances in Social Sciences, Education and Humanities Research*, vol. 121, pp. 6–12.

Karnfelt, M 2017, 'China's tight capital controls fail to address underlying problems', *Financial Times*, 10 November. Available from: www.ft.com/content/1d288888-c613-11e7-b2bb-322b2cb39656. [18 September 2018].

Katsomitros, A 2018, 'The petro-yuan could usher in a new era for global energy', *World Finance*, 16 July. Available from: www.worldfinance.com/markets/the-petro-yuan-could-usher-in-a-new-era-for-global-energy. [12 October 2018].

Kawai, M 1996, 'The Japanese yen as an international currency: performance and prospects', in R Sato, RV Ramachandran & H Hajime (eds), *Organization, performance and equity: perspectives on the Japanese economy*, pp. 305–355, Netherlands: Kluwer Academic Publishers.

Kuo, M 2018, 'RMB internationalization outlook milestones and the BRI', *The Diplomat*, 4 April.

Kwan C 2018, 'Issuing facing renminbi internationalization: observations from Chinese, regional and global perspectives', *Public Policy Review*, Policy Research Institute, Ministry of Finance, Japan, vol. 14, no. 5, pp. 871–900.

Lau, K, Moe, T, Fu, S & Wang, J 2018, 'China musings: RMB depreciation: the bad, the good, and the trade', Goldman Sachs, 28 August.

Law, C & Yuen, D 2019, 'A comparison of investment strategies of China and Japan in infrastructure projects in ASEAN', in F Cheung & YY Hong (eds), *Regional connection under the belt and road initiative*, London and New York: Routledge.

Lee, J 2018, 'China's petro-yuan "thundering into action" as Iran ditches US dollar in oil trade', *Reuters*, 14 May. Available from: www.rt.com/business/426637-china-petroyuan-oil-trade-iran/. [20 October 2018].

Leng, S 2018, 'China pledges to open up financial markets amid threat of US trade war', *South China Morning Post*, 14 April.

Liu, H 2015, 'The trajectory of the dollar and its impacts on RMB internationalization', *Economic review*, Bank of China (Hong Kong) Limited, November.

Lockett, H 2018, 'FTSE Russell to include China A-shares in key indices', *Financial Times*, 27 September. Available from: www.ft.com/content/8c22a60e-c1eb-11e8-95b1-d36dfef1b89a. [20 October 2018].

Lowe, P 2014, 'Some implications of the internationalization of renminbi', Conference on the Internationalization of the Renminbi, Centre for International Finance and Regulation, Sydney.

Ma, G & Villar, A 2014, 'Internationalization of emerging market currencies', *The transmission of unconventional monetary policy to the emerging markets*, BIS Papers, no. 78, pp. 71–86.

Ma, J 2012, 'Roadmap for RMB internationalization', *Asia Economics Special*, Deutsche Bank AG, Hong Kong, 25 June.

McCauley, R & Ma, G 2015, 'Transforming central bank liabilities into government debt: the case of China', *China & World Economy*, vol. 23, no. 4, pp. 1–18.

McDonald, K, Bosshard, P & Brewer, N 2009, 'Exporting dams: China's hydro-power industry goes global', *Journal of Environmental Management*, vol. 90, pp. S294–S302.

McMillan LLP 2017, *China's capital controls – implications for China focused companies*, Global Law Office, January.

MSCI 2014, *Consultation on China A-shares: index inclusion roadmap*, March.

Olsson, D & Fei, A 2018, 'Why international use of RMB is about to be propelled', *King & Wood Mallesons*, 4 April. Available from: www.kwm.com/en/au/knowledge/insights/why-international-use-rmb-will-increase-20180404. [22 October 2018].

Otero-Iglesias, M 2018, 'Renminbi internationalization: stuck in mid-river – for now', *Strategic and International Studies*, Elcano Royal Institute, 4 July.

Overholt, WH, Ma, G & Law, CK 2016, *Renminbi rising: a new global monetary system emerges*, United Kingdom: Wiley.

Park, H 2016, 'China's RMB internationalization strategy: its rationales, state of play, prospects and implications', M-RCBG Associate Working Paper Series, Harvard Kennedy School, no. 63, August.

Prasad, E 2018, 'The slow, uneven rise of the Renminbi', *Cato Journal*, Spring/Summer.

'RMB internationalization gets boost from European Central Bank', 2017, *China Banking News*, 29 June. Available from: www.chinabankingnews.com/2017/06/29/rmb-internationalisation-gets-boost-european-central-bank/. [4 October 2018].

Renmin University of China and International Monetary Institute 2017, *2017 RMB Internationalization Report*, July.

Renmin University of China and International Monetary Institute 2018, *2018 RMB Internationalization Report*, July.

Reuters 2018a, 'China names JPMorgan Chase as yuan clearing bank in U.S', *Reuters*, 13 February. Available from: www.reuters.com/article/us-china-us-yuan-clearing/china-names-jpmorgan-chase-as-yuan-clearing-bank-in-u-s-idUSKBN1FX0T0.   [24 September 2018]

Reuters 2018b, 'China to simplify Panda Bond rules to boost issuance', *Reuters*, 3 July. Available from: www.reuters.com/article/china-bonds-panda/china-to-simplify-panda-bond-rules-to-boost-issuance-idUSL4N1TZ30Z. [24 September 2018].

Santacreu, A & Zhu, H 2017, 'China's foreign reserves are declining. Why, and what effects could this have?', *On the Economy Blog*, Federal Reserve Bank of St. Louis, 3 October.

Setser, B 2018, 'Devaluation risk makes China's balance of payments interesting (again)', *Council on Foreign Relations*, 2 July. Available from: www.cfr.org/blog/devaluation-risk-makes-chinas-balance-payments-interesting-again. [12 November 2018]

Slav, I 2018, 'Petro-yuan not quite yet: Chinese oil futures a risky endeavor', *Wolf Street*, 21 August. Available from: https://wolfstreet.com/2018/08/21/petro-yuan-update-chinese-oil-futures-a-risky- endeavor/. [18 October 2018].

Standard Chartered Bank 2012, 'CNH – introducing the renminbi globalization index', *Global Research*, 14 November.

Standard Chartered Bank 2018, 'Offshore renminbi – depreciation angst', *Global Research*, 6 August.

State Information Center & SINOIMEX 2018, 'Big data report on trade cooperation under the belt and road initiative 2018', May. Available from: www.sic.gov.cn/archiver/SIC/UpFile/Files/Default/20180509162109827517.pdf. [30 November 2018].

Surendran, S 2018, 'Lead story: China acts to make petro-yuan a reality', *Capital, the Edge Malaysia Weekly*, 30 April.

SWIFT 2017, 'RMB internationalization: can the belt and road revitalize the RMB?', *RMB Tracker*, July.

SWIFT 2018a, 'RMB internationalization: where we are and what we can expect in 2018', *RMB Tracker*, January.

SWIFT 2018b, 'RMB progress towards becoming an international currency', *RMB Tracker*, September.

Takagi, S 2012, 'Internationalizing the yen, 1984–2003: unfinished agenda or mission impossible? Currency internationalization: lessons from the global financial crisis and prospects for the future in Asia and the Pacific', *BIS Papers*, No. 61, pp. 75–92.

Takungpao 2018a, '入富提振市場信心', 29 September, pp. A13.

Takungpao 2018b, 'A股國際化快於預期', 29 September, pp. B3.

World Gold Council 2018, 'The Bretton Woods system', *World Gold Council*, 7 November. Available from: www.gold.org/about-gold/history-of-gold/bretton-woods-system. [30 November 2018].

'Xi pledges to bring benefits to people through belt and road initiative', 2018, Xinhua News Agency, 27 August. Available from: www.gov.cn/xinwen/2018-08/27/content_5316913.htm. [12 October 2018].

Yeung, K 2018, 'China's yuan more popular as reserve currency despite trade war, IMF data shows', *South China Morning Post*, 2 October. Available from: www.scmp.com/business/money/wealth/article/2166652/chinas-yuan-more-popular-reserve-currency-despite-trade-war. [14 October 2018]

Yu, H 2014a, 'China's eagerness to export its high-speed rail experience to ASEAN members', *The Copenhagen Journal of Asian Studies*, vol. 32, no.2, pp. 13–36.

Yu, Y 2014b, 'How far can renminbi internationalization go?', *Asian Development Bank Institute,* ADBI Working Paper Series no. 461, February. Available from: www.adb. org/sites/default/files/publication/156316/adbi-wp461.pdf. [30 November 2018].

Yu, Y 2017, 'Why China's capital account liberalization has stalled', *Project Syndicate*, 31 October. Available from: www.project.syndicate.org/commentary/china-capital-account-liberalization-on-hold-by-yu-yongding-2017-10?barrier=accesspaylog.   [7 August 2018].

Zhang, L & Tao, K 2014, 'The benefits and costs of renminbi internationalization', ADBI Working Paper, Asian Development Bank Institute, no. 481, May.

Zhang, S 2018, 'UK index compiler FTSE Russell to add Chinese stocks to its global equity gauges', *South China Morning Post,* 28 September. Available from: www.scmp. com/business/china-business/article/2165903/uk-index-compiler-ftse-russell-add-Chinese-stocks-its-global. [14 October 2018].

Zhang, S & Yeung, K 2018, 'Global index compiler MSCI considers quadrupling Chinese stocks' weightings in its benchmark gauges', *South China Morning Post,* 28 September. Available from: www.scmp.com/business/china-business/article/2165789/global-index-compiler-msci-considers-quadrupling-chinese. [14 October 2018].

4 China's rising consumerism, RMB internationalization, and sustainable growth

Minggao Shen and Jianghui Chen

Introduction

Consumption will bring changes to both China and the world. As a large country with economies of scale, China can achieve domestic consumption and manufacturing upgrades without relying on overseas demand. At the politburo meeting on 23 April 2018, the authorities proposed to expand 'domestic demand' again for the first time in three years. We believe 'domestic demand' might have a different meaning this time around in that expanding domestic consumption is likely to represent the 'new form of domestic demand'.

Over the next 30 years or so, China's modernization will depend upon whether it can increase the proportion of consumption in its economy, while ensuring that its manufacturing sector maintains a stable or slightly increasing global market share. In 2016, China's manufacturing sector accounted for 34.8% of the G20 total, while private consumption achieved just 10%.

China's consumption growth potential represents the resilience of its economic growth. Based on overseas experience, over the next 30 years on a constant price basis, consumer spending in China could grow four to seven times. When inflationary factors are considered, nominal consumption growth could be as high as 18–32 times. Alternatively, renminbi (RMB)-denominated nominal consumption growth might reach 52.5 times over the next 30 years, should the annualized growth of 14.1% over the past 30 years be maintained.

In relation to the consumption structure, current private consumption in China is approximately at the same stage as the US in the 1930s, Japan in the 1950s, and Korea in the 1980s. In the more developed eastern region, the proportion of consumer discretionary spending is close to 60%, similar to the level seen in Japan when it had a comparable per capita GDP. In 30 years, this ratio might reach nearly 80%, while the proportion of consumer staples spending might have shrunk by half.

Consumption will bring various changes to China, the most important three aspects being that: 1) only consumption upgrade can drive manufacturing upgrade, which in turn is a necessary condition for sustainable consumption upgrade; 2) China will transform from a major exporter into a major consumption-driven country and from a trade surplus country to a deficit one; 3) a deficit economy driven by consumption will lend support to the regionalization and subsequent internationalization of the RMB.

If China maintains the kind of consumption growth seen over the past ten years, it might become the world's largest consumption-driven country in 20 years. For China, consumption upgrade is the future. To capture relevant investment opportunities, we highlight keywords such as branding, standardization, cross-generational upgrade, new business models, and world-class companies.

Rising consumerism in China will help rebalance the global economy and unleash sustainable growth in the world. In recent history, Japan's forced rebalancing between consumption and production was a result of suppressed production. China can achieve rebalancing through promoting consumption with the economy of scale, an incremental source of growth not only to China but to the rest of the world.

Trade tensions or 'trade cold wars' initiated by the US might have successfully contained the rise of the former Soviet Union, Germany, and Japan, but this might not work very well on China. Taking full advantage of the economies of scale in its consumption development, China should be able to resolve trade tensions, escape the middle-income trap, and become the world's largest economy.

The logic of China's economic growth in its 'new era' will be changed fundamentally in that consumption, instead of exports or investment, will be the main driver of change for the country.

In fact, such a shift in growth drivers is already underway. Exports have supported China's industrialization over the past four decades, while consumption will provide sustainable momentum for modernization of the country over the next 30 years. Only consumption upgrade can drive manufacturing upgrade, which in turn is a necessary condition for a sustainable consumption upgrade. If successful, over the next 30 years, such a shift will turn China from the world's major exporter into a major consumption-driven country, from a country recording a trade surplus to one with a deficit, and from an industrialized economy to a modernized one.

Sino–US trade tensions will help accelerate this shift of the Chinese economic focus towards consumption. Whatever their specific format, these trade tensions reflect the underlying competition between the world's two major consumption-driven countries, today's US vs. tomorrow's China. As such, China needs to take measures in response to trade tensions or even a 'trade war' initiated by the US. These measures, however, come with a cost, and can break the 'zero-sum game'. Only by encouraging domestic consumption can China put itself in a strategically favorable position, where it carries on with manufacturing upgrade and maintains moderate economic growth domestically while externally mitigates attempts to 'contain China's rise' and even make breakthroughs with RMB internationalization.

China's consumption growth potential

Thanks to economies of scale as a large country, China has to a large extent reached industrialization before its private sector becomes wealthy. Based on estimates by the Maddison Program using purchasing power parities, China's manufacturing sector currently accounts for 34.8% of the G20 total, 25.6 percentage points higher than the percentage for Japan when the latter had a comparable per capita GDP (Figure 4.1). In comparison, China's consumption sector appears relatively weak, at less than 10% of the G20 total in 2016, or less than 30% of the size of its manufacturing sector (Figure 4.2).

Industrialization has driven the rise of the Chinese economy over the past four decades. Using purchasing power parities, China's GDP has outstripped the US, effectively shifting the global economic landscape from one dominated by the US and Europe back to one dominated by China and India (Figure 4.3). On a global scale, consumption and investment pretty much grew at the same pace during 1978–2016 (Figure 4.4). Comparatively speaking, export-driven investment growth was the main engine of China's rise. During this period, China's export, investment, and consumption growth was 29, 18.5, and 7.1 times the global pace of growth.

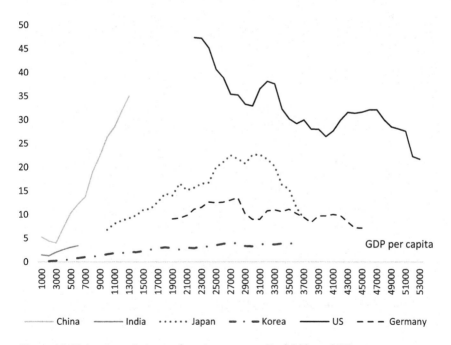

Figure 4.1 Major countries' manufacturing sector as % of G20 total (%)

Source: Maddison (2018), World Bank (2018), Conference Board (2018)

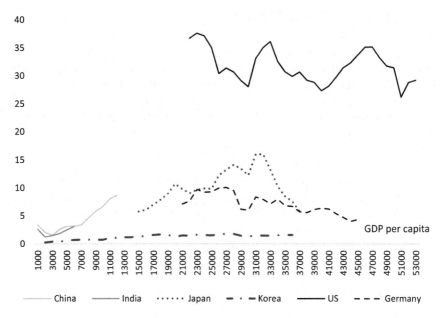

Figure 4.2 Major countries' private consumption as % of G20 total (%)
Source: Maddison (2018), World Bank (2018), Conference Board (2018)

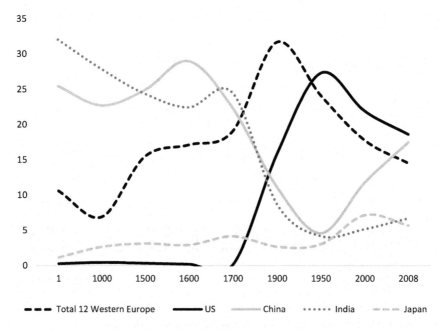

Figure 4.3 Major economies' GDP as % of global total (%, measured in PPP)
Source: Maddison (2018)

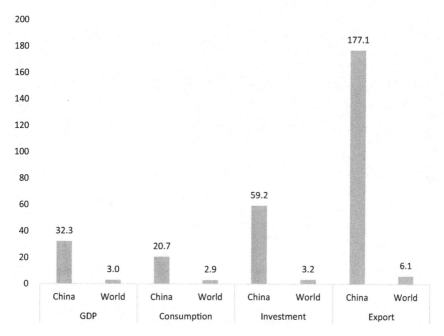

Figure 4.4 China vs. global, 1978–2016 growth (real value, times)
Source: World Bank (2018)

Various data point to the fact that China has underperformed in consumption growth. While the country's exports, investment, and consumption as a proportion of the G20 total increased quickly from 1.6, 2.2, and 1.4% in 1980 to 22.0, 27.9, and 10.1% in 2016 (Figure 4.5), per capita consumer spending was equivalent to just 6.9% of the level in the US in 2016 (Figure 4.6).

In the case of G20 countries, developed countries tend to have a high proportion of consumption relative to GDP, although countries with a high consumption-to-GDP ratio are not necessarily developed ones. In particular, China's consumption-to-GDP ratio is the second-lowest of the G20 emerging markets, just next to Saudi Arabia (Figure 4.7). The potential and scale of China's consumption growth over the next three decades can be estimated using the two methods below.

Per capita consumer spending

China's per capita spending as a proportion of per capita GDP is relatively low. Based on 2010 World Bank data using a constant US dollar, China had per capita consumer spending of US$2,337, representing 36% of per capita GDP (Figure 4.7). There is a strong positive correlation between per capita GDP and

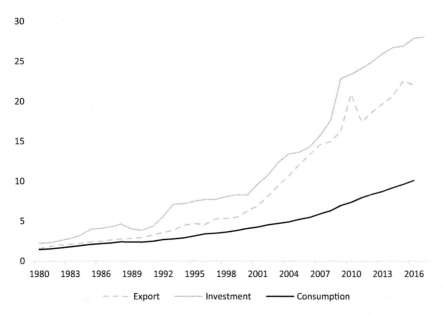

Figure 4.5 China's exports, investment, and consumption as % of G20 total (%)
Source: World Bank (2018)

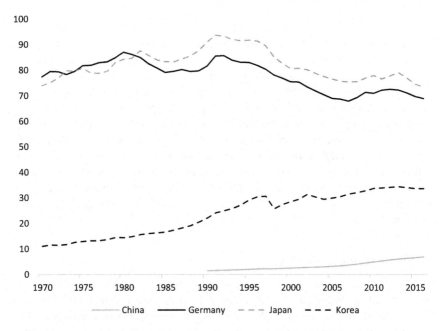

Figure 4.6 Per capita consumer spending of major countries relative to the US (%)
Source: World Bank (2018)

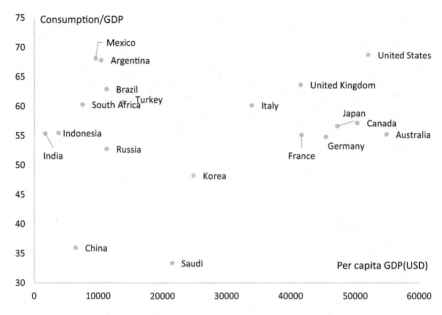

Figure 4.7 G20 per capita GDP and private consumption as % of GDP, 2015 (%)
Source: World Bank (2018)

per capita consumer spending in the 74 countries with a population over ten million (Figure 4.8). Putting China's 2015 per capita GDP into the formula in Figure 4.8, we calculate that China's per capita consumer spending is supposed to reach US$3,765 (2010 constant US dollar) to represent 58% of per capita GDP, which is 22 percentage points higher than the actual figure.

Total consumption

Everything said, China still posted 11.2 times consumption growth over the past 30 years on a low base, much faster than developed countries and other emerging economies (Figure 4.9). China's per capita GDP in 2017 is equivalent to levels in the US in 1934, Japan in 1957, and Korea in 1987. Using a 2010 constant US dollar and referencing the path of development of three countries, China's per capita is supposed to reach a range between US$20,466 (based on US growth path, partly affected by the Second World War) and US$34,332 (based on Japan's growth path) in 30 years.

We can estimate China's per capita consumption in 30 years using two methods.

Method I: correlation between per capita consumer spending and per capita GDP. Putting the per capita GDP of Japan, Korea, and the US into the formula in Figure 4.8 and using a 1.4 billion population base, we arrive at total

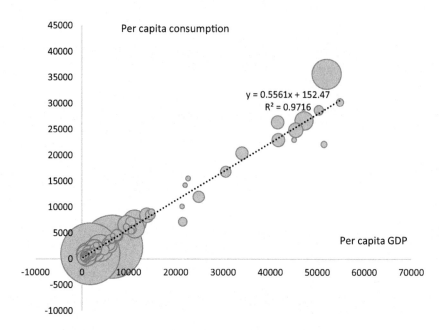

Figure 4.8 Per capita GDP and private consumption, 2015 (US$)
Source: World Bank (2018)

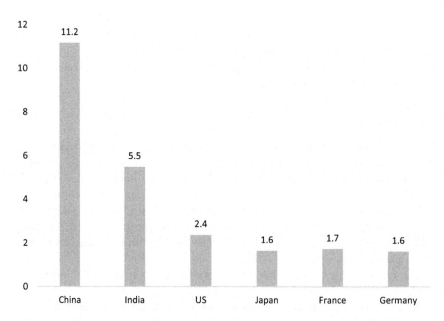

Figure 4.9 Major countries' private consumption growth in 1986–2016 (real value, times)
Source: World Bank (2018)

consumption of US$26.9 trillion, 21.3 trillion, and 16.1 trillion for China in 30 years, which would be equivalent to 7.2 times, 5.7 times, and 4.3 times the country's actual total consumption in 2017.

Method II: per capita consumer spending vs. per capita GDP in corresponding years. Counting 30 years forward from the point when the three referenced countries had the same per capita GDP as today's China, the consumption-to-GDP ratio for the US was 57% in 1964, 55% for Japan in 1987, and 49% for Korea in 2017 (Figure 4.10). Applying a population base of 1.4 billion, we calculate that China's total consumption could reach US$26.3 trillion, 18.4 trillion, and 16.3 trillion in 30 years to represent 7.0, 4.9, and 4.3 times the actual figures in 2017.

This means China's consumption growth has strong potential ahead and is likely to become a key driver of moderate economic growth (4–6%). According to the analysis above, based on constant prices, China's consumer spending is likely to grow four to seven times over the next three decades, nominal growth being likely to reach as high as 18–32 times based on RMB pricing. Alternatively, nominal consumption growth might reach 52.5 times over the next 30 years if nominal growth over the past 30 years is maintained.

It can be expected that unless there are any major policy changes, China could only exceed the US in consumption much later than it can in GDP. As of

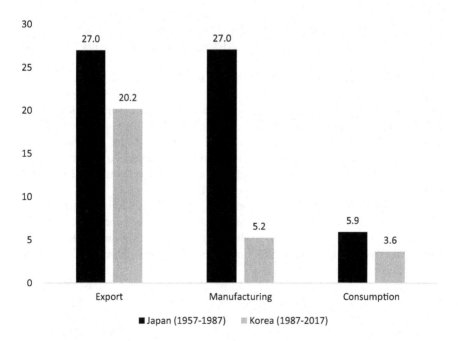

Figure 4.10 Export, manufacturing, and consumption growth in Japan and Korea (real value, times)

Source: World Bank (2018), Conference Board (2018)

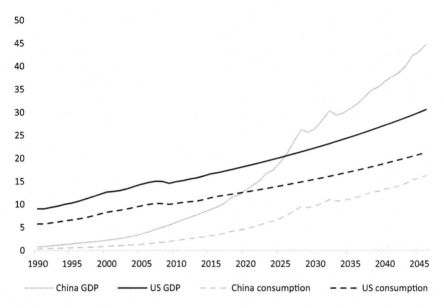

Figure 4.11 Japan growth path: GDP and consumption forecasts, China vs. US (US$ trn)
Source: World Bank (2018)

now, China's consumption has surpassed Japan but only represents 30% of US consumption.

Scenario I: Assuming 1) China follows Japan's path and maintains the kind of growth experienced by Japan during 1957–1987; 2) China maintains a population of 1.4 billion; 3) calculations are based on real values in US dollars, i.e. the current exchange rate; 4) the US maintains its pace of growth over the past ten years, China's GDP will likely surpass the US around 2026. However, a relatively low proportion of private consumption in its economy means that China is unlikely to surpass the US to become the world's largest consumption-driven country within the next 30 years (Figure 4.11).

Scenario II: If we replace assumption (1) above with China maintaining its pace of growth over the past ten years, while assumptions for the US remain unchanged, China's GDP is still likely to surpass the US around 2026, but it might take over the US around 2037 to become the world's largest consumption-driven country (Figure 4.12).

Based on the discussion above, with appropriate policy measures, China needs to, and could, maintain relatively high consumption growth over the next 30 years. Due to manufacturing sector growth weakening, consumption will be the main driver of moderate economic growth. The size of China's consumption might be somewhere between scenarios I and II. More importantly, consumption is by nature a slowly changing variable, and its improvement requires early and

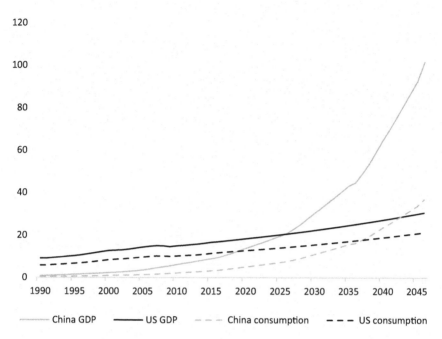

Figure 4.12 China current growth path: GDP and consumption forecasts, China vs. US (US$ trn)

Source: World Bank (2018)

prompt implementation of supportive measures such as accelerated urbanization, significant tax cuts, and substantial enhancement of retirement and health-care protection.

Changes in the consumption structure

China's consumption might have been underestimated, but it appears to be close to the levels for the US, Japan, and Korea when they were at comparable per capita GDP levels based on data for some consumption subcategories (Figure 4.13 and Figure 4.14). Overall, private consumption in China is approximately at the same stage as the US in the 1930s, Japan in the 1950s, and Korea in the 1980s.

In the next 30 years following the above-mentioned times, the proportion of food spending in the US, Japan, and Korea would nearly contract by half, while per-1,000 resident motor vehicle ownership would increase two- to three-fold. Based on overseas experience, consumption subsector performance tends to diverge as per capita GDP continues to grow, spending on consumer staples to be outpaced by discretionary. Owing to a lack of data for the earlier days, we have looked at consumption structural changes in the US during 1976–2006

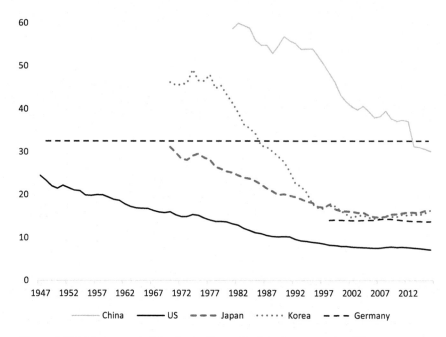

Figure 4.13 Major countries' food spending as % of total consumption (%)
Source: CEIC (2018)

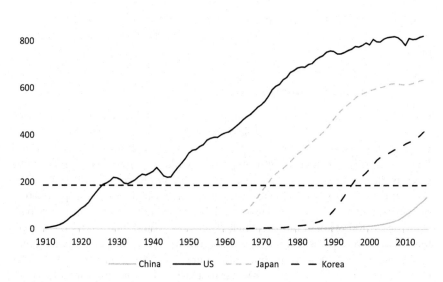

Figure 4.14 Motor vehicles per 1000 residents (unit)
Source: CEIC (2018)

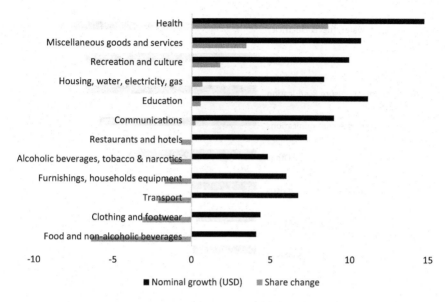

Figure 4.15 US consumption growth and proportion changes (1976–2006, pp)
Source: OECD (2018)

and in Japan during 1970–2000, and have reached a very similar conclusion (Figures 4.15 and 4.16).

Based on a rough categorization where goods whose daily spending as a proportion of total consumer spending continues to decline are categorized as consumer staples, and those with a rising proportion are categorized as consumer discretionary, consumer staples mainly include food, tobacco, liquor and beverages, apparel and shoes, furniture, and home appliances, while consumer discretionary spending includes health care, education, entertainment and recreational products, transportation and telecom, water, electricity and fuel, and housing.

Figure 4.17 demonstrates changes in the proportion of consumer discretionary spending in Japan during the 30 years after 1970: the proportion of spending on housing, water and electricity, health care, education and entertainment, and transportation and telecom nearly doubled, and these are likely to be the fastest-growing consumer subsectors for China over the next 30 years. The proportion of spending on food, tobacco and liquor, apparel and daily necessities shrank by nearly half during the period (Figure 4.18).

Based on China's provincial data, consumption as a proportion of GDP has a U-shaped relationship with per capita GDP, first declining before picking up again as per capita GDP increases (Figure 4.19). At present, the consumption-to-GDP ratio in more developed regions such as Beijing, Shanghai, and Zhejiang has picked up as per capita GDP rises. Food spending as a proportion of GDP

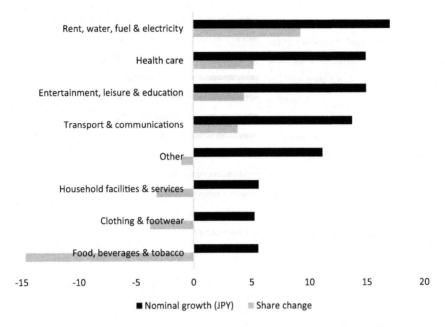

Figure 4.16 Japan consumption growth and proportion changes (1970–2000, pp)
Source: CEIC (2018)

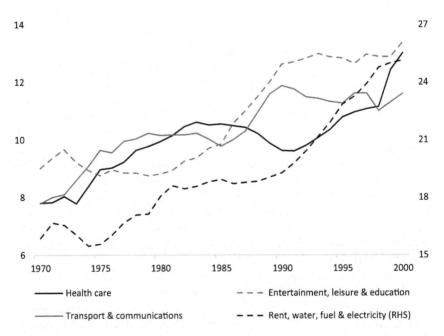

Figure 4.17 Subsectors with a rising proportion in total spending in Japan (%)
Source: CEIC (2018)

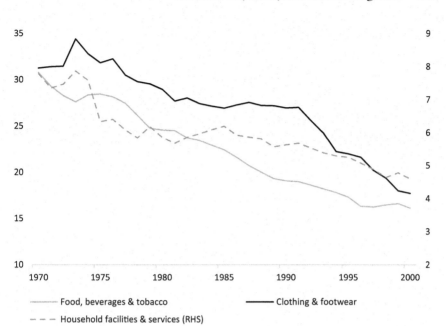

Figure 4.18 Subsectors with a declining proportion in total spending in Japan (%)
Source: CEIC (2018)

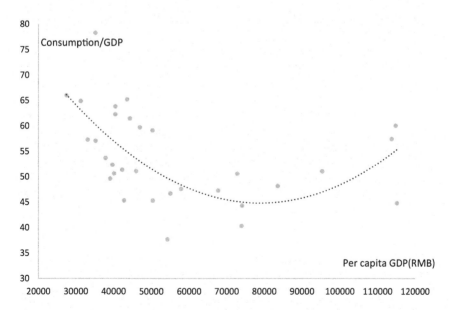

Figure 4.19 Per capita GDP and consumption-to-GDP ratio in different provinces (2016, %)
Source: CEIC (2018), Wind (2018)

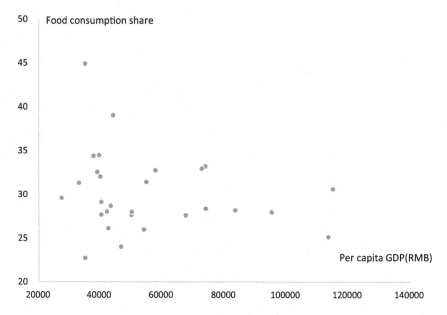

Figure 4.20 Food spending as % of total consumer spending in different provinces (2016, %)

Source: CEIC (2018), Wind (2018)

has a strong negative correlation with per capita GDP and is set to continue to go down (Figure 4.20).

Based on provincial data for food spending as a proportion of total consumer spending and per-1,000 resident vehicle ownership, the more developed provinces of Jiangsu, Zhejiang, and Guangdong are following the paths of Korea, Japan, and the US (Figures 4.21 and 4.22).

Over the past decade or so, consumer staples spending as a proportion of total consumer spending across various regions in China has declined, and at a faster pace especially since 2013 (Figure 4.23). In 2016, consumer staples accounted for 47.1% of total consumer spending in the northwestern region, 3.0 percentage points and 5.5 percentage points higher than the percentages in the central and eastern regions. During 2002–2016, spending on consumer staples grew by 2.6, 3.1, 3.1, and 3.3 times in the eastern, central, western, and northeastern regions, while spending on consumer discretionary grew by 4.8, 4.7, 4.4, and 5.5 times (Figure 4.24).

The proportion of spending on consumer discretionary in the eastern, central, and western regions is basically below the levels for Japan and Korea when their per capita GDP was at comparable levels (Figure 4.25). This proportion in the more developed eastern region has come closer to 60% since 2013 and to the level for Japan when it had a similar per capita GDP. This percentage is likely to reach nearly 80% in 30 years, representing an upside of 20 percentage points.

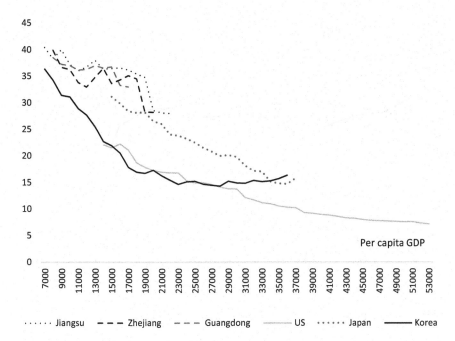

Figure 4.21 Food spending as % of total consumer spending in selected regions (%)
Source: CEIC (2018), Wind (2018)

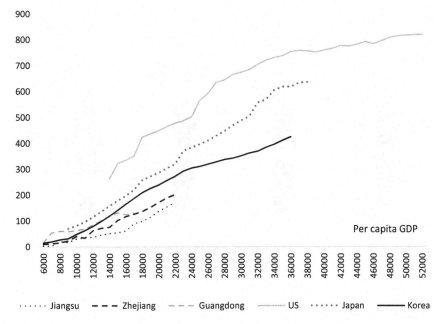

Figure 4.22 Per-1,000 resident vehicle ownership in selected regions (unit)
Source: CEIC (2018), Wind (2018)

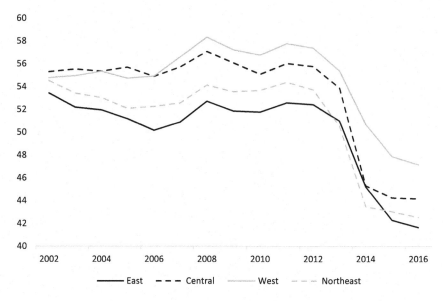

Figure 4.23 Proportion of consumer staples[1] spending by region (%)
Source: Wind (2018)

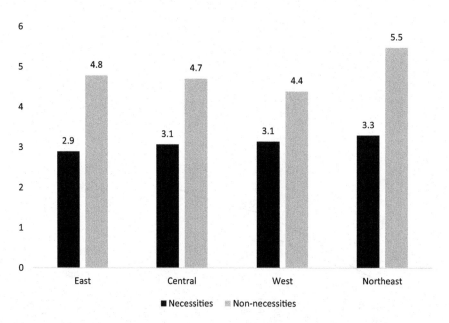

Figure 4.24 Consumer staples and discretionary spending growth by region (2002–2016, nominal value)
Source: Wind (2018)

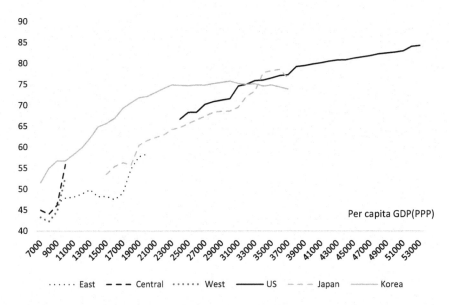

Figure 4.25 Proportion of spending on consumer discretionary in selected regions (%)
Source: CEIC (2018), Maddison (2018), Wind (2018)

While the proportion of spending on consumer staples in China is set to come down, this does not require that the growth upside to consumer staples spending is capped. Given a low base, simply the maintenance of current total retail sales growth of around 10% means cumulative growth of 19.2 times over the next 30 years. Based on the patterns across various provinces, spending on consumer staples is negatively correlated with the household savings rate, meaning that reducing the household savings rate could raise the proportion of consumer staples spending, partly due to the fact that some low-income regions have a relatively high proportion of precautionary savings (Figure 4.26).

What changes will consumption bring to China?

Given economies of scale for a large country and China's current stage of economic development, consumption will bring changes to China as well as to the entire world. It is unlikely that a large country will sustain its modernization process through exports and global consumption. On the contrary, the advantage of being a large country lies in the fact that it can achieve modernization without relying on overseas demand. Based on China's current stage of economic development, consumption, and consumption upgrade will be the core driver of high-quality economic growth.

Consumption will bring various changes to China, the most important three aspects being that: 1) only consumption upgrade can drive manufacturing upgrade,

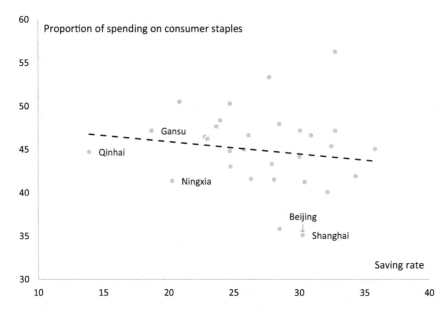

Figure 4.26 Provincial savings rate and proportion of spending on consumer staples (%)
Source: Wind (2018)

which in turn is a necessary condition for sustainable consumption upgrade;
2) China will transform from a major exporter into a major consumption-driven
country, and from a country recording a trade surplus to one with a deficit; and
3) a trade deficit driven by consumption will provide support for the regionalization and subsequent internationalization of the RMB.

Manufacturing upgrade driven by consumption upgrade

Since 2008, there has been a widening gap between China's goods exports and
manufacturing sector as a proportion of their respective G20 total (Figure 4.27).
Accordingly, exports as a proportion of industrial and agricultural total production have continued to decline (Figure 4.28). This implies three options: 1) As
global trade continues to recover, China will mitigate the pressure of overcapacity through increasing exports; 2) China will ensure reasonable demand growth
through encouraging domestic consumption; or 3) China will reduce its manufacturing sector growth and accordingly tolerate slower GDP growth. Of these
three options, we find the encouragement of domestic consumption to be more
constructive: while economic growth will decelerate further, the resilience in consumption growth will help increase the resilience in overall economic growth.

Over the next 30 years or so, China's strategy might be to increase the proportion of consumption in its economy while ensuring that its manufacturing sector

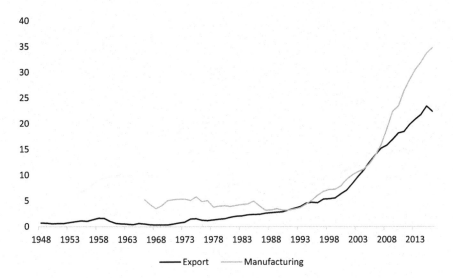

Figure 4.27 Market shares of China's goods exports and manufacturing sector among G20
countries (%)

Source: CEIC (2018), Conference Board (2018)

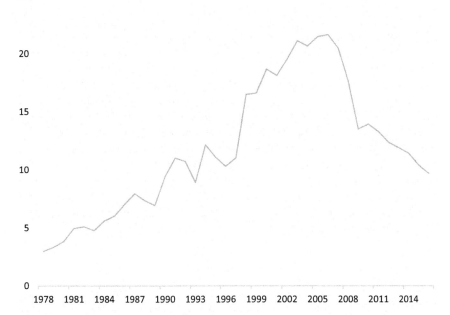

Figure 4.28 China's exports as % of industrial and agricultural total production (%)

Source: CEIC (2018)

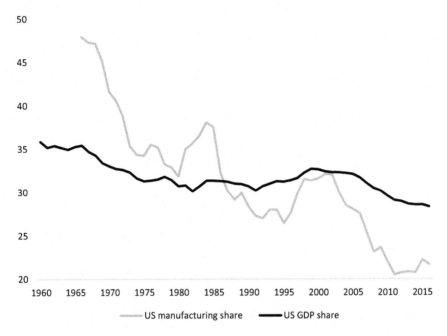

Figure 4.29 US GDP and manufacturing sector as % of G20 total (%)
Source: CEIC (2018), Conference Board (2018)

maintains a stable or slightly increasing global market share. China is facing the mid-/long-term challenge of ensuring that its GDP continues to rise as a proportion of the global total while preventing the market share of its manufacturing sector among G20 countries from increasing significantly. Since the 1960s, the market share of the US manufacturing sector among G20 countries has shrunk by more than 50%. However, the proportion of the country's GDP declined just slightly thanks to the strong support from domestic consumption (Figure 4.29). Based on nominal exchange rates, China has surpassed Japan to become the world's second-largest consumption-driven country. China's global economic position will depend upon whether or not it can become a major consumption-driven country after becoming a major exporter and manufacturer. From this perspective, it can be said that the potential of China's consumption upgrade determines the potential of its manufacturing upgrade.

Consumption upgrade to reduce trade surplus

The process of China transitioning into a major consumption-driven country is basically one of a declining trade surplus as: 1) declining exports following the relocation of low-end manufacturing industries typically happens along with consumption upgrade; 2) consumption upgrade tends to drive import growth.

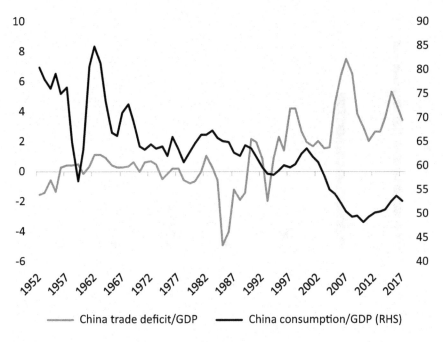

Figure 4.30 China trade deficit vs. consumption, as % of GDP (%)
Source: CEIC (2018)

China is not far from becoming a country with a trade deficit, and a trade deficit is nothing to be fearful of. Based on overseas experience, the proportion of a country's consumption in its GDP is typically negatively correlated with the proportion of trade surplus versus its GDP.

Except for a few years in the 1980s, China has always been a country with a trade surplus. However, in recent years, its trade surplus has shown a declining trend, as the proportion it represents in the country's GDP declined from the peak level of 6.5% to 3.5% in 2017 (Figure 4.30). Looking ahead, China may experience more monthly trade deficits, and the likelihood of China eventually turning into a country with an overall trade deficit will increase substantially.

Consumption to drive RMB internationalization

Several factors are behind the internationalization of a currency. In our view, consumption and a corresponding trade deficit are among the most critical factors. The degree of currency internationalization can be measured by several gauges; in foreign exchange turnover, a country's shares in global consumption and trade can basically explain its currency's degree of internationalization (Figure 4.31). In comparison, owing to regulatory restrictions, the RMB is much less internationalized than it is dictated by economic fundamentals. In other words, the potential of RMB internationalization has yet to fully play out.

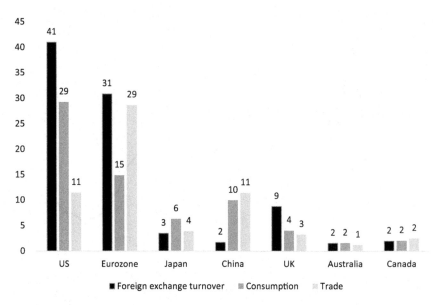

Figure 4.31 Shares of Forex turnover, consumption, and trade, 2016 (%)
Source: BIS (2018), CEIC (2018)

Based on overseas experience, it is more likely for countries with a trade deficit to achieve currency internationalization. Major countries' trade surplus as a proportion of GDP is negatively correlated with their share of total foreign exchange turnover. In other words, the larger trade surplus a country has, the less internationalized is its currency (Figure 4.32). If this experience is applicable to China, a large trade surplus is a constraint on RMB internationalization. To major countries and regions, China is the trade partner with the largest surplus, much larger than Europe, and the US is the largest trade-deficit country (Figure 4.33).

The internationalization of the domestic currency will help the expansion of outward direct investment (ODI) and thereby further promote the internationalization of the currency. Overseas experience indicates that the more internationalized a currency, the larger the share of total ODI the country represents (Figure 4.34). The strategic plan of the Belt and Road Initiative (BRI) is set to be an RMB-centric strategy. RMB internationalization is closely related to domestic reforms and consumption upgrade, but both are slowly changing variables. Therefore, we think that the realization of the BRI initiative will be a gradual long-term process.

Although China on the whole is a trade-surplus country, it has experienced regional trade deficits, which means RMB internationalization will likely start with the regionalization of the currency. Of the G20 countries, China has a trade deficit with most developed countries (excluding Germany, Japan, and Australia) and resource-rich emerging economies, and these goods dominated by Chinese

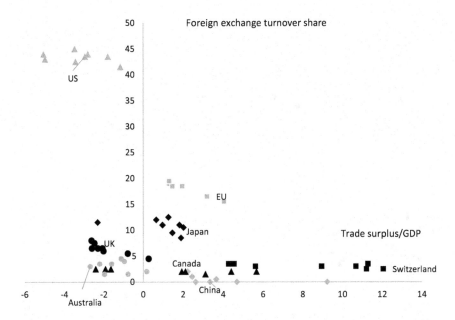

Figure 4.32 Trade-surplus-to-GDP ratio and level of currency internationalization (%)
Source: BIS (2018), CEIC (2018)

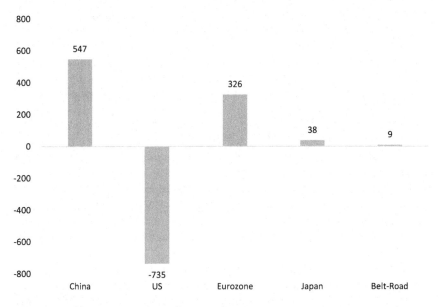

Figure 4.33 Trade surplus/deficit for major regions, 2016 (US$ bn)
Source: BIS (2018), CEIC (2018)

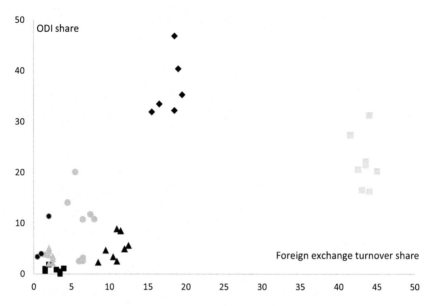

Figure 4.34 Shares of Forex turnover and ODI (%)
Source: BIS (2018), CEIC (2018)

demand are potentially subject to RMB pricing (Figure 4.35). China has a trade deficit with some of the BRI countries (Figure 4.36), and the regionalization of the RMB may start in these countries. Afterwards, the rise in China's consumption power will gradually drive the RMB to become a major global currency. The internationalization of the currency will drive more RMB-denominated ODI; together with China's consumption upgrade and import growth, this will fulfil important prerequisites for achieving the strategic goals of the BRI initiative.

A global consumption centre

At the politburo meeting on 23 April 2018, 'expanding domestic demand' was proposed again for the first time in three years, with an initiative to combine economic restructuring with domestic demand expansion. No doubt this is partly due to the latest uncertainties brought by China–US trade tensions; however, we believe 'domestic demand' might have a different meaning this time around in that expanding domestic consumption is likely to represent the 'new form of domestic demand'.

Promoting consumption is a good solution to China–US trade tensions. Firstly, China's trade surplus will gradually decline along with consumption upgrade and manufacturing relocation; the most intense stage of China–US trade friction will be over soon. From this perspective, risks to the economy caused by China–US trade friction may be resolved. In addition, if trade friction has been deliberately

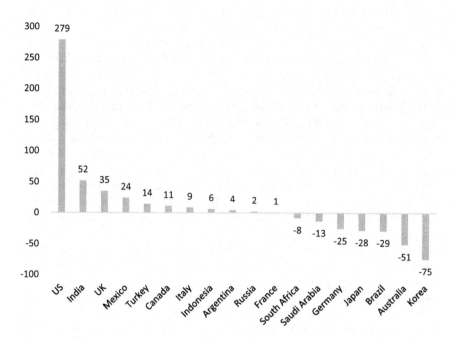

Figure 4.35 China's trade surplus/deficit with G20 countries (2017, US$ bn)
Source: CEIC (2018)

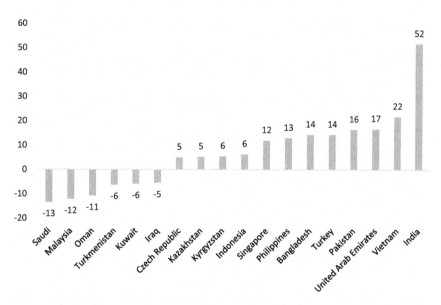

Figure 4.36 China's trade balance with BRI countries (2017, US$ bn)
Source: CEIC (2018)

employed to contain China's rise, domestic consumption growth can offset risks tied to external factors. Consumption upgrade will still promote manufacturing innovation and upgrade in China, and will mitigate political risks.

Secondly, rising consumerism in China will help rebalance the global economy and unleash sustainable growth in the world. China's consumption expenditure share in G20 has risen slowly relative to its manufacturing-value-added share. Their gap has widened from 5.5 percentage points in 2001 to 21.8 percentage points in 2016, a perfect reflection of the US (Figure 4.37). Japan had gone through a similar process of rebalancing though on a much smaller scale. In Japan, the consumption and production share gap had expanded to 6.6 percentage points in 1991, before it started to narrow down to almost zero in recent years. However, the narrowing gap was not due to rising consumption share but the opposite. For China to grow into a global consumption centre, its consumption share in G20 would have to rise, an incremental source of growth not only to China but to the rest of the world.

Trade tensions or 'trade cold wars' initiated by the US might have successfully suppressed the rise of the former Soviet Union, Germany, and Japan, but this might not work very well on China because China still has sufficient room to escape the middle-income trap and become the world's largest economy over the next ten years.

In 20 years, China might become the world's largest consumption-driven economy. For China, consumption upgrade is the future. To capture relevant investment opportunities, we highlight keywords such as branding,

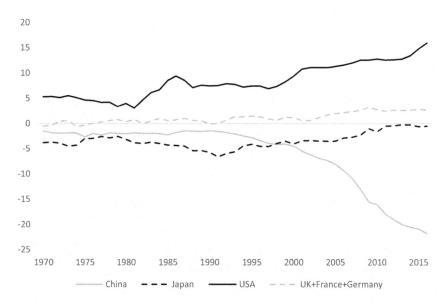

Figure 4.37 Major countries' share gap between consumption expenditure share and manufacturing value added share in G20 total (%)

Source: World Bank (2018), Conference Board (2018)

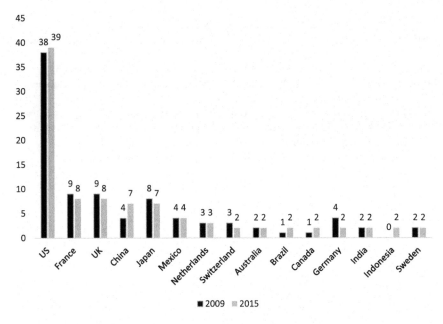

Figure 4.38 Global top 100 retail and consumption companies by country
Source: PWC (2018)

standardization, cross-generational upgrade, new business models, and world-class companies.

During 1996–2016, of the global top 500 companies, the number of Japanese companies dropped sharply from 141 to 52, while the number of Chinese companies surged from 2 to 110. The most important driver behind this was the rise of China's large manufacturing sector. Currently, the vast majority of Chinese companies that have made it among the global top 500 are large state-owned enterprises, and a relatively small proportion of retail and consumer companies. According to statistics, in 2015, among the global top 100 retail and consumer companies, there were 39 US companies and just seven Chinese companies (Figure 4.38). Against the backdrop of consumption upgrade, coupled with China's large domestic market, a number of domestic retail and consumer companies with growth potential are rising. To identify and take positions in these companies in advance will be crucial for value investors.

Note

1. Consumer staples include food, beverages & tobacco, clothing & footwear, household facilities & services. Consumer discretionary includes healthcare, transportation and telecommunications, entertainment, leisure & education, and rental, water, fuel & electricity.

References

BIS Database (accessed April 2018), www.bis.org/statistics/index.htm.

CEIC Database (accessed April 2018), https://insights.ceicdata.com/Untitled-insight/myseries.

Conference Board (accessed April 2018), www.conference-board.org/ilcprogram/.

Maddison Project (accessed April 2018), www.rug.nl/ggdc/historicaldevelopment/maddison/releases/.

OECD Database (accessed April 2018), https://data.oecd.org/.

PWC (accessed April 2018), www.pwc.com/gx/en/industries/consumer-markets.html.

Wind Database (accessed April 2018), www.wind.com.cn/en/edb.html.

World Bank Database (accessed April 2018), https://data.worldbank.org/indicator.

5 Understanding green bond challenges

A stakeholder's perspective

David C. Broadstock, Louis T. W. Cheng, and Tiantian Wang

5.1 Scope and objectives

Green finance has become a hot topic in Hong Kong and China. In March 2018, the Hong Kong government announced that it is expected to launch a green bond issuance programme of up to HK$100 billion to provide funding for its green public works projects. This green initiative echoes well with the mainland government's Belt and Road Initiative as all Belt and Road capital projects should consider using green financing and environmentally sound operations. As an Asian financial centre and the designated international capital market for mainland China, it is important for Hong Kong to create a financial platform for both the supply side (i.e. green bond issuers) and the demand side (i.e. green bond investors) to enhance the primary and secondary green finance market. However, before establishing a world-class green finance market, we need to first understand the challenges of using green finance from the stakeholders' perspectives. Then, hopefully, the Hong Kong government and the private sector can join forces to overcome these challenges.

The main objective of this chapter is to describe these challenges faced by various stakeholders to achieve a successful green finance market. However, before we talk about the challenges, we need to lay out the scope, assumptions we make, and positions we take in our framework.

5.1.1 Scope and assumptions

The International Development Finance Club (IDFC) defines green finance as financial investments flowing into sustainable development projects and initiatives, environmental products, and policies that encourage the development of a more sustainable economy. We take the view that green finance includes various green investment vehicles such as direct investments from governments and non-government organisations (NGOs), green bonds, green notes, green credit, and private equity financing related to green projects. However, for practical purposes, and due to lack of transaction data and public disclosure, we will focus on green bonds in our research and discussion here. In addition, there are many different but similar terminologies. For instance, terms that are used interchangeably include green bonds as opposed to climate bonds; green finance as opposed to climate finance; socially responsible investments (SRIs), environmental, social and governance (ESG) integration, impact investing and sustainable investing. In this chapter, we will simply use green bonds to represent the financing (supply of green bonds) side and ESG investing to reflect the investment side (the demand for green bonds) throughout.

It is important that ESG performance measures must properly reflect green projects funded by green bonds. First, in order to speed up the adoption of green projects using green financing, asset owners play a very critical role in demanding high firm-level ESG performance which gives proper credit in using green bonds. By doing so, green bond issuers will seek ways to warrant an effective monitoring of green bond proceeds to be used in green projects in a proper manner.

5.1.2 Our positioning

We position this chapter as a framework to explore empirically the challenges, and eventually to lead to solutions to establish a sophisticated green bond market, in our case, in the context of Hong Kong. We believe that the key to understanding the friction and obstacles to achieve these goals come from two main aspects: 1) the market (including regulatory) efficiency for issuing and pricing of green bonds with sufficient market depth (i.e. liquidity) for the secondary market; and 2) a commonly acceptable evaluation framework to compute quantifiable key performance indicators (KPIs) to benchmark ESG investment performance.

With these aims, we organize the chapter in the following manner. Section 5.2 introduces the overall market development of green bonds, while 5.3 describes some of the more prominent certifications/definitions of green bonds. In Section 5.4, we raise an argument on differentiating the motivations and subsequently pricing mechanisms between green bonds issued by non-profit organizations including governments/agencies and for-profit organizations (i.e. private firms). Section 5.5 proposes a framework to evaluate the success of green bonds from the issuers' perspective. In 5.6, we suggest a few possible paths for future green bond research and policy development to achieve a successful green bond market. In conclusion, we hope to shed light on the challenges from the perspectives of both the green bond issuers and the investors.

5.2 Market statistics for green bonds

Climate change and environmental issues have gradually become common challenges facing all countries in the world. This has prompted the emergence and development of the market for green bonds. A simple categorization for a green bond is that it is a type of bond instrument that creates new capital flows targeted towards low-carbon economic development – though note that we will review more complete/concrete definitions later in the chapter when it becomes necessary to do so. Compared with ordinary bonds, green bonds not only offer access to the usual economic benefits of traditional financial instruments (i.e. regular bonds), but they can adapt to the new financing environment that stakeholders are expecting from organizations and bring tangible environmental and social benefits. A number of researchers have highlighted the importance of capital markets in supporting sustainable economic development, including, for example, Tian (2018) and Tokareva et al. (2018). Additional discussion on (and definitions for) environmental and climate finance can be found in Anderson (2015) and Lindenberg (2014).

The market for green bonds is broadly recognized to have been established in March 2007. The European Union's Energy Action Plan set ambitious targets in the areas of renewable energy and energy efficiency, urging the European Investment Bank (EIB) to engage in these areas.[1] EIB chose to emphasize its commitment via a climate-related capital market product, fostering public awareness and reaching new investors by issuing the world's first green bond – a 600 million euro-dollar transaction initially labelled as a Climate Awareness Bond – in June 2007.[2] The first corporate green bond was issued by the energy company EDF in November 2013. This was an important turning point in the market, as it arguably signified the point at which private and profit-oriented companies had confidence that green bonds offered a cost-effective yet socially responsible financing strategy. Also in 2013, the International Finance Corporation (IFC) launched a $1 billion green bond to support developing countries in their climate change projects, which stimulated further enthusiasm in the international green bond market.

5.2.1 A summary of the global green bond market

The issuance of green bonds has shown explosive growth globally. To get a sense of the underlying trends of the green bond market, Figure 5.1 plots some

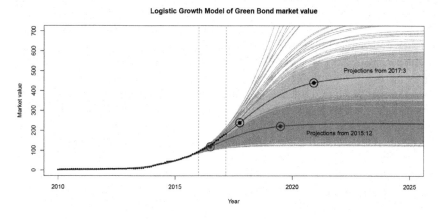

Figure 5.1 Logistic growth curve-based projections of the dollar value of the green bond market: The blue lines (turquoise shaded region) show projections based on data up until 2015:12; The red lines (red shaded region) show projections based on data up until 2017:3

Table 5.1 Summary statistics for bond coupon rates by type of green bonds issuer

	N (%)	Mean	Sd	Median	Min	Max	Se
Agency	143 (9.97%)	2.46	1.95	2	0	8.12	0.16
Corporate	885 (61.67%)	3.3	2.41	3.15	0	11.8	0.08
Govt/Treasury/ Central Bank	7 (0.49%)	2.95	4.66	1.25	0.5	13.48	1.76
Other Gov/ Supra	348 (24.25%)	3.09	2.74	2.25	0	11.75	0.15
Non-US Municipals	38 (2.65%)	1.85	2.56	0.85	0	10.18	0.42

Note: N refers to the number of green bonds issued. The data in brackets '(…)' represent the share of each of the different types of bonds relative to the total.

Source: created by authors using data from Thomson Reuters Eikon

'conservative' market projections on the basis of bonds contained in the Climate Bond Initiative (CBI) data. The annual value of global green bond issuances continued to grow at an annualized growth rate of about 50% from 2012 until 2017. Statistics released by the CBI show that by November 2018, the global green bond market had reached $388.30 billion, where the Eurobond Markets (US$171.05 billion) and the United States (US$80.64 billion) are the first and second largest green bond issuing regions in the world.

Owing to the rapid expansion in the number and scale of green bond issuances, the issuers and types of green bond have gradually evolved and have now become quite comprehensive. The types of issuing institution have developed from initial bank issuances to include a variety of municipal issuances, commercial issuances, enterprise issuances etc. (see Table 5.1). The general categories of green bond include corporate green bonds, agency green bonds, bank green bonds, government green bonds, municipal green bonds, Supra green bonds, and other forms. Of these, corporate bonds account for the largest proportion, 61.67% of the total number of issued bonds and 57.22% of total value of green bonds. At the same time, the categories of green bond 'types' has also diversified, as can be seen by the examples given in Table 5.2. In order to meet the unique needs of different investors, the issuers of green bonds in different countries have gradually refined the types of project financed using a green bond and have made a great effort to clarify the direction of the use of funds (via use of proceeds statements).

As of November 2018, based on the data contained in the Thomson Reuters Eikon database, 1,435 green bonds had been issued globally, the cumulative value total exceeding US$388 billion.[3] Both the number of issuances and the dollar-value of green bonds have increased rapidly since 2013. Prior to this, the Eurobond market was the main market for green bond issuance, but since 2013 the scale and geographical distribution of the issuing countries have gradually expanded.

Table 5.2 Types and examples of green bonds that have been issued

Type	Proceeds raised by bond sale are	Debt recourse	Example
'Use of Proceeds' Bond	Earmarked for green projects	Recourse to the issuer: same credit rating applies as issuer's other bonds	EIB 'Climate Awareness Bond' (backed by EIB); Barclays Green Bond
'Use of Proceed' Revenue Bond or ABS	Earmarked for or refinances green projects	Revenue streams from the issuers though fees, taxes etc. are collateral for the debt	Hawaii State (backed by fee on electricity bills of the state utilities)
Project Bond	Ring-fenced for the specific underlying green project(s)	Recourse is only to the project's assets and balance sheet	Invenergy Wind Farm (backed by Invenergy Campo Palomas wind farm)
Securitization (ABS) Bond	Refinance portfolios of green projects or proceeds are earmarked for green projects	Recourse is to a group of projects that have been grouped together (e.g. solar leases or green mortgages)	Tesla Energy (backed by residential solar leases); Obvion (backed by green mortgages)
Covered Bond	Earmarked for eligible projects included in the covered pool	Recourse to the issuer and, if the issuer is unable to repay the bond, to the covered pool	Berlin Hyp green Pfandbrief; Sparebank 1 Bolligkredit green covered bond
Loan	Earmarked for eligible projects or secured on eligible assets	Full recourse to the borrower(s) in the case of unsecured loans. Recourse to the collateral in the case of secured loans, but may also feature limited recourse to the borrower(s).	MEP Werke, Ivanhoe Cambridge and Natixis Assurances (DUO), OVG
Other debt instruments	Earmarked for eligible projects		Convertible Bonds or Notes, Schuldschein, Commercial Paper, Sukuk, Debentures

Source: www.climatebonds.net/market/explaining-green-bonds

Table 5.3 summarizes the number and value of green bond issuances since 2009 and illustrates the general growth patterns over time and across regions. The total value of green bonds issued by Eurobond markets has reached US$171.05 billion, and the total value of green bonds issued by the United States market has reached US$80.64 billion, accounting for 44.05% and 20.77% of the total value of global green bonds respectively. Other than the United States and Eurobond markets, China has the highest value of green bond issuance. As of November 2018, the value of green bonds issued in mainland China had reached $40.24 billion, accounting for 10.36% of the total value of global green bonds. Next came France and Germany, with cumulative issuance values of US$33.57 billion and US$10.91 billion respectively.

Table 5.4 provides further elaboration on the geographical breakdown of bond issuances, alongside a closer lens on the number and value of issuances per year since 2013, the point at which the market saw major growth. We can see that in 2013, fewer than 50 bonds were issued, whereas from 2014 onwards it was in the hundreds of new issuances per year. The largest proportion of these bonds has been issued within Eurobond Markets (accounting for 41.88% of the total number of green bonds), followed by the United States (21.25%), and mainland China (7.52%) is an emerging major player in the global market.

The average years to maturity of the green bonds that have been issued to date are summarized in Table 5.5. Broadly speaking, green bonds display the characteristics of long maturity and high credit. At the time of issue, average maturity is around 20 years. Across the 'live' bonds, the remaining years to maturity are broadly in the range of 16–23 years. It is worth noting that corporate bonds offer the smallest value for years to maturity at just one year, though other bond issuers also have some cases of short-term bonds, two years as the minimum years to maturity for all other bond issuer types.[4] Green bonds with maturity of less than five years (excluding five years) accounted for 21.36% of the total number of green bonds issued, and a maturity of 5–9 years accounted for 47.86% of the total number of green bonds issued. Long-term bonds with maturity of ten years or more accounted for 30.76% of the total number of green bonds issued.

Table 5.6 summarizes the distribution of issuer types by key countries or geographic regions. The Eurobond Markets, the United States, and China are the top three regions with the highest issuance number and value for green bonds issuances. It can be seen that corporate bonds represent the majority of the bonds issued, particularly in China. The issuance value of corporate green bonds in these three markets has reached US$101.02 billion, US$41.56 billion, and US$36 billion respectively. In addition, the total issuance value of agency bonds is US$68 billion, accounting for 17.53% of the total issuance value of all green bonds. Whereas agency bonds are widely adopted in Europe and the United States, there are only handfuls of agency bonds issued in other markets.

The last feature of the data we will explore briefly is the coupon rate, which reflects the value/price of a green bond (see Table 5.7), though we will also return to questions of pricing in Section 5.4. Bonds issued in India have the

Table 5.3 Green bonds issued in the Eurobond market, United States, and Mainland China (since 2009)

	Global		Eurobond Markets			United States			Mainland China		
	N	Value	N	Value	Va / T_Va	N	Value	Va / T_Va	N	Value	Va / T_Va
2009	4	0.76	2	0.32	42.27%	2	0.43	56.79%	0	0	0
2010	53	2.95	52	2.75	93.23%	1	0.2	6.77%	0	0	0
2011	28	0.82	25	0.41	50.31%	3	0.41	49.69%	0	0	0
2012	19	2.17	12	0.96	43.99%	4	0.57	26.02%	0	0	0
2013	42	11.94	29	3.26	27.34%	8	4.8	40.21%	0	0	0
2014	133	30.44	72	16.23	53.31%	24	6.67	21.93%	2	0.22	0.71%
2015	289	45.48	90	23.53	51.73%	163	15.79	34.72%	0	0	0
2016	223	77.98	94	31.22	40.04%	43	20.02	25.68%	34	18.04	23.13%
2017	357	121.24	128	52.18	43.04%	39	22.23	18.33%	41	12.69	10.47%
2018	283	93.14	94	39.05	41.92%	18	9.53	10.23%	31	9.29	9.97%
Sum (mean for Va)	1,435	388.3	601	171.1	44.05%	305	80.64	20.77%	108	40.24	10.36%

Note: N refers to the number of green bonds issued. Value refers to the value of green bonds issued. Va/T_Va refers to the percentage of the total value of green bonds issued in this market to the total value of global green bonds in that year. The unit of value is US$ billion. The number and value of green bonds in 2018 include only green bonds issued from January to November 2018.

Source: created by authors using data from Thomson Reuters Eikon

Table 5.4 Green bonds issued in different countries/regions by year (after 2013)

	2013		2014		2015		2016		2017		2018		Accumulative Total	
	N	Value	N	Value	N	Value	N	Value	N	Value	N	Value	N	Value
Eurobond Markets	29	3.26	72	16.23	90	23.53	94	31.22	128	52.18	94	39.05	601	171.05
United States	8	4.80	24	6.67	163	15.79	43	20.02	39	22.23	18	9.53	305	80.64
Sweden	2	0.14	14	0.80	13	0.83	26	1.41	34	1.94	51	2.80	140	7.92
Mainland China	0	0	2	0.22	0	0	34	18.04	41	12.69	31	9.29	108	40.24
Malaysia	0	0	0	0	0	0	0	0	49	0.44	3	0.05	52	0.49
Japan	0	0	1	0.04	5	1.85	1	0.09	6	0.58	21	1.74	29	2.45
France	0	0	4	3.56	5	0.47	3	2.61	8	21.70	4	3.20	27	33.57
Norway	0	0	5	0.36	5	1.13	2	0.36	8	0.69	6	3.02	26	4.89
Germany	1	0.29	1	0.57	2	1.16	3	1.70	5	2.83	10	4.38	22	10.91
Australia	0	0	2	0.43	2	0.22	3	0.66	7	2.31	5	2.49	19	7.05
India	0	0	0	0	4	0.17	7	0.32	6	0.41	0	0	17	0.96
Canada	0	0	3	0.94	1	0	1	1.17	3	0.83	8	3.91	16	7.02
Hong Kong	0	0	0	0	0	0	0	0	1	0.57	4	1.41	5	1.97
Others	2	3.44	5	0.61	4	0.33	6	0.38	22	1.84	28	12.29	68	19.14
Global	42	11.94	133	30.44	289	45.48	223	77.98	357	121.24	283	93.14	1435	388.30

Note: N refers to the number of green bonds issued. Value refers to the value of green bonds issued. The unit of value is US$ billion. The number and value of green bonds in 2018 include only green bonds issued from January to November 2018.

Source: created by authors using data from Thomson Reuters Eikon

Table 5.5 Characteristics of different types of bond

Summary statistics according to bond tenor (Years to maturity)

	Mean	Sd	Median	Min	Max	se
Agency	16.79	9.73	19	2	28	0.81
Corporate	18.63	8.88	21.5	1	30	0.30
Govt/Treasury/Central Bank	15.71	10.89	16	2	29	4.12
Non-US Municipals	22.58	6.47	25	2	29	1.05
Other Gov/Supra	19.39	8.73	24	2	29	0.47

Source: created by authors using data from Thomson Reuters Eikon

highest average coupon (6.29), followed by Malaysia (5.55), and then mainland China (4.7). The minimum value of coupon issued by Malaysia was 4.8, which is the highest minimum coupon across all countries or regions. However, it is also worth noting that (i) all green bonds issued in Malaysia are corporate bonds, and (ii) Malaysian bonds also have the smallest standard errors, i.e. most bonds have similar coupon rates. The highest coupon green bond appeared in Nigeria and is a 13.4-coupon bond issued by Nigeria-Federal Republic of (Government) in December 2017. Broadly speaking, we observed that, on average, corporate green bonds have a higher coupon relative to other types of green bond (not shown in the table).

Next we briefly discuss green bond market activity in various global regions.

5.2.2 Europe

Global interest in green bonds originated from the European bond markets, following the first major issue in 2007 by the EIB. The first explosive growth phase in Europe occurred in 2010. In that year, the Eurobond markets issued 52 green bonds with a total value of US$2.753 billion, accounting for 93.23% of the total global green bond issuance. Referring to Table 5.3, which compares the issuance of green bonds in Eurobond markets and the United States since 2009, we observe that by 2014, the Eurobond market accounted for only 27.34% of the global green bond market according to the value of bonds issued. By 2013, the value of green bonds issued by the United States reached US$4.8 billion, accounting for 40% of global green bonds (US$11.94 billion in 2013). The proportion of global green bonds emanating from Europe has been declining steadily since 2014, which means the scale of green bonds and the geographical distribution of the issuing countries have both gradually expanded since that year. Notwithstanding this, we see from Table 5.4 that a number of European countries have joined the green bond market including, for example, France, Germany, and Sweden. Sweden and Germany issuers started utilising green bonds in 2013. Sweden has issued the second-largest number of green bonds except the United States and Eurobond markets, but the total value of green bonds issued

Table 5.6 Distribution of different types of green bond in different countries/regions

	Total		Agency		Corporate		Govt/Treasury/Central Bank		Other Gov/Supra		Non-US Munis	
	N	Value	N	Value	N	Value	N	Value	N	Value	N	Value
Eurobond Markets	601	171.05	64	36.36	282	101.02	2	1.98	243	30.82	10	0.87
United States	305	80.64	46	16.78	193	41.52	0	0	66	22.29	0	0
Mainland China	108	40.24	4	3.74	102	36	0	0	2	0.5	0	0
Sweden	140	7.92	0	0	123	6.99	0	0	5	0.31	12	0.62
Malaysia	52	0.49	0	0	52	0.49	0	0	0	0	0	0
Japan	29	2.45	2	0.39	22	1.84	0	0	1	0.04	4	0.18
France	27	33.57	3	3.12	14	11.32	1	16.77	8	2.02	1	0.34
Norway	26	4.89	2	0.16	19	4.22	0	0	0	0	5	0.51
Germany	22	10.91	6	3.13	16	7.78	0	0	0	0	0	0
Australia	19	7.05	5	3.11	9	2.02	0	0	5	1.93	0	0
India	17	0.96	5	0.32	12	0.64	0	0	0	0	0	0
Canada	16	7.02	1	0.37	7	2.89	0	0	6	3.45	2	0.3
Hong Kong	5	1.97	0	0	5	1.97	0	0	0	0	0	0
Other	68	19.14	5	0.51	29	3.08	4	8.56	12	6.73	4	0.31
Total	1,435	388.30	143	67.99	885	221.78	7	27.31	348	68.09	38	3.13

Note: N refers to the number of green bonds issued. Value refers to the value of green bonds issued. The unit of value is US$ billion. The total number and value of green bonds is up to November 2018.

Source: created by authors using data from Thomson Reuters Eikon

Table 5.7 Summary statistics for green bonds coupon rates by selected countries/geographic regions

	N	Mean	Sd	Median	Min	Max	Se
Eurobond Markets	601	3.28	2.8	2.5	2.96	11.8	0.11
United States	305	3.15	1.69	2.65	3.1	9.75	0.1
China (Mainland)	108	4.7	1.12	4.73	2	7.76	0.11
Sweden	140	0.8	0.85	0.57	0	6	0.07
Malaysia	52	5.55	0.44	5.58	4.8	6.6	0.06
Japan	29	0.5	0.49	0.27	0.02	2.12	0.09
France	27	1.87	1.37	1.39	0.2	5.5	0.26
Norway	26	2.85	2.15	2.03	0.5	9.69	0.42
Germany	22	0.59	0.39	0.56	0.12	1.5	0.08
Australia	19	3.25	0.64	3.25	1.75	4.26	0.15
India	17	6.29	3.64	7.85	0	9.15	0.88
Canada	16	2.83	0.9	2.83	1.65	4.39	0.22
Hong Kong	5	3.74	1.83	4.25	1.62	5.62	0.82
Total	1,367	3.12	2.49	2.65	0	13.48	0.07

Source: created by authors using data from Thomson Reuters Eikon

by Sweden is not very high, accounting for only 2% of the accumulated value of global green bonds.

In 2014, the total value of the four green bonds issued by France reached $3.563 billion, nearly 5.5 times the value issued in 2012, accounting for 11.7% of the total value of global green bonds issued in that year. Norway started issuing green bonds in 2014, and 26 green bonds were issued up to November 2018, with an annual issuance value of no more than $700 million before 2018. And the value of green bonds issued by Norway in the first eleven months of 2018 reached $3.32 billion, which is a marked increase compared with the previous annual total for 2017 of less than $700 million. To this point, the European markets remain the world leader in the overall number and value of green bonds that have been issued.

5.2.3 United States

In the US markets, the International Bank for Reconstruction and Development was responsible for the first green bond with a US$300 million issue in April 2009 (a total of US$430 million in US green bonds were issued that year). Subsequently, the market for green bonds in the US developed steadily, and there was an explosive growth in 2015. In that year, 163 green bonds were issued in the US market, with a total issuance value of US$15.79 billion, more than doubling that in 2014 (US$6.67 billion), representing 34.72% of the total global green bond value in 2015. As of November 2018, the US issued 305 green bonds with a market value of $80.64 billion, making it the second-largest green bond issuer in the world.

The US is the world's largest issuer of green municipal bonds. According to the CBI, a total of US$11 billion in green municipal bonds was issued in the US in 2017, an increase of nearly US$4 billion over the previous year, accounting for nearly half of the total number of green bonds issued in the US in that year. American green municipal bonds started in 2013. The state of Massachusetts first issued US$100 million in green municipal bonds to finance clean water, energy efficiency, and ecological protection projects. Later, California issued US$300 million in green municipal bonds in 2014, to finance water and transportation projects. In July 2014, the District of Columbia Water Authority issued the first green municipal bond with a second opinion and demonstrated the environmental, social, and governance performance of the project. The investors of green municipal bonds in the US are mainly individual investors, which can better disperse investment risks.

In addition, the Massachusetts Institute of Technology is the first university to publicly issue green bonds. In 2014, five buildings of the school were used as collateral to issue green bonds with a value of US$370 million for the construction of environmental protection projects in schools.

5.2.4 Asian demand for green bonds

As early as 2004, Singapore City Developments Ltd issued a US$239 million green corporate bond, but the real development of Asian green bonds began in 2014 when mainland China issued its first green bond. Though starting late relative to Europe and the US, the Asian green bond market has shown strong momentum and development. In particular, the cumulative value of green bonds issued by China (mainland) has reached US$40.24 billion, accounting for 10.36% of the global total value of green bonds. Japan issued its first green bond, worth US$442 million in 2014, and in 2018 the value of green bond issued in the Japanese market reached $1.735 billion (up until November), which is roughly three times the value issued in 2017 (US$579.6 million). Malaysia also started issuing green bonds in 2017, issuing 49 green bonds with a total market value of US$436 million. India started issuing green bonds in 2015, and the cumulative issuance value of green bonds as of November 2018 stands at US$958 million.

5.2.5 A focus on mainland China and Hong Kong

The first green bond issued in mainland China was in May 2014, when CGN Wind Energy Ltd issued the first domestic five-year medium-term note linked to carbon income. Then in January 2015, Société Générale issued US$4.9 billion of special financial bonds for energy conservation and environmental protection projects. In July 2015, Golden Wind Technology issued US$49.02 million of bonds in Hong Kong, and the funds raised were used for renewable energy projects. In that year, nearly 1,000 enterprises operating in green energy, public transport, environmental protection technology, and related fields received more than one trillion RMB of financing through debt financing instruments in the interbank market. Nevertheless, compared with the bank's green credit scale (up to six trillion RMB by the end of 2014), China's green bond market is small in scale, single in variety but had great potential for development.

On 22 December 2015, the People's Bank of China issued the 'Notice on Issue of Green Financial Bonds', marking the formal launch of China's green bond market. Released on the same day was the 'Green Bond Support Project Catalogue (2015 edition)', which was the first document providing a formal definition and classification criteria for green bonds in China. It provides a reference for the approval and registration of green bonds, the evaluation of third-party green bonds, the rating of green bonds, and related information on disclosure requirements. On 31 December 2015, the National Development and Reform Commission issued the 'Guidelines for Issuing Green Bonds', which offered a tailored definition of green *corporate* bonds in China.

In 2016, China issued 34 green bonds, the total value of which reached US$18.03 billion, accounting for 23.11% of the total value (US$77.98 billion in 2016) of global green bonds. This includes two green panda bonds issued by New Development Bank (formerly known as the BRIC Bank) in July 2016 and Beijing Enterprises Water Group Ltd in August 2016. As a result, the issuer of green bonds in China has expanded from the original financial institutions to non-financial enterprises and overseas entities. The variety of bonds issued includes green financial bonds, green corporate bonds, green debt financing tools, green panda bonds, green asset-backed securities, and other types. As of November 2018, 108 green bonds were issued in mainland China, with a total value of US$40.24 billion, reaching 10.36% of the total value of global green bonds. It is also worth mentioning that Hong Kong issued its first green bond worth US$567 million in 2017, and then issued four green bonds worth US$1.41 billion in 2018. Its green bond market is also gradually developing, and The Climate Bonds Initiative (2016) actively discussed pathways to scale up green bond market issuances in China. This contributed to earlier discussions by the World Business Council for Sustainable Development (2015) which talked more generally about the important role of green bonds in scaling up demand and supply of climate financing solutions.

Third-party certification of green bonds has arguably been a key feature underlying domestic market progress. While recognized international institutions, for instance Ernst & Young, provide second opinions for China's green bond issuances, domestic green bond third-party certification agencies with professional knowledge and strength have also begun to emerge. Local institutions such as the Climate and Energy Finance Research Center of Central University of Finance and Economics, China Energy Conservation Consulting Co., Ltd and Business Road Ronglv Green have also begun to provide third-party certification for the issuance of green bonds in China and to examine and evaluate environmental and social impact of green projects, and the direction of fundraising.

5.3 Definitions and certification of green bonds

To this point of the chapter we have given relatively limited attention to the definition of a green bond. To date, there is no universally agreed upon definition for a green bond. This is not entirely unexpected, since the market remains relatively young, and there is still a need to develop a depth of experience among issuers so that good and bad practices can be identified and then regulated. Notwithstanding this, the foundations of a green bond are much the same as any regular bond, and it serves some purpose to provide a brief recap of regular bonds.

A bond is a debt investment in which an investor loans money to an entity (typically corporate or governmental) which borrows the funds for a defined time at a variable or a fixed interest rate. Bonds are used by companies, municipalities, states, and sovereign governments to raise money and finance projects and activities. Owners of bonds are debtholders, or creditors, of the issuer. Bonds are often used when companies, or other entities such as governments of investment banks, need to raise money to finance new projects, maintain ongoing operations, or refinance other existing debt obligations.

The actual market price (value) of a bond depends upon a number of factors including the credit quality of the issuer, the length of time until expiration, and the coupon rate compared to the general interest rate environment at the time. Accordingly, the 'value', and in turn the demand and market price for bonds, can thus vary over time.

5.3.1 *What is a green bond?*

To try to make concrete what distinguishes a green bond from a regular (sometimes known as a 'black') bond, we may look at a number of existing/emerging classification schemes. The International Capital Market Association (ICMA) issued the green bond principles (GBP) on 31 January 2014 (last updated in June 2018). GBP are supported by a global community of over 250 institutions and are used as a reference for best practice in developed and emerging markets. These principles were determined by a voluntary coalition containing equal numbers of underwriters, issuers and investors (25 members in total) of green bonds, providing 'best-practice' advice to feed into the guiding principles. Membership of the coalition arguably was dominated by European and US members; less prominence was given to Asian market players. However, this was more a reflection of the market at the time than any deliberate omission, since early market participation was dominated by European and US issuers.[5] The five principles which form the GBP are as follows:

- **Principle 1**: Use of proceeds: Description of use of proceeds should be included in the legal documentation.
- **Principle 2**: Project evaluation and selection: Issuers should outline the process used in determining project eligibility, including the process, criteria, and environmental sustainability objectives.

- **Principle 3**: Management of proceeds: This recommends the segregation of funds in a separate portfolio (ring fencing of proceeds) and disclosure of intended investments for unallocated proceeds.
- **Principle 4**: Reporting: The reporting should cover use of proceeds reporting and impact reporting.
- **Principle 5**: External review is recommended.

The first principle, which is also the most important, requires that the funds raised must be used for green projects, such as climate change mitigation, climate change adaptation, natural resource conservation, biodiversity conservation, and pollution prevention and control. GBP has a list of eligible green project categories, captures the most commonly used types of project supported by, or expected to be supported by, the green bond market. The issuer should describe the intended use of proceeds in legal documents, such as the solicitation instructions, to ensure that the green projects invested into can produce material environmental benefits.

Secondly, the selection of green projects must follow a strict/well-defined evaluation process. The issuer of a green bond should clearly communicate to investors: the environmental sustainability objectives; the process by which the issuer determines how the projects fit within eligible green projects categories; the related eligibility criteria, including, if applicable, exclusion criteria or any other process applied to identify and manage potentially material environmental and social risks associated with the projects.

Thirdly, the collection of funds must be subject to supervision and tracking. The net proceeds of the green bond, or an amount of these net proceeds should be credited to a sub-account, moved to a sub-portfolio or otherwise tracked by the issuer in an appropriate manner. The issuers should set a retrospective management and monitoring mechanism, involving a formal internal verification process to retrospectively evaluate and document the actual use of process, so it may be objectively verified that the relevant funds are used for the investment and operation of green projects, as they should be. The issuer may also make appropriate investments in the idle funds, but it has to disclose them to investors.

The fourth principle is that issuers must disclose the report on the use of the raised funds at least once a year, including a list of the green items to which the raised funds are invested, a brief description of the project, the total expenditure of the raised funds, and the expected impact of the project. GBP recommends that issuers should better use qualitative and quantitative performance indicators (e.g. energy capacity, electricity generation, greenhouse gas emissions reduced/avoided, number of people provided with access to clean power, decrease in water use, reduction in the number of cars required) in their regular reports to measure the environmental impact of specific investments, if it is feasible.

The GBP do not impose mandatory requirements on the certification of green bonds, but certified climate bonds can gain stronger trust from investors and help issuers obtain lower interest rate financing. GBP recommends that issuers use external review to ensure that the issued green bonds meet the requirements of the above principles. Issuers can use the independent status and professional services of third parties to complete the project evaluation and screening process, as well as to verify the allocation of funds raised. External review forms can be diversified, such as second opinions issued by well-known research institutions, audit reports issued by audit institutions, third-party certification reports issued by non-profit organizations, and rating reports issued by rating agencies.

5.3.2 Perspective of some major ratings agencies

After the market for green bonds began to display the characteristics of early-stage maturity, major global rating agencies started to develop their own perspectives on what defines a green bond. The objectives of the rating agencies differ from those underlying the green bond principles, since the agencies are typically trying to develop market tracker indices, using a variety of 'screens' to ensure that the created indices are genuinely reflective of pricing dynamics of green bonds. Here we will take the index screens/definitions used by Standard & Poor's (S&P), and Moody's, as representative examples of the definitions being applied, how they have evolved and how they differ. We then offer some remarks on the planned additions to the repertoire of standards by reflecting on the intended standards to be launched by the International Standards Office (ISO).

5.3.2.1 Standard and Poor's

S&P were possibly the first of the major ratings agencies to develop a bespoke green bond index. The index takes the universe of bonds that have been issued, then screens out first those that do not fulfil the following criteria:

- **Disclosure:** The issuer must clearly demarcate a bond as being green, which can be done through a number of channels.
- **Country/currency:** Any country/currency is viable.
- **Green Flag:** Bonds must be certified green by the CBI.
- **Maturity:** Maturity must be greater than one month within the rebalancing period; no bond expires within the index.
- **Coupon type:** Various types are permissible including fixed, zero-coupon, step-up, floaters, and fixed-to-float.
- **Pricing:** Bid price data are required from specified providers. Bonds not priced by Thomson Reuters or Securities Evaluations | ICE Data Services are not eligible for index inclusion.

(Note that the above is not a comprehensive list of the criteria but summarizes the core features that make it unique in identifying green bonds.)

It is evident from the green flag requirement the prominent role assigned to CBI by leading global financial institutions such as S&P. The role of the CBI here is to provide a form of due diligence. Not only must a firm itself declare that a bond is a green bond, but S&P require external verification from the CBI that the bond satisfies their own criteria to be formally flagged as a green bond.

Among the interesting features within the original S&P criteria are the somewhat relaxed maturity requirements and, to a lesser extent, the open currency requirements. The requirement that a bond need only have more than one month to maturity during any portfolio rebalancing allows the potential for some inappropriate exploitation of green bonds, or 'greenwashing'. Greenwashing is the phenomenon in which a corporate entity tries to take advantage of the reputation, and in turn, value gains that might arise from being seen to be green. There was speculation in the early phase of the corporate era of green bonds that greenwashing may be occurring. These fears were heightened by the emergence of short maturity bond issuances. However, from their inception, green bonds were arguably intended to support more significant green projects that would naturally require longer than two years to complete and hence require longer maturities.

In February 2017, S&P refined their green bond index (to become the green bond 'select' index), adding to or modifying the list of screening criteria. The various modifications may not have been motivated by a desire to avoid representing corporate greenwash in the index, yet the modifications are apparently more strongly in favour of ensuring that the index reflects investment grade bonds. Some of the changes in the criteria are as follows:

- **Currency and market of issue:** Bonds issued in non-G10 currencies in the native market of that currency *are not* eligible. Bonds issued in non-G10 currencies issued in global markets (foreign, global, Eurobond) are eligible without any specific restrictions.
- **Maturity:** Each bond must have at least 24 months to final maturity at the time of issuance, in addition to one month to expiry to remain on the index.
- **Optionality and exclusions:** Various efforts are taken to ensure that optionality does not 'contaminate' the underlying bond price trend.
- **Credit rating quality:**
  o **New issues:** must be rated by a rating agency (S&P, Moody's or Fitch).
  o **Non-rated and defaulted bonds:** are removed.
  o **Investment grade:** Minimum credit rating is BBB–/Baa3/BBB–.
  o **High-yield:** Maximum credit rating BB+/Ba1/BB+.

These various modifications therefore narrow the focus of the green bond index. One might initially interpret these changes as S&P supporting a view that green bonds should reflect a certain type of investment grade bond. What is perhaps surprising, though, is the desire to screen out low-yield bonds and cap the credit-rating at BB+. Many green bonds have higher ratings, since they are large scale, and in many cases issued by investment banks with significant resources.

5.3.2.2 Moody's

Ratings agency Moody's have also developed their green bond assessment (GBA) criteria, which were made public around December 2016. Moody's GBAs assign the following weights in their evaluations:

- **Use of proceeds** is the most significant, and it counts for 40% of the assessment score.
- **'Organization' element** of a green bond accounts for 15%.
- **Ongoing reporting and disclosure** accounts for 20%.
- **Disclosure** relating to the use of proceeds is 10%.
- **Management of proceeds**, 15%.

On the basis of these criteria, Moody's appear to remain closer to the green bond principles introduced earlier in this chapter. Therefore, in comparison, S&P and Moody's take quite different classification schemes. Although some differences are of course to be expected – they are, after all, competitors that need to find a unique selling point – it is noteworthy the style and depth of information they feed into their respective classifications.

5.3.3 *Other screens/classifications*

Without any formal and/or universally adopted screens/definitions as to what constitutes a green bond, various alternative indexes and possible standards are being presented to the market. For example, Bloomberg/Barclays/MSCI have worked together to produce their own 'Green Bond Index', which was highlighted by CBI as the best green bond index in 2018! The Solactive Green Bond Index was the first index aimed at allowing investors to capture the performance of investment-grade labelled green bonds that are denominated in EUR and USD. Vaneck are rumoured to have created a green bond exchange traded fund (ETF) which may be the first green bond ETF. The importance of the ETF is not to be understated since it reflects a higher level institutional demand for green bonds.

The growth and importance the green bond market, alongside the concerns that come attached to the existence of alternative definition, standards, and screening criteria have attracted the interest of the ISO. The ISO is actively developing a global green bond standard, with input from Luxflag. 'The label will complement [green bond] second opinion providers,' according to Annemarie Arens, general manager of Luxflag. The label requirements are still under development, but for a bond to secure the Luxflag 'Green Bond' label it must adhere to or recognize the following standards which are in development:

- ISO 14030-1 'Green Bonds – Environmental performance of nominated projects and assets'
- ISO 14030-2 'Green Bonds – Taxonomy of eligible investment categories'
- ISO 14030-3 'Green Bonds – Verification requirements'

Once complete, these standards will provide an unambiguous and globally recognized set of standards that will make participation in the global green bond market, both by the issuers and the suppliers of capital (investors), much easier and more transparent.

5.3.4 Summary

To summarize, in this brief review we have outlined the main issues and stages of development of green bond definitions and standards. While the market is now more than a decade old, and although there are widely adopted green bond principles, there remains a lack of formal definition. It is likely that this will be resolved fairly soon (before 2025). The informal tutelage and oversight of the green bonds market by the CBI has provided a solid foundation in definition and has provided confidence to major financial institutions, such as S&P, which use CBI recognition within their own screening criteria for their green bond index products. The commitment by the ISO to develop official standards should co-align with a new phase of the green bond market and help promote market liquidity, increasing investor confidence through comparability and transparency.

5.4 Understanding green bond pricing and the differentiation between NGOs (non-profit) and private sector (for-profit) issues

One of the main challenges for green bond (GB) funding, as perceived by the market, is the pricing issue. Whether GBs should carry a higher, lower, or identical yield (i.e. return) compared to their regular counterpart is a very heated debate among investment professionals. For GB new issues (i.e. IPO market), Schroders' Mihkel Kase (2015) argued that green bonds have the additional risk of environmental default and 'greenwashing', leading to an additional risk premium. Experts suggest that no clear connection between the green bonds designation and favourable pricing can be found. Furthermore, DuPont, Levitt, and Bilmes (2015) from Harvard concluded that GBs experience high demand, leading to an increased willingness to pay a price premium and therefore lower yield over time. In fact, a similar debate can be found for the secondary GB market where liquidity and the loss of green credentials are the main concerns. Evidence is beginning to emerge that green bonds are possibly being invested in by larger institutions under buy and hold strategies, limiting liquidity (and potentially price efficiency) due to reduced levels of trade. Leading investment banks such as HSBC – who are at the forefront of green bond issuances in Asia – also express caution, since the absence of in-depth international standards in GB labelling and monitoring makes it a challenge to accurately and fairly price GBs. Although, as discussed earlier in this chapter, there is positive forward progress on defining globally recognized standards, it is intuitive that the pricing debate will continue for some time.

One of the most recent contributions to the pricing debate is a report by MSCI released in December 2018 (MSCI 2018) entitled 'Does high-yield receive the

ESG credit it deserves: The relevance of ESG across fixed income'. This report provides an interesting twist on the pricing and valuation debate. It is shown that green bonds maintain a closer parity with treasury bonds than regular bonds do. The inference is that regular bonds need to offer a higher yield relative to treasury bonds in order to attract investors into taking the risk. However, green bonds do not need to offer the same high-yield. This is therefore advantageous from the issuer's perspective to verify that raising capital through green bonds is cheaper than raising capital through regular bonds. Earlier market reports reviewing cost/value concerns in green bonds also included Barclays (2015) and Bloomberg (2015). The Climate Bonds Initiative and HSBC (2016) collaborated to summarize the state of the market up until 2016.

One additional route we can take to understand pricing characteristics is to make a more general contrast between regular (or black) bonds and green bonds, to evaluate the index level pricing trends. We do, however, note that these aggregate indices lose focus in the distinction between for-profit and non-profit issuers and instead bundle them together to provide an overall market perspective. For this purpose we will consider the trends from some of S&P's core bond index products, specifically: SPSUSGRN which tracks the performance of the US green bond market and was the first green bond index issued by S&P[6]; SPGRNSLT, a refined version of the S&P green bond index, was developed, designed to track trends in the global market[7]; SPUSAGGT, which is an index designed to track the performance of the overall market for bonds[8]; and SPBDXUTR compiled by S&P/Citigroup which is intended to reflect the performance of bonds issues by non-US developed market countries.[9] These series are shown in Figure 5.2.

When contrasting the domestic and global market price trends, we observe very different patterns. In comparing the series, we need to remain mindful that these are index series, based at 100, though as downloaded, not guaranteed to be

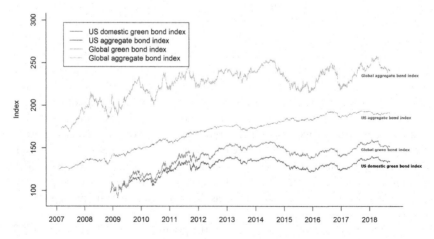

Figure 5.2 S&P Bond Indices over time – daily data spanning Jan. 2007 to Oct. 2018

based in the same year. As such, care should be taken to compare the trends in the data rather than the specific levels. Taking first the US domestic green bond index and comparing it against the US aggregate bond index, we can observe that the green bond index appeared to have a more rapid growth from 2009 to 2013 compared with the aggregate bond index, but after this the index value appeared to stabilize at around 125 points. In contrast, the aggregate bond index has, broadly speaking, witnessed a more sustained growth pattern. The consequence of this is that a pricing wedge has emerged at the index level.

The next point of comparison is the difference between the US domestic green bond index and the global green bond index. These index series share the same base, so a more direct comparison can be made. From mid-2009 onwards, the global index has maintained a higher value than the US domestic index, and a clear separation of the indices was visible by 2012 and remains in place until now. In Section 5.2 we discussed the various differences between regional markets, and these might in part explain some of the pricing differences. The last point of comparison is the global aggregate bond index, from which we can distil insights into the volatility of bond prices. Comparing the global green and black bond price series, the evidence points to green bonds having significantly lower pricing volatility. This is consistent with the idea that green bonds are less liquid (recalling earlier discussions that institutions might be adopting a buy and hold strategy for green bonds), resulting in fewer price movements and hence having a likelihood of lower price volatility. Further, and more technical, descriptions of index level pricing and volatility patterns can be found in Pham (2016), Febi et al. (2018), and Reboredo (2018).

5.4.1 Non-profit versus for-profit (private) issuers

Table 5.8 considers the evidence on pricing differentials for bond issuers with and without profit-driven motivations. This table compares the issuances from 2013 onwards, around the time corporate green bonds started to be issued; only 15 corporate green bonds were issued globally in 2013. For the sake of this table we treat non-profit entities as corporate issuers, which have a duty to their stakeholders to maximize their revenues. Non-profit organizations are all other issuers that are not corporate. Issuers with for-profit and non-profit objectives might reasonably have different objectives for issuing bonds. Similarly, investors may themselves seek and/or assign different attributes and values to issuers with different underlying motivations for raising capital. Table 5.8 offers a revealed-perspective on this issue and highlights the fact that there is a clear for-profit pricing premium that needs to be paid by issuers. In 2013, both for-profit and non-profit green bonds could attract investors using similar coupon rates. However, by 2014, this had changed, and the coupon rate for for-profit bonds was 3.37, compared with just 2.30 for bonds from non-profit issuers. This pricing premium does not appear to be incidental, and it can be seen that for all years since 2014, for-profits bonds have held an average coupon rate that is demonstrably larger than for bonds from non-profit issuers. Averaging of all years,

Table 5.8 Coupon rates for green bonds issued by for-profit and non-profit organizations in the Eurobond market, United States, and Mainland China (since 2013)

	All bonds		For-profit (corporate)		Non-profit (non-corporate)	
	N	Coupon	N	Coupon	N	Coupon
2013	42	2.79	15	2.79	27	2.79
2014	133	2.87	73	3.37	60	2.30
2015	289	3.60	199	3.77	90	3.22
2016	223	2.77	136	2.93	87	2.53
2017	357	3.41	264	3.55	93	3.01
2018	283	2.52	209	2.80	74	1.73
Sum	1,327		896		431	
Mean	221.17	2.99	149.33	3.20	71.83	2.60

Source: created by authors using data from Thomson Reuters Eikon

the mean coupon rate on for-profit green bonds (3.20) is 23.1% higher than on non-profit green bonds (2.60).

To establish a more concrete understanding of the revealed coupon differentials between these types of issuer, Figure 5.3 plots histograms of the coupon rates separately by for-profit and non-profit issuers. The scales on the x- and y-axes are held constant to ease comparison. The unique difference in the histograms is in the large frequency of for-profit green bonds with coupon rates between three and six. This is not with bonds issued by non-profit issuers. In addition, we can see that the highest discount rates are not offered by for-profit bond issuers. Taken together, we can conclude that the higher average coupon rate on for-profit green bonds is not being driven by a small number of high coupon bonds but instead by a fundamental difference in the underlying pricing mechanisms and expectations.

5.5 Redefining bond issues success of green bonds: an issuer's perspective

We now turn our attention to developing a simple empirical investigation of the decision by firms to issue a green bond. We implement a discrete choice modeling exercise to establish some baseline understanding as to whether there might be some form of marketing benefits to being green, i.e. whether firms that have existing brand status and reputation might see some form of incremental value (increased probability) to issuing a green bond.

The potential value to firms of 'being green' has been the topic of various discussions, culminating in an academic debate about how firms are capable of 'doing well by doing good'; see, for example, Ariely et al. (2009), Bénabou & Tirole (2010), and Cheng et al. (2013). Doing good here refers to being

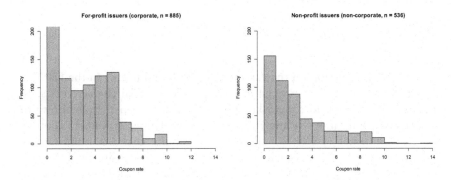

Figure 5.3 Coupon rates on green bonds from for-profit issuers (left panel) and non-profit issuers (right panel), 2013–2018

environmentally and socially responsible; doing well refers to maintaining business profitability. There is rich literature related to this debate including contributions from Barth et al. (1997), Belu and Manescu (2013), Cavaco and Crifo (2009, 2014), Clarkson et al. (2011), Di Giuli and Kostovetsky (2014), Ferrell et al. (2016), Kim and Lyon (2011), Li et al. (1997), Noh (2018), Roslen et al. (2017), Van't Veld and Kotchen (2011), and Wagner (2010), who cumulatively discuss various aspects of the decision to disclose environmental performance (or liabilities).

There is also existing literature discussing incentives to adopt green finance from different perspectives and by issuers of different types, e.g. Bowen et al. (2017), Bracking (2015), Byrne et al. (2017), Cheng et al. (2014), Clapp (2018), Corfee-Morlot et al. (2012), Ferguson et al. (2016), Flaherty et al. (2017), Glomsrød and Wei (2018), Karpf and Mandel (2018), Konar and Cohen (2001), Mathews and Kidney (2012), McInerney and Johannsdottir (2016), Ng (2018), Ng and Tao (2016), Paranque and Revelli (2017), Sudo (2016), and Zhou et al. (2017).

5.5.1 Research design

We employ a simple two-stage analysis framework. The first stage involves describing the factors that coincide with a firm achieving the status of being a global brand. Achieving such a status requires a concerted effort and considerable dedication and resources to maintain. The decision to maintain such a brand may feasibly be (possibly endogenously) related to the choice to issue a green bond. This follows from the premise that issuing a green bond will be seen as a positive contribution to a firm's corporate social responsibility (CSR) activities, which will only work in the direction of improving a firm's brand image. The decision to maintain a global brand is modelled as:

$$pr.[Brand = 1 = 1] = a_0 + c_0 ESG + a_1 \ln(MCAP) + a_2 DvdYLD + a_3 CAGR + a_4 OPM$$
$$+ a_5 DE + a_6 WACCD + a_7 PE + a_8 IDOB + a_9 WOB + a_{10} CEOTENURE$$
$$+ a_{ind} factor(SECTOR) + a_{year} factor(Year)$$

$$(1)$$

Detailed information on the variables can be found below. In the first line of equation (1) we have a range of firm-specific financial characteristics. In the second line we add several key board-level characteristics. In the third line we control for industry and year-fixed effects. This equation also controls for environmental (ESG) to reflect the possibility that the motivations/requirements for brand recognition are potentially increasing in ESG performance, since higher ESG scores may well coincide with higher corporate visibility.

The main equation of interest then explains the probability of issuing a green bond, while incorporating the roles of brand recognition, and its potential interaction with ESG performance. The interaction effect reflects the logic that firms with better ESG scores and global brand recognition at the same time are afforded additional incentives to maintain visible socially responsible credentials and would therefore increase the likelihood of issuing a green bond. We therefore estimate the following model structure:

$$pr.[Green\ bond = 1] = b_0 + c_1 BRAND + c_2 ESG + c_3 (BRAND * ESG) + b_1 \ln(MCAP) +$$
$$b_2 DvdYLD + b_3 CAGR + b_4 OPM + b_5 DE + b_6 WACCD + b_7 PE +$$
$$b_8 IDOB + b_9 WOB + b_{10} CEOTENURE + b_{ind}\ factor(SECTOR) +$$
$$b_{year} factor(Year) + b_{US} US + b_{EU} EUROPE$$

$$(2)$$

The advantage of estimating the brand equation is that it can be used to control for the potentially endogenous selection process that firms might face of first deciding whether to pursue a global brand and, following this, deciding whether to issue a green bond. We treat the estimation problem as a standard Heckman selection problem and incorporate into our bond equation the inverse Mills ratio (MILLS) calculated after estimating the brand equation (1). The resulting model is:

$$pr.[Green\ bond = 1] = b_0 + c_1 BRAND + c_2 ESG + c_3 (BRAND * ESG) +$$
$$b_1 \ln(MCAP) + b_2 DvdYLD + b_3 CAGR + b_4 OPM + b_5 DE +$$
$$b_6 WACCD + b_7 PE + b_8 IDOB + b_9 WOB + b_{10} CEOTENURE +$$
$$b_{ind}\ factor(SECTOR) + b_{year} factor(Year) + b_{US} US + b_{EU} EUROPE +$$
$$d_{MILLS} MILLS$$

$$(3)$$

The Mills ratio operates in a similar way to standard 2SLS, in that its inclusion into the bond equation serves to control for the coefficient biases that may be driven by endogeneity. Estimated this way, there is no need to substitute the potentially endogenous variables with the fitted values obtained from the brand equation.

5.5.2 Key steps in the data construction

The data include a range of variables intended to capture company-specific features covering financial performance and governance structures, industry and country controls including:

- 'GREEN_BOND': This is our main variable of interest and is a dummy variable taking the value 1 if the company is a green bond issuer or not. This value is intended to capture the timing that the firm switch to a 'greener capital structure'. Once a firm has issued a green bond it 'switches' value from 0 to 1 and can never reverse.
- 'BRAND': This reflects whether a company enjoys a strong international brand reputation (BRAND = 1) or does not (BRAND = 0). To determine this, we refer to global brand recognition data available from websites such as www.brands.com from which we are able to identify companies with strong global brand recognition, i.e. within the top 500 global brands, and companies with strong regional brand recognition, i.e. the leading brands in their country. Companies with recognized high-level international or regional brand recognition are deemed strong brand companies, i.e. BRAND = 1.
- 'ESG': This refers to the environmental, social, and governance disclosure score reported by Bloomberg LLC. This is Bloomberg's proprietary score developed on the basis of firms' disclosure of ESG-related information. Note that ESG reports are often not mandated company filings, and as discussed below many companies still choose not to disclose such reports.
- A range of other more standard firm level controls are used in the analysis including: 'MCAP' the market capitalization of a firm; 'DvdYLD', the dividend yield; 'CAGR' the cumulative average growth rate of sales over the preceding 12 months; 'OPM', the operating profit margin; 'DE', the net debt to equity ratio; 'WACCD', the weighted average cost of debt faced by a firm; 'PE', the price to earnings ratio; 'IDOB', the percentage of independent directors on the board; 'WOB', the percentage of women on board; and lastly 'CEOTENURE', the CEO tenure as a percentage of financial year earnings.

We note that in our final estimation sample, all firms have ESG scores available. On a global scale, ESG reporting is still largely limited. At this time, Bloomberg reports ESG scores for nearly 30,000 firms globally. They conclude that about 50% of firms in the US provide governance reports, but only 17% of US firms offer sufficient environmental reporting information to be able to have environmental disclosure scores. Thus, it is by no means guaranteed that in our data we should be able to observe such a high prevalence of ESG scores. We do not see any pragmatic steps we can take to reflect this in our modeling strategy, but it is something to be mindful of.

In addition to these 'traditional' variables, following recent studies in behavioural finance and environmental economics, we control for the effects of climate related variables. To construct these variables, we obtain a range of climatic variables from the Weather Underground website (using their API interface, www.wunderground.com), for the final day of each month of the year, for all countries represented in our sample. We use a relatively crude assumption with regard to the geography of our observations, choosing either the largest/capital city where possible, but where data access does not permit this, we use recordings made at the largest international airport within the country of the issuer. For instance, Weather Underground does not provide easy access to (non-airport based) monitoring stations in Beijing, so in this case we use the capital airport monitoring reports to capture the climate data. We acknowledge some imprecision in our assumptions here but note that our approach captures sufficient variation between countries and over time to suit our needs.

We concentrate on using (i) temperatures – arguably the most eponymous indicator of climate change featured in both research and the popular press and (ii) visibility – which reflects how far you can see in kilometres and which will decrease with pollution, as well as other weather conditions. The variables used in the analysis are:

- 'TEMP_MEAN': The annual average temperature of the country of the issuer over the 12 months of the year. This measure is useful in making broad comparisons of average climate but neglects important swings in temperature ranges between summer and winter, which could get averaged out.
- 'TEMP_RANGE': The range variable is intended to serve as a measure of the variability of weather conditions. TEMP_RANGE is therefore used to complement TEMP_MEAN and not instead of it. This variable is constructed as the average of the range for each of the 12 months, where the range for a given month is defined as the difference between the maximum observed temperature and the minimum observed temperature.
- 'VIS_MEAN': This variable is constructed in a similar manner to the TEMP_MEAN variable, but instead of averaging over temperatures, we average over the reported visibility levels.
- 'VIS_RANGE': This variable is constructed in a similar manner to the TEMP_RANGE variable and is similarly intended to be used in combination with VIS_MEAN.

Additional information on the steps involved in creating the dataset used in this empirical example are outlined in Table 5.9.

We note that the unit of observation for our study is the bond issuer and not the specific bonds. We do not contain information on individual bonds for this reason and because a single issuer may issue more than one bond, even within the same year. Accounting for such bond-level data will likely increase the complexity of the analysis, but we think in the present case it would not materially alter our conclusions. Notwithstanding, it remains an important direction for future research to tackle the bond-level data more directly.

Table 5.9 Key steps in the data construction

Data processing step	Sample information
Phase 1: Bond sample construction	
Generate a list of green bonds based on the Bloomberg database list of green bonds, cross-verified against the Climate Bonds Initiative (CBI) certified bond list	Circa. **1000** green bonds up until the 2016 sample cut-off date
Of which we then isolate the corporate issuances. Most green bonds up until the end of our sample period were by non-corporate issuers, thereby eliminating many observations from the sample.	Giving a sample of **338** corporate green bonds in total, issued across a sample of 108 unique firms from across the globe
Create a matched sample of black bonds from the universe of international corporate bonds issuances over the sample period, taken from Datastream.	Circa **250,000** corporate black bonds identified over the sample period
Implement a 3:1 propensity score based matching of black bonds against the green bonds on a range of bond-level characteristics including coupon, term, whether bond type is perpetual or fixed, currency of issue, industry of issue, and country of issuer.	**1,358** corporate bond issuances identified, from **651** unique firms
The matching process is constrained to identify black bonds only from companies that have no history of issuing a green bond, such that we do not compare green and black bonds from the same company.	Note: GB mean coupon rate = 3.221 BB mean coupon rate = 3.316 GB St. Dev. of coupon rate = 2.288 BB St. Dev. of coupon rate = 2.647 BB = black bond
Phase 2: Construction of firm level indicators	
Obtain a range of firm level accounting and corporate governance variables. Data are hand-collected from the Bloomberg database, availability of consistently measured international data, Bloomberg's proprietary disclosure measures, and corporate governance variables are the main factors reducing sample size.	From the **651** unique firms we potentially have **1,953** firm-year observations available for estimation.
Global brand ranking classifications are identified using information from http://interbrand.com. This website provides access to comprehensive global and regional brand ranking data. We hand-collect all global and country-specific ranking reports over the sample period, then carefully match brand names against corporate names. (Where necessary, brand information was allocated to the parent company, if the brand belongs to a subsidiary of the parent company.)	**138** of the firms in the sample are identified as having a strong global brand, of which **31** are green bond issuers (i.e. roughly 22.5% of firms with global brand recognition issued a green bond in our sample).
Lack of availability of key estimation variables limits the sample size available for estimation. Key variables for which only limited data is available include: - PE ratio: 1,083 missing cases - ESG disclosure scores: 1,115 missing cases - CEO tenure: 1,313 missing cases	After (case-wise) deletions, we arrive at a pooled cross-section of **452** firm-year observations for estimation of our most general model specifications.

Source: created by authors.

5.5.3 *Analysis (results) and discussion*

The estimation results are summarized in Table 5.10. The table of results contains a lot of rich information though here we will summarize only the most important features of the results. First we verify that global brand recognition is associated with the propensity to issue a green bond, confirming an important strategic marketing dimension to firms' decisions to 'green their capital structure'. Second is that we find evidence to support the process of corporate social responsibility reporting catalyses this effect. Specifically, we observe that firms' average ESG disclosure scores positively influence the probability of issuing a green bond, which by itself is very intuitive. However, global brand recognition serves to reduce the probability of issuance. This is to say there is a potential tension which exists between being green and maintaining global brand recognition.

5.6 Future directions of green bond research and the latest developments in ESG/green investment practices

The connection between green bond and ESG performance at the firm level can be viewed as a feedback loop. The firm issuing a green bond obtains financing for implementing green projects. This green effort is integrated into the firm's overall ESG performance, leading to a higher ESG rating for the firm. Asset owners and institutional investors who value sustainability would then see this as a positive signal and pursue this firm, leading in turn to a stronger demand for the firm's stock. Such a green bond-ESG stock connection becomes a loop which would strengthen the firm's desire to issue more green bonds in the future (see Figure 5.4).

We have positioned this chapter as a framework to explore empirically the challenges and eventually lead to solutions to establish a sophisticated green bond market. We believe that the key to understanding the friction and obstacles to achieve these goals come from two main aspects: 1) the market (including regulatory) efficiency for issuing and pricing of green bonds with sufficient market depth (i.e. liquidity) for the secondary market; and 2) a commonly acceptable evaluation framework to compute quantifiable KPIs to benchmark ESG investment performance.

By reviewing the existing global trends and context of the market for green bonds, and through our empirical analysis, we hope to have shed light on the opportunities and challenges from both the green bond issuers' and the investors' perspectives. Research questions and priorities have been identified, and future work should seek to better understand the value and role of green bonds within the wider remit of ESG investing.

5.6.1 *ESG investments*

ESG investment is the process by which investment decisions are underpinned or directed by a variety of screens that help identify investment opportunities

Table 5.10 Estimation results

	Stage 1 Brand equation Pr.(BRAND=1)		Stage 2 Green Bond issuance equation Pr.(GREEN_BOND=1)			
			Without endogeneity control		With control for endogeneity	
	(1)		(2)		(3)	
	Coefficient	Std. Error	Coefficient	Std. Error	Coefficient	Std. Error
BRAND			−4.292***	(1.118)	−4.366***	(1.143)
ESG	0.007	(0.006)	0.010	(0.012)	0.014	(0.012)
BRAND*ESG			0.090***	(0.021)	0.090***	(0.021)
Ln(MCAP)	0.592***	(0.070)	0.045	(0.093)	0.338	(0.272)
DvdYLD	−0.029	(0.049)	0.124**	(0.051)	0.102*	(0.054)
CAGR	0.002	(0.005)	0.010	(0.006)	0.008	(0.006)
OPM	−0.013***	(0.005)	0.003	(0.003)	−0.005	(0.007)
DE	−0.0005	(0.0003)	−0.001	(0.001)	−0.001	(0.001)
WACCD	0.224**	(0.114)	−0.235*	(0.128)	−0.151	(0.140)
PE	−0.014**	(0.007)	0.001	(0.003)	−0.009	(0.009)
IDOB	−0.002	(0.005)	−0.008	(0.007)	−0.007	(0.007)
WOB	0.018**	(0.008)	0.032***	(0.012)	0.043***	(0.015)
CEOTENURE	−0.008	(0.012)	−0.032	(0.020)	−0.035*	(0.020)
TEMP_RANGE			0.022	(0.044)	0.023	(0.044)
VIS_RANGE			−0.060**	(0.030)	−0.065**	(0.030)
TEMP_MEAN			0.038**	(0.017)	0.040**	(0.017)
MURKINESS			0.143**	(0.065)	0.135**	(0.065)
US			−0.604*	(0.359)	−0.643*	(0.363)
EUROPE			−1.045***	(0.386)	−1.054***	(0.388)
Inverse Mills ratio					0.759	(0.651)
Intercept	−6.605***	(0.837)	−1.863	(1.950)	−6.029	(4.112)
Observations	458		452		452	
Region dummies	Yes		Yes		Yes	
Year dummies	Yes		Yes		Yes	
Industry dummies	Yes		Yes		Yes	
Log-likelihood	−207.881		−108.127		−107.480	
Chi-square test	Pass		Pass		Pass	
Chi-square for exclusion of Brand and/or ESG variables	Fail		Pass		Pass	
Pseudo R^2	0.29		0.42		0.42	

Source: created by authors

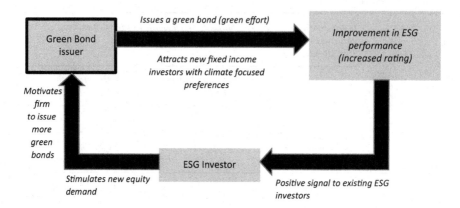

Figure 5.4 The green-bond/ESG investment loop

with positive environmentally responsible attributes. The main challenge for ESG investment is to construct a comprehensive rating system or measure to evaluate the ESG performance of a firm. We propose a quantifiable composite measure which integrates social returns with financial returns to form a single indicator for the decision-making of asset owners. In this section, we will explain the difference between SRI and ESG investment. Then we will explore future directions for industry and academic research.

5.6.1.1 From SRI to ESG: the path to sustainable investments

SRI has been around for over 90 years, but ESG factors are a relatively new. ESG became prominent in 2006 with the launch of the UN PRI (Principles for Responsible Investment). There are three main dimensions by which SRI and ESG differ:

1) Investment focus:
   a   SRI: Principles focused
       Investments established on SRI objectives are driven first by ethical principles, then may be extended into religious, cultural, and organization values.
   b   ESG: Returns focused
       Investments based on ESG criteria incorporate long-term sustainability factors in research to identify firms with higher investment potential.
2) Investment screens
   a   SRI: Use negative screens
       Removes investment choices that do not need organizational value (e.g. remove tobacco firms).

    b   ESG: Use positive screens

        Assigns scores to ESG factors to guide investment choices instead of exclusion, i.e. prioritize investment opportunities.

3) Investment Boundary

    a   SRI: Different criteria

        SRI screens vary substantially among investors and are organization specific (e.g. health screen removes tobacco; religious screen removes alcohol and gambling); i.e. SRI-based investment screens are somewhat subjective.

    b   ESG: Universal approach

        Factors related to E, S, and G should all be considered as independent positive screens, so the investment priorities are universal and clear, i.e. ESG screening criteria are quite objective. Of course the emphasis of E, S, and G may vary by different investors.

5.6.1.2 ESG investment as an asset class

Current academic/industry research has no guidance on the risk positioning of ESG investment as an asset class. ESG portfolio development currently emphasizes social return with acceptable financial return but is silent on risk characteristics. We need a better definition of a composite matrix and methodology to integrate social returns and financial returns in a scientific manner. This is needed to construct ESG as asset classes before we can fairly and comprehensively evaluate their risk–return characteristics. In short, ESG funds and ESG portfolios should not be measured purely by financial performance. Finally, social return is subjective but important in ESG investments.

5.6.1.3 ESG as a screen to select investments

ESG screens are very popular among asset managers as a solution to impact investing demanded by asset owners. Different operators use different proprietary data to generate ESG screens. Of E, S, and G, the G factor has received the largest share of research and is used in a sophisticated manner. E is becoming important but still very industry specific. S is more difficult to quantify and abstract to measure. In conclusion, investment community including asset managers, analysts, and risk managers will continue to pursue ESG screens to maintain flexibility in pursuing returns.

    For future research, measuring ESG investment performance and constructing benchmarks are the key challenges. The investment profession has to jointly integrate social and financial returns into a composite performance indicator (Figure 5.5). Large-scale research to profile ESG preferences of investors according to their underlying utility function is needed to form a scientific database to construct benchmarks related to ESG investments.

    We have positioned this chapter as a framework to explore empirically the challenges and eventually lead to solutions to establish a sophisticated green bond

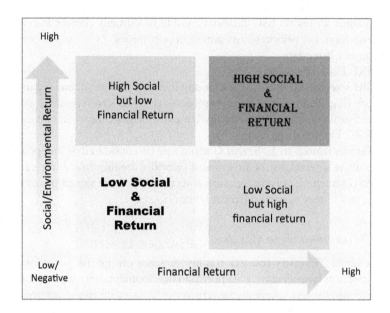

Figure 5.5 Integrating social and financial returns into a composite performance indicator

market. We believe that the key to understanding the friction and obstacles to achieve these goals come from two main aspects: 1) the market (including regulatory) efficiency for issuing and pricing of green bonds with sufficient market depth (i.e. liquidity) for the secondary market; and 2) a commonly acceptable evaluation framework to compute quantifiable KPIs to benchmark ESG investment performance.

By reviewing the existing global trends and context of the market for green bonds, and through our empirical analysis, we hope to have shed light on the opportunities and challenges from both the green bond issuers' and the investors' perspectives. Research questions and priorities have been identified, and future work should seek to better understand the value and role of green bonds within the wider remit of ESG investing.

5.6.2 Appendix: List of firms used in the empirical work in Section 5.5.

Appendix 1 List of green bond issuers included in the 'Brands to Green' sample

500 Georgia Office Partnership	ABN Amro Bank NV	Acciona Financiacion Filiales Sau
Alliander NV	Apple Incorporated	Arise AB
Atrium Ljungberg AB	Bahia Sul HLDG GmbH	Banco Nacional de Costa Rica
Bank of America Corporation	Bank of China Ltd (London Branch)	Bank of China Ltd (Luxembourg Branch)

Appendix 1 Cont.

Bank of China Ltd (New York Branch)	Bank Sinopac Company Ltd	Berlin Hyp AG
BKK AS	Bpce SA	BRF SA
Castellum AB	City Developments Limited	Cooperatieve Centrale Raiffeisen Boerenleenbank BA
Credit Agricole Corporate and Investment Bank SA	CTBC Bank Company Ltd	Deutsche Kreditbank AG
Digital Realty Trust LP	DNB Bank ASA	E Sun Commercial Bank Ltd
Electricite de France SA	Energia Eolica SA	Engie SA
Enna Energia SRL	Entra ASA	Fabege AB
Fastighets AB Forvaltaren	Fibria Overseas Finance Limited	Fonciere des Regions SA
Fortum Varme Holding Samagt MED STHLMS Stad Publ	AB Georgia Power Company	Goldwind New Energy HK Investment Ltd
Green Bancorp Inco	Greenko Investment Company	Hera SpA
HSBC France SA	Hyundai Capital Services Incorporated	Iberdrola Finanzas SA
Iberdrola International BV	Icpf Finance Pty Ltd	ING Bank NV
Innovatec SpA	Intesa Sanpaolo SpA	Inversiones CMPC SA
Investa Office Fund	Kaiser Foundation Hospitals	KGI Bank Company Ltd
Latvenergo AS	Link Finance Cayman 2009 Ltd	LM Group Holding AS
LTC GB Limited	Lyse AS	Mexico City Airport Trust
Mitsubishi UFJ Financial Group Incorporated	Modern Land China Company Ltd	Morgan Stanley
MTR CI Corporation Ltd	National Australia Bank Limited	National Bank of Abu Dhabi
Nomura Research Institute Limited	Nordea Bank AB	NRG Yield Operating LLC
NTPC Limited	NYA Svensk Fastighetsfinansiering Publ AB	Paprec Holding SA
Pattern Energy Group Inco	QBE Insurance Group Limited	Rapid Holding GmbH
Regency Centres Limited Partnership	Rikshem Publ AB	Rodamco Sverige AB
SBAB Bank Publ AB	SCA Hygiene AB	Scatec Solar ASA
Schneider Electric SE	Shanks Group PLC	Skandinaviska Enskilda Banken AB
Skanska Financial Services AB	Société Générale SA	Solarcity Corporation
Southern Power Company	Stangastaden AB	Stockland Trust Management Limited
Sumitomo Mitsui Banking Corporation	Svensk Fastighetsfinansiering II Publ AB	Tennet Holding BV

(*continued*)

Appendix 1 Cont.

Terraform Global Operating LLC	Terraform Power Operating LLC	Turkiye Sinai Kalkinma Bankasi AS
Unibail Rodamco SE	Unilever PLC	United Photovoltaics Group Ltd
Uppsalahem AB	Vardar AS	Vasakronan Publ AB
Verbund AG	Vestas Wind Systems A/S	Vornado Realty LP
Wallenstam AB	Westar Energy Incorporated	Westpac Banking Corporation

Source: created by authors

Notes

1   A summary of the early history of green bonds can be found at www.climatebonds.net/market/history and www.environmental-finance.com/content/the-green-bond-hub/green-bond-reporting.html.

2   Climate bonds are now considered a general class of environmentally focused bonds, green bonds being a subset of climate bonds. Other climate bonds include, for example, water bonds. For more information, please refer to the Climate Bonds Initiative website at www.climatebonds.net/.

3   It is worth noting that there are different databases summarizing the green bond market. Here for most of our remaining analysis we shall stick with summarizing information contained in either the Thomson Reuters Eikon database, which permits us to have a detailed exploration of the pricing characteristics, or the CBI green bond database, through which we can get an alternative benchmark on the number of bond issuances and their value.

4   We should remain mindful of formal definitions in finance for bonds versus notes, or bills/commercial paper. Typically, ten years or larger maturity for a new issue requires that issue to be termed a 'bond'. New issues of between one and nine years maturity (normally three, five, or eight years) are typically termed as 'notes'. Issues with less than one year to maturity are called a 'bill' if issued by the US Treasury, or 'commercial paper' if issued by firms. We note, however, that the CBI do not make clear distinctions and call issues with less than ten years maturity bonds. Similarly, Thomson Reuters Eikon do not actively distinguish green bonds on the basis of maturity, and many shorter-term issues are demarcated as bonds, when a more formal definition might in fact label them as notes. Similar to CBI and Thomson Reuters Eikon, we make no further distinctions between these more nuanced bond types.

5   Available at: www.eib.org/attachments/green-bond-market-development-and-eib.pdf

6   Available at: http://us.spindices.com/indices/fixed-income/sp-green-bond-index

7   Available at: http://us.spindices.com/indices/fixed-income/sp-green-bond-select-index-usd

8   Available at: https://us.spindices.com/indices/fixed-income/sp-us-aggregate-bond-index

9   Available at: https://us.spindices.com/indices/fixed-income/sp-citigroup-international-treasury-bond-ex-us-index

References

Anderson J 2015, 'Environmental finance', Chapter 15 in V Ramiah & GN Gregoriou (eds), *Handbook of environmental and sustainable finance*. Academic Press, Elsevier, pp. 307–333.

Ariely, D, Bracha, A & Meier, S 2009, 'Doing good or doing well? Image motivation and monetary incentives in behaving prosocially', *American Economic Review*, vol. 99, no. 1, pp. 544–555.

Barth, ME, Mcnichols, MF & Wilson, GP 1997, 'Factors influencing firms' disclosures about environmental liabilities', *Review of Accounting Studies*, vol. 2, pp. 35–64.

Belu, C & Manescu, C 2013, 'Strategic corporate social responsibility and economic performance', *Applied Economics*, vol. 45, no. 19, pp. 2751–2764.

Bénabou, R & Tirole, J 2010, 'Individual and corporate social responsibility', *Economica*, vol. 77, no. 305, pp. 1–19.

Bowen, A, Campiglio, E & Herreras Martinez, S 2017, 'An "equal effort" approach to assessing the North–South climate finance gap', *Climate Policy*, vol. 17, no. 2, pp. 231–245.

Bracking, S 2015, 'Performativity in the green economy: how far does climate finance create a fictive economy?', *Third World Quarterly*, vol. 36, no. 12, pp. 2337–2357.

Byrne, J, Taminiau, J, Kim, KN, Lee, J & Seo, J 2017, 'Multivariate analysis of solar city economics: impact of energy prices, policy, finance, and cost on urban photovoltaic power plant implementation', *Wiley Interdisciplinary Reviews: Energy and Environment*, vol. 6, no. 4, p. e241.

Cavaco, S & Crifo, P 2009, 'The CSP-CFP missing link: complementarity between environmental, social and governance practices?', *Journal of Economic Literature*, vol. 14, no. L21, p. C33.

Cavaco, S & Crifo, P 2014, 'CSR and financial performance: complementarity between environmental, social and business behaviours', *Applied Economics*, vol. 46, no. 27, pp. 3323–3338.

Cheng, B, Ioannou, I & Serafeim, G 2014, 'Corporate social responsibility and access to finance', *Strategic Management Journal*, vol. 35, no. 1, pp. 1–23.

Cheng, IH, Hong, H & Shue, K 2013, 'Do managers do good with other people's money?', no. w19432. National Bureau of Economic Research.

Clapp, C 2018, 'Investing in a green future', *Nature Climate Change*, vol. 8, no. 2, p. 96.

Clarkson, PM, Li, Y, Richardson, GD & Vasvari, FP 2011, 'Does it really pay to be green? Determinants and consequences of proactive environmental strategies', *Journal of Accounting and Public Policy*, vol. 30, pp. 122–144.

Corfee-Morlot, J, Marchal, V, Kauffmann, C, Kennedy, C, Stewart, F, Kaminker, C & Ang, G 2012, 'Towards a green investment policy framework: the case of low-carbon, climate-resilient infrastructure', OECD Environment Working Papers, no. 48, OECD Publishing, Paris, https://doi.org/10.1787/5k8zth7s6s6d-en..

Di Giuli, A & Kostovetsky, L 2014, 'Are red or blue companies more likely to go green? Politics and corporate social responsibility', *Journal of Financial Economics*, vol. 111, no. 1, pp. 158–180.

Febi, W, Schäfer, D, Stephan, A & Sun, C 2018, 'The impact of liquidity risk on the yield spread of green bonds', *Finance Research Letters*, vol. 27, pp. 53–59.

Ferguson, I, Levetan, L, Crossman, ND & Bennett, LT 2016, 'Financial mechanisms to improve the supply of ecosystem services from privately owned Australian native forests', *Forests*, vol. 7, no. 2, p. 34.

Ferrell, A, Liang, H & Renneboog, L 2016, 'Socially responsible firms', *Journal of Financial Economics*, vol. 122, no. 3, pp. 585–606.

Flaherty, M, Gevorkyan, A, Radpour, S & Semmler, W 2017, 'Financing climate policies through climate bonds–a three-stage model and empirics', *Research in International Business and Finance*, vol. 42, pp. 468–479.

Glomsrød, S & Wei, T 2018, 'Business as unusual: the implications of fossil divestment and green bonds for financial flows, economic growth and energy market', *Energy for Sustainable Development*, vol. 44, pp. 1–10.

Karpf, A & Mandel, A 2018, 'The changing value of the "green" label on the US municipal bond market', *Nature Climate Change*, vol. 8, no. 2, p. 161.

Kim, E-H & Lyon, TP 2011, 'Strategic environmental disclosure: evidence from the DOE's voluntary greenhouse gas registry', *Journal of Environmental Economics and Management*, vol. 61, no. 3, pp. 311–326.

Konar, S & Cohen, MA 2001, 'Does the market value environmental performance?', *Review of Economics and Statistics*, vol. 83, no. 2, pp. 281–289.

Li, Y, Richardson, GD & Thornton, DB 1997, 'Corporate disclosure of environmental liability information: theory and evidence', *Contemporary Accounting Research*, vol. 14, no. 3, pp. 435–474.

Lindenberg, N 2014, *Definition of green finance*, German Development Institute, published online, available at www.die-gdi.de/uploads/media/Lindenberg_Definition_green_finance.pdf.

Mathews, JA & Kidney, S 2012, 'Financing climate-friendly energy development through bonds', *Development Southern Africa*, vol. 29, no. 2, pp. 337–349.

McInerney, C & Johannsdottir, L 2016, 'Lima Paris action agenda: focus on private finance–note from COP21', *Journal of Cleaner Production*, vol. 126, pp. 707–710.

Ng, AW 2018, 'From sustainability accounting to a green financing system: institutional legitimacy and market heterogeneity in a global financial centre', *Journal of Cleaner Production*, vol. 195, pp. 585–592.

Ng, TH & Tao, JY 2016, 'Bond financing for renewable energy in Asia', *Energy Policy*, vol. 95, pp. 509–517.

Noh, HJ 2018, 'Relationship between climate change risk and cost of capital', *Global Business and Finance Review*, vol. 23, pp. 66–81.

Paranque, B & Revelli, C 2017, 'Ethico-economic analysis of impact finance: the case of green bonds', *Research in International Business and Finance*, vol. 47, pp. 57–66.

Pham, L 2016, 'Is it risky to go green? A volatility analysis of the green bond market', *Journal of Sustainable Finance & Investment*, vol. 6, no. 4, pp. 263–291.

Reboredo, JC 2018, 'Green bond and financial markets: co-movement, diversification and price spillover effects', *Energy Economics*, vol. 74, pp. 38–50.

Roslen, SNM, Yee, LS & Ibrahim, SAB 2017, 'Green bond and shareholders' wealth: a multi-country event study', *International Journal of Globalisation and Small Business*, vol. 9, no. 1, pp. 61–69.

Sudo, T 2016, 'Domestic and international finance in a regional perspective', in Anbumozhi V., Kalirajan K., Kimura F., Yao X. (eds) *Investing on low-carbon energy systems*, pp. 435–462. Springer, Singapore.

Tian, H 2018, 'Role of capital market to accelerate the transition to low-carbon energy system', in Anbumozhi V., Kalirajan K., Kimura F. (eds) *Financing for low-carbon energy transition*, pp. 211–238. Springer, Singapore.

Tokareva, GF, Shalina, OI & Barkova, EE 2018, 'The role of financial sector in providing sustainable development goals', in *IOP conference series: earth and environmental science*, vol. 107, no. 1, p. 012138. IOP Publishing.

Van't Veld, K & Kotchen, MJ 2011, 'Green clubs', *Journal of Environmental Economics and Management*, vol. 62, no. 3, pp. 309–322.

Wagner, M 2010, 'The role of corporate sustainability performance for economic performance: a firm-level analysis of moderation effects', *Ecological Economics*, vol. 69, no. 7, pp. 1553–1560.

Zhou, J, Xiong, S, Zhou, Y, Zou, Z & Ma, X 2017, 'Research on the development of green finance in Shenzhen to boost the carbon trading market', in IOP *conference series: earth and environmental science*, vol. 81, no. 1, p. 012073. IOP Publishing.

[Related reports/'non-academic' publications]

Barclays 2015, 'Credit research – the cost of being green', 18 September, Barclays, available at www.environmental-finance.com/assets/files/US_Credit_Focus_The_Cost_of_Being_Green.pdf.

Bloomberg 2015, 'Green bonds: Mobilising the debt capital markets for a low-carbon transition', December, OECD and Bloomberg Philanthropies policy perspective, available at www.oecd.org/environment/cc/Green%20bonds%20PP%20%5bf3%5d%20%5blr%5d.pdf.

Climate Bonds Initiative 2016, 'Roadmap for China: scaling up green bond market issuance', Climate Bonds Initiative and International Institute for Sustainable Development, available at www.climatebonds.net/resources/roadmap-for-china/april/2016/paper2.

Climate Bonds Initiative and HSBC 2016, 'Bond and climate change: the state of the market 2016', Climate Bonds Initiative and HSBC, available at www.climatebonds.net/resources/publications/bonds-climate-change-2016.

duPont, C.M., Levitt, J.N., and Bilmes, L.J.. "Green Bonds and Land Conservation: The Evolution of a New Financing Tool." Harvard Kennedy School Faculty Research Working Paper Series RWP15-072, December 2015. Available at https://papers.ssrn.com/sol3/papers.cfm?abstract_id=2700311##

Kase, M April 2015, 'The fix: green bonds – are they colouring investors' judgements?', Schroders. Available from: www.schroders.com/en/SysGlobalAssets/schroders/sites/au/insights/20150429-the-fix_green-bonds.pdf [17 June 2016]

MSCI 2018, 'Does high-yield receive the ESG credit it deserves: the relevance of ESG across fixed income'. Available at www.msci.com/www/research-paper/does-high-yield-receive-the-esg/01193137629

National Development and Reform Commission 2015, 'Guidelines for issuing green bonds' 《綠色債券發行指引》. Available at: www.bourse.lu/documents/pdf-LGX-SSL-NDRC.pdf

People's Bank of China 2015, 'Green bond endorsed project catalogue' 《綠色債券支持項目目錄》. Available at: www.greenfinance.org.cn/displaynews.php?cid=79&id=468

People's Bank of China 2015, 'Notice on issue of Green financial bonds'. Available at: www.syntaogf.com/Menu_Page_EN.asp?ID=21&Page_ID=150.

World Business Council for Sustainable Development 2015, 'WBCSD leadership program 2015: green bonds 002°C a guide to scale up climate finance', WBCSD Education. Available at www.wbcsd.org/Projects/Education/Resources/GREEN-BONDS-002-C-A-guide-to-scale-up-climate-finance

Green energy, technology, and manufacturing

6 Advancement of environmental sustainability through LNG

The case of Qatar–China relations[1]

Steven Wright

Despite Qatar's small geographical size, it has a magnified international importance given it is the world's largest exporter of liquefied natural gas (LNG), gas to liquid fuels (GTL), in addition to helium. China emerged in 2017 as the leading global consumer of LNG which is a cleaner fuel source that can contribute towards environmental sustainability. This underlines the importance of Qatar in China's calculations as it is a significant source of this energy. As Qatar is also a member of the Belt and Road Initiative (BRI), it is appropriate to use it as a case study in examining how individual states, which are part of the BRI, are engaged with it, and how this relationship has evolved, driven by the trade in LNG which is a product of China's drive towards advancing environmental sustainability through switching to cleaner fuels. This is especially so given the strategic role of Qatar as a major energy supplier to China, which brings particular dynamics to the bilateral relationship. Indeed, given the manner in which the BRI seeks to achieve larger economic and political connectivity, it is also important that focus is given to the manner in which China will acquire the natural resources it needs to drive its own economic development, and how trade has accelerated based on environmentally driven needs for cleaner energy sources. Also, it is clear that a central feature of China's long-term economic development strategy is its commitment to achieving this but with greater consideration towards environment sustainability by mitigating the adverse effects of air and water pollution. It is on this basis that the role of cleaner fossil fuels such as LNG and GTL will necessarily have greater importance as part of China's energy mix.

The central argument of this chapter is that Qatar's foreign and economic relations have demonstrated increasing connectivity with China on the basis of trade in LNG, and this trend is expected to continue and will be complemented by the BRI and by Chinese efforts towards procuring fuels that can help it achieve an environmentally sustainable future. The premise of this chapter is that such connectivity can be conceptually understood through the model of complex interdependence as outlined by Robert Keohane and Joseph Nye (1977). The bilateral relationship between these two countries has progressively developed on the basis of LNG, but the relationship has broadened into multiple areas based on the central pillar of trade in energy and has deepened based on China's need for cleaner fuels which help it achieve its environmental sustainability goals. With the unveiling of the BRI in 2013, a new dimension has been added to the bilateral relationship which warrants examination. While the BRI has potential for greater economic integration for its member countries, the relationship with Qatar has to also be contextualized in the strategic trade in LNG. It is on this basis that an examination of the evolving character of the global and regional LNG markets is justified in analysing and contextualizing how Qatar will integrate and engage with the BRI.

Complex interdependence

As a theoretical framework, the 'complex interdependence' model as proposed by Robert O. Keohane and Joseph S. Nye in the 1970s offers a synthesis of liberal and realist perspectives in international relations and forms a basis of the neoliberal school of thought on contemporary world politics (Keohane and Waltz 2000). It rests on the premise that societies have become inherently interconnected in several forms and interaction takes place over a number of issues (Keohane and Nye 1977). In the contemporary period, that interaction is no longer simply on issues relating to warfare and security but should also be understood through the impact of environmental concerns, in addition to global communications, international organizations, trade, knowledge sharing, and transnational threats among others. Given the nature of globalization and regionalization, it is appropriate to understand the multilateral and bilateral relationships through the complexity of layers which inform priorities and trajectories in such relations, and that 'issue areas' have to be conceptualized within the broader context of key matters that impact the given relationship.

As a model, its importance lies in the challenge it has made to pre-existing assumptions within the realist tradition of international relations, that hard power, and through military and economic capacity, was a primary determinant of bilateral and multilateral foreign policies, given that they will be used as instruments of state policy. Complex interdependence is a theory which challenges this: it stresses that trans-governmental politics necessitates that goals of states vary by issue and that bilateral relationships between states are far more complicated. Here, Keohane and Nye (1977) argue that states will use a variety of extensions of power at their disposal to achieve their objectives, which will include international organizations, international actors, economic ties, and soft power linkages. While realism would see an agenda formation as stemming from shifts in the balance of power and security threats, complex interdependence argues that change in priorities is induced from a variety of means that are specific to the bilateral relationship and issue area (Grieco 1988). Keohane and Nye (1977) argue that connectivity between transnational actors, issues relating to sensitivities over interdependence, and the distribution of power resources, all play a role in shaping the agenda between different parties.

In attempting to provide a conceptualization for analysis on Qatar's relations with China and its relationship to the BRI, complex interdependence is an appropriate theoretical framework, given the manner in which it is able to account for the differential motivating factors by the two states for closer political and economic relations and the varied manner in which that relationship is developing. Given this, the following section will seek to provide discussion on the nature of Qatar's relations with China and how they have evolved, before moving on to a discussion of the impact of the BRI on the bilateral relationship.

Pre-BRI phase: development of China–Qatar relations

Despite formal diplomatic relations through the establishment of an embassy only developing from the late 1980s, bilateral trade began around the 1950s and was mainly in fertilizer and petrochemical exports from Qatar to China (Park 2017). To illustrate the manner in which trade has developed rapidly, in 2000, the total trade levels was around US$400 million; by 2010 it had reached around US$4 billion and peaked in 2014 (prior to the global decline in the price of crude oil) at US$13 billion (Park 2017). What is important here is that the rapid spike in trade relations that took place is primarily a product of bilateral trade through Qatar becoming a strategic supplier of LNG and petrochemicals for China.

Qatar's trade with China through LNG can be understood as a relatively recent phenomenon, as the activation of a memorandum of understanding signed in 1994 for the supply of LNG only occurred in 2009 (Ahmed 2016). This slow development was largely a product of the lack of LNG terminals to receive shipments in China; however, with their progressive development and the drive by Beijing towards cleaner fuels, LNG has emerged as a clear growth area in catering for China's domestic energy needs. The initial LNG sales agreement with China was made in 2008 between Qatargas and the China National Offshore Oil Corporation for the supply of two million tons annually over a 25-year period. Increasing ties between China and Qatar developed during this period and was cemented by a visit to Qatar by the then Vice President Xi Jinping in 2008 (Ahmed 2016). Based on this collaboration, the China National Offshore Oil Corporation opened an office in Qatar in March 2009, and this was reciprocated by Qatargas, which opened an office in Beijing in November that year. On the basis of these growing ties, a further agreement for the supply of three million tonnes annually of LNG was achieved with PetroChina, and delivery of supplies began in 2011. Subcontracts were later expanded in 2009, with both China National Offshore Oil Corporation, for an additional five million tonnes annually, and PetroChina for an additional supply of two million tonnes annually. These agreements constituted the core of China's early relationship with Qatar, because prior to this the volume of trade and political ties was marginal.

It is worth recognizing that such cooperation prior to the announcement of the BRI was taking place on the basis of mutual commercial interest. By 2010, Qatar Petroleum signed a 30-year exploration and production-sharing agreement with Shell and PetroChina for the development of Qatar's Block-D field. What is important here is that PetroChina was able to secure a 25% stake in this field. Additional exploration and production-sharing agreements were signed with

China National Offshore Oil Corporation in 2009, and a further agreement signed with PetroChina in 2012. These agreements are significant in that they created stakeholders in Qatar's natural gas sector, and the volume of trade that such joint ventures develop play a fundamental role in the relationship.

By 2011, Qatar Petroleum International, China National Offshore Oil Corporation, and Shell (China), signed a broad cooperation framework agreement in Taizhou, Zhejiang province, located in the middle of the East China Sea coast, for the development of a refinery and petrochemical complex for the production of refined fuels and associated petrochemicals. This project was instructive, as it demonstrated an attempt by Qatar to invest on the Chinese mainland in its petroleum sector. While this project was ultimately cancelled owing to environmental concerns, it underlines the manner in which the initial agreements signed over the supply of LNG to China allowed for a broad array of trade and investment to take place (Park 2017). Nevertheless, one observation that can be made on the nature of the national oil companies (NOCs) of Qatar and China is that they operate in an autonomous manner from the national foreign policy positions, as their primary motivation is commercial gain.

It is important to appreciate that even in the period preceding the announcement of the BRI, Qatar's relations with China had taken on the character which can best be conceptualized through complex interdependence, whereby mutually beneficial trade and investment began to flourish centered on the natural gas and petroleum sectors. It is based on this that Qatar's trade with China has been growing exponentially: between 2008 and 2013 the volume of trade tripled. The main driver of this expansion in trade was demand from China for natural gas. As of 2017, Qatar was supplying around 11% of China's natural gas imports, which located it as the third-largest supplier of natural gas to China after Turkmenistan and Australia respectively. Qatar can be understood as having special importance for China's energy security, and therefore the character of Qatar's relations with the BRI has to be understood within this context. China emerged in 2017 as the world's largest importer of LNG ahead of both Japan and South Korea. This trend for greater consumption is set to continue: the vast majority of projected LNG demand globally is expected to come from China, which translates to it being the target market for any growth in supply from Qatar. Indeed, access to a reliable and cheap energy source is essential for Chinese economic growth, and given that Qatar supplies a significant proportion of China's natural gas needs, the manner in which this trade can be expected to develop warrants close attention, which we will provide in the subsequent sections.

Qatar and the Belt and Road Initiative: A driver of interdependence?

In accordance with the complex interdependence theory, a broad array of trade, investment and connectivity was able to develop following the primary ties being developed through the supply of LNG and petrochemicals. This trade was to provide the basis on which further interdependence could be developed through the BRI. The BRI was unveiled in 2013 as a major initiative that draws inspiration from the ancient Silk Road, and in its modern incarnation it has come to redefine China's foreign policy and engagement with partner countries (Huang 2016). The basis of China's foreign policy through the BRI gives focus to mutual prosperity, inclusiveness, and international collective benefit and has been characterized by President Xi Jinping as a policy agenda which embodies a new model of international relations. The scale of the project is unprecedented in that it encompasses more than 60 nations but cumulatively accounts for more than half of the global population and under a third of global GDP.

At a geopolitical level, the BRI seeks to provide connectivity between Asia, Europe, and through to Africa. It embodies major infrastructure projects, which include logistical hubs such as ports, airports, railways, and roads, in addition to industrial development areas, energy pipelines, and electricity generation. Other infrastructural projects include telecommunications, financial cooperation, and general trade supporting such linkages. Given the breadth of the engagement, it rests on the principle of interconnectivity towards yielding mutual economic gain. The BRI has five pillars of cooperation: policy coordination, facilities connectivity, unimpeded trade, financial integration, and people-to-people ties. It is based on this breadth of ties, under which it led to greater connectivity through economic linkages, that it is appropriate to apply Keohane and Nye's model of complex interdependence to conceptualize the evolving manner in which countries interact with China and the BRI.

On a strategic level, the BRI can be understood as a response to the United States' Pivot to Asia in 2011, under the presidency of Barack Obama, given that it was interpreted as a means of expanding the US presence around China's periphery, thereby constituting a form of containment. China's economic position rests heavily on its maritime trade routes; around 40% of China's total trade is maritime based, and 80% of its energy imports of crude oil passed through the Malacca Strait. The perception of US moves towards achieving a containment of China through the projection of naval power may be understood as a motivation for the BRI to use geo-economic linkages as a means of catering for China's national security. On this basis, it can be seen as a counterweight to the possible risks of US disruption to access routes which would significantly impact China's economy and thereby its political stability. Crucially, however, it is a geo-economic rather than a political means of power projection and can be understood as characterizing China's national security strategy (Beesen 2018). The adoption of the BRI, therefore, has strategic value in catering for Chinese trade and economic development through a broader trade strategy which offsets the risk of US-led containment. The scale of the BRI is highly significant: China is predicting trade flows of around US$2.5 trillion by 2025, and it would constitute the majority of global trade by 2050. On this basis, the significance of the BRI is that it has the potential to redefine the concept of globalization and multilateral trade, yet it remains to be seen if it will deliver on such expectations and integrate effectively within the Middle Eastern geopolitical arena (Ehteshami 2018).

Nevertheless, the Gulf region has special importance given its geographic location and energy resources for the BRI (Qian and Fulton 2017).

Qatar's inclusion in the BRI is significant, given Doha's economic character and geographic location. Ties between Qatar and China only developed in 1988, yet trade has developed progressively, China emerging as Qatar's third largest trading partner by 2017, with a total trade level of US$10.6 billion. The completion of Hamad Port in 2017 underlined the significance of Qatar's strategic location in importance for the BRI. With a total capacity of 7.5 million twenty-foot equivalent units (TEU), it is the second-largest port within the Middle East after Dubai's Jebel Ali. Given its strategic location and capacity, it is poised to have importance for the BRI for entrepôt trade across the region. This supports Qatar's own ambitions to become a regional trade hub. Therefore, attracting a greater proportion of shipping from China and BRI-linked countries has a particular value as part of Qatar's own needs to diversify its income sources away from oil and natural gas export revenue.

Following the launch of the BRI in 2013, Qatar established the first renminbi (RMB) clearing centre in the Middle East, Qatar Renminbi Centre (QRC), which allows for the clearance of transactions using RMB. This initiative was significant in that it challenged the pre-eminence of the US dollar as the global reserve currency yet underlined the outlook by Qatar that the broader regionalization that would take place through the BRI as well as the economic linkages which Qatar could benefit from would have fed into the strategic decision to establish Qatar at the forefront of China–Middle Eastern relations. The QRC allows for the direct settlement of trades through the Industrial and Commercial Bank of China, and this has the further impact of allowing greater exposure by Qatar-based corporations to the Chinese market (Fulton 2018). The significance of this should not be underestimated: the QRC has become the third-largest Chinese currency clearing facility globally through the Industrial and Commercial Bank of China, after Singapore and Luxembourg. Following the launch of the QRC, the United Arab Emirates established an RMB clearing facility in 2017 in Dubai. Both initiatives further enhance and underline the manner in which trade between China and the Middle East is leading to increased economic ties (Fulton 2018).

Building on the QRC establishment, the Qatar Investment Authority (QIA), which is Qatar's sovereign wealth fund, established an initial fund in 2014 amounting to US$10 billion, that was equally funded by both the QIA and the Industrial and Commercial Bank of China, as a means of promoting investments within the Middle East region. It was on the basis of this that further opportunities were to develop whereby the Qatar Central Bank (QCB) was given greater access to China's bond market which allowed for investment within mainland China. This catered for currency swap agreements and was further reinforced through QIA investments in Chinese IPOs.

Qatar's political economy can be differentiated from the majority of BRI partner countries whose economies lack the capital available for large infrastructure-based projects. Qatar has one of the highest GDPs per capita values globally, and by virtue of its oil and natural gas exports its economy has capital available for investment. Despite this ability to finance its own infrastructure projects, its economic strategy is to attract foreign direct investment, thereby allowing it the option to invest its own capital resources in high-return projects internationally. Moreover, attracting foreign direct investment is an effective means of providing for economic liquidity. Therefore, the BRI has strategic value to Qatar in capital acquisition and investment. In this respect, the strategic value of establishing the QRC is clear, as it will enable trade and investment from China while also becoming a regional hub for currency transactions in RMB.

In accordance with the complex interdependence theory, strategic collaboration in a specific area can yield to overspill, which will infuse the bilateral relationship in other areas. Several examples are available to demonstrate this, including the manner in which Qatar Airways has expanded its frequency of operations to six destinations in mainland China. Such measures are important as connectivity through travel caters for tourism, but also Qatar has sought to expand awareness of the Middle Eastern region by providing an endowment of US$10 million to Peking University.

Given the recognition that the central pillar in Qatar's relations with China remains its energy trade, despite the BRI catering for a broadening and deepening of that relationship into a more sustainable strategic partnership, it is appropriate at this stage to give attention to both the nature and strategy underpinning Qatar's energy policy, in addition to providing a geopolitical assessment of how change can be expected to shape Qatar's linkages with China.

Qatar's energy strategy

A remarkable aspect of Qatar's natural gas sector is that its development was strategically grounded in a long-term vision. Discovered in 1971, Qatar's North Field is the largest non-associated gas field globally, with an estimated reserve of 900 trillion cubic feet (TCF). Despite its discovery, the energy market was primarily focused on the demand for crude oil rather than natural gas. Indeed, demand for natural gas was fairly limited, and as such a sizeable proportion of natural gas was typically flared by oil producers. Nevertheless, in 1984 a strategic decision was made to develop the gas reserves. This saw the establishment of Qatargas based on the decision to exploit the field for domestic need and for export purposes. Moves towards developing the field began in 1987, and the first production started in 1991. It was recognized within Qatar that this was a strategic asset, and the challenge would be one of trying to develop and find markets for natural gas, thereby providing Qatar with the ability to capitalize on its natural resource.

The decision for Qatar to capitalize on its natural gas sector saw it invest in a gas hub in Ras Laffan, in order to enable Qatar to export its gas. This cost around US$2 billion, which Qatar had to draw from international financing in order to fund the project. It did this primarily in partnership with Mobile Oil (later

ExxonMobil), yet the long-term nature of the strategy was for Qatar to become a major supplier of natural gas on a global basis. In order to achieve this, three pillars were identified in Qatar's natural gas sector for this to be achieved.

Firstly, it had to adopt a fully integrated gas sector, which entailed adopting a new method for supplying LNG whereby production, gas liquefaction, transportation, and finally a receiving terminal and re-gasification would be provided for. In this sense, Qatar's natural gas sector was a fully integrated industry which facilitated access to markets and adoption of gas as an energy fuel source.

The second pillar of Qatar's LNG strategy was for cost optimization. The approach here was to use its engagement in all sectors as a means of lowering the costs of producing and delivering LNG to the customer. Strategies that were adopted included maximizing the proportion of natural gas that could be extracted from the bore wells. It was recognized here that cost optimization serves the purpose not only of maximizing revenue for Qatar but also of lowering cost of natural gas to consumers, which serves the purpose of helping expand the market and demand for this commodity. This was particularly important during the early stages of Qatar's LNG development, given that the liquefaction costs were particularly high. Yet also in relation to supplying natural gas, shipping costs were particularly high for this to be achieved, and the approach adopted by Qatar was to significantly increase the size of the LNG tankers and to adopt innovative approaches such as having a reliquification plant on board the tanker itself. By using both an integrated approach and seeking cost optimization, these innovations proved successful and made the production price of Qatar's LNG the lowest in the world.

The final pillar rested on reliability. By developing a brand that is linked to the pillar of reliability, price competitiveness, and quality of delivery, Qatar was able to capitalize on this as a means of securing long-term energy supply agreements with strategic consumers. This final pillar is particularly important in that the provision of natural resources for energy security purposes involves calculations that go beyond mere price. Therefore, a fundamental basis for Qatar's energy policy was that it would always be able to deliver its shipments on time and unhindered. Therefore, this was critical for its future success, the reputation of the company and access to new markets.

While the strategic decision to develop Qatar's LNG sector has proved highly successful, one challenge which was always present that could undermine Qatar's reputation as a reliable supplier concerned its geopolitical neighbourhood. The Middle East and North Africa can be understood as the most complex geopolitical area globally, which is beset by a range of security concerns. The Gulf region itself can generally be considered as having a greater degree of stability than its wider geopolitical neighbourhood, yet it also has historically suffered from insecurity. Following the revolutionary upheaval in Iran 1979, the region was gripped by a war between Iran and Iraq from 1980 to 1988, an invasion by Iraq into Kuwait in 1990, followed by a US-led invasion of Iraq in 2003. Despite the seriousness of these periods of geopolitical upheaval and the existing risk, the development of Qatar's natural gas sector and the willingness for international consumers to secure supplies through long-term contracts has not been impacted. It is therefore instructive at this stage to recognize that Qatar's national economic interests depend on the promotion of regional peace and security.

When these strategic issues are taken into consideration, it is possible to identify that a key strategic approach of Qatar has been to progressively expand global consumption of LNG and to diversify supply on a global basis. Moreover, with concerns over environmental degradation rising, Qatar has sought to market its LNG as a cleaner alternative to other fossil fuels such as oil or coal. Given this, it has been able to benefit from concerns over environmental sustainability, as this has helped drive demand for its LNG.

While Qatar's initial growth was driven by its oil sector, it was only following the discovery of Qatar's North Field, which is the largest non-associated gas field globally, that Qatar became distinguished as the country having the third-largest natural gas deposits after Russia and Iran. As Qatar has emerged as a gas-driven economy, its trade relations with major gas-consuming countries have special importance in the context of any analysis of its international relations. What is clear is that Qatar's bilateral ties with China have a strategic character based on mutual interests. As China has emerged as the leading consumer of LNG, this has clear importance to Qatar. Moreover, as China, Japan, and South Korea are the largest consumers of LNG globally, this has necessitated Qatar having a 'look-East' orientation for its natural gas sector. Conversely, for China, LNG is a cleaner fuel source, so increased use and trade of LNG contributes towards China's goal of environmental sustainability. Nevertheless, it is important to locate this as part of the complex interdependence framework by examining, in the following section, how the global market is evolving, and what ramifications this has on Qatar's trade relations with China.

The impact of a changing global energy market

For energy exporting countries, whose national economies draw a significant proportion of their GDP from such exports, the changing nature of the global energy market has special importance. Over the past decade, the global energy market has gone through a rapid transformation (Lynch 2018). The emergence of the US as the world's largest producer of oil, in addition to becoming an exporter of natural gas, has heralded a new era whereby the US has achieved energy independence (Grigas 2017). The implications of this are significant in that it signals a shift in the manner in which the national security and economic interests of the US are calculated (Medlock et al. 2014). The impact of this can be understood as a new era away from the security of natural resources playing an important role in foreign policy calculations, which has been a central feature of US engagement with the Middle East region since the end of the Second World War. The emergence of the US as a major player in the global energy market also heralds greater supply and competition. This has been driven through the exploitation of shale in the US and has served to have a dampening effect on global prices for oil. The key beneficiary of this has been major energy-importing countries such as China, as cheaper oil has fuelled economic growth and dulled inflation.

With the US emerging as a net exporter of LNG, its export capacity will be helping grow the global LNG market which feeds into Qatar's overall strategy for enhancing the adoption of LNG on a global level. Based on the US's geographical location, the 2016 completion of a widening of the Panama Canal has greatly facilitated the ability for the US LNG exporters to have a global reach and supply (Wright 2017). The US$5.3 billion expansion of the Panama Canal has reduced the transit cost from the US, and decreased the transit time by a third. Shipments to China can now be completed in 14 days, which allows both the US west coast and the Gulf coast products to be competitive in their supply to China, given its role as the main growth market for LNG globally (Moryadee et al., 2014).

While the changing fortunes of the US have certainly had a global impact, a broader pattern that can be observed is that there is a shift in the centre of gravity for energy demand at a global level, and this is primarily characterized by the move in demand from OECD to non-OECD nations, with particular emphasis on China and India. This shift in demand has been a trend since the 1990s and has been driven by rising levels of the economic prosperity of billions of people in developing countries (Grigas 2017). Given the size of China and India's population, they have proven to be the largest drivers in global demand for oil between 2007 and 2017. For natural gas, it is China that has proven to be the largest driver of demand over the past decade, and this trend is projected to continue. Yet at a geopolitical level, it is important to recognize that south and northern East Asia constitutes the majority of global demand for natural gas, which is relevant to this chapter. The combined demand from China, Japan, South Korea, and India, constitute more than 60% of global demand. It is based on this that these markets hold special importance for Qatar and other leading LNG suppliers, in both current and future market demand.

Although it is clear that there has been a shift in the centre of gravity in demand from OECD to non-OECD nations, it is important to recognize that supply of LNG is also growing. Australia has emerged as a leading producer of LNG and has in 2018 exported a comparative amount to that of Qatar, which is the world's leading producer. While Qatar's gas supplies are from non-associated natural gas fields, in the case of Australia, it is from coal-seam gas and has been enabled by significant investment into the sector during a period of high oil prices. While some predictions had indicated that Australia would overtake Qatar is the world's leading producer, Qatar announced in September 2018 that it would increase its LNG output (at 77 million tonnes per year in 2018) to 110 million by 2024. This is despite a parallel growth in global LNG output globally.

This expansion would ensure Qatar's dominance as the leading global supplier of LNG; yet of equal importance is the strategy behind this expansion in the face of a rise in global output. While it is accurate that global demand is projected to increase, there are indications that the scale of supply may be outstripping demand, which will lead to depressed prices. At a strategic level, Qatar's outlook on the growth in supply to the LNG market is that it would essentially grow the market for LNG consumption globally. This is an important provision, which has a bearing on China in that a greater output of LNG would firstly make it more affordable, and given its nature as being a cleaner fuel source, it is an attractive option over crude oil and coal. As a major exporter of natural gas and associated products, a key distinguishing feature of Qatar's energy export strategy is that its long-term approach is to grow the size of the consumer market rather than engaging in uncompetitive pricing strategies which provide short-term gain at the expense of longer-term demand in the interests of sustainability.

A further major player in the post-2020 period will be Russia, when it expands its LNG export capacity. Russia is already a leading producer of natural gas, but thus far it has been characterized by the unrealized potential in LNG as the focus has been on natural gas. The genesis behind this change in direction was in 2013, as the Russian parliament relaxed the role of the natural gas company Gazprom in producing and exporting gas globally. This liberalization has fostered competition, and the Russian LNG market is a natural area for growth. In March 2017, President Putin stated that 'without a doubt Russia not only can but will become the largest producer of liquefied natural gas in the world.' This underlines the political drive for a rapid increase in Russia's export capacity, especially given its need to bolster national revenue (Wright 2018).

The significance of a Russian expansion of LNG exports stems from its geographic location (Charap et al. 2017). Given the rising LNG consumption of China, Russia has the potential to supply its needs through pipeline-based supply, in addition to the Japanese market. Such a shift towards the East Asian market by Russia has been precipitated by the growing application of sanctions by the European Union since March 2014, when Russia was condemned for a violation of Ukrainian sovereignty. The increased tensions, coupled with the inherent challenges faced by the Russian economy, have provided a motivator for increased Russian engagement with its East Asian neighbours.

On a strategic level, the growth in the market and adoption of LNG by encouraging greater demand, also caters for two primary objectives: firstly, the expertise that Qatar has developed within its NOC with regard to the natural gas sector places it in a highly competitive position to take on a character akin to that of an IOC through technology development and innovation, and its becoming a stakeholder in projects on a global basis. The advantage of this for Qatar is that it would enhance its revenue stream for the country. It is, in essence, a classic example of state capitalism. Secondly, Qatar's support for growing the LNG market also has the potential for allowing it to engage in energy swap agreements. This essentially would involve a partner country supplying LNG on behalf of another country and vice versa. It is an innovative approach towards providing natural gas but would also allow countries to capitalize on pipelines, reduce transit periods and cost, in addition to reconciling energy security considerations with practical supply agreements for the supply of energy on a global basis. When Qatar's relations with China are taken into consideration, this could allow for greater access to the Chinese market by engaging in collaborative projects with China's northern and western neighbours. Indeed, this is an important consideration, given the manner in which pipeline-based supply is being exploited between Russia and China. On this issue, Daojiong and Meidan (2015) comment:

> Such developments are certainly welcome news for China, though future prospects for China's 'One Belt, One Road' project will also be conditioned by the pursuit of global diversification by Middle Eastern economies. Meanwhile, China continues to hedge against over-reliance on the Middle East as a source of energy supply. The signing in May 2014 of a 30-year deal to import Russian pipeline gas through the Power of Siberia pipeline was widely seen as a landmark deal. Some experts believe that 'Russia's share of the Northeast Asian natural gas market [will] never [rise] above 9% by 2030 and in the next decade [will have] difficulty exceeding 3%'. But the more pertinent point is that China has various options for dealing with energy suppliers around the world. The successful negotiation of the gas pipeline, facilitated by Moscow's souring ties with its traditional oil and gas consumers in Europe, suggests that more Russian oil and gas will find its way to Asia, and especially China.
>
> (Daojiong and Meidan 2015: 10)

Are Gulf regional dynamics an unintended driver?

Qatar's LNG trade is global in orientation, and only a marginal volume of its LNG supply is to its regional neighbours. In Table 6.1, a breakdown of Qatar's supply agreements is listed, and this underlines that the principal global consumers of Qatar's LNG exports are Japan, South Korea, and Taiwan. Qatar's Dolphin Pipeline extends to the United Arab Emirates (UAE) and to Oman. The proportion of gas that transits through the pipeline is small in comparison to Qatar's main customers and this underlines that Qatar's LNG strategy is commercially driven.

What is important in the LNG supply agreements that Qatar has is that 95% of the contracts are long-term, and the majority will be up for renewal between 2017 and 2022. Globally, the trend is towards shorter contracts, which reflects the 'supply glut' in the LNG sector. The global average in 2017 for supply contract length fell below seven years. It is based on this that the LNG market can be understood to be one that is evolving, yet it remains different from the crude oil market given that the majority of LNG is traded on a long-term basis rather than through spot trading. Moreover, the LNG market can be further differentiated from the crude oil market in that LNG is priced on a regional basis rather than on a global index. The reason for regional indexing is largely a legacy of regional trade and the manner in which it is contracted; yet, as greater supply capacity comes onto the global market, the scope for a growth in spot trading of gas, coupled with a common pricing index, grows.

As highlighted in the table, the global context is evolving in a manner that promises to see a much greater degree of LNG supply reach the global market. It is on this basis that while Qatar's strategy can be understood as focused on

Table 6.1 Qatar LNG supply agreements

Operator	Trains	mn t/y	Start-up	Shareholders	Key Customers (Destinations)
Qatargas 1	T1-3	9.6	1997	• QP (65%) • ExxonMobil (10%) • Total (10%) • Marubeni (7.5%) • Mitsui (7.5%)	• Japanese utility companies (Japan)
Qatargas 2	T1	7.8	2009	• QP (70%) • ExxonMobil (30%)	• ExxonMobil (UK)
Qatargas 2	T2	7.8	2009	• QP (65%) • ExxonMobil (18.3%) • Total (16.7%)	• CNOOC (China) • Total (various destinations)
Qatargas 3	T1	7.8	2010	• QP (68.5%) • ConocoPhillips (30%) • Mitsui (1.5%)	• Centrica (UK) • CNOOC (China) • Chubu (Japan)
Qatargas 4	T1	7.8	2011	• QP (70%) • Shell (30%)	• Shell (various destinations) • PetroChina (China) • Marubeni (Japan)
Total Qatargas: 7 trains, 40.7 mn t/y cap.					
Rasgas 1	T1&2	6.6	1999–2000	• QP (63%) • ExxonMobil (25%) • KORAS (5.0%) • Itochu (4.0%) • LNG Japan (3.0%)	• Kogas (Korea)
Rasgas 2	T1, 2	2×4.7	2004, 05	• QP (70%) • ExxonMobil (30%)	• Petronet (India) • Edison (Italy)
Rasgas 2	T3	4.7	2007	• QP (65%) • ExxonMobil (30%) • CPC (5.0%)	• CPC (Taiwan), • EDF, Eni (Belgium)
Rasgas 3	T1	7.8	2009	• QP (70%) • ExxonMobil (30%)	• Kogas (Korea), • Petronet (India)
Rasgas 3	T2	7.8	2010	• QP (70%) • ExxonMobil (30%)	
Total Rasgas: 7 trains, 36.3 mn t/y cap.					

Source: Middle East Economic Survey; author's calculations.

(Note: Rasgas formally merged with Qatargas on 1 January 2018.)

growing global demand for LNG, the evolving market context can be expected to have a lowering effect on prices due to excess supply. Given the rising population of the non-OECD countries, a low-cost energy source is an enabler of economic development. Low prices also serve to increase demand over the longer term. However, it is noted that overly low prices will deter other producers from entering the market if their production costs impact their ability to generate profit: this is already a market force which is serving as a cap on shale producers in the US. In this sense, the LNG market is one that is regulated by the market, while the crude oil market operates in a more anticompetitive manner given the cartel role of OPEC, which leads to artificial price inflation.

A second factor that will impact Qatar during the period when its contracts come up for renegotiation is that the nature of its supply linkages will also necessarily fluctuate, based on energy security considerations. Although Qatar has the lowest LNG production cost globally, each country differs in its energy security approach, thereby necessitating different degrees of import diversification by source. When these are taken into consideration, Qatar may lose some market share and thereby necessitate it targeting emerging markets instead, which further reinforces the importance of China due to its projected growth in demand for LNG and the impact that the BRI may have on being a driver of future growth in demand.

In target markets, thus far Qatar's supply linkages have been global in orientation, yet growing supply coupled with the majority of its supply contracts being due for retendering by 2022 translates to the medium term being a period of flux. It is therefore appropriate to recognize the demand areas for future LNG which Qatar could target. As outlined above, a shift in the centre of gravity in demand has, at a broad level, been taking place between OECD and non-OECD countries. This demand is led by growth from China, yet as a geopolitical area, it is the Middle Eastern region that also demonstrates significant demand. This is primarily a product of the high birth rates across countries within the Middle East and North Africa. Therefore, this raises the question of whether Qatar will increasingly target its regional neighbourhood as a growth market based on the factors highlighted above, thus posing an alternative to increased integration of supply with China as part of the BRI.

It is of particular significance that despite the Gulf region being oil rich, with the exception of Qatar and Iran, the region is 'gas poor' and countries are increasingly reliant on gas imports to meet their domestic needs for electricity. Indeed, the UAE and Kuwait have begun importing gas from the US, which raises questions as to why this gas was not sourced from Qatar given its geographical proximity.

It is noteworthy that during the initial stages of Qatar's developing its natural gas sector, it sought to construct pipelines to its regional neighbours and beyond. Such an approach had merit not only on a commercial level but also that it could foster greater cooperation between states within the region and provide economic advantages through the supply of cheaper and cleaner energy. Indeed, Saudi Arabia's energy mix stands out in that the majority of its electricity production is achieved through oil-fired power stations. Given that this is Riyadh's main export commodity, one could argue that it would be economically advantageous to the kingdom to have opted to import gas to cover its electricity production needs, thereby freeing up capacity that could be used for export purposes (Krane and Wright 2014).

Both in demand for gas from Qatar by its regional neighbours and the construction of gas pipelines, only limited success has been achieved. The construction of the Dolphin pipeline linking Qatar to the UAE and Oman did achieve a degree of integration, yet it is not used to full capacity. This is largely a product of an additional factor in relation to the creation of a Gulf-gas market, which is that Qatar's neighbouring states have shown that they want that gas provided at a discounted rate, which comes with an opportunity cost to Qatar given that it can supply LNG to the global market at a much higher rate of return.

Of the issues highlighted relating to Qatar integrating into supply within its regional geopolitical area, the main reason for both the economic rationale not being capitalized on and pipelines not being permitted for construction across neighbouring countries' land and territorial waters can be reduced to regional political competition which is induced by centralized elite-level decision-making rather than being institutional. By virtue of the centralized nature of decision-making in the Arab Gulf countries, even though an economic and political logic may exist for a particular course of action, the idiosyncrasies of the ruling elite personalize the decision-making, making it inherently political. This is particularly so for the Arab Gulf countries that are monarchical. Prejudices, therefore, feed into decision-making, which has hindered the realization of a regional market for natural gas, thereby necessitating that Qatar opted for a global approach in the supply of its natural gas. This context has historically served to support Qatar's integration with East Asian consuming countries rather than with its regional market (Piet and Wright 2016).

Adding to the context outlined above, the severance of diplomatic relations and enactment of an embargo on Qatar on 5 June 2017 in a coordinated campaign by Saudi Arabia, UAE, Bahrain, and Egypt can be understood from the outset as negating any possibility for greater regional integration through regional grade in Qatar's gas. While it is accurate that regional tensions and periodic crises had emerged historically among the Arab Gulf monarchies, the 2017 Gulf crisis crystallized into fundamentally incompatible outlooks on regional order. Essentially, Qatar's outlook has been one of gradualist and progressive-pragmatism through pluralism, as it sees a greater emphasis on popular self-determination, the rule of law, and an opening of civil society, to be at the forefront of what the region needs for development and security to be achieved. Comparatively, the Saudi-led group is seeking maintenance of the traditional monarchical status quo, as social or political liberalism, and an opening of civil society is viewed as a threat to their national security and dynastic rule. Indeed, the manner in which the 2011 uprisings took place, in addition to a resurgent Iran, has heightened a sense of insecurity that has sharpened this interpretation of the risks of progressive pluralism and gradualist liberalism.

It is on the basis of these incompatible views on regional order that the strategic objective of the blockade can be interpreted as seeking regime change in Qatar. While Qatar has proved resilient to the blockade, in how this impacts Qatar's trade in LNG and its relations with China, the regional dynamics only serve to accelerate and motivate greater integration by Qatar within the BRI framework. Indeed, on a political level, by providing for an increased share in China's LNG energy security needs, it also has a strategic by-product of fostering Chinese national security interests in seeing stability within the Gulf region, and between Qatar and its neighbours specifically.

Scope for untapped initiatives to increase Qatar–BRI connectivity?

The Paris Agreement on climate change formally entered into force in November 2016. Carbon capture and storage (CCS) has become an increasingly important factor for reducing the carbon footprint of respective countries (Cho et al. 2017). One area which can be exploited further between Qatar and China is through CCS. While Qatar already practices CCS, CO_2 storage from China has the potential for reinjection to Qatar's oil fields, thus allowing Qatar to be both a CO_2 sink and an exporter of fossil fuels causing CO_2 emissions.

A distinguishing feature of Qatar is that it is the world's largest player in the LNG tanker industry, accounting for around 10% of the global total. Qatar's Nakilat has 65 wholly and joint-owned LNG vessels, plus four LPG vessels. The return leg of the trade offers an opportunity for Qatar to transport back liquid CO_2 for subsequent enhanced oil recovery (EOR) and enhanced gas recovery (EGR), and CO_2 storage. Qatar may therefore transform from a major CO_2 source to a CO_2 sink for mitigating against climate change.

Transporting CO_2 from China to be used for CCS within Qatar and for oil field injection promises to have environmental benefits and to enhance the strategic linkages between China and Qatar. It is noted, however, that the use of Qatar's tankers to transport CO_2 in liquid form may not be possible on LNG tankers given the pressure/temperature that they will need to withstand, yet it is viable on LPG tankers. Therefore, this is an area that can be identified as warranting further consideration by both countries as part of a broader logic which is fostering connectivity and economic interdependence.

Concluding observations

When Qatar's relations with China are taken into consideration, what is clear is that the relationship is explainable through the framework of complex interdependence. The central area of cooperation of the relationship has been the trade in LNG which is an impact feature in China's strategy for promoting environmental sustainability. Despite it being a strategic goal, this chapter has underlined that although the trade in LNG was not initially driven by concerns over environmental sustainability, complex interdependence has risen and Chinese calculations on trade with Qatar has taken on a new dynamic driven by the desire to import 'cleaner' fuels. This has fed into cooperation in multiple sectors in accordance with the complex interdependence framework. Given the standing of Qatar as the world's largest supplier of LNG, and that China has evolved into the world's largest importer of LNG, a partnership on a strategic level has a logic that is to the advantage of both parties. It is noteworthy, however, that this relationship was initiated prior to the unveiling of the BRI, yet the BRI can be understood as an accelerant, which adds a strategic dimension for greater sociocultural connectivity, trade, and financial cooperation while contributing to the strategic aim of an environmentally sustainably future for China within the BRI context. Qatar's strategic location and development of its port infrastructure allow it to be a logistical hub for trade from China for entrepôt trade, primarily from Kuwait, Iraq, and Iran, despite competition existing from Dubai's Jebel Ali port. With Qatar also offering a well-established regional RMB clearing hub, this strategic value to the BRI seems assured.

While the foundation of the bilateral relationship rests on the trade in LNG, and it can be expected to develop in both scope and intensity based on the BRI and Chinese goals for environmental sustainability, it is also important to recognize here that both global geopolitical dynamics relating to LNG supply and the nature of Qatar's relations with its neighbours can be understood as a contributing driver for greater bilateral integration. As highlighted in the above discussion, at a global level, rising centres of LNG supply are emerging which is increasing the supply of LNG to the global market. While supply increases, a global shift in the consumption of LNG is also underway from OECD to non-OECD nations, primarily dominated by China's demand. With Qatar's energy strategy focusing on increasing its supply of LNG to the global market, the primary market for Qatar on a strategic level is China, which further underlines the importance of the relationship.

The regional geopolitics of the Gulf region, which has witnessed a breakdown in relations between Qatar and the neighbouring states of Saudi Arabia, UAE, and Bahrain, has also worked against the potential for Qatar providing LNG to a growing regional market. It is on this basis that Qatar's export focus will necessarily remain globally orientated. The majority of its long-term energy contracts will expire by the early 2020s. Those that are not renewed will yield excess supply and therefore reinforce the importance of China as a consumer market.

It is on the basis of these multiple factors that an identifiable strategic rationale and motivation exist for Qatar's increased engagement with China, which will further motivate its integration within the BRI. The strength of the BRI and renewed Chinese goals for environmental sustainability is that it promises to serve as a catalyst for greater integration in a manner which can be conceptualized through the complex interdependence framework.

Note

1 This article was made possible by a National Priorities Research Program Standard (NPRP-S) 12th Cycle grant no. NPRP12S-0210-190067 from the Qatar National Research Fund (a member of Qatar Foundation). The findings herein reflect that work, and are solely the responsibility of the author.

References

Ahmed, G 2016, 'In search of a strategic partnership: China-Qatar energy cooperation from 1988 to 2015', in T Niblock, A Galindo Marines & D Sun (eds), *The Arab states of the Gulf and BRICS: new strategic partnerships in politics and economics*. Gerlach Press, Berlin, pp. 57–85.

Beesen, M 2018, 'Geoeconomics with Chinese characteristics: the BRI and China's evolving grand strategy', *Journal of Economic Political Studies,* vol. 6, pp. 240–256.

Charap, S, Drennan, J & Noël, P 2017, 'Russia and China: a new model of great-power relations', *Survival,* vol. 59, pp. 25–42.

Cho, W, Yu, H & Mo, Y 2017, 'CO2 conversion to chemicals and fuel for carbon utilization', in Y. Yun, *Recent advances in carbon capture and storage.* Intechopen, London, pp. 193–208.

Daojiong, Z & Meidan, M 2015, *China and the Middle East in a new energy landscape.* Chatham House, London.

Ehteshami, A 2018, 'Gold at the end of the rainbow? The BRI and the Middle East', *Global Policy,* vol. 9, No. 3, pp. 387–397.

Fulton, J 2018, 'Striking a balance between economics and security: China's relations with the Gulf monarchies', in J. Fulton and L. Sim (eds), *External Powers and the Gulf Monarchies.* Routledge, London, pp. 140–158.

Grieco, J 1988, 'Anarchy and the limits of cooperation: a realist critique of the newest liberal institutionalism', *International Organization,* vol. 42, pp. 485–507.

Grigas, A 2017, *The new geopolitics of natural gas.* Harvard University Press, Boston, MA.

Huang, Y 2016, 'Understanding China's Belt & Road initiative: motivation, framework and assessment', *China Economic Review,* vol. 40, pp. 314–321.

Keohane, RO & Nye, JS 1977, *Power and interdependence: world politics in transition.* Little Brown, New York.

Keohane, RO & Waltz, KN 2000, 'The neorealist and his critic', *International Security,* vol. 25, pp. 204–205.

Krane, J & Wright, S 2014 *Qatar 'rises above' its region: geopolitics and the rejection of the GCC gas market.* No. 35. LSE Kuwait Programme, London.

Lynch, M 2018, 'New energy and the geopolitics of the future', in J. Considine and K. Paik (eds), *Handbook of energy politics.* Edward Elgar Publishing, Cheltenham, pp. 276–287.

Medlock, KB, Jaffe, AM & O'Sullivan, M 2014, 'The global gas market, LNG exports and the shifting US geopolitical presence', *Journal of Energy Strategy Reviews,* vol. 5, pp. 14–25.

Moryadee, S, Gabriel, SA & Rehulka, F 2014, 'The influence of the Panama Canal on global gas trade', *Journal of Natural Gas Science Engineering,* vol. 20, pp. 161–174.

Park, R 2017, *A comparative assessment of the role of energy in Qatar's East Asian foreign relations: case studies on China, Japan and South Korea.* Qatar University.

Piet, R & Wright, S 2016, 'The dynamics of energy geopolitics in the Gulf and Qatar's foreign relations with East Asia', in L Lester (ed.), *Energy relations and policy making in Asia.* Palgrave Macmillan, London.

Qian, X & Fulton, J 2017, 'China-Gulf economic relationship under the "Belt and Road" initiative', *Asian Journal of Middle Eastern Islamic Studies,* vol. 11, pp. 12–21.

Wright, S 2017, 'Qatar's LNG: impact of the changing East-Asian Market', *Middle East Policy,* vol. 24, pp. 154–165.

Wright, S 2018, *Shifting markets of liquid gas: emerging producers and alternative geostrategies.* Al Jazeera Centre for Studies, Doha.

7 Technological assessment of CO_2 capture and EOR/EGR/ECBM-based storage

Guoping Hu, Kai Jiang,
Rui Wang, and Kevin Gang Li

7.1 Introduction

The total amount of carbon on earth is constant and its distribution between the lithosphere, the atmosphere, and the biosphere has remained relatively constant in human history until the industrial era (Yang et al. 2008). The subsequent emission of CO_2 into the atmosphere from human activities is recognized as the main cause of climate change, including global warming, rising sea levels, extreme weathers, agricultural problems and etc. (Motz et al. 2001, Chu and Majumdar 2012, Hegerl and Stott 2014, Howard-Grenville et al. 2014, Rutgersson et al. 2014). With the growth of the global population and living standards, the increased need for food, water, and energy, results in even larger quantities of CO_2 being emitted into the atmosphere (Hüsler and Sornette 2014). Therefore, overwhelming attention has been paid to the development of various low carbon technologies across every aspect of human activities (Chu and Majumdar 2012), though much more effort is needed to meet emission targets (Pachauri and Meyer 2014).

In particular, the energy sector is the biggest contributor to anthropogenic carbon emissions. Fossil fuels such as coal, oil, and natural gas will remain as major sources of energy in the near future owing to their affordable price, high availability, high security, and stability in their utilization systems (Bachu 2008). It is almost inevitable that emissions of CO_2 into the atmosphere will continue, and lead to even more severe climate change effects (Chu 2009) in next few decades without our taking countermeasures that have to be economical, environmentally friendly, and viable in large scale.

Many methods have the potential to reduce global CO_2 emissions. Some of them can accelerate the sink of carbon dioxide directly from atmosphere, such as re-forestation, ocean fertilization, and CO_2 mineral carbonation (Yamasaki 2003, Druckenmiller and Maroto-Valer 2005, Maroto-Valer et al. 2005a, Maroto-Valer et al. 2005b, Edenhofer et al. 2011). These processes can simultaneously capture and sequester CO_2 at low energy costs, which however, alone are not sufficient to significantly curb CO_2 emissions. Some other technologies have been developed to tackle the industrial carbon emissions, namely various carbon dioxide capture

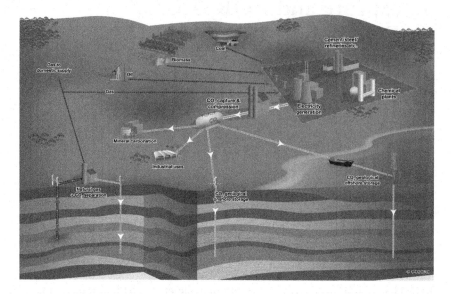

Figure 7.1 A schematic diagram of carbon capture and storage (Image courtesy of
CO2CRC, with permission to reuse)

and storage technologies (CCS, Figure 7.1). CCS is a full industry chain that
covers the following steps at least (Rochelle et al. 2002, Gibbins and Chalmers
2008, Chu 2009, Chalmers 2019):

- capture of CO_2 from its emission sources or air
- compression of CO_2 into storable formations
- transportation of CO_2
- storage of the captured CO_2 in suitable geographical storage sites

Quite often, pre-storage survey of the geosequestration sites, planning of
transportation, and post-storage monitoring are also important components to
the development of CCS.

CCS provides an efficient way to reduce industrial CO_2 emissions to the
atmosphere, while allowing the consumption of fossil fuels and securing sufficient energy supply for society (Edenhofer et al. 2011). Given that renewables
may take decades to dominate the energy market, CCS is believed to be the only
transitional technology that can decarbonize the economy and sustain its growth
in the meantime, without compromising the living standard of rich countries or
sacrificing the "right of development" of developing nations. However, the high
capture and compression costs, e.g. 23–35 US\$/tCO_2 to capture, 0–5 US\$/

tCO$_2$ for delivery, and 0.6–8.3 US\$/tCO$_2$ for geological storage and monitoring (Herzog et al. 2018), and identifying appropriate storage sites must be resolved before its large scale deployment (Abu-Zahra et al. 2007, Bachu 2008, Gibbins and Chalmers 2008).

The Belt and Road Initiative (BRI) is a historic geopolitical strategy that aims to establish and strengthen multinational trade corridors and provide mechanisms for ongoing cooperation and engagement. BRI involves significant numbers of countries and regions far beyond the traditional Silk Road in the exchange of commodities, technologies, and culture. Apart from driving the development of regional economies, environmental issues particularly greenhouse gas emission have also drawn much attention among BRI countries under the Paris Agreement (Huang 2016). With more than 130 countries now reported to have signed the agreement, BRI provides an unparalleled platform to integrate the CCS value chain from emission sources to storage sites between its member countries. The BRI has also facilitated the development of transportation infrastructures including pipelines, sea freight, and high-speed railways. These infrastructures have created a tremendous delivery network, significantly decreasing logistics costs and have enabled a better framework for carbon trade. For example, oil and gas delivery trucks, trains, and ships are often empty when they return to oil and gas export destinations. On this basis, these empty containers could be filled with captured CO$_2$, which would then be delivered to oil and gas fields and injected underground for enhanced oil recovery (EOR) or enhanced gas recovery (EGR). While a small part of the injected CO$_2$ may be prone to migration to atmosphere after many years, the majority of the CO$_2$ will be trapped underground permanently.

7.2 Carbon capture

Carbon capture is a process of separating CO$_2$ from gas mixtures (mostly nitrogen or methane), allowing the capture of CO$_2$ in either power generation or other industry sectors that rely on the combustion or processing of carbon based fuels. The separation of CO$_2$ is a very important industrial process in various industry sectors, such as hydrogen upgrading, unconventional natural gas treatment, syngas purification, and many refinery processes (Sholl and Lively 2016). The capture technologies (Figure 7.2) are similar for all these sectors and include absorption, adsorption, membrane, cryogenic separation, mineralization, or a combination of these techniques (Lee et al. 2006, Trachtenberg et al. 2009, Endo et al. 2011, Tuinier et al. 2011, Masoumi et al. 2013, Scholes et al. 2013, Liu et al. 2014, Khalilpour et al. 2015).

Although CCS is being intensively investigated as an efficient and effective way to reduce CO$_2$ emissions to the atmosphere, the cost of carbon capture has to be reduced to a manageable level before it can be deployed at an industrial scale (Hu et al. 2016). Carbon capture processes, depending on the operation conditions, can be classified into three configurations, including pre-combustion, oxyfuel combustion, and post-combustion. Pre-combustion involves a gasification

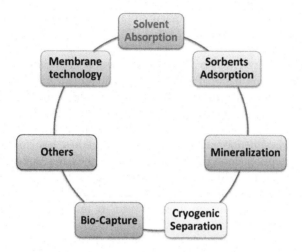

Figure 7.2 Technologies for CO_2 capture (Hu 2018; with permission to reuse)

process to convert a carbon-based fuel into a carbon free gaseous fuel through, for example, water gas shift reaction with CO_2 captured before the combustion of hydrogen, which is often known as integrated gasification combined cycle (IGCC). Oxyfuel combustion is a process of fuel burning using enriched or pure oxygen as the oxidant; thereafter the CO_2 streams are often quite pure and ready for transportation and storage. Post-combustion refers to CO_2 capture from the flue gases after fuel burning, which deals with relatively low concentration of CO_2 (less than 15 vol %) but enables much easier retrofitbility owing to little modification being required for existing processes.

Chemical looping combustion (Fan 2011, Fennell and Anthony 2015) is a special combustion technique classified as a modified oxyfuel process where it requires an oxygen carrier, i.e. solid metal oxides (Me_xO_y), serving as an oxidant for the burning of fuels. Since no air is directly introduced into the combustion chamber, the CO_2 streams are generally pure enough for transportation and storage after water removal.

7.2.1 Solvent absorption

The absorption of CO_2 into a solvent has been investigated for decades, and was first used for purifying gases, such as hydrogen gas, natural gas, and synthesis gas (Shrier and Danckwerts 1969), and more recently for reducing CO_2 emissions (Lee et al. 2006). A typical solvent absorption process is presented in Figure 7.3, in which a mixture gas flows through an absorber, and CO_2 is captured in the solvent by physical solvation (physical absorption) or chemical reaction (chemical absorption); then the CO_2-loaded solvent is flashed or heated to regenerate the solvents and obtain high purity CO_2. Physical absorption, such as Selexol™

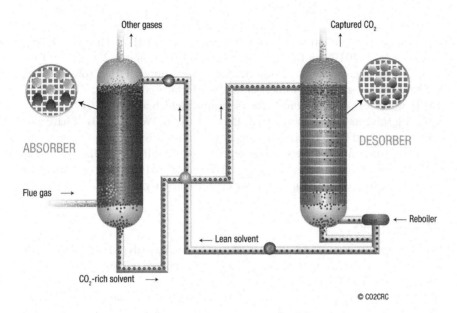

Figure 7.3 A solvent absorption process for CO₂ capture (Image courtesy of CO2CRC, with permission to reuse)

and Rectisol™, often requires high CO₂ partial pressure to achieve a relatively high CO₂ absorption capacity. It is very rarely used in post-combustion carbon capture owing to its low solubility at low pressures and the tendency of solvent evaporation. Many chemical solvents have been investigated for carbon capture, including monoethanolamine (MEA) (Rochelle et al. 2002), diamines (Zhou et al. 2010), piperazine and its derivatives (Bishnoi and Rochelle 2002, Freeman et al. 2009, Li et al. 2014), ammonia (Collett et al. 2011), amino acid salts (Hu et al. 2018), ionic liquids (Blanchard et al. 1999), and their blends (Bishnoi and Rochelle 2002, Dugas and Rochelle 2009). Among them, MEA is the benchmark solvent for carbon capture. However, the use of MEA brings some disadvantages, such as a high energy penalty for solvent regeneration, high degradation rate, and its high corrosivity (Lim et al. 2014, Wang et al. 2015). Some research has been conducted from the perspective of reducing energy costs, such as utilizing solar energy in power plants to supplement the total energy requirements (Zhao et al. 2014). However, for the purpose of industrial CCS, the energy consumption needs to be further reduced, and drawbacks of solvent degradation and corrosion must be addressed before the large-scale deployment MEA-based techniques. In most aqueous solvent absorption processes, pre-water removal is not required owing to water evaporation during the regeneration step. However, pre-removal of SO$_x$ and NO$_x$ may be necessary owing to the high reactivity between solvents and SO$_x$/NO$_x$ causing potential degradation of solvents.

Overall energy consumption for amine based carbon capture is around 2–4 MJ/kg CO_2. The evaporation of water may account for 25–45% of the regeneration energy varying with L/G ratio (Oexmann et al. 2012). The latest report (Rochelle et al. 2019) on the overall energy consumption was 2.1 MJ/kg CO_2 using 5 M piperazine with an advanced flashing stripper. Other solvents such as phase change solvents (Pinto et al. 2014, Machida et al. 2018, Zhang et al. 2019), water-lean or even nonaqueous solvents (Heldebrant et al. 2017) and precipitating solvents (Smith et al. 2013, Hu et al. 2016, Wu et al. 2017) have also been investigated to minimize the energy loss in sensitive heat and water evaporation. Furthermore, amines can be regenerated via different methods, such as electrochemically mediated regeneration (Wang et al. 2019a, Wang et al. 2019b), to minimize the cycle time and enhance energy efficiency.

7.2.2 Adsorption

In adsorption processes, CO_2 is adsorbed on porous materials (adsorbent) from its sources (Figure 7.4) and then released via either a reduction in pressure (pressure swing adsorption, PSA, or pressure vacuum swing adsorption, PVSA), an increase in temperature (temperature swing adsorption, TSA), or a combination of both (pressure-temperature swing adsorption, PTSA). Both physical (physisorption) and chemical (chemisorption) adsorption can be used for CO_2 capture, and many adsorbents have been investigated for this purpose, such as activated carbon (Plaza et al. 2010), silica (Tao et al. 2019), zeolites (Xiao, et al. 2008), amine sorbents (Xian, et al. 2016), metal oxides (Kim et al. 2015), metal-organic frameworks (MOFs) (Raksakoon et al. 2015), and carbonates (Zhao et al. 2013).

The development of materials and processes is the most significant topic in adsorption. The operating capacity of CO_2 and the selectivity of CO_2/N_2 are major factors to characterize the performance of adsorbents in the laboratory. Figure 7.5 shows a typical adsorption isotherm graph of N_2 and CO_2 at two temperatures. In a PSA process (assuming temperature is maintained as constant, T_1), pressure is increased from P_2 to P_1 for adsorption, then decreased from P_1 to P_2 for desorption. In this scenario, the apparent selectivity of CO_2/N_2 of this adsorbent can be written as V_1/V_1', which varies with temperature and the partial pressure of N_2/CO_2. The adsorption capacity of CO_2 for this adsorbent is $(V_1 - V_2)$ at T_1 from P_1 to P_2. In a TSA process (assuming pressure is maintained as constant, P_2), adsorption occurs at a lower temperature, T_1. Then adsorbents are heated up to T_2. The adsorption capacity of CO_2 for this adsorbent is $(V_2 - V_3)$ at P_2 from T_1 to T_2. It should be noted though, that adsorption is often accompanied by heat exchange and transfer, and temperature swings occur along with partial pressure changes. Although PSA and TSA indicate that the dominant operating variables are pressure and temperature, respectively, most adsorption processes are indeed PTSA if analysis becomes strict.

Physisorption is favoured in post-combustion carbon capture processes via PSA owing to its rapid swing speed and capability of being employed in a large scale (as high as 100,000 m^3/h – Webley 2014). In low CO_2 concentration scenarios

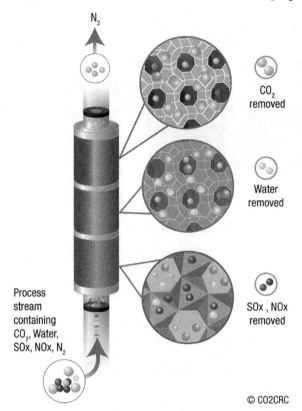

Figure 7.4 A typical sorbent adsorption process for capturing CO_2 (Image courtesy of CO2CRC, with permission to reuse)

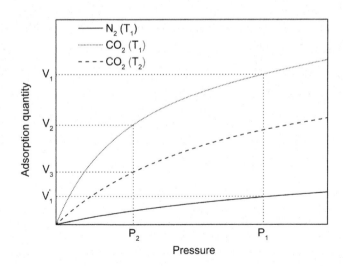

Figure 7.5 A representative of adsorption isotherm ($T_1 < T_2$)

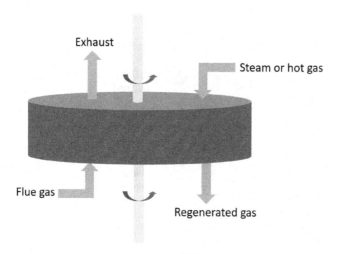

Figure 7.6 A schematic diagram of a rotary TSA facility

(natural gas power plants and direct air capture), chemisorption is favoured owing to its high selectivity and strong chemical bonding. The chemisorption process is mostly achieved by TSA to break the strong chemical bond between CO_2 and basic groups at higher temperatures to regenerate adsorbents, where the temperature change may be tens to hundreds kelvin. Thus, process intensification is necessary to achieve high heat and mass transfer, and thus, short cycle time. This can be achieved by material design or process innovation, such as hollow fibre adsorbents (Lively et al. 2009, Sujan et al. 2018), 3D printed adsorbents, and fluidization (using a fluidized bed to replace the fixed bed).

Rapid TSA also attracts much attention owing to technical innovation and engineering breakthroughs. The rotary wheel TSA drum (Figure 7.6, VeloxoTherm™) is usually packed with structured adsorbents and it rotates to shift from adsorption to desorption periodically. More flow streams are possible to achieve other adsorption steps, such as purge. The facility developed by Inventys Inc. is as fast as 60 seconds per cycle, at 30 tons per day, and currently targets $15 per ton of CO_2. The adsorption column, packed with structured sorbent, rotates to switch between adsorption of feed gas and desorption using steam for regeneration, via direct heating. Furthermore, Inventys Inc. is targeting a gigaton scale for future development.

7.2.3 Membranes

Membrane separation is a technology that can selectively separate different components from a mixture of gases and liquids via thin film materials. Membrane materials can be polymeric (e.g. cellulose acetate, polysulfone, and polyimide), inorganic (e.g. ceramic and metallic membranes) or a mixture of both (e.g. zeolite membranes, MOF membranes etc.) (Baker 2004, Powell and Qiao 2006, Chung et al. 2007). The separation of gases using membranes can be by both physical and chemical processes. The permeability of CO_2 and the selectivity of CO_2/N_2 are important parameters from the perspective of materials, while driving forces and mass transfer rates are extremely important for process operation. In membrane separation processes for carbon capture, the major driving force is the CO_2 partial pressure (i.e. pressure times CO_2 concentration) gradient. The separation mechanisms of gas molecules through a membrane can be categorized into five models: Knudsen diffusion, molecular sieving, solution-diffusion model, surface diffusion, and capillary condensation (Scholes et al. 2009) (Figure 7.7).

The PolarCap™ process, using polymeric membrane (Polaris™) developed by Membrane Technology and Research (MTR) Inc., has been demonstrated on a 1 ton CO_2/day scale, although the most economical run is still based on a 50–60% capture rate. Innovation in membrane materials has drawn significant interests to improve their performance, such as ultra-thin membranes to increase permeability (Tan et al. 2015) and mixed matrix membranes (MOF, ZIF) to increase selectivity (Xie et al. 2018). These membranes are, however, still very far from industrial application. Novel processes have also attracted much attention for achieving similar targets, such as the membrane contactor concepts being proposed and demonstrated, including the solvent gas-membrane (Scholes et al. 2014) and solvent microalgal-membrane systems (Zheng et al. 2016) to enhance the selectivity and driving force, and thus the mass transfer rate.

7.2.4 Chemical looping

Chemical looping (Fan 2011, Fennell and Anthony 2015) is a special technique that may be classified as one of the oxyfuel combustion methods. It was first proposed by Lewis et al. (1951) for the production of CO_2 from coal using an oxygen-carrier technique, and later proposed by Ishida and Jin (1994) as a solution to the mitigation of greenhouse gas. It requires an oxygen carrier, e.g. transition metal oxides (Me_xO_y), serving as an solid oxidant for the burning of fuels. The exhaust gas generally contains CO_2 and water only, making it ready for transportation and storage after water removal. Many chemicals have been investigated as oxygen carriers, such as monometallic oxides – e.g. Mn_2O_3/Mn_3O_4, CuO/Cu_2O, Fe_2O_3/Fe_3O_4, NiO/Ni, $CaSO_4/CaS$, and Co_3O_4/CoO (Mattisson et al. 2009) – or combined metal oxides, such as $(Mn_yFe_{1-y})O_x$, $(Mn_ySi_{1-y})O_x$, and $CaMnO_{3-\delta}$ (Rydén et al. 2014). The combustion process (Figure 7.8) can be described by the following reactions (*1* & *2*). In the first step (*1*), oxygen carrier (Me_xO_y) is oxidized by oxygen gas. Thereafter, the oxidized carrier (Me_xO_{y+1}) reacts with fuel ($C_\alpha H_\beta$) to generate heat (*2*). The gas exhaust is mainly CO_2 and H_2O, and pure CO_2 can be easily obtained by water vapour condensation.

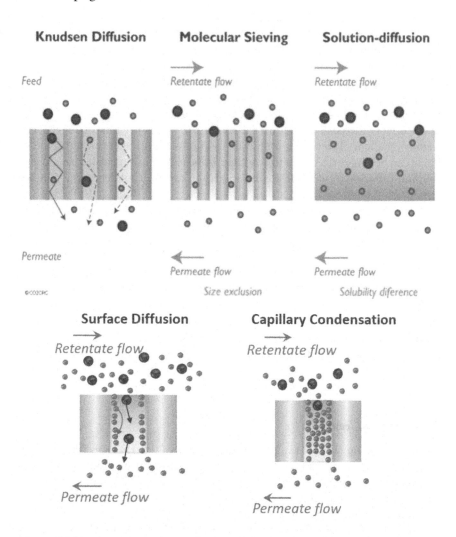

Figure 7.7 Membrane separation mechanisms (Image courtesy of CO2CRC, with permission to reuse)

$$2Me_xO_y + O_2 \rightarrow 2Me_xO_{y+1} \tag{1}$$

$$(2\alpha + 0.5\beta)Me_xO_{y+1} + C_\alpha H_\beta \rightarrow (2\alpha + 0.5\beta)Me_xO_y + \alpha CO_2 + 0.5\beta H_2O \tag{2}$$

Chemical looping enables the minimization of gas separation costs, owing to the high CO_2 purity in its exhaust stream; however, it may significantly reduce the overall power efficiency (Abanades et al. 2015). The estimated capture costs are expected to be ~US$22 per ton of CO_2 (Abanades et al. 2015). Investigations

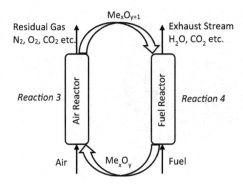

Figure 7.8 A simplified schematic chemical looping process

on more reactive, low-cost oxygen carriers, and efficient reactors are critical to achieving this low-cost target.

7.2.5 *Mineral carbonation*

Mineral carbonation is a method for capturing and storing CO_2 at the same time. The mineral materials for capturing CO_2 can be mineral wastes (e.g. metallurgy wastes or fly ash) or metal oxides (i.e. Me_xO_y, such as CaO and MgO, often mixtures) (Maroto-Valer et al. 2005a, Romanov et al. 2015). The major barrier for this technology is the slow reaction kinetics, which can be overcome by elevating temperature or adding a catalyst, such as carbonic anhydrase enzyme (Figure 7.9) in an aqueous solution (Wang 2015). The availability of these mineral wastes is another challenge, the geographical mismatch between CO_2 and mineral waste is also a barrier to the large-scale deployment of carbonization for CCS.

The carbonation process also provides a pathway for capturing CO_2, while reusing oxides, known as carbonate looping (Sun et al. 2016, Wang 2015). Similar to chemical looping, carbonate looping (Figure 7.10) requires two reactors, one for carbonation (Carbonator, 3), another for regeneration (Calciner, 4). Taking calcium looping as an example, the operation temperature in the carbonator is often elevated to ~600–700°C to achieve high reaction kinetics, while the regeneration process requires an even higher temperature of ~900–1000°C. The regeneration temperature could be reduced if a vacuum condition was imposed on the calcination system (Ball and Sceats 2010). Carbonate looping is specially suitable for high temperature gas sources, but these high temperature requirements inevitably incur a high energy penalty.

$$Me_xO_y + CO_2 \rightarrow Me_xCO_{y+2} \qquad (3)$$

$$Me_xCO_{y+22} \rightarrow Me_xO_y + CO_2 \qquad (4)$$

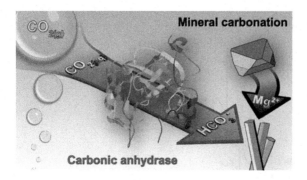

Figure 7.9 A carbonic anhydrase catalyzed mineralization process of MgO (Power et al. 2016; with permission to reuse)

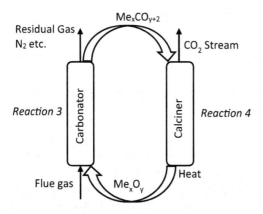

Figure 7.10 A simplified schematic of the carbonate looping process

7.2.6 Cryogenic distillation

Cryogenic distillation (low temperature distillation, Figure 7.11) is a method to condense CO_2 at a low temperature to produce concentrated liquid CO_2 for transport and storage, while the other gases (mainly N_2) flow through to the atmosphere (Surovtseva et al. 2011, Scholes et al. 2013). The advantage of cryogenic distillation is that the CO_2 can be captured with an extremely high purity (99.999%) and compressed in one step. Cryogenic is also technically mature in regards to super-large-scale gas separations (hundreds of millions of tons per annum).

7.2.7 Other techniques

There are other technologies being developed for carbon capture, including algae cultivation (Zheng et al. 2016) or a combination of the different technologies

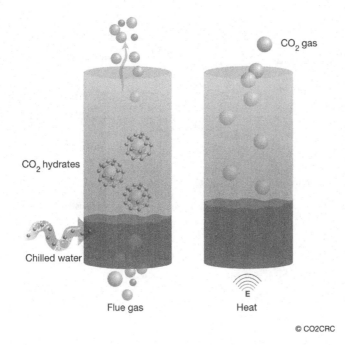

CO₂ gas

CO₂ hydrates

Chilled water

Flue gas

Heat

E

© CO2CRC

Figure 7.11 A simplified diagram of cryogenics distillation (Image courtesy of CO2CRC, with permission to reuse)

mentioned above (Yong et al. 2016). However, more efforts are needed to make these technologies competitive with those mentioned so far (7.2.1–7.2.5). currently, there are many active projects focusing on direct air capture (DAC). Although the overall costs are still relatively high, they are expected to be reduced significantly in the years to come. For example, the CEO of Carbon Engineering Ltd., Steve Oldham, states that they are aiming for US$100 per ton of CO_2 (Energy Transition Climate Action Summit).

7.3 Carbon storage

Once CO_2 is captured via the techniques discussed above, it is compressed to a 'supercritical state', which is analogous to the form of CO_2 at least 800 metres underground (Intergovernmental Panel on Climate Change 2005), and then transported by pipeline or storage tanks to be injected into sedimentary basins, where CO_2 will be stored securely and permanently. Ideal sequestration structures are suggested to have high CO_2 injectivity and storage capacity, impermeable caprock, and stable stratum structure (Bachu 2000). Depleted oil and gas reservoirs, unmineable coal seams, and deep saline reservoirs (Figure 7.12) have been proved to be reliable storage formations by *the Intergovernmental Panel on Climate Change (IPCC) Special Report on CCS,*[1] because they have naturally

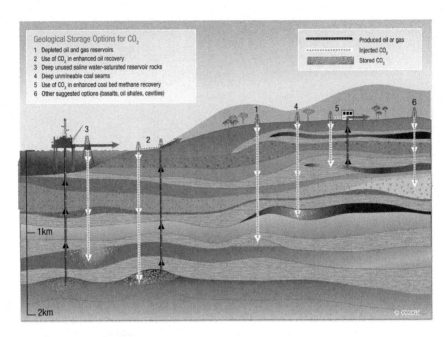

Figure 7.12 CO₂ geological storage options (Image courtesy of CO2CRC, with permission to reuse)

stored crude oil, natural gas, brine over millions of years (Intergovernmental Panel on Climate Change 2005). To date, the overall high cost of CCS is still the largest challenge. Thus, enhanced oil recovery (EOR), enhanced gas recovery (EGR), and enhanced coal seam gas (an unconventional nature gas) recovery (ECBM) (Figure 7.12) have attracted increasing interests and been broadly deployed as win-win opportunities for CO_2 sequestration owing to the financial benefits and carbon reductions that can be achieved.

Depleted oil and gas reservoirs are considered to be the most suitable underground formations owing to their long history of exploration and production, large amount of reservoir data, and reusable infrastructure such as injection and surface facilities (Tomić et al. 2018). These advantages can reduce storage costs, enable the evaluation of the precise storage capacity, and bring minimal risk and uncertainty of leakage. Deep saline aquifers are also considered as target repositories owing to their large storage capacity. However, storage projects in these formations are not widely deployed due to the relative high costs, impacts on seismicity, and the logistics of sequestration (Tao and Clarens 2013).

7.3.1 CO₂ storage mechanisms

The storage of CO_2 falls into two categories: physical/displacement storage and chemical storage. Physical/displacement storage includes stratigraphic and

Table 7.1 Characteristics of physical and chemical trapping mechanism (Bradshaw et al., 2007) (with permission to reuse)

Trapping mechanism	Characteristics			
	Nature of Trapping	Effective Timeframe	Occurrence in Basin	Capacity
Stratigraphic and structural	CO_2 remains as a fluid below the seal rock	Immediate	Dependent on basins' tectonic evolution	Significant
Residual	CO_2 fills the spaces between pores of the grains of the rocks	Immediate	Along migration pathway of CO_2	Very large
Adsorption	CO_2 preferentially adsorbs onto coal surface	Immediate	Thick coal seams	Low
Dissolution	CO_2 dissolves into formation fluid	Immediate	Along migration pathway of CO_2 both up and down dip	Very large
Mineralization	CO_2 reacts with rock to form new stable precipitates	Tens to thousands of years	Along migration pathway of CO_2	Significant

structural trapping and residual trapping, while chemical storage refers to dissolution trapping and mineral precipitation trapping (Sun et al. 2018). The comparison of the two mechanisms and their characteristics are illustrated in Table 7.1.

7.3.1.1 Stratigraphic and structural trapping

Stratigraphic and structural trapping is the primary storage mechanism at the CO_2 injection stage (Zhang and Song 2014). Theoretically, the buoyancy of injected CO_2 is smaller than that of other liquids present in the pore space, and therefore it will percolate up through the porous rocks until reaching the top of the formation, which would be impermeable caprock (Bachu et al. 1994). CO_2 will then accumulate in this location with both vertical and lateral seals (Figure 7.13).

7.3.1.2 Residual trapping

Residual trapping is intrinsically linked with stratigraphic and structural trapping, and it generally takes place after injection (Bachu et al. 2007). This mechanism is based on the irreducible gas saturation, left by the migrated CO_2 stream or plume when water returns to pore spaces, after which CO_2 is partially expelled from the pore space by H_2O and partially resides in the pore space (Figure 7.14). More specifically, owing to buoyancy forces, the injected CO_2 flows to the top of the

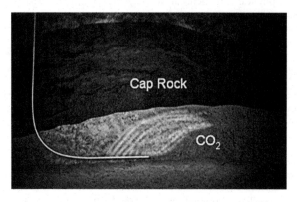

Figure 7.13 Stratigraphic and structural trapping mechanism (CO_2 Capture Project (CCP 2015), with permission to reuse)

Figure 7.14 Residual trapping mechanism (CO_2 Capture Project (CCP 2015), with permission to reuse)

aquifer through porous rocks, which leads to an increase in CO_2 saturation and creates vertical and lateral migration paths. When the injection stops, CO_2 continues to flow upward and displace other liquids at the leading edge of the plume owing to its low density, while at the trailing edge fluids in turn displace CO_2 (Juanes et al. 2006). In this process, the CO_2 phase is disconnected and become residual and immobile.

7.3.1.3 Solubility trapping

Solubility trapping (Figure 7.15) is the process where CO_2 mixes with and then dissolve in brine through diffusion, dispersion, and convection (Bachu et al. 2007). In solubility trapping, water first comes to contact with CO_2, and will

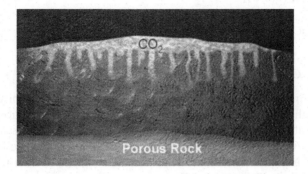

Figure 7.15 Solubility trapping mechanism (CO₂ Capture Project (CCP 2015), with permission to reuse)

be saturated very quickly. Then the CO_2-saturated water will sink, owing to its higher density than the original liquid; thereafter, more fresh water will contact CO_2 and dissolve it. Thus, CO_2 can be stored in a quite secure and dissolved state (Gluyas and Mathias 2013, Nardi et al. 2013).

7.3.1.4 Mineral trapping

Mineral trapping occurs on the interface of mineral grains (silicate or carbonate) and the CO_2 dissolved in water. The dissolution of CO_2 in water can produce a weak carbonic acid (H_2CO_3) and ionic substances, for example bicarbonate (HCO_3^-), both of which chemically react with the mineral grains present in rock to form solid carbonate minerals (Gunter et al. 2004). This process can be rapid or extremely slow, but effectively and permanently stabilizes CO_2 to rock (Grobe et al. 2009). One example is the magnesium in rock grain, producing the solid mineral $MgCO_3$ on the grain's surface through a chemical reaction with CO_3^{2-} in water. Several common chemical reactions of mineralization trapping are listed in Equations 5–11.

$$CO_2 + H_2O \leftrightarrow H_2CO_3 \tag{5}$$

$$H_2CO_3 = H^+ + HCO_3^- \tag{6}$$

$$HCO_3^- \leftrightarrow CO_3^{2-} + H^+ \tag{7}$$

$$Ca^{2+} + HCO_3^- = CaCO_3(S) + H^+ \tag{8}$$

$$Ca^{2+} + CO_3^{2-} = CaCO_3(S) \tag{9}$$

$$Mg^{2+} + HCO_3^- = MgCO_3(S) + H^+ \qquad (10)$$

$$Mg^{2+} + CO_3^{2-} = MgCO_3(S) \qquad (11)$$

7.3.2 Mechanisms of CO₂-EOR/EGR/ECBM-based storage

CO_2-EOR has been investigated for a few decades. When injected CO_2 mixes with crude oil at high pressure, the interfacial tension between them reduces, evidently, and gradually minimizes to near zero, which leads to a miscible state (Ampomah et al. 2016, Hosseini et al. 2018). CO_2 can also reduce the viscosity of crude oil, making it a qualified solvent. Thus it could swell and liberate the remaining trapped oil in the fluid (Yin 2015).

CO_2-EGR is a relatively new area under discussion which has not been studied as comprehensively as CO_2-EOR. The CO_2-EGR technology has three principal mechanisms. The first one is to maintain pressure when the natural gas field is depleted (Amer et al. 2018). Then the injected fluid re-pressurizes the gas reservoir, producing more hydrocarbon gas. Moreover, the density of CO_2 is higher than natural gas by 2–6 times, as a result, the injected CO_2 migrates downwards, displacing the natural gas upwards (Kuuskraa et al. 2013). Third, the viscosity of CO_2 is higher than that of methane, which is conducive to establishing a relatively stable displacement front owing to the relatively lower mobility ratio (Shi et al. 2017). The primary mechanism of CO_2-ECBM is competitive adsorption. The absorbability of CO_2 to coal seams is much higher than that of methane (CH_4) (Jiang et al. 2015), and the adsorption of CO_2 to shale surface is stronger than that of CH_4 in shale gas (Mohagheghian et al. 2019).

CO_2 storage mechanisms for EOR/EGR/ECBM differ from that for deep saline aquifers, which stems from the influence of the oil and gas underground. The first storage mechanism is the replacement effect that is correlated with CO_2-EOR/EGR/ECBM mechanisms mentioned above. The pore space produced by oil and gas extraction is filled with CO_2, which is similar to the void replacement effect. Other storage mechanisms, like stratigraphic and structural trapping, residual trapping, solubility trapping, and mineral precipitation, also occur in CO_2 utilization-based storage. However, some slight differences should be highlighted. The performance of CO_2 in single brine or oil phase is different from that in the co-existence of oil and gas, and the CO_2 solubility and CO_2 partition coefficients in oil/gas-water are different (Atia and Mohammedi 2018). Furthermore, the mineralization trapping of CO_2 is less evident in oil/gas reservoirs, since the oil/gas film on the surface of the pore structure which isolates the contact between mineral grains and weak carbonic acids (Zhou et al. 2019).

The injected CO_2 is trapped by at least one of the above mechanisms that take place at different rates, from days to years to thousands of years, for any storage formation. When, which, and how long the trapping type occurs are determined by the CO_2 flow behaviour and the timescale involved. With increasing time

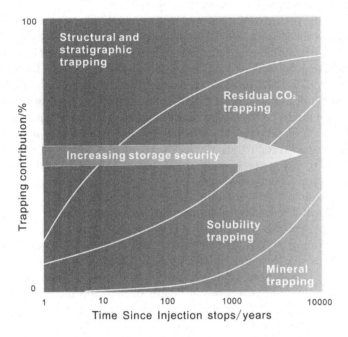

Figure 7.16 CO₂ trapping mechanisms and timescales (Intergovernmental Panel on Climate Change 2005; with permission to reuse)

and migration, the predominant storage mechanism changes, during which an increasing volume of CO_2 binds residually in the pore spaces, dissolved in the water, or precipitated with mineral grains, and so sequestration becomes more and more secure (Figure 7.16) (Intergovernmental Panel on Climate Change 2005, Gluyas and Mathias 2013, Nardi et al. 2013, Zhang and Song 2014).

7.3.3 Overview of CO₂-EOR/EGR/ECBM technology

CO_2-EOR was proposed in 1952 in a patent (Whorton et al. 1952) in the US. Then the first commercial CO_2-EOR flood was launched in the SACROC field in 1972 (Merchant 2017). By far most of the operational and completed CO_2-EOR projects are located in the Permian Basin in the US. These projects had produced oil at around 350,000 barrels a day (or 10 million tons per year), accounting for nearly 6% of the total onshore oil production in the US (Nuñez-López and Moskal 2019). More than 70% of the injected CO_2 is from nearby natural CO_2 fields and reservoirs where CO_2 can be exploited at a low cost (McGlade 2019). This is particularly evident in Colorado State, New Mexico State, and Arizona State. Other CO_2 sources are anthropogenic facilities where CO_2 can be captured, for example, the Century and Petra Nova plants in Texas (McGlade 2019).

CO_2-EOR could improve oil recovery by 8–15% theoretically, and meanwhile 30–40% of the injected CO_2 is stored underground (Zhang et al. 2016). A typical project is the Weyburn-Midale in Saskatchewan (Canada) where CO_2 is sourced from a gasification plant in North Dakota, then transported by pipeline to improve the production of oil (Cavanagh and Rostron 2013). In 2018, there were about 375 EOR projects across the US, Canada, China, Brazil, Croatia, Turkey, Saudi Arabia, United Arab Emirates, and other countries, 98 of which were carried out by CO_2 flooding. The experience from these applications suggests that 6–15% of the original oil in place can be recovered using CO_2 flooding. The increased production is more than 2 million barrels oil per day, which is predicted to increase to 4.5 million barrels per day by 2040, with a share of 4% of total oil production (IEA 2019).

CBM is very widely distributed in many nations such as the US, Canada, Australia, and China. The traditional production method is to reduce the pore pressure within the coalbeds by drilling wells, imposing vacuum pressure, then pumping water (King Abdullah Petroleum, Al-Fattah et al. 2011) or CO_2 into dewatered coalbeds underground. In the CONSOL project in the US, CO_2 was injected into coalbeds from 2001 to 2014. More than 3, 000 tons of CO_2 were injected into two thin coal seams at depths of 375–500 metres by May 2013. No leakage has been observed since then, indicating that the injected CO_2 remains stored in the coal seams (Meier and Sharma 2015). In China, a single well micro-pilot CO_2-ECBM test was implemented in southern Qinshui Basin in 2004 (Figure 7.17). A total of 19.2 tons of liquid CO_2 was successfully injected into the N°3 coal seam (at a depth of 478 metres), and meanwhile, the CBM recovery has increased by more than 40% compared to the drainage production (Jiang et al. 2015). However, many problems postpone the deployment of CO2-ECBM technology, for example, coal swelling around injection wells during the injection process.

The availability of reservoir data and the presence of sealed caprocks in gas fields is beneficial to CO_2-EGR. Nevertheless, CO_2-EGR is still in a very early stages of development (Jiang et al. 2014). Few experiments or simulations on mechanisms have been conducted (He 2008, Rafiee and Ramazanian 2011, Yang, et al. 2012, Dali et al. 2013, Guo et al. 2015). The feasibility study on CO_2-EGR in the tight gas field of the Ordos basin in China indicates that it is theoretically feasible (Shi et al. 2017). The numerical simulation on EGR and CO_2 sequestration in western Poland has also been investigated, which confirms that CO_2-EGR is technically feasible but also presents challenges that it lacks economic feasibility (Klimkowski et al. 2015). Supercritical CO_2-based fracturing technology, associated with enhanced shale gas recovery, is also promising because it consumes less water and has a large potential for CO_2 sequestration (Mohagheghian et al. 2019, Zhou et al. 2019). To date, three CO_2-EGR pilot tests (the CSEGR pilot test in The Netherlands, the Budafa Szinfelleti in Hungary, and the Krechba in Algeria) are in operation to examine the feasibility of CO_2 storage in the process of CO_2-EGR in medium and high permeability gas fields (Shi et al. 2017).

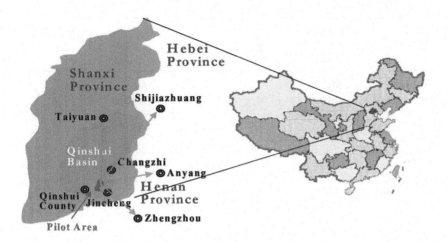

Figure 7.17 Location of China's CO_2-ECBM pilot (Wong et al. 2006; with permission to reuse)

7.3.4 Screening criteria for CO₂-EOR/EGR/ECBM storage sites

The purpose of site selection is to identify basins suitable for CO_2 storage and further evaluate the storage capacity, which is fundamental for storage deployment. As mentioned at the beginning of Section 7.3, desired geological structures should have sufficient storage capacity, large CO_2 injectivity, and impermeable caprocks. Accordingly, screening criteria are discussed at the basin scale, sub-basin scale, and country/region scale (Bachu 2003, Wei et al. 2013). However, uniform standards at a certain level are not likely to be established across the world, since the deposits and the particular characteristics, such as the lithological heterogeneity, thickness, density, and permeability, of each continent, or even each basin, are complicated and generally unique. In addition to geological features, reservoir conditions, such as reservoir type and rock wettability, are also of great significance when screening sites. Broadly, applicable selection criteria for CO_2-EOR/EWR/ECBM based storage sites are provided in Table 7.2.

7.3.5 Storage capacity

Many organizations (US Department of Energy, Carbon Sequestration Leadership Forum, and ECOFYS, etc.) and scholars (Stefan, 2008; Zhou et al. 2008, Shen et al. 2009, De Silva and Ranjith 2012, Jiang et al. 2018, Sun et al. 2018) have proposed calculation methodologies towards general or specific basins to estimate the storage capacity in different formations. A pyramid model proposed by the Carbon Sequestration Leadership Forum (CSLF) is very well accepted.

Table 7.2 Screening criteria for CO_2-EOR/EGR/ECBM-based storage sites

Criteria	CO_2-EOR		CO_2-EWR	CO_2-ECBM
	Miscible	Immiscible		
Capacity	>4 Mt	—	>2 Mt	>1 Mt
Reservoir type	Sandstones and carbonates	—	Sandstones and carbonates	—
Rock wettability	Water wet or week oil wet	—	—	—
Depth	>450 m	600–900 m	800–2,500 m	300–1, 500 m
Thickness	<40 m	10–0 m	> 20 m	> 10 m
Temperature	60–121°C	>35°C	>3°C	>35°C
Pressure	>Minimum miscibility and < fracture pressures	>7.5 MPa	>7.5 MPa	>7.5 MPa
Porosity	>3%	>3%	>10%	>5%
Permeability	>5 mD	>0.1 mD	>20 mD	>1 mD
Caprock thickness	>10 m	>10 m	>20 m	>10 m
Ash content	—	—	—	<25%
Oil density	<0.88	>0.9	—	—
Oil viscosity	<10 mPa·s	10–1,000 mPa·s	—	—
Oil saturation	>0.3	0.3–0.7	—	—
Salinity	—	—	>3 g/L	—
Methane content	—	—	—	2.5–50 m³/t
Coal rank	—	—	—	0.6–1.5%

Sources: (Sun et al. 2018, Tapia et al. 2016, Wei et al. 2013, Bachu 2003, Gluyas and Mathias 2013, Baines and Worden 2004, Grobe et al. 2009)

It involves the uncertainties of geological and economic conditions and therefore defines storage capacity at four levels: theoretical, effective, practical, and matched (Figure 7.18). The theoretical capacity is the maximum capacity given that all injected CO_2 can be stored, which is an ideal condition with great uncertainties. The effective capacity is smaller because it takes a number of technical restrictions and reservoir conditions into account. Non-technical considerations, such as legal and policy, infrastructure, as well as financial challenges, are included in the practical level. The matched level is the smallest; however, it is the closest to actual capacity, which depends on CO_2 sources, storage sites, injectivity rate, and other issues.

So far, CO_2 storage potential in many countries has been evaluated (Table 7.3). Among the four storage options, the deep saline aquifer option has a larger storage capacity than oil/gas fields and coal seam reservoirs. It should be particularly noted though that shale gas resources (not illustrated in Table 7.3) have high storage capacities. With a total of 188 Tcm (trillion cubic metres) of shale

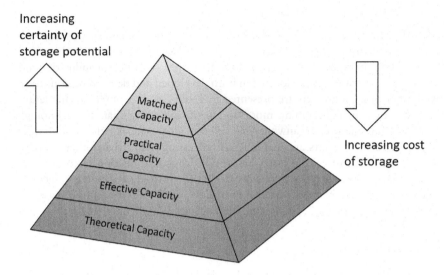

Figure 7.18 The pyramid model of storage capacity (Stefan et al. 2007; with permission to reuse)

Table 7.3 Storage capacity in some countries (unit: Gt)

Country/region	Deep Saline Aquifers	Oil Reservoirs	Gas Reservoirs	Coal Beds	Total
China	1,826.1	4.9	4.3	10.8	1,846.1
the US	2,379.0–21,633.0	186.0–232.0		54.0–113.0	2,619.0–21,978.0
Australia	210.1–685.4	16.5 (offshore: ~15.6)		—	226.6–701.9
Canada	400.0	4.0		2.0	406.0
Europe	350.0	30.0		1.5	381.5
United Kingdom	4.6–46.7	1.1–3.6	6.3	—	11.8–56.6
Japan	142.6	3.5		—	146.1
Global				487.6	

Sources: (Sun et al. 2018, Abdul-Razzak 2008, Folger 2017, Takahashi et al. 2009, Carbon Storage Taskforce 2009)

gas resources (not illustrated in Table 7.3) being potentially recoverable globally, CO_2-EGR can contribute as much as 71 Tcm and store 281 Gt (gigaton) of CO_2 economically (Godec et al. 2014). Regarding total storage capacity, the US presents the largest in the world, at 2,619.0–21,978.0 billion metric tons. The storage capacity in China, which is the largest CO_2 emitter, is estimated to be 1846.1 Gt of CO_2, which is approximately 140 times the amount of its carbon emissions in 2017 (13.1 Gt).

7.4 Snapshot of international projects

In 2018, there were 43 large-scale facilities (18 in commercial operation, 5 under construction, and 20 in various stages of development) around the world (Global CSS Institute 2018). These projects centre on different industries and components of CCS and are located in both developed and developing countries. A number of CCS projects are presented in Table 7.4. It is observed that large-scale deployment is becoming more dominant, indicating that the technology is increasingly mature. Meanwhile, the primary CO_2 sources before 2014 were power generation plants and natural gas processing. After that, other sources, such as the coal-to-liquid industry and the hydrogen production sector are also considered. More recently, deploying CCS in the iron and steel industry seem to become a research frontier, which is worth investigation in the future. (Cormos 2016, Leeson et al. 2017, Griffin and Hammond 2019, Xi et al. 2019).

7.5 Challenges

CCS has been investigated for many decades, and significant achievements have been made towards its deployment. However, the overall scale of CCS projects is still significantly lower than a so-called 'meaningful scale', i.e. a relatively small-scale power plant in China (500 MWh) generates ~8,000–10,000 tons of flue gas (~15 vol.%) per day, which is well beyond the capacity of current mature technologies to capture (absorption, adsorption, and membrane). In this case, cryogenics may be the only capable technique to capture CO_2 from flue gases on such a scale.

CO_2 utilization and geological storage have been encouraged in recent years owing to increased climate changes. However, it is not completely similar to traditional CO_2-EOR/EGR/ECBM. Firstly, most of the traditional CO_2 injection projects still utilize natural CO_2 sources, e.g. from natural gas fields, rather than anthropogenic CO_2 emissions. Secondly, their ultimate objectives are different. The principal target for oil and gas companies is to maximize oil and gas extraction, rather than solving environmental concerns. Nevertheless, these injection trials accumulate experience for CO_2 storage, and in the short term facilitate emissions reduction. However, the enhanced oil/gas extraction will increase greenhouse gas emissions, as it is likely to be used in fossil fuel production. As such, it becomes a dilemma for these companies in balancing fossil-fuel production and emissions reduction. This has become vaguer, as the software that is used for reservoir simulation and production optimization in the oil/gas sector currently is unable to reflect the exact storage-based production process, consider CO_2 storage, which makes it difficult for these enterprises to confirm the management of maximum benefits under the pressure of climate change.

Although CO_2-EOR is a mature technique, the US has proposed the Next Generation CO_2-EOR technology to meet future demands (Kuuskraa et al. 2013). This prospect has higher requirements in terms of robust reservoir characterization, enhanced fluid injectivity via near-well completion, and extensive

Table 7.4 Significant global CCUS projects

Project	Country	Year of Operation	Main Area	Scale	Capture Capacity (Mt/year)	Status	Industry
Sleipner CO$_2$ Storage	Norway	1996	Capture and dedicated storage	Large-scale	1.00	Operational	Natural gas processing
Ketzin Pilot Project	Germany	2004	Dedicated storage	Pilot	0.01	Completed	Power generation
Pembina Cardium CO$_2$ Monitoring Pilot	Canada	2005	Capture and CO$_2$-EOR	Pilot	0.02–0.03	Completed	Natural gas processing
Sinopec Zhongyuan Carbon Capture Utilization and Storage Pilot Project	China	2006	Capture and CO$_2$-EOR	Pilot	0.12	Operational	Chemical production
Renfrew Oxy-fuel (Oxycoal 2) project	UK	2007	Capture	Pilot	N/A	Completed	Power generation
Jilin Oil Field EOR Demonstration Project	China	2008	CO$_2$-EOR	Demonstration	0.10–0.35	Operational	Natural gas processing
Snøhvit CO$_2$ Storage	Norway	2008	Capture and dedicated storage	Large-scale	0.70	Operational	Natural gas processing
CO2CRC Otway	Australia	2008	Capture and dedicated storage	Demonstration	0.01	Operational	Natural gas processing
Karlshamn Field Project	Sweden	2009	Capture	Demonstration	0.01	Completed	Power generation

(continued)

Project	Country	Year of Operation	Main Area	Scale	Capture Capacity (Mt/year)	Status	Industry
CO_2 Sequestration Field Test: Deep Unamenable Lignite Seam	USA	2009	CO_2-ECBM	Pilot	N/A	Completed	N/A
Cranfield Project	USA	2009	Monitor and dedicated storage	Pilot	N/A	Operational	N/A
Chongqing Hechuan Shuanghuai Power Plant CO_2 Capture Industrial Demonstration Project	China	2010	Capture and utilization	Demonstration	0.10	Operational	Power generation
Brindisi CO_2 Capture Pilot Plant	Italy	2010	Capture	Pilot	N/A	Completed	Power generation
Shenhua Group Ordos Carbon Capture and Storage (CCS) Demonstration Project	China	2011	Dedicated storage	Demonstration	0.10	Completed	Coal-to-liquids
La Pereda Calcium Looping Pilot Plant	Spain	2012	Capture	Demonstration	N/A	Completed	Power generation
CarbFix Project	Iceland	2012	Dedicated storage	Demonstration	N/A	Operational	Power generation
Callide Oxyfuel Project	Australia	2012	Capture	Demonstration	N/A	Completed	Power generation

Project	Country	Year	Type	Scale	Capacity	Status	Industry
Boundary Dam CCS	Canada	2014	Capture and CO_2-EOR	Large-scale	1.00	Operational	Power generation
Hadong – Dry-sorbent CO_2 Capture System Test	South Korea	2014	Capture	Demonstration	0.05	Operational	Power generation
Port Jerome CO_2 Capture Plant	France	2015	Capture	Demonstration	0.10	Operational	Hydrogen production
Quest	Canada	2015	Capture and dedicated storage	Large-scale	1.00	Operational	Hydrogen production
Karamay Dunhua Oil Technology CCUS EOR Project	China	2015	CO_2-EOR	Demonstration	0.10	Operational	Chemical production
Tomakomai CCS Demonstration Project	Japan	2016	Capture and dedicated storage	Demonstration	0.10	Operational	Hydrogen production
Abu Dhabi CCS (Steel industries)	United Arab Emirates	2016	Capture and CO_2-EOR	Large-scale	0.80	Operational	Iron and steel
Illinois Industrial CCS	USA	2017	Capture and dedicated storage	Large-scale	1.00	Operational	Ethanol production
Geothermal Plant with CO_2 Re-injection	Croatia	2018	Capture	Demonstration	0.05	Operational	Power generation
Haifeng Carbon Capture Test Platform	China	2018	Capture	Large-scale	0.03	Operational	N/A
Gorgon Carbon Dioxide Injection	Australia	2019	Capture and dedicated storage	Large-scale	3.40–4.00	Operational	Natural gas processing

monitoring, diagnostics, and process control, all of which are significant for reducing the unproductive channelling of CO_2 through high permeability reservoir flow paths (Kuuskraa et al. 2013). Regarding CO_2-ECBM, several obstacles are observed after a large body of laboratory experiments and fields tests. They include: a lack of guidelines that define "unmineable coals" in the basin scale, and insufficient geological and reservoir data to identify favourable settings for CO_2 injection and storage in coal, particularly deep coal seams. The other challenge is, a weak ability to develop site or location models for coal swelling when the pores contain multiple fluids (e.g. methane, N_2, water, and CO_2), which is crucial to understand the dynamics of CO_2/methane exchange under actual reservoir conditions (Li and Fang 2014). As for CO_2-EGR technology, it is still under pro-active study. The issues caused by mixing CO_2 and natural gas are believed to be a critical reason as to why the CO_2-EGR process has received far less attention. In the case of gas-gas mixing, the injected CO_2 makes its way to the production wells, which is called CO_2-breakthrough. At this stage, natural gas production starts to drop noticeably, while the production rate of CO_2 begins to increase significantly (Atia and Mohammedi 2018).

Economically, it should be noted that the cost of capture and storage is still high, which restricts the deployment of large-scale demonstration projects. Despite this, CO_2-EOR projects have been operated widely in the US, the successful operation of which is aided by incentive policies and tax subsidies. The US government provides an example of how policy incentives facilitate CO_2-EOR deployment. In the 1980s, encountered the declining domestic oil production, the America Crude Oil Windfall Profit Tax 1980 kick-started the EOR industry by significantly reducing its tax burden (Friedmann and Mayer 1980). More recently, the 45Q tax credit in America has been amended to provide a tax reduction of \$35/t CO_2 for 12 years for CO_2 utilization and geological storage projects (Fan et al. 2019). By contrast, most of the world has not implemented economic stimulus measures yet to promote this carbon reduction technology.

The other challenge is the low perception of CO_2 storage projects among the public. Most people have a general knowledge of climate change and CO_2, but their understandings of the scientific dimensions are much lower (Itaoka et al. 2013). The primary reason is the safety of sequestration. Research has revealed that earthquakes, and CO_2 leakage caused by accidents or fluid migration in poorly sealed formations, are extremely harmful to human beings (Wallquist et al. 2011), surface water (Smith et al. 2011), and plants and animals (Polson et al. 2012). These risks are likely to lead to a delay in CCS deployment and transitioning to a low-carbon society (Palmgren et al. 2004, Wassermann et al. 2011) because the public believes that CCS should not be used before more sustainable solutions become widely available (van Alphen et al. 2007). In addition, cost plays a role in individuals' attitudes towards CO_2 storage. Investment in energy technologies is highly encouraged by the public, but this support decreases when cost information is offered (Curry 2005). Moreover, if consumers are required to be responsible for the construction of additional infrastructure in some form, which may result in increasing electricity prices, they might in turn express little enthusiasm

(Wallquist et al. 2012). Furthermore, from the perspective of emission reduction measures, renewable energy options are the most preferred solution (Curry et al. 2007, de Best-Waldhober et al. 2011), while the public is unfamiliar with CCS and CCUS in many countries (Curry et al. 2007, Tokushige et al. 2007).

7.6 Future trends

CCS has been internationally accepted as a key component in technological roadmaps to mitigate anthropogenic climate change along a relatively fast and cheap route. It is believed that CO_2 utilization and geological storage technologies will play a key role in meeting both this climate target and energy demand in the years to come. CO_2-EOR, which has been investigated thoroughly since the 1950s, is considered the most economical way at present, as it is relatively mature and its benefit of enabling additional crude oil production can partially offset the costs of CO_2 capture, transport, and storage.

Several issues should be highlighted to promote the deployment of CCS effectively and securely. Foremost, integrity of CO_2 storage should be ensured to avoid CO_2 migrating back to the surface and thence to the atmosphere. Several actions are recommended: identifying sites with suitable geology that traps CO_2, screening and avoiding wells that would create a conduit for CO_2 to reach the surface, and enhancing monitoring and field surveillance to detect leakage.

The cost of full chain CCS and CCUS has so far prevented them from entering mainstream use. The technical assessment of larger scale capture techniques is essential for meeting the demands of real, industrial scale power plants. Economic assessment of industrial scale capture technologies is also essential, as capture costs drop significantly with scale. Only the oil/gas sector is profitable in the full life cycle, depending on the increased fossil fuel production.

There are two measures for developing storage projects and even CCS and CCUS deployment. The first is strengthening research to overcome the above challenges and further improve production, leading to larger profits. The second is implementing political and economic intervention, either incentives or tax relief, to increase enterprise enthusiasm, particularly for CO_2-EGR and CO_2-ECBM technologies that are relatively far from commercial application.

To increase individuals' awareness of CO_2 geological storage, several actions may be effective. As the general public expresses positive responses when benefits are introduced (Ashworth et al. 2012, L'Orange Seigo et al. 2014), information related to 'CC(U)S enabling an effective transition to sustainable energy future' or 'the deployment providing local benefits like new employment' could make CCS projects more attractive. Moreover, trust has been seen as an essential element to public support, so the context and reputation of leaders are important elements for building that trust (Terwel et al. 2009, Li et al. 2017). It is therefore suggested to ask people or a media outlet with high reputations in the community near the deployment location to publicize the benefits of CO_2 storage.

To conclude, in the future, economical capture techniques, efficient utilization, and geological storage of CO_2 may be the best way for carbon emission reduction, and CO_2-EOR is an inevitable choice and will surely have great prospects in countries with carbon-intensive policies and integration of regional CC(U)S chains such as China and other BRI countries.

Note

1 This is the first international report that incorporating CO_2 capture, transportation, and storage into the CCS system and systematically introducing CCS from technical, economic, environmental, public, and legal perspectives.

References

Abanades, JC, Arias, B, Lyngfelt, A, Mattisson, T, Wiley, DE, Li, H, Ho, MT, Mangano, E & Brandani, S 2015, 'Emerging CO_2 capture systems', *International Journal of Greenhouse Gas Control*, vol. 40, pp. 126–166.

Abdul-razzak, S 2008, *Carbon Capture and Sequestration: In the Canadian Context*. Available: www.eng.mcmaster.ca/sites/default/files/uploads/carbon_capture_and_sequestration.pdf.

Abu-zahra, MRM, Niederer, JPM, Feron, PHM & Versteeg, GF 2007, 'CO_2 capture from power plants part II. A parametric study of the economical performance based on mono-ethanolamine', *International Journal of Greenhouse Gas Control*, vol. 1, pp. 135–142.

Amer, MA, Ghazi, S, Ali, S, Zafar, T & Riaz, M 2018, 'Enhanced gas recovery by CO_2 injection method in depleted gas reservoirs', *Archives of Petroleum & Environmental Biotechnology*, vol. 144, p. 1.

Ampomah, W, Balch, R, Cather, M, Rose-coss, D, Dai, Z, Heath, J, Dewers, T & Mozley, P 2016, 'Evaluation of CO_2 storage mechanisms in co_2 enhanced oil recovery sites: application to morrow sandstone reservoir', *Energy & Fuels*, vol. 30, pp. 8545–8555.

Ashworth, P, Bradbury, J, Wade, S, Ynke Feenstra, CFJ, Greenberg, S, Hund, G & Mikunda, T 2012, 'What's in store: Lessons from implementing CCS', *International Journal of Greenhouse Gas Control*, vol. 9, pp. 402–409.

Atia, A & Mohammedi, K 2018, 'A review on the application of enhanced oil/gas recovery through CO_2 sequestration', in I Karamé (ed) *Carbon Dioxide Chemistry, Capture and Oil Recovery*, pp. 241–253.

Bachu, S 2000, 'Sequestration of CO_2 in geological media: Criteria and approach for site selection in response to climate change', *Energy Conversion and Management*, vol. 41, pp. 953–970.

Bachu, S 2003, 'Screening and ranking of sedimentary basins for sequestration of CO_2 in geological media in response to climate change', *Environmental Geology*, vol. 44, pp. 277–289.

Bachu, S 2008, 'CO_2 storage in geological media: role, means, status and barriers to deployment', *Progress in Energy and Combustion Science*, vol. 34, pp. 254–273.

Bachu, S, Bonijoly, D, Bradshaw, J, Burruss, R, Holloway, S, Christensen, NP & Mathiassen, OM 2007, 'CO_2 storage capacity estimation: methodology and gaps', *International Journal of Greenhouse Gas Control*, vol. 1, pp. 430–443.

Bachu, S, Gunter, WD & Perkins, EH 1994, 'Aquifer disposal of CO_2: Hydrodynamic and mineral trapping', *Energy Conversion and Management*, vol. 35, pp. 269–279.

Baines, SJ & Worden, RH 2004, 'Geological storage of carbon dioxide', *Geological Society, London, Special Publications,* vol. 233, pp. 1–6.

Baker, RW 2004, *Membrane Technology and Applications.* California, John Wiley & Sons, Ltd.

Ball, R & Sceats, MG 2010, 'Separation of carbon dioxide from flue emissions using endex principles', *Fuel,* vol. 89, pp. 2750–2759.

Bishnoi, S & Rochelle, GT 2002, 'Absorption of carbon dioxide in aqueous piperazine/ methyldiethanolamine', *Aiche Journal,* vol. 48, pp. 2788–2799.

Blanchard, lA, Hancu, D, Beckman, EJ & Brennecke, JF 1999, 'Green processing using ionic liquids and CO$_2$', *Nature,* vol. 399, pp. 28–29.

Bradshaw, J, Bachu, S, Bonijoly, D, Burruss, R, Holloway, S, Christensen, NP & Mathiassen, OM 2007, 'CO$_2$ storage capacity estimation: Issues and development of standards', *International Journal of Greenhouse Gas Control,* vol. 1, pp. 62–68.

Carbon Storage Taskforce 2009, *National Carbon Mapping and Infrastructure Plan– Australia.* Canberra: Department of Resources, Energy and Tourism.

Cavanagh, A & Rostron, B 2013, 'High-resolution simulations of migration pathways and the related potential well risk at the ieaghg weyburn–midale co$_2$ storage project', *International Journal of Greenhouse Gas Control,* 16, pp. s15–s24.

CCP 2015, *CO$_2$ trapping mechanisms* [online]. Available: www.co2captureproject.org/ co2_trapping.html [22 october 2015].

Chalmers, H 2019, 'Fundamentals point to carbon capture', *Nature Climate Change,* vol. 9, pp. 348–348.

Chu, S 2009, 'Carbon capture and sequestration', *Science,* vol. 325, pp. 1599–1599.

Chu, S & Majumdar, A 2012, 'Opportunities and challenges for a sustainable energy future', *Nature,* vol. 488, pp. 294–303.

Chung, T-s, Jiang, lY, Li, Y & Kulprathipanja, S 2007, 'Mixed matrix membranes (MMMS) comprising organic polymers with dispersed inorganic fillers for gas separation', *Progress in Polymer Science,* vol. 32, pp. 483–507.

CO2CRC Limited. Available: www.co2crc.com.au/.

Collett, JR, Heck, RW & Zwoster, AJ 2011, 'Dissolved carbonic anhydrase for enhancing post-combustion carbon dioxide hydration in aqueous ammonia', *Energy Procedia,* vol. 4, 240–244.

Cormos, C-c 2016, 'Evaluation of reactive absorption and adsorption systems for post-combustion CO$_2$ capture applied to iron and steel industry', *Applied Thermal Engineering,* vol. 105, pp. 56–64.

Curry, T, Reiner, DM, Ansolabehere, S & Herzog, HJ 2005, How aware is the public of carbon capture and storage? In ES Rubin, DW Keith, CF Gilboy, M Wilson, T Morris, J Gale, & K Thambimuthu (Eds.), *Greenhouse Gas Control Technologies 7* (pp. 1001– 1009). Oxford: Elsevier Science Ltd.

Curry, TE, Ansonlabehere, S & Herzog, H 2007, 'A survey of public attitudes towards climate change and climate change mitigation technologies in the United States: analyzes of 2006 Results', US, MIT carbon sequestration initiative.

Dali, H, Lihui, G, Haocheng, I, Meizhu, Z & Feifei, C 2013, 'Dynamic phase behavior of near-critical condensate gas reservoir fluids', *Natural Gas Industry,* vol. 33, pp. 68–73.

De Best-waldhober, M, Paukovic, M, Brunsting, S & Daamen, D 2011, 'Awareness, knowledge, beliefs, and opinions regarding ccs of the dutch general public before and after information', *Energy Procedia,* vol. 4, pp. 6292–6299.

De silva, PNK & Ranjith, P 2012, 'A study of methodologies for CO_2 storage capacity estimation of saline aquifers', *Fuel,* vol. 93, pp. 13–27.

Druckenmiller, ML & Maroto-valer, MM 2005, 'Carbon sequestration using brine of adjusted PH to form mineral carbonates' *Fuel Processing Technology,* vol. 86, pp. 1599–1614.

Dugas, R & Rochelle, G 2009, 'Absorption and desorption rates of carbon dioxide with monoethanolamine and piperazine', *Energy Procedia,* vol. 1, pp. 1163–1169.

Edenhofer, O, Pichs-madruga, R, Sokona, Y, Seyboth, K, Matschoss, P, Kadner, S, Zwickel, T, Eickemeier, P, Hansen, G, Schlömer, S & Stechow, CV 2011, 'IPCC, 2011: Summary for policymakers. Ipcc special report on renewable energy sources and climate change mitigation', *Mitigation, Climate Change.* Cambridge: Cambridge University Press.

Endo, K, Nguyen, QS, Kentish, SE & Stevens, GW 2011, 'The effect of boric acid on the vapour liquid equilibrium of aqueous potassium carbonate', *Fluid Phase Equilibria,* vol. 309, pp. 109–113.

Fan, J-L, Xu, M, Yang, L, Zhang, X & Li, F 2019, 'How can carbon capture utilization and storage be incentivized in China? A perspective based on the 45q tax credit provisions', *Energy Policy,* vol. 132, 1229–1240.

Fan, L-S 2011, *Chemical Looping Systems for Fossil Energy Conversions.* Columbus: John Wiley & Sons Ltd.

Fennell, P & Anthony, B 2015, *Calcium and Chemical Looping Technology for Power Generation and Carbon Dioxide (CO_2) Capture.* Cambridge: Elsevier.

Folger, P 2017, 'Carbon Capture and Sequestration (CCS) in the United States', in Congressional Research Service, pp. 7–5700.

Freeman, SA, Dugas, R, Van Wagener, D, Nguyen, T & Rochelle, GT 2009, 'Carbon dioxide capture with concentrated, aqueous piperazine', *Energy Procedia,* vol. 1, pp. 1489–1496.

Friedmann, PA & Mayer, DG 1980, 'Energy tax credits in the energy tax act of 1978 and the crude oil windfall profits tax act of 1980', *Harvard Journal on Legislation,* vol. 17, p. 465.

Gibbins, J & Chalmers, H 2008, 'Carbon capture and storage', *Energy Policy,* vol. 36, pp. 4317–4322.

Global CSS Institute 2018, *Global Status of CCS 2018.* Melbourne, Australia: Global Carbon Capture and Storage Institute.

Gluyas, J & Mathias, S 2013, *Geological Storage of Carbon Dioxide (CO_2): Geoscience, Technologies, Environmental Aspects and Legal Frameworks.* Philadelphi: Woodhead Publishing.

Godec, M, Koperna, G, Petrusak, R & Oudinot, A 2014, 'Enhanced gas recovery and co_2 storage in gas shales: a summary review of its status and potential', *Energy Procedia,* vol. 63, pp. 5849–5857.

Griffin, PW & Hammond, GP 2019, 'Industrial energy use and carbon emissions reduction in the iron and steel sector: A UK perspective', *Applied Energy,* vol. 249, pp. 109–125.

Grobe, M, Pashin, JC & Dodge, RL 2009, 'Carbon Dioxide Sequestration in Geological Media. State of the science', Tulsa: American Association of Petroleum Geologists.

Gunter, WD, Bachu, S & Benson, S 2004, 'The role of hydrogeological and geochemical trapping in sedimentary basins for secure geological storage of carbon dioxide', *Geological Society, London, Special Publications,* vol. 233, pp. 129–145.

Guo, P, Xu, H & Wang, Z 2015, 'Calculation of multi-component gas-gas diffusion coefficient', *Natural Gas Industry,* vol. 35, pp. 39–43.

He, S 2008, 'Technical problems and countermeasures of developing the puguang gas field with high H_2S and CO_2 content', *Natural Gas Industry,* vol. 28, p. 82.

Hegerl, G & Stott, P 2014, 'Atmospheric science. From past to future warming', *Science,* vol. 343, pp. 844–845.

Heldebrant, DJ, Koech, PK, Glezakou, VA, Rousseau, R, Malhotra, D & Cantu, DC 2017, 'Water-lean solvents for post-combustion co₂ capture: fundamentals, uncertainties, opportunities, and outlook', *Chemical Reviews,* vol. 117, pp. 9594–9624.

Herzog, G, Smekens, K, Dadhich, P, Dooley, J, Fujii, Y, Hohmeyer, O, Riahi, K, Akai, M, Hendriks, C, Lackner, K, Rana, A, Rubin, E, Schrattenholzer, l & Senior, B 2018, 'Chapter 8: Cost and Economic Potential', *Cost and Economic Potential* (IPCC), pp. 339–362.

Hosseini, SA, Alfi, M, Nicot, JP & Nuñez-lopez, V 2018, 'Analysis of CO_2 storage mechanisms at a CO_2-EAR site, Cranfield, Mississippi', *Greenhouse Gases: Science and Technology,* vol. 8, pp. 469–482.

Howard-grenville, J, Buckle, SJ, Hoskins, BJ & George, G 2014, 'Climate change and management', *Academy of Management Journal,* vol. 57, pp. 615–623.

Hu, G 2018, *Novel Promoters for Carbon Dioxide Absorption in Potassium Carbonate Solutions.* Doctorate, The University of Melbourne.

Hu, G, Nicholas, NJ, Smith, KH, Mumford, KA, Kentish, SE & Stevens, GW 2016, 'Carbon dioxide absorption into promoted potassium carbonate solutions: A review', *International Journal of Greenhouse Gas Control,* vol. 53, pp. 28–40.

Hu, G, Smith, KH, Wu, Y, Mumford, KA, Kentish, SE & Stevens, GW 2018, 'Carbon dioxide capture by solvent absorption using amino acids: A review', *Chinese Journal of Chemical Engineering,* vol. 26, pp. 2229–2237.

Huang, Y 2016, 'Understanding China's belt & road initiative: Motivation, framework and assessment', *China Economic Review,* vol. 40, pp. 314–321.

Hüsler, AD & Sornette, D 2014, 'Human population and atmospheric carbon dioxide growth dynamics: Diagnostics for the future', *The European Physical Journal Special Topics,* vol. 223, pp. 2065–2085.

IEA 2019, *IEA Updates EOR Project Data, Doubling Output Forecast* [online]. Oil & Gas Journal. Available: www.ogj.com/home/article/17222807/iea-updates-eor-project-data-doubling-output-forecast [2019].

Intergovernmental Panel on Climate Change 2005, 'Carbon dioxide capture and storage', in B Metz, O Davidson, HD Coninck, M Loos & I Meyer (eds) *Intergovernmental Panel on Climate Change (IPCC) Special Report.*

Ishida, M & Jin, H 1994, 'A novel combustor based on chemical-looping reactions and its reaction kinetics' *Journal of Chemical Engineering of Japan,* vol. 27, pp. 296–301.

Itaoka, K, Dowd, A-m, Saito, A, Paukovic, M, De Best-waldhober, M & Ashworth, P 2013, 'Relating individual perceptions of carbon dioxide to perceptions of ccs: an international comparative study', *Energy Procedia,* vol. 37, pp. 7436–7443.

Jiang, J, Shao, Y & Younis, RM 2014, 'Development of a multi-continuum multi-component model for enhanced gas recovery and CO_2 storage in fractured shale gas reservoirs.' SPE improved oil recovery symposium, Society of Petroleum Engineers.

Jiang, K, Dou, HE, Shen, P & Sun, T 2015, 'China's CCUS progresses and a new evaluation method of CO_2 storage capacity in coalbed reservoirs', Carbon management technology conference.

Jiang, K, Zhang, S & Dou, HE 2018, 'Method of evaluating CO_2 storage capacity in coal seams using exploration databases, with application to china', 14th Greenhouse Gas Control Technologies Conference, Melbourne, pp. 21–26.

Juanes, R, Spiteri, E, Orr Jr, F & Blunt, M 2006, 'Impact of relative permeability hysteresis on geological CO_2 storage', *Water Resources Research,* vol. 42, w12418.

Khalilpour, R, Mumford, K, Zhai, H, Abbas, A, Stevens, G & Rubin, ES 2015, 'Membrane-based carbon capture from flue gas: a review', *Journal of Cleaner Production,* vol. 103, pp. 286–300.

Kim, H, Jang, HD & Choi, M 2015, 'Facile synthesis of macroporous li_4sio_4 with remarkably enhanced co_2 adsorption kinetics', *Chemical Engineering Journal,* vol. 280, pp. 132–137.

King Abdullah Petroleum Studies, Al-Fattah, S M., Barghouty, M. F. & Dabbousi, B. O. 2011, *Carbon Capture and Storage: Technologies, Policies, Economics, and Implementation Strategies.* CRC press.

Klimkowski, Ł, Nagy, S, Papiernik, B, Orlic, B & Kempka, T 2015, 'Numerical simulations of enhanced gas recovery at the Załęcze gas field in poland confirm high CO_2 storage capacity and mechanical integrity', *Oil & Gas Science and Technology,* vol. 70, pp. 655–680.

Kuuskraa, VA, Godec, ML & Dipietro, P 2013, 'CO_2 utilization from "next generation" CO_2 enhanced oil recovery technology', *Energy Procedia,* vol. 37, pp. 6854–6866.

L'orange Seigo, S, Dohle, S & Siegrist, M 2014, 'Public perception of carbon capture and storage (CCS): A review', *Renewable and Sustainable Energy Reviews,* vol. 38, pp. 848–863.

Lee, SC, Choi, BY, Lee, TJ, Ryu, CK, Ahn, YS & Kim, JC 2006, 'CO_2 absorption and regeneration of alkali metal-based solid sorbents', *Catalysis Today,* vol. 111, pp. 385–390.

Leeson, D, Mac Dowell, N, Shah, N, Petit, C & Fennell, P 2017, 'A techno-economic analysis and systematic review of carbon capture and storage (CCS) applied to the iron and steel, cement, oil refining and pulp and paper industries, as well as other high purity sources', *International Journal of Greenhouse Gas Control,* vol. 61, pp. 71–84.

Lewis, WK, Gilliland, ER & Sweeney, MP 1951, 'Gasification of carbon-metal oxides in a fluidized powder bed', *Chemical Engineering Progress,* vol. 47, p. 251.

Li, H, Moullec, YL, Lu, J, Chen, J, Marcos, JCV & Chen, G 2014, 'Solubility and energy analysis for co_2 absorption in piperazine derivatives and their mixtures', *International Journal of Greenhouse Gas Control,* vol. 31, pp. 25–32.

Li, Q, Liu, G, Cai, B, Leamon, G, Liu, L-c, Chen, Z-a & Li, X 2017, 'Public awareness of the environmental impact and management of carbon dioxide capture, utilization and storage technology: The views of educated people in China', *Clean Technologies and Environmental Policy,* vol. 19, pp. 2041–2056.

Li, X & Fang, Z-m 2014, 'Current status and technical challenges of co_2 storage in coal seams and enhanced coalbed methane recovery: An overview', *International Journal of Coal Science & Technology,* vol. 1, pp. 93–102.

Lim, J, Aguiar, A, Scholes, CA, Dumée, lF, Stevens, GW & Kentish, SE 2014, 'Monoethanolamine reclamation using electrodialysis', *Industrial & Engineering Chemistry Research,* vol. 53, pp. 19313–19321.

Liu, H, Liu, B, Lin, l C, Chen, G, Wu, Y, Wang, J, Gao, X, lv, Y, Pan, Y, Zhang, X, Zhang, X, Yang, l, Sun, C, Smit, B & Wang, W 2014, 'A hybrid absorption-adsorption method to efficiently capture carbon', *Nature Communications,* vol. 5, p. 5147.

Lively, RP, Chance, RR, Kelley, BT, Deckman, HW, Drese, JH, Jones, CW & Koros, WJ 2009, 'Hollow fiber adsorbents for CO_2 removal from flue gas' *Industrial & Engineering Chemistry Research,* vol. 48, pp. 7314–7324.

Machida, H, Ando, R, Esaki, T, Yamaguchi, T, Horizoe, H, Kishimoto, A, Akiyama, K & Nishimura, M 2018, 'Low temperature swing process for CO_2 absorption-desorption using phase separation CO_2 capture solvent', *International Journal of Greenhouse Gas Control*, vol. 75, pp. 1–7.

Maroto-valer, MM, Fauth, DJ, Kuchta, ME, Zhang, Y & Andrésen, JM 2005a, 'Activation of magnesium rich minerals as carbonation feedstock materials for CO_2 sequestration', *Fuel Processing Technology*, vol. 86, pp. 1627–1645.

Maroto-valer, MM, Tang, Z & Zhang, Y 2005b, 'CO_2 capture by activated and impregnated anthracites', *Fuel Processing Technology*, vol. 86, pp. 1487–1502.

Masoumi, S, Keshavarz, P, Ayatollahi, S, Mehdipour, M & Rastgoo, Z 2013, 'Enhanced carbon dioxide separation by amine-promoted potassium carbonate solution in a hollow fiber membrane contactor', *Energy & Fuels*, vol. 27, pp. 5423–5432.

Mattisson, T, Lyngfelt, A & Leion, H 2009, 'Chemical-looping with oxygen uncoupling for combustion of solid fuels', *International Journal of Greenhouse Gas Control*, vol. 3, pp. 11–19.

McGlade, C 2019, Commentary: can CO_2-EOR really provide carbon-negative oil? International Energy Agency.

Meier, B & Sharma, S 2015, 'Using stable carbon isotopes to track potential leakage of carbon dioxide: Example from an enhanced coal bed methane recovery site in West Virginia, USA', *International Journal of Greenhouse Gas Control*, vol. 41, pp. 107–115.

Merchant, D 2017, 'Enhanced oil recovery–the history of CO_2 conventional wag injection techniques developed from lab in the 1950's to 2017', Carbon management technology conference.

Mohagheghian, E, Hassanzadeh, H & Chen, Z 2019, 'CO_2 sequestration coupled with enhanced gas recovery in shale gas reservoirs', *Journal of CO₂ Utilization*, vol. 34, pp. 646–655.

Motz, I, Koch, I, Kutzbach, HD & Stahr, K 2001, 'Measurement of greenhouse gases: air-conditioned perspex chambers for the measurement of soil respiration and trace gases in undisturbed plant populations', *Agrartechnische Forschung*, vol. 7, pp. e28–e31.

Nardi, A, Abarca, E, Grandia, F & Molinero, J 2013, *CO₂ Storage Trapping Mechanisms Quantification*. Barcelona, Spain: Amphos 21.

Nuñez-lópez, V & Moskal, E 2019, 'Potential of CO_2-EOR for near-term decarbonization', *Frontiers in Climate*, vol. 1, p. 5.

Oexmann, J, Kather, A, Linnenberg, S & Liebenthal, U 2012, 'Post-combustion CO_2 capture: chemical absorption processes in coal-fired steam power plants', *Greenhouse Gases: Science and Technology*, vol. 2, pp. 80–98.

Pachauri, RK & Meyer, LA 2014, 'Climate change 2014: Synthesis report'. Geneva, Switzerland: IPCC.

Palmgren, C, Morgan, M, De Bruin, W & Keith, D 2004, 'Initial public perceptions of deep geological and oceanic disposal of carbon dioxide', *Environmental Science & Technology*, vol. 38, pp. 6441–6450.

Pinto, D, Knuutila, H, Fytianos, G, Haugen, G, Mejdell, T & Svendsen, HF 2014, 'CO_2 post combustion capture with a phase change solvent. Pilot plant campaign', *International Journal of Greenhouse Gas Control*, vol. 31, pp. 153–164.

Plaza, MG, García, S, Rubiera, F, Pis, JJ & Pevida, C 2010, 'Post-combustion CO_2 capture with a commercial activated carbon: comparison of different regeneration strategies', *Chemical Engineering Journal*, vol. 163, pp. 41–47.

Polson, D, Curtis, A & Vivalda, C 2012, 'The evolving perception of risk during reservoir evaluation projects for geological storage of CO_2', *International Journal of Greenhouse Gas Control,* vol. 9, pp. 10–23.

Powell, CE & Qiao, GG 2006, 'Polymeric CO_2/N_2 gas separation membranes for the capture of carbon dioxide from power plant flue gases', *Journal of Membrane Science,* vol. 279, pp. 1–49.

Power, IM, Harrison, AL & Dipple, GM 2016, 'Accelerating mineral carbonation using carbonic anhydrase', *Environmental Science & Technology,* vol. 50, pp. 2610–2618.

Rafiee, MM & Ramazanian, M 2011, 'Simulation study of enhanced gas recovery process using a compositional and a black oil simulator', SPE enhanced oil recovery conference. Society of Petroleum Engineers.

Raksakoon, C, Maihom, T, Probst, M & Limtrakul, J 2015, 'The hydration of carbon dioxide in copper-alkoxide functionalized metal-organic frameworks: A DFT study', *The Journal of Physical Chemistry c,* vol. 119, pp. 3564–3571.

Rochelle, GT, Goff, G, Cullinane, T & Freguia, S 2002, 'Research results for CO_2 capture from flue gas by aqueous absorption/stripping', *Proceedings of the Laurance Reid Gas Conditioning Conference,* pp. 131–152.

Rochelle, GT, Wu, Y, Chen, E, Akinpelumi, K, Fischer, KB, Gao, T, Liu, C-t & Selinger, JL 2019, 'Pilot plant demonstration of piperazine with the advanced flash stripper', *International Journal of Greenhouse Gas Control,* vol. 84, pp. 72–81.

Romanov, V, Soong, Y, Carney, C, Rush, GE, Nielsen, B & O'Connor, W 2015, 'Mineralization of carbon aioxide: A literature review' *Chembioeng Reviews,* vol. 2, pp. 1–27.

Rutgersson, A, Jaagus, J, Schenk, F & Stendel, M 2014, 'Observed changes and variability of atmospheric parameters in the baltic sea region during the last 200 years', *Climate Research,* vol. 61, 177–190.

Rydén, M, Leion, H, Mattisson, T & Lyngfelt, A 2014, 'Combined oxides as oxygen-carrier material for chemical-looping with oxygen uncoupling', *Applied Energy,* vol. 113, pp. 1924–1932.

Scholes, CA, Ho, MT, Wiley, DE, Stevens, GW & Kentish, SE 2013, 'Cost competitive membrane-cryogenic post-combustion carbon capture', *International Journal of Greenhouse Gas Control,* vol. 17, pp. 341–348.

Scholes, CA, Kentish, SE & Stevens, GW 2009, 'Effects of minor components in carbon dioxide capture using polymeric gas separation membranes', *Separation and Purification Reviews,* vol. 38, pp. 1–44.

Scholes, CA, Qader, A, Stevens, GW & Kentish, SE 2014, 'Membrane gas-solvent contactor pilot plant trials of co_2 absorption from flue gas' *Separation Science and Technology,* vol. 49, pp. 2449–2458.

Shen, P, Liao, X & Liu, Q 2009, 'Methodology for estimation of CO_2 storage capacity in reservoirs', *Petroleum Exploration and Development,* vol. 36, pp. 216–220.

Shi, Y, Jia, Y, Pan, W, Huang, L, Yan, J & Zheng, R 2017, 'Potential evaluation on CO_2-EGR in tight and low-permeability reservoirs', *Natural Gas Industry b,* vol. 4, pp. 311–318.

Sholl, DS & Lively, RP 2016, 'Seven chemical separations to change the world', *Nature,* vol. 532, pp. 435–437.

Shrier, A & Danckwerts, P 1969, 'Carbon dioxide absorption into amine-promoted potash solutions', *Industrial & Engineering Chemistry Fundamentals,* vol. 8, pp. 415–423.

Smith, J, Durucan, S, Korre, A & Shi, J-q 2011, 'Carbon dioxide storage risk assessment: analysis of caprock fracture network connectivity', *International Journal of Greenhouse Gas Control,* vol. 5, pp. 226–240.

Smith, K, Quyn, D, Indrawan, N, Thanumurthy, J, Guow, N, Nicholas, A, Lee, K, Mumford, C, Anderson, B, Hooper, S, Kentish, G & Stevens, G 2013, 'Pilot Plant for Capturing CO_2 Using a Precipitating K_2CO_3 Solvent', Chemeca 2013: Challenging Tomorrow.

Stefan, B 2008, 'Comparison between methodologies recommended for estimation of CO_2 storage capacity in geological media'. Cape Town, South Africa: Capacity and fairways subgroup of the geologic working group.

Stefan, B, Didier, B, John, B, Robert, B, Niels, PC, Sam, H & Odd-magne, M 2007, *Estimation of CO_2 Storage Capacity in Geological Media*. Melbourne, Australia: Task force on CO_2 storage capacity estimation for the technical group of the carbon sequestration leadership forum.

Sujan, AR, Koh, D-y, Zhu, G, Babu, VP, Stephenson, N, Rosinski, A, Du, H, Luo, Y, Koros, WJ & Lively, RP 2018, 'High-temperature activation of zeolite-loaded fiber orbents', *Industrial & Engineering Chemistry Research,* vol. 57, pp. 11757–11766.

Sun, L, Dou, H, Li, Z, Hu, Y & Hao, X 2018, 'Assessment of CO_2 storage potential and carbon capture, utilization and storage prospect in China', *Journal of the Energy Institute,* vol. 91, pp. 970–977.

Sun, Z, Wang, J, Du, W, Lu, G, Li, P, Song, X & Yu, J 2016, 'Density functional theory study on the thermodynamics and mechanism of carbon dioxide capture by CAO and CAO regeneration' *Rsc Advances,* vol. 6, pp. 39460–39468.

Surovtseva, D, Amin, R & Barifcani, A 2011, 'Design and operation of pilot plant for CO_2 capture from IGCC flue gases by combined cryogenic and hydrate method', *Chemical Engineering Research and Design,* vol. 89, pp. 1752–1757.

Takahashi, T, Ohsumi, T, Nakayama, K, Koide, K & Miida, H 2009, 'Estimation of CO_2 aquifer storage potential in Japan, *Energy Procedia,* vol. 1, pp. 2631–2638.

Tan, S, Nam, E, Cui, J, Xu, C, Fu, Q, Ren, JM, Wong, EH, Ladewig, K, Caruso, F, Blencowe, A & Qiao, GG 2015, 'Fabrication of ultra-thin polyrotaxane-based films via solid-state continuous assembly of polymers', *Chemical Communications,* vol. 51, pp. 2025–2028.

Tao, L, Xiao, P, Qader, A & Webley, PA 2019, 'CO_2 capture from high concentration CO_2 natural gas by pressure swing adsorption at the CO2CRC Otway site, Australia', *International Journal of Greenhouse Gas Control,* vol. 83, pp. 1–10.

Tao, Z & Clarens, A 2013, 'Estimating the carbon sequestration capacity of shale formations using methane production rates', *Environmental Science & Technology,* vol. 47, pp. 11318–11325.

Tapia, JFD, Lee, J-y, Ooi, REH, Foo, DCY & Tan, RR 2016, 'Optimal CO_2 allocation and scheduling in enhanced oil recovery (EOR) operations', *Applied Energy,* vol. 184, pp. 337–345.

Terwel, BW, Harinck, F, Ellemers, N & Daamen, DDL 2009, 'Competence-based and integrity-based trust as predictors of acceptance of carbon dioxide capture and storage (CCS)', *Risk Analysis,* vol. 29, pp. 1129–1140.

Tokushige, K, Akimoto, K & Tomoda, T 2007, 'Public perceptions on the acceptance of geological storage of carbon dioxide and information influencing the acceptance', *International Journal of Greenhouse Gas Control,* vol. 1, pp. 101–112.

Tomić, L, Maričić, VK, Danilović, D & Crnogorac, M 2018, 'Criteria for CO_2 storage in geological formations', *Underground Mining Engineering,* vol. 32, pp. 61–74.

Trachtenberg, MC, Cowan, RM, Smith, DA, Horazak, DA, Jensen, MD, Laumb, JD, Vucelic, AP, Chen, H, Wang, L & Wu, X 2009, 'Membrane-based, enzyme-facilitated, efficient carbon dioxide capture', *Energy Procedia,* vol. 1, pp. 353–360.

Tuinier, MJ, Hamers, HP & Van Sint Annaland, M 2011, 'Techno-economic evaluation of cryogenic CO_2 capture-a comparison with absorption and membrane technology', *International Journal of Greenhouse Gas Control*, vol. 5, pp. 1559–1565.

Van Alphen, K, Van Voorst Tot Voorst, Q, Hekkert, MP & Smits, REHM 2007, 'Societal acceptance of carbon capture and storage technologies', *Energy Policy*, vol. 35, pp. 4368–4380.

Wallquist, L, Seigo, SLO, Visschers, VHM & Siegrist, M 2011, 'Public acceptance of ccs system elements: A conjoint measurement' *International Journal of Greenhouse Gas Control*, vol. 6, pp. 73–88.

Wallquist, L, Seigo, SLO, Visschers, VHM & Siegrist, M 2012, Public acceptance of CCS system elements: A conjoint measurement. International Journal of Greenhouse Gas Control, 6, 77–83. doi:10.1016/j.ijggc.2011.11.008

Wang, J 2015, 'More efficient sequestration of carbon dioxide: a new approach enables the enzyme to more efficiently catalyze the conversion of carbon dioxide to calcium carbonate', *Tribology and Lubrication Technology*, vol. 71, pp. 14–15.

Wang, M, Hariharan, S, Shaw, RA & Hatton, TA 2019a, 'Energetics of electrochemically mediated amine regeneration process for flue gas CO_2 capture', *International Journal of Greenhouse Gas Control*, vol. 82, pp. 48–58.

Wang, M, Rahimi, M, Kumar, A, Hariharan, S, Choi, W & Hatton, TA 2019b, 'Flue gas CO_2 capture via electrochemically mediated amine regeneration: System design and performance', *Applied Energy*, vol. 255, 113879.

Wang, T, Hovland, J & Jens, KJ 2015, 'Amine reclaiming technologies in post-combustion carbon dioxide capture', *Journal of Environmental Sciences*, vol. 27, pp. 276–289.

Wassermann, S, Schulz, M & Scheer, D 2011, 'Linking public acceptance with expert knowledge on CO_2 storage: Outcomes of a delphi approach', *Energy Procedia*, vol. 4, pp. 6353–6359.

Webley, PA 2014, 'Adsorption technology for CO_2 separation and capture: A perspective', *Adsorption*, vol. 20, pp. 225–231.

Wei, N, Li, X, Wang, Y, Dahowski, RT, Davidson, CL & Bromhal, GS 2013, 'A preliminary sub-basin scale evaluation framework of site suitability for onshore aquifer-based CO_2 storage in China', *International Journal of Greenhouse Gas Control*, vol. 12, pp. 231–246.

Whorton, L, Brownscombe, E & Dyes, A 1952, 'Method for producing oil by means of carbon dioxide'. *USA Patent*, vol. 2, p. 30.

Wong, S, Law, D, Deng, X, Robinson, J, Kadatz, B, Gunter, WD, Jianping, Y, Sanli, F & Zhiqiang, F 2006, 'Enhanced coalbed methane, micropilot test at South Qinshui, Shanxi, China', *International Journal of Greenhouse Gas Control*, vol. 1, pp. 215–222.

Wu, Y, Mirza, NR., Hu, G, Smith, KH, Stevens, GW & Mumford, KA 2017, 'Precipitating characteristics of potassium bicarbonate using concentrated potassium carbonate solvent for carbon dioxide capture. Part 1. Nucleation', *Industrial & Engineering Chemistry Research*, vol. 56, pp. 6764–6774.

Xi, L, Qianguo, L, Hasan, M, Ming, L, Qiang, L, Jia, L, Alisa, W, Muxin, L & Francisco, A 2019, 'Assessing the economics of CO_2 capture in China's iron/steel sector: A case study', *Energy Procedia*, vol. 158, pp. 3715–3722.

Xian, S, Xu, F, Zhao, Z, Xia, Q, Xiao, J, Li, Y, Wang, H & Li, Z 2016, 'A novel carbonized polydopamine (c-pda) adsorbent with high CO_2 adsorption capacity and water vapor resistance', *Aiche Journal*, vol. 62, pp. 3730–3738.

Xiao, P, Zhang, J, Webley, P, Li, G, Singh, R & Todd, R 2008, 'Capture of CO_2 from flue gas streams with zeolite 13x by vacuum-pressure swing adsorption', *Adsorption*, vol. 14, pp. 575–582.

Xie, K, Fu, Q, Xu, C, Lu, H, Zhao, Q, Curtain, R, Gu, D, Webley, PA & Qiao, GG. 2018, 'Continuous assembly of a polymer on a metal–organic framework (cap on mof): A 30 nm thick polymeric gas separation membrane', *Energy & Environmental Science*, vol. 11, pp. 544–550.

Yamasaki, A 2003, 'An overview of CO_2 mitigation options for global warming-emphasizing CO_2 sequestration options', *Journal of Chemical Engineering of Japan*, vol. 36, pp. 361–375.

Yang, H, Xu, Z, Fan, M, Gupta, R, Slimane, RB, Bland, AE & Wright, I 2008, 'Progress in carbon dioxide separation and capture: A review', *Journal of Environmental Sciences*, vol. 20, pp. 14–27.

Yang, S, Du, Z, Sun L, S, Tang, Y & Pan, Y 2012, 'Phase behavior of CO_2 sequestration and the enhanced natural gas recovery', *Natural Gas Industry*, vol. 5, pp. 39–42.

Yin, M 2015, *CO_2 Miscible Flooding Application and Screening Criteria*. Masters dissertation. Missouri University of Science and Technology.

Yong, JKJ, Stevens, GW, Caruso, F & Kentish, SE 2016, 'In situ layer-by-layer assembled carbonic anhydrase-coated hollow fiber membrane contactor for rapid CO_2 absorption' *Journal of Membrane Science*, vol. 514, pp. 556–565.

Zhang, D & Song, J 2014, 'Mechanisms for geological carbon sequestration' *Procedia Lutam*, vol. 10, pp. 319–327.

Zhang, L, Li, X, Ren, B, Cui, G, Zhang, Y, Ren, S, Chen, G & Zhang, H 2016, 'CO_2 storage potential and trapping mechanisms in the h-59 block of Jilin oilfield China' *International Journal of Greenhouse Gas Control*, vol. 49, pp. 267–280.

Zhang, S, Shen, Y, Wang, L, Chen, J & Lu, Y 2019, 'Phase change solvents for post-combustion CO_2 capture: principle, advances, and challenges', *Applied Energy*, vol. 239, pp. 876–897.

Zhao, C, Chen, X, Anthony, EJ, Jiang, X, Duan, L, Wu, Y, Dong, W & Zhao, C 2013, 'Capturing CO_2 in flue gas from fossil fuel-fired power plants using dry regenerable alkali metal-based sorbent', *Progress in Energy and Combustion Science*, vol. 39, pp. 515–534.

Zhao, L, Zhao, R, Deng, S, Tan, Y & Liu, Y 2014, 'Integrating solar organic rankine cycle into a coal-fired power plant with amine-based chemical absorption for CO_2 capture', *International Journal of Greenhouse Gas Control*, vol. 31, pp. 77–86.

Zheng, Q, Martin, GJO & Kentish, SE 2016, 'Energy efficient transfer of carbon dioxide from flue gases to microalgal systems', *Energy & Environmental Science*, vol. 9, pp. 1074–1082.

Zhou, J, Hu, N, Xian, X, Zhou, L, Tang, J, Kang, Y & Wang, H 2019, 'Supercritical CO_2 fracking for enhanced shale gas recovery and co2 sequestration: Results, status and future challenges', *Advances in Geo-energy Research*, vol. 3, pp. 207–224.

Zhou, Q, Birkholzer, JT, Tsang, C-f & Rutqvist, J 2008, 'A method for quick assessment of CO_2 storage capacity in closed and semi-closed saline formations', *International Journal of Greenhouse Gas Control*, vol. 2, pp. 626–639.

Zhou, S, Chen, X, Nguyen, T, Voice, AK & Rochelle, GT 2010, 'Aqueous ethylenediamine for CO_2 capture', *Chemsuschem*, vol. 3, pp. 913–918.

8 Meeting the green challenges and opportunities of Hong Kong manufacturers in China's Belt and Road pathway

The Pearl River Delta experiences

Ning Liu, Carlos Wing-Hung Lo, and Pansy Hon Ying Li

Introduction

As ecological, societal, and political demands to reduce pollution have steadily increased during China's quest for sustainable development, Hong Kong manufacturers must develop strategies to build and enhance their corporate environmental management capacity in order to survive and prosper in these challenging contexts. Their environmental management capacity affects the extent to which Hong Kong manufacturers can seize the opportunities of the Belt and Road Initiative unveiled by the Chinese government in 2013 to foster inter-regional cooperation between related countries and regions (Dong et al. 2016). This chapter identifies their green evolution in operating their manufacturing plants in the Pearl River Delta (PRD) region, in order to shed light on their capacity and preparedness to pursue a green path of industrial development along the Belt and Road region.

Hong Kong manufacturers have been contributing to the environmental degradation in the PRD region since the 1980s when they relocated their polluting operations from Hong Kong to various locations there. In response to serious pollution problems nationwide, the Chinese government has been imposing increasingly stricter regulatory control on industrial enterprises over pollution, creating considerable compliance challenges for Hong Kong manufacturers. Local communities have also become more concerned with industrial pollution, and local protests against industrial polluters have become common occurrences nationwide. By drawing on two rounds of questionnaire survey conducted in 2007 and 2013 with respondents from members of the Federation of Hong Kong Industries (FHKI) with manufacturing operations in the PRD region, we examine the changes in corporate environmental management in these two periods under growing pollution regulatory pressure. On this basis, we assess the progress that Hong Kong manufacturers have made in greening their manufacturing operations. Their greening experiences will shape their corporate strategies and operations in managing their environmental footprint in future industrial investment in other Belt and Road localities.

Corporate environmental management and strategies

Sizable literature exists on corporate environmental compliance and strategies. The two key research questions in this literature are: (1) What strategies can an enterprise adopt in relation to its impact on the environment? (2) What array of factors, both internal and external to the enterprise, can affect its environmental strategies and performance? A third question, which has not been addressed much in the existing literature but is important in the context of China, is what types of challenge are enterprises facing in their efforts to comply with environmental regulations?

Types of corporate environmental strategy

In the existing literature, there are many different approaches to characterizing corporate environmental strategies, often reflecting the specific research questions that the particular studies address and the data and methods that they use. In most policy-oriented studies on the antecedents of regulatory compliance, the attention is often simply on an enterprise's degree/extent of compliance, as measured by the specific number of concrete facilities and steps that an enterprise uses to meet a certain regulatory requirement (Winter and May 2001; May 2005). An alternative focus is on an enterprise's actual pollution abatement efforts as measured by such variables as pollutant emissions (Hettige et al. 1996), actual annual abatement expenditure (Aden et al. 1999), or participation in voluntary environmental programmes (Liu et al. 2018b; Potoski and Prakash 2005; Rivera 2004).

Management and business strategy studies tend to be more sophisticated in their conceptualization and measurement of corporate environmental strategies (Christmann 2004; Sharma 2000). In their synthesis of the literature on environmental management and corporate social responsibility, Henriques and Sadorsky (1999), for example, propose a four-category classification of a business firm's approach to the natural environment: reactive, defensive, accommodative, and proactive. They hypothesize that firms with a proactive environmental profile differ from other firms in their perception of the influence of different stakeholders. Other scholars have taken a more 'inductive' approach by categorizing specific strategies they identify through interviewing managers and reviewing company publications. Bansal (2004), for example, codes 22 items describing principles of sustainable development adopted by forestry companies in Canada, and groups these items into the three categories of environmental integrity, economic prosperity, and social equity.

In our research, we have chosen not to adopt a specific classification as a starting point for our inquiry, because much of the current literature is based mainly on the experiences in Western countries, and it is unclear whether classifications in those settings are equally applicable to the transitional context of China. Instead, we have asked three sets of questions in our surveys, which help us identify elements of an enterprise's environmental management strategy. The first set of questions examines the personal knowledge and awareness of the owners/managers on a number of environmental concepts and frameworks such as ISO 14000, green purchasing requirements, and the precautionary principle. The second set concerns the company's orientation to the environment, including such questions as whether the company considers the environmental impact of the production process and whether it plans to use more environmentally friendly components in its products and production processes. The third set deals with the firm's activities in corporate environmental management, including such items as sponsorship of events related to environmental protection, routine environmental audits, and setting environmental performance objectives as part of annual business plans.

Factors affecting corporate environmental strategies

Both the literature on public policy and that on business strategy include many excellent studies examining motivating factors for corporate environmental strategies. These studies look at three major sets of variables. The first set concerns institutional and stakeholder influences: the enforcement style of the regulatory regime (Aden et al. 1999; Liu et al. 2018a; May 2005); pressures from investors, communities, and interest groups (Aden et al. 1999; Harrison and Antweiler 2003; Hettige et al. 1996; Liu et al. 2010; Zhu, Cordeiro and Sarkis 2013); local institutional networks (Marshall et al., 2005); the saliency of ecological issues (Bansal and Roth, 2000); and industry pressure (Delmas and Toffel 2004).

The second set concerns individual- and organizational-level factors. One major focus is on the attitude of top executives toward environmental issues, for example, whether the top management acknowledges an ethical obligation to environmental pollution control and whether they are interested in launching and implementing environmental management measures within the firm (Branzei et al. 2004; Marshall et al. 2005; May 2005; Petts et al. 1999). The other focus relates to internal organizational structures and processes, for example, whether ideas on pollution control are shared freely among the employees at various levels within the firm and whether the firm has an environmental manager at the senior level (Bansal 2004; Halme 2002; Prakash 2001; Roy et al. 2001).

The third set concerns managerial perceptions of the potential outcomes associated with the implementation of better environmental management practices; for example, whether they believe those practices will lead to improved production efficiency, enhanced business reputation, a higher employee commitment, a lower risk of lawsuits, and enhanced competitive advantages (Bansal and Roth 2000; Chatterji and Toffel 2010; Henriques and Sadorsky 1999). One may hypothesize that managers' perceptions about potential outcomes are variables that mediate the effects of institutional and stakeholder influences and individual- and firm-level factors on corporate environmental strategies.

Difficulties enterprises face in complying with environmental regulations

Most public policy studies focus on the difficulties that government agencies encounter when they try to enforce environmental regulations, but they seldom explicitly look at the difficulties that enterprises face in their efforts to comply with environmental regulations. Some studies in the literature on business strategy have looked at the difficulties encountered by enterprises but only in the context of how these difficulties affect an enterprise's commitment to environmental protection (e.g. Tilley 1999). In the proposed study, we examine this issue in a more direct way by asking our survey and interview respondents about the specific challenges they face in complying with environmental regulations, such as whether the pollutant discharge fees system is too complicated for a manger to understand, whether the local environmental protection bureau (EPB) is inconsistent in its enforcement of environmental regulations, and whether there has been insufficient direct communication between the enterprise and the local EPB.

This longitudinal study of corporate environmental management among Hong Kong manufacturers in the PRD region is built on two sets of previous research by the investigators that focuses on environmental regulation enforcement and corporate environmental management in China. The first set is based on a series of surveys of enforcement officials in local EPBs in both urban and suburban cities in the Pan-PRD region. The research shows that local environmental protection agencies have been able to improve their enforcement effectiveness by securing greater government and social support, and they have gradually tightened up regulatory control over polluting enterprises (Lo, Fryxell and van Rooij 2009; Lo and Tang 2006). In our longitudinal study of regulatory enforcement in Guangzhou with surveys and interviews conducted in 2000 and 2006 respectively, a clear linkage of changes was demonstrated between institutional environments and regulatory enforcement style. Specifically, regulatory enforcement officials in the Guangzhou EPB were found to be putting more emphasis on educational, formalistic, and coercive regulatory approaches (Lo et al. 2009) and contextualizing the enforcement strategies in more dynamic and diversified settings (Zhan et al. 2014). These findings provide us with the background knowledge for understanding the political, economic, societal and institutional contexts of corporate environmental management and compliance in China (Lo and Fryxell 2003, 2005).

Another set of previous research studies is based on surveys and interviews of business managers in several large metropolitan areas – Beijing, Dalian, Guangzhou, and Shanghai – focused on enterprise managers' sense of environmental responsibility (Chung et al. 2005; Lo et al. 2010; Liu et al. 2016). One line of our research focusing on Hong Kong-owned manufacturing enterprises in the PRD region and explored the way these firms perceive the impact of the legal, political, economic, and social environment on their environmental practices (Yee et al. 2013). Using the theoretical model developed in our earlier study, we traced how, in response to environmental impacts and top management motivations for environmental protection (EP), demands from different stakeholders, affect the adoption of environmental management programmes within enterprises in China. We found substantial differences in the way distinct stakeholder groups influence top managements' motivations for EP. Local government demands for EP are positively related to perceptions of risk from noncompliance. The impact of industry pressure is broader but also enhances a belief in the 'business case' for such programmes, as well as top management's commitment to EP. Yet societal pressure is negatively correlated with enterprise motivations for EP (Lo et al. 2010).

Data collection and sample

This longitudinal study was conducted in collaboration with the FHKI and collected data from its 2,284 members in 2007 and 2,150 members in 2013. Questionnaires were addressed to the most senior corporate executives listed in the FHKI's 2007 and 2013 members directories. In total, 568 Hong Kong manufacturers responded to the 2007 survey and 334 to the 2013 survey, a response rate of 25% and 16% respectively. Comparisons (number of employees and industry category) indicated that responding corporations were not different from non-respondents. Although the survey was administered to all members (both Hong Kong and mainland China), only those with factories in the PRD region were selected for this study. The resulting samples were 377 out of a sample size of 1,800, yielding a response rate of 20% in the 2007 survey, and 192 out of a sample size of 1,816, yielding a response rate of 10.5% in the 2013 survey. All questions were measured using a seven-point Likert-scale.

Survey findings

We divide findings from the two surveys into four parts, as presented and discussed below.

Environmental performance and practices

We examined Hong Kong manufacturers' environmental performance and practices in two ways. First, we asked firm executives to reflect on the operation situation of various environmental programmes and activities. Following the existing literature, we offered respondents a list of sixteen environmental practices to evaluate. As shown in Table 8.1, two lines of interesting findings emerge. First, some established activities such as recycling, end-of-pipe control, and environmental audits remained stable during the study period, while other practices (e.g. incorporate ecological themes in marketing, measure key aspects of our business's

Table 8.1 A comparison of HK-based manufacturers' environmental performance and practices in 2007 and 2013

Indicate the strength of your agreement (or disagreement) with the following items	2007	2013	
The operation situation of our company's environmental management programs and activities:	Mean	Mean	T-test statistic
1. Sponsorship of events about environmental protection	3.21	3.48	−1.71
2. Company displays about environmental programmes	3.32	3.60	−1.57
3. Incorporation of ecological themes when marketing some of our products	**3.46**	**3.85**	−2.17*
4. Routine environmental audits	4.16	4.56	−2.33
5. Recycling of waste streams	4.55	4.62	−0.44
6. Environmental training for managers	3.98	4.23	−1.53
7. Environmental training for operatives	3.94	4.12	−1.15
8. Using filters and other emission controls in our production processes	**4.52**	**4.88**	−2.27*
9. Participation in government-sponsored environmental programmes	3.04	3.72	−3.91***
10. Setting environmental performance objectives as part of our annual business plans	3.64	3.93	−1.62
11. Measuring key aspects of our business' environmental performance	**3.67**	**4.09**	−2.41*
12. Preparation and release of environmental reports	2.86	3.08	−1.29
13. Developing a certifiable EMS (environmental management systems) (e.g. ISO 14001)	**3.45**	**4.11**	−3.14**
14. Including environmental performance measures in our management evaluations	3.48	3.72	−1.33
15. Scientifically assessing the life-cycle impact of our products	2.98	3.16	−1.01
16. Making investments in clean production technologies	**3.44**	**4.14**	−4.00***

Source: compiled by the authors.

Note: * Significant < .05; ** Significant < .01; *** Significant < .001.

environmental performance) were getting adopted on an increasingly wider scale. Second, we observed that there were significantly greater efforts and progress in practices that could signal market and government stakeholders. For example, the mean perception of 'participation in government-sponsored environmental programmes' and 'making investments in clean production technologies' (as part of a flagship government-sponsored environmental programme, cleaner production) increased significantly from 3.04 to 3.72, and from 3.44 to 4.14, respectively. Developing a certifiable environmental management system such as the ISO 14001 was also more favoured by Hong Kong manufacturers.

Notwithstanding this progress, however, the majority of the examined environmental practices were only marginally adopted, as the results suggest that firm executives' perceived level on average was mostly between 'level 3 (experimented with, but did not adopt)', 'level 4 (have adopted, but does not seems to be a priority)', and 'level 5 (adopted and emphasized)'. The highest two scores in the 2013 survey were below 5 and were found in the two basic and established practices: recycling (mean value = 4.62) and end-of-pipe emission control (mean value = 4.88). Taken together, findings here corroborate the emerging literature that emphasizes the heterogeneity of environmental programme sponsorship in altering corporate environmental behaviors (Darnall et al. 2009) while also cautioning that such behavioural changes are likely to be ceremonial rather than actual commitment (Boiral 2007).

Second, we asked respondents to compare their performance and actions with those of local firms and industrial peers. Results are presented in Table 8.2. Surveyed Hong Kong enterprises considered themselves to perform better than local enterprises perform in various resource consumption and pollution emission. For example, the average responses to 'producing more pollutants and waste' were between '2 (very much disagree)' and '3 (disagree)', perceptions remaining stable across the two surveys. In energy consumption, our respondents considered themselves to be no different from local enterprises, but this gap enlarged across the two surveys. Overall, they believed their operation had a trivial impact on the

Table 8.2 A comparison of HK-based manufacturers' environmental performance and practices with peer firms in 2007 and 2013

Indicate the strength of your agreement (or disagreement) with the following items	2007	2013	
Relative to most other enterprises in China, our company:	*Mean*	*Mean*	*T-test statistic*
1. produces large amounts of water pollutants	2.17	2.15	0.18
2. produces large amounts of air pollutants	2.16	2.21	0.42
3. produces large amounts of solid waste	2.45	2.60	−1.09
4. produces large amounts of chemical or other hazardous waste	1.81	1.97	−1.35
5. uses relatively little energy	**4.08**	**4.44**	−2.67**
6. uses large amounts of mineral resources	**2.53**	**2.24**	1.98*
7. uses relatively few biological resources	5.00	4.96	0.22
8. has a trivial impact overall on the environment	4.93	5.18	−1.78
Relative to *most other enterprises in our industry,* our company:			
1. is environmentally friendly	**5.00**	**5.30**	−2.37*
2. has made significant progress in reducing our impact on the environment	**4.89**	**5.15**	−2.46*
3. has an outstanding record in environmental protection	**4.44**	**4.68**	−2.13*

Source: compiled by the authors.

Note: * Significant < .05; ** Significant < .01; *** Significant < .001.

environment compared to the local enterprises. Similar findings are also found in comparing with most other enterprises in the industry. Interestingly, this superior performance witnessed a significant increase during our study period. These findings thus extend the literature by revealing a more dynamic view of how diffusions of pro-environmental initiatives within industry and within jurisdiction may evolve (Liu et al. 2018b).

Outcomes of environmental protection measures

We then examined the executives' expected outcomes of adopting the various environmental protection measures mentioned above. In doing so we classified the potential outcomes into expected compliance outcomes and economic outcomes. Results are shown in Table 8.3. We first noticed that all outcome indicators remained stable during the study period, except for one market-related respect that underwent a significant drop. Executives became less confident in the 2013 survey as to whether adopting better environmental protection measures would allow their companies to 'attain competitive advantages over our nearest competitors'. The mean value of this perception dropped from 4.69 in 2007 to 4.41 in 2013. Overall, average expectations on both compliance and economic outcomes fell between 4 (neutral) and 5 (agree), the highest score in 'better compliance' (mean = 5.62, 2007 survey) and the lowest score in 'lower production

Table 8.3 A comparison of HK-based manufacturers' perceived outcomes of environmental measures in 2007 and 2013

Indicate the strength of your agreement (or disagreement) with the following items.	*2007*	*2013*	
By adopting better environmental protection measures, our company can:	*Mean*	*Mean*	*T-test statistic*
1. lower production costs	4.24	4.34	-0.68
2. improve our corporate reputation	5.47	5.56	-0.88
3. improve the quality of our products	4.88	4.84	0.33
4. enhance our employees' commitment	4.49	4.48	0.05
5. serve our customers better	5.10	5.02	0.63
6. better comply with existing environmental regulations	5.62	5.54	0.71
7. avoid facing stricter environmental regulations in the future	5.05	4.92	1.05
8. reduce the risk of lawsuits	5.18	5.12	0.59
9. avoid negative publicity	5.23	5.14	0.80
10. attain better relations with government officials	5.18	5.04	0.32
11. increase the customer base of our products	5.13	4.91	1.81
12. attain competitive advantages over our nearest competitors	**4.69**	**4.41**	1.99*

Source: compiled by the authors.

Note: * Significant < .05; ** Significant < .01; *** Significant < .001.

cost' (mean = 4.24, 2007 survey). In general, we found that Hong Kong-based manufacturers believed that investment in environmental protection measures served more to reduce non-compliance cost than to improve market competency.

Internal management

Top management's environmental awareness is a critical contributor to environment-related investment and environmentally friendly measures adoption. As shown in Table 8.4, we examined top executives' personal awareness and knowledge of the 14 environmental concepts/frameworks as identified in the extant literature and practical trend. We observed the highest score in 'ISO14000' (mean = 4.49, 2013 survey), which has been the most popular environmental management system (EMS) practice in the past decades, and the lowest score in 'Factor 4' (mean = 1.84, 2007 survey). Four indicators are seen significantly increasing executive awareness and knowledge: full-cost accounting, life cycle analysis, clean development mechanisms under the Kyoto Treaty, and clean production technologies for my industry. On average, top executives consider themselves to be somewhere between 'Have just a little knowledge of it' and 'Have some knowledge of it' in relation to these four concepts/programmes. Increasing top management attention to cleaner production technologies is

Table 8.4 A comparison of HK-based manufacturers' environmental awareness in 2007 and 2013

How would you rate your personal awareness and knowledge of the following environmental concepts/ frameworks on the scale provided?	*2007* Mean	*2013* Mean	T-test statistic
1. ISO 14000	4.36	4.49	−0.96
2. Industrial ecology	2.77	2.83	−0.42
3. Principles of sustainable design	2.96	3.21	−1.70
4. Full-cost accounting	2.93	3.38	−2.95**
5. Life-cycle analysis	3.22	3.63	−2.80**
6. Global reporting initiative (GRI)	2.74	2.68	0.48
7. Eco labels	4.06	3.88	1.38
8. Global compact	3.01	2.74	1.89
9. Precautionary principle	3.19	2.98	1.39
10. Environmental management systems (EMS)	3.53	3.76	−1.50
11. Green purchasing requirements	3.80	3.81	0.09
12. Clean production technologies for my industry	3.28	3.98	−4.40***
13. Clean development mechanisms under Kyoto Treaty	2.53	2.84	−2.34*
14. Factor 4	1.84	1.80	0.38

Source: compiled by the authors.

Note: * Significant < .05; ** Significant < .01; *** Significant < .001.

consistent with what we observed earlier, that Hong Kong-based enterprises were performing better in response to local government-initiated voluntary environmental programmes.

Table 8.5 further reveals that in addition to increasing top management attention and involvement in environmental-related issues, other aspects of internal support witnessed some improvement. For instance, the surveyed Hong Kong-based enterprises were more involved in educating their employees to the need to protect the environment. Although overall efforts to share environmental knowledge and information at different levels remain unchanged during the survey period, our respondents showed significantly more disagreement with the statement 'Most employees in our company are totally unaware of the need to protect the environment'. Such a finding hence indicates a lagging influence of initiatives to engage general employees in corporate environmental management. Surveyed managers also see fewer barriers in accessing knowledge of environmental technologies and accurate data of their pollution level.

Table 8.5 A comparison of HK-based manufacturers' internal management in 2007 and 2013

	2007	2013	
Our company's situation	*Mean*	*Mean*	*T-test statistic*
1. Many top-level managers in our company are personally and actively involved in developing environmental policies and monitoring their implementation	**4.57**	**4.80**	−2.01*
2. Ideas on pollution management are shared freely among lower, middle, and upper levels within our company	4.40	4.43	−0.26
3. Our company has an environmental officer at the senior management level	**4.02**	**4.31**	−2.07*
4. Environmental managers or those chiefly responsible for environmental management in our company have adequate authority to influence capital investment decisions	**3.82**	**4.13**	−2.44*
5. We currently have complete knowledge on what pollution control technologies are available	**3.94**	**4.34**	−3.61***
6. Most employees in our company are totally unaware of the need to protect the environment	**3.85**	**3.30**	4.72***
7. Our company has been extremely effective in protecting the environment	4.55	4.71	−1.51
8. It is very difficult for us to get accurate data on the pollution levels of our operation	**3.82**	**3.52**	2.51**

Source: compiled by the authors.

Note: * Significant < .05; ** Significant < .01; *** Significant < .001.

Table 8.6 A comparison of HK-based manufacturers' perceived external influence in 2007 and 2013

	2007	*2013*	
The following groups have made demands on our company to develop better environmental protection measures:	*Mean*	*Mean*	T-*test statistic*
1. The local government (e.g. mayor, local people's congresses)	**4.28**	**4.60**	−2.33*
2. The local EPB (i.e. through fines, fees)	4.44	4.49	−0.36
3. Environmental interest groups	3.68	3.89	−1.53
4. The community via legal action	**3.30**	**3.83**	−3.60***
5. The community via other means (e.g. Internet, bloggers, or boycotts)	**3.00**	**3.53**	−3.78***
6. Media organizations (e.g. newspapers and broadcast media)	**3.19**	**3.62**	−3.06**
7. Customers (e.g. via purchasing requirements or other means)	4.19	4.41	−1.46
8. Employees	**3.61**	**3.90**	−2.21*
9. Major competitors (i.e. through fear of losing business to them)	**3.59**	**3.98**	−2.61**
10. Shareholders / investors	**3.92**	**4.20**	−1.96*
11. Industry associations	3.91	4.11	−1.45
Partnership with External Groups			
1. If approached by local government environmental agencies, our company would be willing to collaborate on corporate environmental protection projects	**5.15**	**4.92**	−2.40*
2. If the FHKI approached us with projects related to corporate environmental protection, our company would be willing to participate	5.12	5.01	1.19
3. If local environmental organizations approached us with ideas for improving corporate pollution, our company would be willing to work with them on corporate environmental protection projects	5.02	4.91	1.16
4. We are willing to work with other firms on projects related to corporate environmental protection	4.98	4.81	1.82
5. We are willing to work closely with academic institutions on projects related to corporate environmental protection	5.01	4.92	0.91

Source: compiled by the authors.

Note: * Significant < .05; ** Significant < .01; *** Significant < .001.

External influence

Hong Kong-based enterprises may experience greater and more complex external influences than their mainland counterparts on their environmental protection decision-making. In our surveys, we first used a traditional stakeholder perspective to look at pressures from various external stakeholders. As shown in Table 8.6, surveyed top executives agreed that their enterprises were under pressure from about half of the eleven stakeholder groups. We found that the top three strongest influences came from local government, EPB, and customers. In particular, our respondents suggested that they experienced significantly more government demand to develop better environmental protection measures. They also became more convinced that it was significantly easier for local EPBs to detect regulatory violations. On the other, respondents either did not agree that there was demand from stakeholders such as environmental interest groups, actions from local community (both legal and others), media organizations, employees, and major competitors or remained neutral on the issue. However, we observed that most of these stakeholders had become more influential during the study period. For instance, the average perception of demand from the community via legal actions had significantly risen from 3.0 (mean value) to 3.53. These findings on the perceptions of stakeholder influence generally resemble what we observed in surveying local-based enterprises in the PRD region (Liu et al. 2016).

The second set of findings indicates an emerging willingness and potential to develop collaboration between regulated enterprises and stakeholders. On average, the surveyed top executives exhibited interest in working with local EPBs, the FHKI, local environmental organizations, other firms, and academic institutions. The mean value of such willingness remains stable during our two surveys, except that the intention to collaborate with local EPB dropped a bit from 5.15 in 2007 to 4.92 in 2013.

Analysis and discussion

In our empirical investigation, we focused on changes over time in two major respects: (1) Hong Kong manufacturers' environmental initiatives/performance and likely outcomes, and (2) internal and external factors may explain firms' green behaviours. First, Hong Kong manufacturers showed a stronger belief in the 2013 survey that their operations in the PRD region had an overall trivial impact on the natural environment, compared to enterprises in the mainland. Although their pollution emission during this period remained largely unchanged, they considered themselves to be more environmentally friendly and made greater efforts in reducing environment externality as compared to other enterprises in the industry. Such changes are mainly reflected in less consumption of mineral resources and greater adoption of environmental practices such as sponsoring events about environmental protection, incorporating ecological themes when marketing some of their products, conducting routine environmental audits, and participating in voluntary environmental programmes. The motivations behind these efforts remained consistent in the two surveys, except that they were less confident in believing that better environmental protection measures could increase the customer base for their products or could attain competitive advantages over their nearest competitors. Future research may consider using multiple data sources with more sophisticated design to explore how diffusions of environmental practices evolve across different industrial sectors within the Belt and Road regions.

Second, for internal factors that explain Hong Kong manufacturers' environmental footprints, we detected both visible organizational stabilities and changes. The attitude of the top management towards EP remained stably high from 2007 to 2013. Their awareness of several particular environmental concepts/frameworks had also enhanced, including full-cost accounting, life cycle analysis, clean production technologies, and clean development mechanisms. In general, there had been greater top management support and employee awareness of environmental issues. At the same time, barriers to related information and technologies had also reduced. Regarding external demands, Hong Kong manufacturers were under greater pressure from various stakeholders, demanding that they develop better environmental protection measures. Particularly, they believe that it has been significantly easier for local EPBs to detect regulatory violations. It will be an interesting research direction to investigate to what extent convergence is observed among Hong Kong-based and local enterprises in conforming to local regulations and stakeholder demands along the Belt and Road regions.

Overall, this research provides important insights into the way Hong Kong-based enterprises have continuously adjusted their corporate environmental management strategies and practices to pursue green manufacturing operations in response to growing local demands for cleaner production in order to acquire environmental corporate citizenship. By observing the effects over time of the various green technical programmes and managerial initiatives adopted by Hong Kong-owned enterprises in the PRD region, our research brings to light both managerial and policy implications on the prospect of Hong Kong manufacturers' adoption of a green strategy and operation in their future industrial investment in the Belt and Road localities.

Projection: Green challenges and opportunities for Hong Kong Manufacturers in China's Belt and Road strategic framework

The Chinese government unveiled the strategic plan for the Belt and Road Initiative in 2013. The New Silk Road Economic Belt aims to link China with Europe through Central and Western Asian countries. The 21st Century Maritime Silk Road connects China with South East Asian countries, Africa, and Europe (see the action plan on the Belt and Road Initiative). Through collaborative efforts to boost economic development along the Belt and Road, this roadmap aims to further integrate China into the world economy and strengthen its influence in these regions.

Environmental protection and pollution control are key elements of developing a cooperative and sustainable business environment in the Belt and Road Initiative. First, many polluting enterprises within the involved regions are still in non-compliance, and they have been subject to increasingly stringent regulatory control for the past decade (Liu et al. 2016; van Rooij 2006; Zheng and Kahn 2013). Second, political commitment to welcome foreign direct investment (FDI), as identified in the Belt and Road Initiative, will attract more foreign investors, including firms with sound environmental reputations and those looking for low environmental standards and preferential treatment in regulatory enforcement. The experience of the past, however, mainly reveals that FDI as an engine of economic growth exacerbated environmental pollution problems in China (Wang and Chen 2014). Last, the strategic plan, as put forward by the central government and the Ministry of Environmental Protection, took a step forward to encourage the outward FDI (*zouchuqu*) of environmentally sound Chinese enterprises in connected regions in the Belt and Road Initiative (Dong et al. 2016). Overall, the new roadmap of the Belt and Road Initiative poses both unprecedented challenges and opportunities for Hong Kong-owned enterprises operating in the involved jurisdictions, both economically and environmentally.

A sizable number of Hong Kong-owned enterprises are operating in the core zones of the Silk Road Economic Belt (SREB) and the Maritime Silk Road (MSR). Taking Quanzhou in Fujian province as an example, Hong Kong-owned enterprises accounted for around half the city's FDI by 2010, over 2,500 new entrants between 2000 and 2010. Similarly, data show that the amount of FDI from Hong Kong has also outnumbered that of other origins of FDI in the cities of Ningbo (Zhejiang province), Chengdu (Sichuan province), and Chongqing in recent years. Collectively with local-based industrial companies, these enterprises emit tremendous quantities of pollutants and exploit China's diminishing stocks of natural capital at an unsustainable rate. This poses a number of serious challenges to Hong Kong and the region as a whole:

1   On aggregate, these enterprises are producing large quantities of pollutants nationwide. These pollutants have adversely affected not only the region's quality of life but also its prospects for long-term sustainable development.
2   As a part of the MSR region, Hong Kong is a recipient of many air- and water-borne pollutants emitted by these enterprises.
3   Many Western countries, that import products from the region, have been developing tougher legal restrictions on products that are not manufactured in environmentally acceptable ways.
4   Many polluting enterprises, including those owned by Hong Kong investors, have increasingly been targeted by local EPBs in their improved environmental regulatory enforcement.
5   Residents in many local communities have increasingly targeted polluting enterprises as objects of collective protests, and environmental degradation is creating environmental refugees to large urban centres.

Consequently, to survive and prosper, Hong Kong-owned enterprises that are operating in the Belt and Road regions should realize that they must adopt strategies that enhance their corporate environmental management capacity. This is not only desirable from a societal perspective but also reflects 'good management', as the costs of environmental irresponsibility can be very high indeed for a firm, especially as officials of mainland EPBs have recently improved their capacity for regulatory enforcement. In addition, the benefits to a firm of good environmental stewardship in their mainland operations are as yet not adequately appreciated. Certain investments in environmental technologies can repay very quickly and clearly (e.g. investments in energy efficiency), while others may be less obvious but even more compelling (e.g. the financial benefits, flexibility, and risk reduction that accompany a good corporate reputation). For instance, the 2015 Belt and Road Environmental Leadership Recognition Award winner, D&G Technology Holding Co Ltd, has strived to manufacture environmentally friendly and energy-saving products, which have been widely adopted in companies along the Belt and Road (see BOCHK Corporate Environmental Leadership Awards). It should be clear that all Hong Kong-owned firms in China must not only begin to meet basic environmental regulatory requirements but should also begin to position themselves as pioneers in the 'greening of industry' in China. In short, they should not repeat the polluting development pathway, which was once widely practised by their predecessors in the PRD region, in seeking business opportunities in the developing Belt and Road localities.

Acknowledgement

This work was partially supported by the General Research Fund project "A Longitudinal and Comparative Study of Corporate Compliance with Environmental Regulations in China" (Project No: CUHK 542413) and the Early Career Scheme project "Government-Sponsored Voluntary Environmental Programs and Firm Exits: A Longitudinal and Comparative Study" (Project No. CityU 21610019) of the Research Grants Council of the Hong Kong Special Administrative Region.

References

Aden, J, Kyu-Hong, A & Rock, MT 1999, 'What is driving the pollution abatement expenditure behavior of manufacturing plants in Korea?', *World Development*, vol. 27, no. 7, pp. 1203–1214.

Bansal, P 2004, 'Evolving sustainability: a longitudinal study of corporate sustainable development', *Strategic Management Journal*, vol. 26, pp. 197–218.

Bansal, P & Roth, K 2000, 'Why companies go green: a model of ecological responsiveness', *Academy of Management Journal*, vol. 43, no. 4, pp. 717–736.

Boiral, O 2007, 'Corporate greening through ISO 14001: a rational myth?', *Organization Science*, vol. 18, no. 1, pp. 127–146.

Branzei, O, Ursacki-Bryant, TJ, Vertinsky, I & Zhang, W 2004, 'The formation of green strategies in Chinese firms: matching corporate environmental responses and individual principles', *Strategic Management Journal*, vol. 25, pp. 1075–1095.

Chatterji, AK & Toffel, MW 2010, 'How firms respond to being rated', *Strategic Management Journal*, vol. 31, no. 9, pp. 917–945.

Christmann, P 2004, 'Multinational companies and the natural environment: determinants of global environmental policy', *Academy of Management Journal*, vol. 47, no. 5, pp. 747–760.

Chung, SS, Fryxell, GE & Lo, CWH 2005, 'A survey on corporate environmental policy statements in mainland China: to what extent do they reflect the environmental commitment of a corporate?', *Environmental Management*, vol. 35, no. 4, pp. 468–482.

Darnall, N, Potoski, M & Prakash, A 2009, 'Sponsorship matters: assessing business participation in government-and industry-sponsored voluntary environmental programs', *Journal of Public Administration Research and Theory*, vol. 20, no. 2, pp. 283–307.

Delmas, M & Toffel, MW 2004, 'Stakeholders and environmental management practices: an institutional framework', *Business Strategy and the Environment*, vol. 13, pp. 209–222.

Dong, Z, Ge, C, Wang, J, Yan, X & Chen, C 2016, 'Strategic implementation framework for the greening development of the Belt and Road Initiative', *Chinese Journal of Environmental Management*, vol. 8, no. 2, pp. 31–35.

Halme, M 2002, 'Corporate environmental paradigms in shift: learning during the course of action at UPM-Kymmene', *Journal of Management Studies*, vol. 39, no. 8, pp. 1087–1109.

Harrison, K & Antweiler, W 2003, 'Incentives for pollution abatement: regulation, regulatory threats, and non-governmental pressures', *Journal of Policy Analysis and Management*, vol. 22, no. 3, pp. 361–382.

Henriques, I & Sadorsky, P 1999, 'The relationship between environmental commitment and managerial perceptions of stakeholder importance', *Academy of Management Journal*, vol. 42, no. 1, pp. 87–99.

Hettige, H, Huq, M & Wheeler, D 1996, 'Determinants of pollution abatement in developing countries: evidence from South and Southeast Asia', *World Development*, vol. 24, no. 12, pp. 1891–1904.

Liu, N, Tang, SY, Lo, CWH & Zhan, X 2016, 'Stakeholder demands and corporate environmental coping strategies in China', *Journal of Environmental Management*, vol. 165, pp. 140–149.

Liu, N, Tang, SY, Zhan, X & Lo, CWH 2018a, 'Political commitment, policy ambiguity, and corporate environmental practices,' *Policy Studies Journal*, vol. 46, no. 1, pp. 190–214.

Liu, N, Tang, SY, Zhan, X & Lo, CWH 2018b, 'Policy uncertainty and corporate performance in government-sponsored voluntary environmental programs.' *Journal of Environmental Management*, vol. 219, pp. 350–360.

Liu, X, Liu, B, Shishime, T, Yu, Q, Bi, J & Fujitsuka, T 2010, 'An empirical study on the driving mechanism of proactive corporate environmental management in China', *Journal of Environmental Management*, vol. 91, no. 8, pp. 1707–1717.

Lo, CWH and Fryxell, GE, 2003, Enforcement styles among environmental protection officials in China. *Journal of Public Policy*, pp. 81–115.

Lo, CWH & Fryxell, GE 2005, 'Governmental and societal support in environmental enforcement in China: an empirical study in Guangzhou', *The Journal of Development Studies*, vol. 41, no. 4, pp. 558–589.

Lo, CWH, Fryxell, GE & Van Rooij, B 2009, 'Changes in enforcement styles among environmental enforcement officials in China', *Environment and Planning A*, vol. 41, no. 11, pp. 2706–2723.

Lo, CWH & Tang, SY 2006, 'Institutional reform, economic changes, and local environmental management in China: the case of Guangdong province', *Environmental Politics*, vol. 15, no. 2, pp. 190–211.

Lo, CWH, Fryxell, GE & Tang, SY 2010, 'Stakeholder pressures from perceived environmental impacts and the effect on corporate environmental management programmes in China', *Environmental Politics*, vol. 19, no. 6, pp. 888–909.

Marshall, RS, Cordano, M & Silverman, M 2005, 'Exploring individual and institutional drivers of proactive environmentalism in the US wine industry', *Business Strategy and the Environment*, vol. 14, pp. 92–109.

May, P 2005, 'Regulation and compliance motivations: examining different approaches', *Public Administration Review*, vol. 65, no. 1, pp. 31–44.

Petts, J et al. 1999, 'The climate and culture of environmental compliance within SMEs', *Business Strategy and the Environment*, vol. 8, pp. 14–30.

Potoski, M & Prakash, A 2005, 'Green clubs and voluntary governance: ISO 14001 and firms' regulatory compliance', *American Journal of Political Science*, vol. 49, no. 2, pp. 235–248.

Prakash, A 2001, 'Why do firms adopt 'beyond-compliance' environmental policies?', *Business Strategy and the Environment*, vol. 10, pp. 286–2999.

Sharma, S 2000, 'Managerial interpretations and organizational context as predictors of corporate choice of environmental strategy', *Academy of Management Journal*, vol. 43, no. 4, pp. 681–697.

Rivera, J 2004, 'Institutional pressures and voluntary environmental behavior in developing countries: evidence from the Costa Rican hotel industry', *Society and Natural Resources*, vol. 17, no. 9, pp. 779–797.

Roy, MJ, Boiral, O & Lagace, D 2001, 'Environmental commitment and manufacturing excellence: a comparative study within Canadian industry', *Business Strategy and the Environment*, vol. 10. p. 257–268.

Tilley, F 1999, 'The gap between the environmental attitudes and the environmental behaviour of small firms', *Business and the Environment*, vol. 8, pp. 238–248.

Van Rooij, B, 2006. 'Regulating land and pollution in China: lawmaking, compliance, and enforcement: theory and cases', *Amsterdam University Press*.

Wang, DT & Chen, WY 2014, 'Foreign direct investment, institutional development, and environmental externalities: evidence from China', *Journal of Environmental Management*, vol. 135, pp. 81–90.

Winter, SC & May, PJ 2001, 'Motivation for compliance with environmental regulations', *Journal of Policy Analysis and Management*, vol. 20, no. 4, pp. 675–698.

Yee, WH, Lo, CWH & Tang, SY 2013, 'Assessing ecological modernization in China: stakeholder demands and corporate environmental management practices in Guangdong province', *The China Quarterly*, vol. 213, pp. 101–129.

Zhan, X, Lo, CWH & Tang, SY 2014, 'Contextual changes and environmental policy implementation: a longitudinal study of street-level bureaucrats in Guangzhou, China', *Journal of Public Administration Research and Theory*, vol. 24, no. 4, pp. 1005–1035.

Zheng, S & Kahn, ME 2013, 'Understanding China's urban pollution dynamics', *Journal of Economic Literature*, vol. 51, no. 3, pp. 731–772.

Zhu, Q, Cordeiro, J & Sarkis, J 2013, 'Institutional pressures, dynamic capabilities and environmental management systems: investigating the ISO 9000–environmental management system implementation linkage', *Journal of Environmental Management*, vol. 114, pp. 232–242.

Section 4

Green development and public-private partnership

9 Greening China's Belt and Road Initiative

A role for Chinese NGOs to go global?

Kathinka Fürst

Implications for domestic NGOs of a global Chinese nation state

Since the early 2000s, the Chinese government has taken steps to "go out" by making China's foreign aid closely intertwined with its "go global" strategy.[1] China's Going Global strategy (走出去战略) is an embodiment of the urgency behind China's economic transformation. In moving away from a planned economy in the 1980s, China began to export resources and capital to the rest of the world. The Going Global strategy sought to bid farewell to the Mao-era mindset of self-reliance, urging Chinese firms to take advantage of booming world trade to invest in global markets. It promotes the deployment of investment in overseas markets to support economic development at home, leading to the internationalization of Chinese enterprises while helping the development of the third sector. Over the past two decades, the policy has provided an overarching framework for actors seeking resources and markets offshore and has been recognized as a significant factor stimulating the unprecedented growth of China's economy.

From 2000 to 2014, China's financial expenditure on foreign aid topped 354.3 billion RMB, which is 267.3 billion more than the total expenditure on foreign aid over the 50 years before 2000.[2] From 2010 to 2014, China's foreign aid stood at 169 billion RMB.[3] The lion's share has come from China's state finances, while the rest was provided by the Export-Import Bank of China, as designated by the Chinese government.[4] Many scholars have examined the breadth of Chinese foreign expenditure and assistance, which entails a number of areas – the structure of the system, the interaction among agencies, and the influence on aid recipients (Zhang & Smith 2017; Norris 2016; Brautigam & Xiaoyang 2012) – but what has been less studied is the role that Chinese NGOs play in delivering foreign aid and their overall position in Chinese (civil) foreign diplomacy. In reality, however, there is ample, at least anecdotal, evidence that suggests that Chinese NGOs are carrying out activities in South East Asian and African countries funded by state Chinese foreign aid, and that through such initiatives these organizations are fostering civil society dialogue and potentially enriching "civil diplomacy."[5] Here, the "Mekong Bright Action" project is a representative example. During the first meeting of the Lancang-Mekong River Cooperation in 2016, China promised to cultivate talent in the field of public health and carry out operations to help poor cataract patients in Cambodia, Laos, Burma, Thailand, and Vietnam to regain their eyesight. Later in the year, the project was carried out by the NGOs China Public Diplomacy Association and the China Charity Alliance, and a total of 800 patients were cured through free operations (Hou 2016). This is just one of several examples illustrating how as China has "gone global," some Chinese NGOs are also embarking on a "going global" trajectory. Anecdotal evidence aside, we know little about the scope and implications of this outward-looking trajectory of Chinese NGOs. Research conducted by China Development Brief suggests that by August 2014, 37 organizations have been part of this trend. Among these organizations, 27 of them provided monetary assistance, 18 of them started programmes overseas, and five of them have staff outside of China.[6]

In the following section, we will take a closer look at the relatively short history of Chinese NGOs going global and analyse some of the characteristics of the phenomenon. But before we do that, a short introduction, focusing on the development and current status of NGOs within Chinese borders is required, with a focus on the environmental sector.

A brief introduction to environmental NGOs in China

Environmental NGOs (eNGO) were among the first type of social organization to emerge after the Chinese government permitted social organization registration in the mid-1990s (Turner 2003). Though dispute remains as to which eNGO was the first social organization established in China, undoubtedly, eNGOs have been a model of inspiration for many other kinds of civil society groups, for not only were they the first to emerge, but they have also been creative in expanding their scope of activity and interacting with different kinds of stakeholders. During the past three decades, Chinese eNGOs have evolved significantly in both quantity and quality. Numbering from zero to approximately 8000 in 2012, eNGOs are experiencing substantial growth as the state has adopted more favourable policies and societal environmental awareness has increased over the years. In addition, eNGOs have started to take actions outside their traditional fields, venturing into areas like policy advocacy and environmental public interest litigation. The complex and dynamic relationship between Chinese eNGOs and other stakeholders is also worth exploring. Unlike NGOs in the western world, Chinese NGOs, especially eNGOs, tend to carry out activities in a non-confrontational manner. The powerful state is both a blessing and a curse as it exerts great influence on Chinese eNGOs' capacity building, resource management, and overall effectiveness. Challenges facing eNGOs can also arise from this aspect, such as difficulties in securing funding, the complex nature of registration, lack of human capital, infrequent cooperation and increased competition, restrictive local politics regarding the environment, and difficulties in obtaining environmental data.

Defining the meaning of NGOs in China

Determining what "NGO" means conceptually creates a definitional difficulty for anybody who studies civil society issues in China. Firstly, the use of a concept developed in a western context to describe organizations that exist in the context of China's authoritarian state is problematic. Historically, the notion of civil society is traced back to the rise of a capitalist economy, the separation of state and church, and the establishment of bureaucratic systems, all of which contributed to the development of modern Europe (Brook & Frolic, 1997; Frolic, 1997). Central to our understanding of civil society is the fact that it gives individuals and groups opportunities to meet around shared interests, independent of the state or government, and not necessarily connected to family life or working life. Civil society and NGOs[7] are thus often understood as something separate from, and at other times in opposition to, the state (Brook & Frolic, 1997). When the notion that civil society exists, in some respects, in opposition to the state, is applied to non-democratic regimes, scholars often struggle to reconcile the discrepancies between theory and reality (Gleiss 2014). In China, as in other authoritarian states, most scholars agree that NGOs and the civil society that they are a part of, can only be understood in terms of a state system set up to limit their independence and autonomy (Alagappa 2004, p.37). Indeed, "State-led," "semi-civil," "embedded," "incorporated," "contained," "nascent," and "limited" are all terms commonly used to describe civil society organizations in authoritarian China (Unger & Chan, 1995; Frolic, 1997; Kang & Feng 2006; Ma 2006; Ho 2001). For example, Hsu (2010 p. 259) argues that "the relationship between Chinese NGOs and the State is often one of strategic alliances and interdependence" and that Chinese NGO leaders note that "the purpose of their NGOs is not to weaken or replace the State, but instead to strengthen the State and help it fulfil its responsibilities to its citizens." This view is echoed by Wexler et al. (2006), who claim that Chinese civil society organizations seek close and cooperative relations with the government more than autonomy, although autonomy is not irrelevant for them.

Given the elusive boundary between the state and civil society in many authoritarian regimes, a central argument in the literature is that civil society in authoritarian states should be conceptualized not based on what it is, but on what it does (Gleiss 2014). In fact, it is not uncommon to argue against applying a single definition or framework for civil society and State-society relations in China; for example, Saich (2000: 138) argues that China is "a country where multiple models of State-society relations may be operating at the same time." So, instead of starting out with a predefined notion of what constitutes an NGO and letting that definition guide their research, China scholars have developed a number of strategies to define the types of organizations included in their studies. Some utilize existing definitions of "NGO," modifying them to fit the reality in China. Wu (2013) for example, builds on the well-recognized definition of civil society organizations developed by Salamon and Anheier in 1997,[8] but adds two specific modifications: first, due to the fact that current Chinese law makes it extremely difficult for non-profit organizations to obtain official status, Wu does not look closely at the formal status, but rather focuses on the actual work and organizational nature of a grassroots group to determine whether or not it is an NGO. Regardless of whether an organization is legally registered, Wu (2013) considers any publicly recognized social organization to be an NGO, as long as it is in practice volunteer-based, not-for-profit, and autonomous. Second, Wu (2013) focuses on groups established outside of the state apparatus and differentiates them from quasi-governmental, state-affiliated organizations, or government organized NGOs (Wu 2013). Other scholars have adopted different strategies to narrow down the type of organizations included in their studies of civil society in China. One such approach is to look at key aspects of the organizations and divide them accordingly. Lu (2007), for example, divides environmental groups into those that avoid confrontation with the government and those that are less fearful of causing offence (Lu 2007).

Providing a definition for the term "NGO" in the Chinese setting is further complicated by the fact that a number of Chinese language terms can mean "NGO." The direct translation of NGO into Chinese is *fei zhengfu zuzhi/jigou* (非政府组织/机构). This expression is not used much in Chinese due partly to the connotation of the Chinese term *fei* (非), which is strongly associated with the notion of opposition. Instead, many NGO staffers simply use the English term "NGO" when talking about the organization they work for.

Chinese law defines three types of civil society organizations. According to China's Ministry of Civil Affairs, all civil society organizations should be registered in one of the following three categories: (1) social organization (社会团体or社团); (2) private non-enterprise unit (民办企业单位); or (3) foundation (基金会). "Social organizations" are officially defined as "non-profit organizations which are formed voluntarily by Chinese citizens in order to realize the shared objectives of their members and which carry out activities according to their charters."[9] "Private non-enterprise units" are officially defined as "non-profit social organizations which are using non-State assets and formed by social enterprise units, social organizations and other social forces or citizens."[10] "Foundations" are officially defined as "non-profit juristic persons who utilize the assets denoted by natural persons, juristic persons or other organizations to improve the commonwealth."[11] In addition to these three types of legally defined entities, "civil organizations" (民间组织) and "social associations" (社会组织) are commonly used in official documentation to refer to one or several of the above listed categories of civil society organization (Xu & Zhao 2010). In addition to these official designations, the terms "grassroots organization" (草根组织) and "government-initiated organization" (官办组织) are also used to describe a variety of organizations that operate in NGO-like ways in China. Spires (2011) defines "grassroots organizations" as those organizations located outside the vertical control mechanisms that the party has tried to impose. These grassroots groups are, according to Spires (2011: 10), "organized by Chinese citizens without the government's initiative or approval, congealing in the social spaces where the government is absent, impotent, or unwilling to act." "Government initiated organizations," often referred to as GONGOs, are organizations with strong institutional ties to government bodies. These organizations or groups were created by the state at different administrative levels to serve as support mechanisms. According to Wu (2003) the government's initiative to establish the group is the core criterion differentiating a GONGO from a genuine civil societal group. An important distinction between GONGOs and the state apparatus is that GONGOs do not implement projects directly through formal administrative systems (Wu 2003). Wu (2003) notes how the function of GONGOs is changing in China. Although these organizations were originally initiated by the state apparatus, GONGOs are gaining greater organizational autonomy (Wu 2003: 40).

A second challenge that makes it difficult to define accurately what we mean by the term NGO in China is the variety of scales, outreach modes, types, and formats of activities implemented by civil society organizations. These groups in China are now highly diverse in terms of their missions, organizational structures, degree of autonomy, and influence. Even organizations engaged in roughly similar activities can have very different organizational characteristics, depending on where they are located or whether they work at the local, regional, or national level. In fact, if we had to choose a single word to describe the broad panorama of NGOs and their activities in China today, it would be "diverse." Getting a bird's eye view of Chinese civil society organizations today is therefore a "Herculean task" (Wang & He 2004 p. 10).

The definition of NGO used in this chapter is synthesized from the work of Chinese scholar Jia (2004: 7–13): organizations which are largely non-governmental, formally organized, not for profit, public value oriented, self-governed, and based on voluntary participation.

Chinese eNGOs: from domestic conservationists to civil diplomats

Responding to challenges posed by socio-economic transformation, accompanying environmental deterioration, and decentralization of decision-making and enforcement power, the Chinese government has provided Chinese eNGOs with economic and political space to engage in environmental work (Tang & Zhan 2008; Fei 2016). Many Chinese provinces and cities, especially those located in well-developed areas, have become increasingly open and have begun to acknowledge the important role played by eNGOs, although it should be noted that the space for eNGOs to operate and implement activities is constantly fluctuating.[12]

According to the latest statistical report from the Ministry of Civil Affairs (2019), there are now over 819,000 registered social organizations in China, three times more than there were ten years ago. NGOs are "at the forefront of civil society development" (Turner 2003: 1). The number of eNGOs has risen from zero in 1994 to 7881 in 201, and their scope of activity has expanded from environmental education and natural resource protection to policy advocacy and environmental public interest litigation. When it comes to which organization can claim to be the first environmental NGO operating in China, there is some ambiguity. The Chinese Society for Environmental Sciences (CSES) was founded in May 1978 by environmental authorities, and some scholars argue that this was China's first NGO (Cao 2010). A year later, in 1979, the World Wildlife Fund (WWF) made its debut in China with a programme calling for the preservation of giant pandas (Xie 2011), making the WWF one of the pioneers of the NGO community in China. In 1991, the Saunders Gull Conservation Society registered in Panjin, Liaoning province. Some consider this organization to be the first real "independent NGO" in China (Cao 2010). Others consider the Daosit Club for Green Civilization, established in Sichuan in 1993, or the Shandong-based Green Civil Association, established in Weihai City in the same year, to be the joint-pioneer NGOs in China (Zhao 1993: 28–9). However, the establishment of Friends of Nature (FoN) in 1994 is generally considered a milestone in the history of environmental activism in China, as most scholars in the field regard FoN to have been China's first NGO (Knup 1997; Ho 2001; Economy 2004; Schwartz 2004; Yang 2005). FoN was founded by Liang Congjie, a descendant of Liang Qichao, a prominent reformer of the late Qing Dynasty, and a member of the Chinese People's Political Consultative Conference (CPPCC). He was no doubt aided, even protected, by his lineage and his connections with China's elite (Larson 2010). In 1995, Global Village Beijing (GVB) was established by Liao Xiaoyi, a graduate in philosophy, in Beijing. That same year the Association for Green Volunteers of Chongqing City was established by Wu Deming, whose wide-ranging work experience prior to establishing the NGO included time in the Chinese army. In 1997, Wang Yongchen, a journalist and a former member of FoN, established Green Earth Volunteers (GEV) in Beijing. FoN, GVB, and GEV are recognized by many as the forerunners that led the way in organizing NGOs and mobilizing the public for environmental protection in Beijing and beyond (Xie 2011). The following few years saw a rapid growth of green civil society organizations throughout the country. The number of formally registered NGOs in Beijing alone doubled from 9 to 18 from 1995 to 1996 (Ho 2001: 901).

In industrial countries such as Japan, NGOs were active from the very beginning of industrialization in the fight against industrial pollution, and same is true in the US. In China, however, the pioneer NGOs began with wildlife protection, water conservation, and other ecology-related activities (Gong 2009). Much NGO activity during the early stage of NGO development in China focused on environmental education, nature appreciation, and protection of the environment. In this period China's NGOs initiated a series of wide-ranging publicity campaigns calling for the protection of endangered species (Cao 2010), such at the giant panda, the golden monkey, and the Tibetan antelope. The campaign to protect the Yunnan golden monkey was begun by nature photographer Xi Zhinong, who reported in 1995 that logging practices were destroying the habitat of the monkey. His efforts drew the attention of a number of environmental activists in Yunnan and other parts of the country, including the founder of FoN, Liang Congjie. FoN mobilized its members to write letters and send petitions to central government officials and launched a media campaign to raise public awareness of

Increase in numbers of civil society organizations and eNGOs over time

Formally registered environmental social organizations in Beijing	No.	9	+9 →	18
	Yr.	(1995)		(1996)
Grassroots environmental groups according to Guobing Yang	No.		+69 →	
	Yr.	(1997)		(1999)
Student environmental groups according to Lu Hongyan	No.	10	+172 →	182
	Yr.	(1996)		(2002)
Grassroots eNGOs at the Global Environmental Facility's conference	No.		→	60
	Yr.			(2002)
Registered eNGOs in the country according to the All China Environmental Federation	No.		→	>3500
	Yr.			(2008)
Registered eNGOs in China	No.	5678	+38,8% →	7881
	Yr.	(2007)		(2012)

Figure 9.1 Increase in number of eNGOs

the plight of the endangered monkeys. Chinese Premier Zhu Rongji responded in 1998 by expressing his anger at large-scale logging in Yunnan. Soon afterward a commissioner in Yunnan was dismissed from his position for his failure to ban logging in mountain areas (Liu 2006). FoN also claims to have exacted a promise from local officials to reconsider earlier decisions to permit logging, and ultimately withdraw such permits. Knup (1997: 12) argues that

> the significance of this activity lies not in the promise to reconsider the logging decisions but in the form of advocacy Liang and FoN created. They identified a problem which the central government itself recognized but which it was ill equipped or unwilling to address. They mobilized citizens and the media in support of stated government goals for sustainable development practices, and compelled the government to enforce its own policies.

By 2000, a surge of new NGO development was underway in China, with the majority of these NGOs being organized by former staff members of the earlier groups (Xie 2011). Data on the number of NGOs operating in China in the period between 2000 and 2005 varies. Wu (2009) estimates that the total number of grassroots, volunteer-based environmental associations had reached 200 by 2006, and that these organizations were dispersed throughout all provinces of the country. In 2005, Economy (2005) claimed that there were approximately 2,000 environmental groups officially registered as NGOs in China, with perhaps as many more registered as for-profit business entities or not registered at all. The discrepancy in the numbers presented by the two scholars can be attributed to different definitions of what constitutes an environmental group. Even if we take

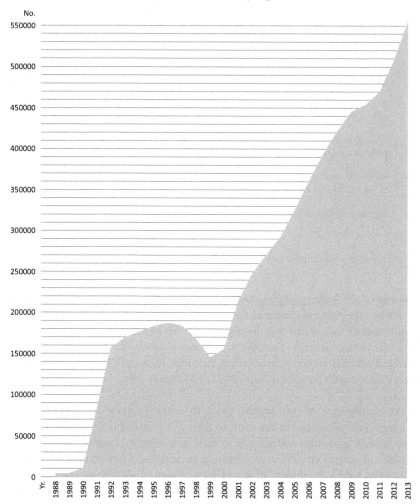

Increase in numbers of civil society organizations over time

Figure 9.2 Increase in number of civil organizations

Wu's (2009) lower estimate, it is clear that the number of NGOs increased rapidly in the first part of the 2000s.

After the start of the new millennium, China's NGOs began engaging in more coordinated actions (Cao 2010). For example, during the summer of 2004, many Beijing-based NGOs jointly launched a campaign to persuade hotels and other large public buildings to keep their thermostats at 26°C in an effort to conserve energy and ultimately to encourage government policymakers to create legislation requiring enterprises to set thermostats to 26°C (Economy 2005). Over 50

NGOs around the country joined the rollout of the campaign. In June 2005, the campaign achieved its goal when the government issued a statute stipulating that air-conditioning should be set at or above 26°C in public buildings during the summer (Qiao & Wang 2005).

By the mid-2000s networks of environmental groups able to undertake coordinated action were coming into existence. One example is the China Youth Climate Action Network (CYCAN), which was established in 2007 by seven university and college-based NGOs. Since 2007 more than 450 colleges and universities have participated in activities organized or sponsored by CYCAN. According to CYCAN, more than ten thousand people have been directly involved in these activities and more than one million people have been affected indirectly.[13] The use of internet technology and online social media platforms also started to play a role in NGO activities during the mid-2000s. In 2006, for example, the Institute of Public and Environmental Affairs launched the China Water Pollution Map, a user-friendly online resource that allows the public to access thousands of environmental quality and pollution infraction records released by various government agencies. A report published by the All China Environmental Federation in 2008 put the number of registered NGOs in the country at more than 3,500 (All China Environmental Federation 2008). According to the All China Environmental Federation, by 2012, 7,881 NGOs had registered in China, meaning the number of registered NGOs had more than doubled between 2007 and 2012 (Shen 2013).

At the time of writing, we are also witnessing a new trajectory for NGOs operating in China, namely those focusing on and implementing activities outside Chinese boarders. However, compared with their peers in other fields, such as health and education, Chinese eNGOs have joined the "going global" trajectory fairly late. In the following section we will briefly examine the outward-looking trajectory of NGOs in China, before analysing Chinese eNGOs "going global" in more detail later in the chapter.

The Chinese NGO "Going Global" Pioneers: disaster relief, health and education from the 1950s

Up until quite recently, most of the effort of Chinese NGOs' engagement outside of the borders of China has been in the fields of poverty relief, education, health, and humanitarian assistance. Many of these organizations had an official background, with funds or employees from the government; so-called government organized non-governmental organizations (GONGOs).[14] A majority of these organizations provide humanitarian assistance in emergency situations such as the One Foundation,[15] the Amity Foundation,[16] China Foundation for Poverty Alleviation and its rescue team, China Social Welfare Foundation and its Blue Leopard rescue team,[17] and the Blue Sky Rescue team.[18] These organizations commonly carry out rescue operations, provide disaster risk assessment, solicit and deliver goods and materials to disaster-impacted areas, arrange relief for disaster victims, and contribute in post-disaster reconstruction. For instance, in the devastating Nepal earthquake in 2015, The Blue Sky Rescue Team sent Chinese professional medical personnel and disaster relief experts to affected areas where they joined forces with local efforts in carrying out rescue activities. In the aftermath of the same earthquake, the China Foundation for Poverty Alleviation provided water, shelters, and medical assistance to the displaced people. This type of humanitarian aid has extended far beyond countries close to Chinese borders. Following the 2016 earthquake in Ecuador and 2015 floods in Myanmar, Chinese NGOs actively provided disaster relief and assistance. The undertaking by Chinese NGOs is often supported, and always endorsed by the Chinese government. Chinese media tend to portray stories of Chinese "heroes" contributing to rescue efforts far outside of the Chinese national jurisdiction. And as such, these efforts play a role in building a positive international image of China globally while contributing to national pride domestically. When viewed subjectively, it is difficult to tell to what extent these efforts are a part of, either by design or convenience, an orchestrated effort, led by the state to strengthen national pride. Objectively, however, Chinese NGOs emerged within the context of an authoritarian state and as such, interaction with the state is sometimes inevitable. Unlike Western NGOs, Chinese NGOs may not have the capacity to implement their goals and strategies without the government's support, especially overseas (Hsu et al. 2016).

It is not only in disaster relief that Chinese NGOs have been active in the international arena in the earlier years of their outbound-focused activities. Several Chinese NGOs have also provided health care aid overseas. The main organizations carrying out health care activities overseas are the Red Cross Society of China and China Foundation for Peace and Development. For example, the China Foundation for Peace and Development implemented a number of series of "Tour of Sight" activities in Myanmar, Mongolia, and other countries, offering free cataract operation programmes and sending local medical staff from host countries to China for training, and they have also provided relevant equipment for surgical eye operations. In Myanmar alone, 977 cataract patients were cured.[19]

In addition, in this same time period, a very limited number of Chinese NGOs have been engaged in educational activities outside of the borders of China. To the best of the knowledge of this author, only two NGOs, namely the China Foundation for Poverty Alleviation and the China Youth Development Foundation, have implemented such activities overseas. Their primary activities include school construction and scholarship and financial aid distribution. For instance, the China Foundation for Poverty Alleviation has provided financial aid to students in Mandalay, Myanmar. This NGO has also implemented a project to provide lunch to primary school students in Sudan and Ethiopia. In a similar approach, the China Youth Development Foundation expanded its flagship Project Hope[20] programme to Africa and conducted their first pioneering projects in Kenya, Tanzania, Burundi, and Rwanda, assisting youths to continue their education. According to the latest data, China Youth League Foundation received a targeted donation of 34.122 million RMB and built 22 Project Hope primary schools across these countries.[21]

In short, when working overseas, Chinese NGOs are more likely to focus on traditional fields like health and education. Compared with sensitive areas, such as labour, security, and human rights, these fields are politically and culturally safer, which no doubt provides more opportunities for NGOs to gain support from both the Chinese and foreign governments. Be that as it may, as the depth of China's exchanges with the world increases, calls for Chinese NGOs to move abreast with the BRI are on the rise. With them, come new opportunities and challenges.

Changing trajectory: going out to green the Belt and Road?

In comparison with NGOs that work in traditional areas, such as poverty alleviation and health, there are very few NGOs that focus on the environmental and social arenas in the international context. Until very recently, however, domestic Chinese NGOs have not emphasized the environmental and social impacts brought by China's overarching "going global" strategy. This situation partly resulted from the limited number of Chinese eNGOs domestically. According to the Bulletin of Statistics on the Development of Social Services (2017) published by the Ministry of Civil Affairs, the proportion of eNGOs among civil society organizations is only 0.86%, paling into insignificance when compared with NGOs focused on education (30.06%) or health (4.77%).[22] However, we are now witnessing some early signals indicating that the Belt and Road Initiative is becoming a driving force pushing Chinese eNGOs to adopt a more outward-looking approach. To argue that the environmental impacts of the BRI are contested would be an understatement at best. Concerns over negative externalities, such as deforestation, species invasion, biodiversity loss, and unsustainable resource management are mounting ('China's BRI' 2019). A couple of examples can be listed to illustrate how the environmental impacts of the BRI have been contested. Take for example the Myitsone Dam in Myanmar. From the start of its construction, the transparency of environmental impact assessment (EIA) was heavily suspect. For local Burmese, the Myitsone area symbolizes their local culture, and a high dam is a violation of their sacred place. Eventually in 2011, the construction of the dam was suspended, though the project has remained controversial since then. After the National League for Democracy took power in 2016, the Burmese government set up a 20-member commission, including the chief minister of Kachin, to review the project, including its environmental and social impacts (Thousands 2019). Despite widespread opposition, anecdotal evidence shows that China in 2019 was trying to revive the dam project[23] (Myitsone 2019). Similarly, BRI-backed power plant projects in Mongolia were strongly opposed by Russia, which was concerned about the negative impact on Lake Baikal (one of the deepest freshwater lakes in the world, which has been a focal point historically for environmental protest within Russia/Soviet Union), which finally led to its suspension. From the perspective of proponents of the BRI however, BRI infrastructure development does not always have negative impacts on the environment. For instance, new infrastructure has accelerated transition to cleaner energy sources in a number of South Asian countries ('The BRI's environmental challenges' 2019) and, using its invaluable experience, China made substantial contributions to alleviating desertification in countries along the route.[24]

Chinese foreign direct investment has been taking place for many years already, but it is only recently that Chinese eNGOs have started to pay attention to this and begun playing a role. This prompts the question: Why is it only now that we are seeing Chinese eNGOs taking an outward-looking trajectory?

State facilitated opportunities: the Chinese state pushing for a Green BRI

The Chinese government has made a strong commitment to ensuring that the BRI is conducted in an environmentally sustainable manner. For instance, in the national document *"Guiding Opinion on Promoting Construction of a Green 'One Belt One Road'"* published in April 2017, the principles of ecological civilization[25] were laid out for the direction of the BRI. The *Guiding Opinion* promises, among other things, global cooperation on a low-carbon economy, ecological conservation, green production, green finance, and green consumerism.[26] One month after the release of the *Guiding Opinion*,[27] in May 2017 at the Belt and Road Forum in Beijing, Chinese officials again pledged that the government would ensure that the BRI will be operating in line with the environmental objectives set in the Guiding Opinion.

In addition, numerous measures have been taken to ensure that the BRI remains a "green" initiative, both through policy development and through financial mechanisms. For instance, in September 2016, the National Development and Reform Commission (NDRC)[28] signed an MoU and Action Plan for the BRI with the United Nations Development Programme China (UNDP China). The collaboration aims to align and accelerate the United Nation's sustainable development goals with the effort from the BRI and, furthermore, to link Belt and Road countries in order to develop mutual understanding of policies and regulations. In April 2018, NDRC had a joint conference with UNDP China, in which the implementation of the MoU and Action Plan were discussed, and the focus of work has now shifted towards research cooperation and capacity building.[29]

In 2017, four departments (Ministry of Commerce, National Development and Reformation Commission, Ministry of Foreign Affairs, and Ministry of Environmental Protection) issued *Guidance on Promoting Green Belt and Road*, aimed at enhancing environmental protection during the BRI project. Also, in April 2019, the International Coalition for Green Development on the Belt and Road was established on The Belt and Road Forum for International Cooperation; it focuses on creating communication bridges between stakeholders and providing theoretical and policy support for green BRI. According to Xinhua Net (Li 2019), the Coalition will concentrate its effort on nine areas, including renewable energy, green finance, and environmental information disclosure. All the above measures indicate that engagement from society has been an integral part of the BRI since the outset of this endeavour, and as such also an important aspect of the green BRI. In September 2017, the Industrial and Commercial Bank of China (ICBC) issued its first One Belt One Road Green Climate Bonds offshore in Luxembourg. The bonds, issued in USD and EUR, raised USD 2.15 billion.[30]

While having these policies in place might be better than not having them at all, the jury is still out as to whether or not these policies, guidelines, and initiatives will be sufficient in ensuring that the BRI really will be "green." Without sufficient and effective monitoring mechanisms, liability clauses, and reliable avenues to claim compensation against those who fail to comply with these, there is a real risk, some argue, that such initiatives, opinions, and guidelines will merely be hollow promises. Jinmei Liu, an environmental lawyer at ClientEarth, has serious doubts that China is only paying lip service to greening the BRI. She is concerned about BRI's lack of overarching environmental policy and has pointed to the fact that the Chinese government has developed many guidelines that are not legally binding.[31] In short, the global concern on the part of global NGOs/IOs that the BRI lacks the mechanisms to provide oversight and prevent environmental externalities has provided not only an opportunity, but also a need for eNGOs in China to take their initiatives and social engagement to a "global" level.

Chinese eNGOs going global: who is doing what, and where?

Motivated by the need to do so, Chinese eNGOs have started to look globally rather than locally, and some of these organizations have, in recent years, made determined efforts to engage effectively in this new scope of work. The overall landscape of eNGOs joining the "going global" phenomenon suggests a number of trends pertaining to the BRI and eNGOs that we will analyse in more depth in the following parts of this chapter. First, we see a notable distinction in terms of the social structure of BRI related NGO initiatives stemming from China:

- Top-down: people to people exchange.
- Bottom-up: domestic grassroots eNGO collaboration to green the BRI.
- Chinese eNGOs with an international presence.

In the following sections we will examine these three emerging trends.

Top-down: people to people exchange

From the outset of the BRI design, there has been an awareness from the Chinese state about the prominence, at least in appearance, of civil diplomacy as an integral part of the BRI. The Chinese state prefers to describe this as "people to people exchange." In 2017, China issued the *Plan for Social Organizations to Promote People to People Exchange (2017–2020)*, encouraging social organization and NGO involvement in the BRI. It has focused on seven main areas for "people to people" exchange, including poverty alleviation, disaster reduction, and climate change mitigation and adaption. Among the 90 organizations included in the *Plan for Social Organizations to Promote People to People Exchange (2017–2020)*, there are seven eNGOs,[32] all of which have an official background. Three of them are regional environmental organizations, respectively from Chongqing and Hebei.

As a mechanism to foster social organization engagement across the globe on BRI issues, the Silk Road NGO Cooperation Network has been established by the China NGO Network for International Exchanges. A Silk Road NGO Cooperation Network Forum will be held every two years in China, while the regional forums will be held in the years between the main forum in one of the member countries. In early 2019, the second Network Forum was held in Beijing, where 170 representatives from 22 countries attended the forum and had wide-ranging discussions on BRI cooperation. The outcomes of the forum focused on five aspects, which include livelihood cooperation and donation, capacity building, and talent exchanges and cultural exchange.[33]

Another main mechanism for NGOs to participate in BRI is provided through the China NGO Network for International Exchanges (CNIE). CNIE was established in October 2005 as a national non-profit civil society organization with independent legal person status. It is mainly composed of national NGOs and peoples from various social fields engaged in research and practice in peace and disarmament, social development, science and education, culture and art, health care, environmental protection, democracy and human rights, ethnic and religious affairs, policy advocacy and law, business and commerce, public welfare and charity, poverty alleviation and disability assistance, and women and youth affairs. To enhance people-to-people communication and collaboration between China and South East Asian countries, CNIE initiated China-Southeast Asia High-Level People-to-People Dialogue in 2013 which, since then, has been held twice, in China and Indonesia, respectively. CNIE has also hosted Cross-Himalaya Dialogue for China, India and Nepal, and other bilateral events like China–Myanmar Roundtable on People-to-People Exchanges and China–Mongolia People-to-People Dialogue, all with the purpose of consolidating social foundation and garnering public support for the development of state-to-state relations between China and relevant countries.[34]

Another significant initiative comes from the China Council for International Cooperation and Environment Development (CCICED), an organization with an official background, which signed a long-term strategy cooperation MoU with the World Resources Institute (WRI) on priority cooperation in Green Belt and Road. It also started a project on Green One Belt One Road and SDG to 2030, and cooperated with experts from the International Union for Conservation of Nature (IUCN).

Some more concrete projects have been carried out under the umbrella of "people to people" exchange. For instance, the All-China Environmental Federation and China Ecological Civilization Research and Promotion Association has held communicating activities with local NGOs in Laos; discussing projects conducted and social responsibilities of enterprises. To promote communication between young people, China Charity Federation also has projects organizing students from Cambodia, Laos, Myanmar, Thailand, Vietnam, and Mongolia to visit China. Funded openly or covertly by the Chinese government, no doubt, these activities are designed to foster mutual understanding between China and BRI countries, paving the way for the BRI.

Overall, it is clear that "people-to-people exchange" form an integral part of the BRI, and as such, is designed to perform an essential role in China's strategic development. In this process, NGOs act as a service provider. Pursuing the goal established by the government, "going out" is relatively easy for NGOs of this kind as they are supported not only financially, but also politically by the Chinese state.

Bottom-up: domestic grassroots eNGOs in collaboration to Green the BRI

The situation is quite different for more grassroots organizations in China with more bottom-up efforts seeking to "green" the BRI. Here, we will take a closer look at some of these initiatives.

In September 2016, the Belt and Road Green Development Partnership[35] was launched to provide policy recommendations for sustainable development under the BRI by bringing together Chinese and international thinktanks, eNGOs, and foundations. Greenovation: Hub[36] acts as a coordinator of the Belt and Road Green Development Partnership. The Platform has 14-member domestic eNGOs that focus on greening the BRI. The Partnership aims to fulfil the goals set by the 2030 Agenda for Sustainable Development and the Paris Climate Agreement, focusing on issues of ecological protection, climate change, energy transition, green finance, and industry cooperation. By working with the international community to promote sustainable development under BRI, the Partnership hopes to help China leverage and improve its leadership in global green governance.

The Partnership plays a role in many areas, such as: providing an enabling environment for participating institutions to facilitate extensive exchange on green development of BRI; facilitating experts to provide professional guidance on topics under BRI; submitting research results and policy recommendations to relevant departments and agencies to maximize the usability and impact of BRI outcomes; and expanding cooperative partnerships with institutions at home and abroad to enhance China's international influence in environmental and climate change governance. With a vision of promoting the implementation of the Paris Climate Agreement and the achievement of the United Nations 2030 SDGs, they aim to use BRI as an opportunity to develop China's capacity for green governance and to build a foundation for the joint consultation and development of BRI and facilitate the sustainable, balanced, and inclusive development of different countries around the world. Their goal is to help China improve its green leadership through global cooperation and development for BRI as well as build a diverse, multi-layered, and effective exchange partnership to promote cross-sectoral dialogue and cooperation, and to build consensus among multiple stakeholders.

The Belt and Road Green Development Partnership plays an important role domestically in China. However, it does not implement activities outside of China. Here we take a look at some cases of domestic grassroots eNGOs that have actually done work outside of China's border seeking to ensure a green BRI.

The Global Environmental Institute and its efforts to green BRI in South East Asia

The Global Environmental Institute (GEI) was founded in 2004 with the aim of securing sustainable development within the country's borders and abroad. Based in Beijing, it works alongside key policymakers, businesses, scientists, civil society leaders, and local communities to foster dialogue and innovative solutions to protect the environment and enhance economic opportunity within China as well as in South East Asia and Africa.

GEI has conducted independent research leading to the publication of reports on investment assessment in Vietnam, Laos, and Myanmar. Those reports include introductions on the current condition of investment, elaboration on environmental laws and policies, and typical case studies. The organization has carried out field research in Myanmar pertaining to the Myitsone Dam investment project,[37] and collected data on the timber trade in Myanmar. In addition, GEI has established a broad cooperation network with other organizations, including governments, enterprises, and other NGOs. For instance, in November 2014, GEI signed an agreement with the Department of Forestry in Myanmar, to conduct a project against illegal timber trading, which they claim is the first project with cooperation between a Chinese NGO and a foreign government. In addition, GEI also has a programme focusing specifically on capacity building among enterprises pertaining to overseas investment. Working with the Center for Climate Strategies and Guangzhou Institute of Energy Conversion, Chinese Academy of Science, from 2013 to the present, GEI has issued renewable energy planning tool packages and guidances on capacity building among senior executives in Myanmar.

Chinese eNGOs with an international presence

In addition to the two above-mentioned trends, with the development of China's "going global," another new kind of eNGO has emerged. They are founded in China, but have branches overseas, and carry out programmes on the international arena. Unlike other domestic eNGOs, these organizations prioritize their overseas projects and often operate in countries that are not covered by the BRI.

China House

China House, an NGO founded in 2014, is a typical example of an internationally orientated eNGO. It focuses on wildlife protection, China–Africa collaboration, and Chinese enterprise "going out." They are targetted towards youth, organizing young people to conduct surveys and research in Africa, Latin America, and South East Asia. Compared to policy recommendation, these research actions are more orientated towards educating and raising awareness among youth. For example, in 2016, partnering with WWF, China House organized a group of young people who successfully conducted research on the corporate social responsibility (CSR) strategies adopted by Chinese mining companies in Kenya, Tanzania, and Zambia; they also analysed labour relations and human resource management, environmental protection, and community relations of Chinese companies operating in Africa. Also, since 2015, China House has worked with the Kenya-based Africa Network for Animal Welfare (ANAW) to organize over 50 de-snaring activities with over 1,000 Chinese volunteers.[38]

Paradise Foundation Africa Projects

Paradise Foundation has launched multiple projects in Africa, the most prominent being the "African Ranger Awards" plan which seeks to raise awareness about the need to conserve Africa's wildlife, emphasizing the critical role that front-line rangers play in conservation. Under the ten-year African Ranger Awards programme, 50 African front-line wildlife rangers will be officially recognized each year. Each winner will be awarded US$3,000.[39] Another example is the Virunga Bamboo Charcoal Program. The Paradise Foundation helped the Virunga National Park in the Democratic Republic of Congo establish a bamboo charcoal factory in 2019, aiming to encourage local people to plant bamboo and produce bamboo charcoal to replace fuelwood to combat deforestation. One reason is that the bamboo forest will slow down habitat loss, and another is that the factory will create more employment opportunities for local people, bringing poverty alleviation. Also, in August 2018, the Paradise Foundation signed a cooperation agreement with the local African conservation organization Mara Elephant Project to jointly carry out the Greater Maasai Mara Program, which aims to provide protection for elephants in an area of 4,000 square kilometres outside the Maasai Mara National Reserve by developing and managing eight anti-poaching patrol units. In the meantime, Paradise works to design and tailor Mara eco-tourism products to local needs, explore the Chinese market, and establish a mechanism that channels profits from tourism back into conservation.

These initiatives are completely outside the of realm of civil diplomacy, driven by completely different motives and serving different purposes. Compared with people-to-people exchange, the motivations behind these activities are less ambiguous and more independent.

What potential is there for effective environmental civil diplomacy stemming from China?

Not many NGOs are actually carrying out work overseas, several factors inhibiting them from doing so effectively, and as such the idea that they can play a strong role in civil diplomacy needs to be questioned, at least in the environmental field.

Many of the impeding factors are generic, such as: political constraints on the scale and range of NGO activities (Fürst & Holdaway 2015; Ashley & He 2008; Enserink & Koppenjan 2007; Han & Zhang 2006; Martens 2006; Schwartz 2004); complicated NGO registration processes (Liu et al. 2011; Ashley & He 2008;); limited financial resources (Zhao 2013; Tang & Zhan 2008); and difficulty recruiting and retaining professional staff (Fürst & Holdaway 2015). Beyond these generic difficulties, a couple of challenges are particularly pertinent for Chinese eNGOs seeking to play a more active role abroad, such as political risks of vested interests, language, cultural and logistical barriers, and limited capacity to take on overseas projects when there is so much to tackle at home. These are the focus of our discussion here.

Political risks of vested interests and lack of knowledge about local conditions

Besides the numerous obstacles, there are also abundant opportunities for NGOs to engage in. As a platform to show the social responsibility of the Chinese government and enterprises, the idea of the green BRI is promoted. According to the "people-to-people exchange" plan, collaboration between NGOs is greatly encouraged. Using its fund, the "South-South Cooperation Grant" supports domestic social organizations to conduct projects, which will alleviate pressure on funding. Universities and institutions provide capacity building activities for NGOs and assist with expertise.

Chinese eNGOs operate in a tight political space. Involvement in potentially contested BRI projects outside of China with unknown vested interests could be a risky game for NGOs, and even though such activities occur outside Chinese borders, there is no reason to believe that engagement in such activities would not have negative spin-off effects on the work that the NGOs conduct inside China. Furthermore, there is the risk of Chinese NGOs being perceived as being embedded in the Chinese state, undermining their independence in seeking to engage in outbound activities.

Language, cultural, and logistical barriers

Language barriers, specific knowledge, and culture diversity bring huge challenges to collaboration with local NGOs in BRI countries. Most BRI countries have their own official language. To conduct research, experienced, multi-lingual elites with expertise in one or more fields such as law, policy, environmental science, management, and publicity are needed.

Experience is also a great obstacle. Lacking experienced employees is prevalent among grassroots NGOs. An investigation on full-time employees' welfare in NGOs showed that 51.45% of investigated people had worked in this field for less than three years. (Lin & Zhang, 2016). As for international cooperation, most grassroots NGOs have no experience in this area, even for old employees.

Limited capacity to take on overseas project, when there is so much to tackle at home

Many eNGOs believe that owing to the above-mentioned restrictions, their limited time and capacity is better spent trying to address domestic environmental issues. The social impact of these organizations is limited in the first place, and many organizations have a hard time documenting and legitimizing their positive impact domestically. Implementing projects overseas would make it even harder for these organizations to make a strong impact (and thus validate the legitimacy of the work conducted by the organization) domestically. This might seem a mundane issue, but in fact, it has major implications for the choice, design and implementation of project activities (as these are mostly dependent on external funding).

Discussion & conclusion

Clearly the BRI has promoted more domestic eNGOs to at least think about, or to try to, take their activities outside of the national jurisdiction. Despite the fact that there are several impediments that seriously undermines these efforts, this trend, albeit nascent at this stage, is likely to continue to grow.

While the future is predicted to be difficult, based on past experiences and observations of the Chinese NGO field over the last two decades, this community and group of organizations are likely to find creative ways to overcome the challenges and continue to push for more NGO engagement overseas in the green BRI realm. A couple of things are, in the opinion of this author, likely to occur in the foreseeable future. First, more thematic groups or networks consisting of both domestic and international NGOs are likely to emerge. Organizations working on green finance will continue to develop their capabilities of green finance and carbon emissions trade; animal protection organizations will further address impacts on wild animals and habitats caused by new infrastructure such as roads and railways; river protection organizations will work on international river conservation and dams, etc. The Belt and Road Green Development Partnership, established by the Greenovation: Hub is an illustrative example. In 2016, seeking to provide policy recommendations for sustainable development of BRI, the Partnership brought together members from domestic and international thinktanks, eNGOs, and foundations to work on issues like climate change, energy transition, green finance, and industry cooperation. So far, 25 organizations have joined the Partnership and eight issues of *Going Green: The World and China*, which reports the output of the Partnership, have been published.

In addition, it is not unreasonable to expect that regional groups and/or networks will also emerge out of this process as regional cooperation is proposed. Different bonds have been established in South East Asia and Africa. In South East Asia, ASEAN collaboration has become a major platform. For example, the Nanjing-based China-ASEAN EXPO has been held since 2004. There are also other various China-ASEAN forums, which help to establish win-win economic diplomacy, which is welcomed in countries such as the Philippines. The Lancang-Mekong Environmental Cooperation Center was established in 2016 under the Lancang-Mekong Dialogue and Cooperation Mechanism. Since its establishment, it has conducted several projects, such as the Great Lancang-Mekong Plan. Under this, joint research on freshwater ecosystem management and sustainable infrastructure investment and green finance has been conducted. Although most of these activities are carried out by officials, international NGOs like WWF, The Nature Conservancy (TNC), Environmental Defense Fund (EDF), and Conservation International are also involved in this platform by facilitating workshops and seminars on capacity building. In Africa, with the development of the China–Africa relationship, cooperation has been more frequent and closer, even beyond the scope of BRI, while remaining consistent and scaling up. For example, the China-Africa Forest Governance Project has been carried out for five years and generated abundant outputs, under the cooperation of IIED, GEI, WWF, and several local NGOs. Despite these somewhat positive trends, it is unlikely that we will see a sudden surge and increased efficiency for effective engagement from Chinese NGOs to green the BRI. This is mainly due to the fact that there still remain several severe impediments hindering such a development.

Certain areas still remain neglected. There are few activities concerning Central Asia, and little emerging effort to start programmes. These difficulties largely result from the obstacles mentioned in the previous section. Sufficient funding, adequate political space, effective cooperation between domestic and international organizations could be the keys issues to be coped with.

There is no chance that NGOs will tackle all the challenges and problems they face alone. Support from different stakeholders is indispensable for NGOs struggling in China's relatively unfavourable environment. Universities, for example, can provide crucial help to NGOs in terms of capacity building and expertise training. Scholars from Tsinghua University and China University of Political Science and Law have played a critical role in NGOs' legal training. Furthermore, a win-win relationship can be built between NGOs and enterprises. With mutual trust and understanding, NGOs can help enterprises maintain sustainable development and reduce potential environmental and financial risks. In addition, public engagement is of vital importance. Public support can provide a solid foundation for NGO development, and awareness of the importance of environmental protection and sustainable development is a prerequisite for any fundamental change.

Political and legal support from the government is also required. What current policies are achieving is far from enough. Politically, there are two aspects that need further improvement. To begin with, the government should be more proactive in understanding the capabilities of NGOs. Attending conferences hosted by NGOs and improving communication with them can not only allow NGOs to realize their potential, but can also give them the opportunity to obtain relevant information and deepen their understanding of the goals of government. Furthermore, funding is the lifeblood of NGOs. An increase of public consultation and procurement can enable NGOs to think and act more globally while encouraging their engagement to green the BRI.

From the perspective of legal support, there are two points worth mentioning. One of the most salient problems confronting Chinese eNGOs today is the fundraising restrictions imposed by law. Few laws have been promulgated by the government to encourage philanthropic giving (Gallagher 2004; Schwartz & Shieh 2009; China Development Brief 2017). The strict and fragmented charitable solicitation regulation severely limits eNGOs' fundraising ability. According to the China Development Brief (2017), by April 2017, only half of the provinces in China had begun accrediting charities. Further improvement in the public fundraising regulation and its enforcement may be needed in the future. Another problem, in this regard, is the gap that exists in overseas corporate behaviour regulation. The guidance on greening BRI is not legally binding. With adequate legal or regulatory binding on environmental standards, environmental impact assessment, and supervision mechanisms of foreign investment, corporations will be pushed to behave in a more environmentally friendly way. Moreover, eNGOs can engage in this, and act as supervisors through information disclosure, or even by prosecution.

Notes

1 Global Environmental Institution. Environmental and Social Challenges of China's Going Global: Beijing: China Environmental Science Press. 2013.57
2 Data source: Retrieved from https://china.aiddata.org/ on January 20, 2020.
3 Data source: The State Council Information Office of the People's Republic of China. China's Foreign Aid (2011), China's Foreign Aid (2014).
4 According to China's Foreign Aid (2011), "[f]inancial resources provided by China for foreign aid mainly fall into three types: grants (aid gratis), interest-free loans and concessional loans" and "[b]y the end of 2009, China had provided a total of 256.29 billion yuan in aid to foreign countries, including 106.2 billion yuan in grants, 76.54 billion yuan in interest-free loans and 73.55 billion yuan in concessional loans."
5 Civil diplomacy can be understood as a long-term strategy focusing on establishing relationships with varied stakeholders through foreign exchanges and activities initiated by non-governmental actors.
6 These organizations are: China Children and Teenagers Fund, China Youth Development Foundation, China Foundation for Poverty Alleviation, China Foundation for Peace and Development, and China Friendship Foundation for Peace and Development.
7 In this chapter the concepts of civil society organizations and NGO will be used interchangeably.
8 In theory, civil society organizations are volunteer-based, not-for-profit, private and civic organizations that exhibit a minimum level of self-governance see: Salamon and Anheier (1997).
9 According to article two in the State Council Order No. 250 "Regulations on the Registration and Administration of Social Organizations" (Shehui tuanti dengji guanli tiaoli 社会团体登记管理条例). See www.mca.gov.cn/article/zwgk/fvfg/mjzzgl/200709/20070900001725.shtml.

10 According to article two in the State Council Order No. 251 "Regulations on the Registration and Administration of Private non-enterprise Units" (Minban feiqiye danwei dengji guanli tiaoli 民办非企业单位登记管理条例). See www.mca.gov.cn/article/zwgk/fvfg/mjzzgl/200709/20070900001726.shtml.

11 According to article two in the State Council Order No. 400 "The Regulations on the Registration and Administration of Foundations" (Jijinhui guanli tiaoli 基金会管理条例) See www.mca.gov.cn/article/zwgk/tzl/200711/20071100003953.shtml.

12 Please see more in Hildebrandt, T. (2013). Social Organizations and the Authoritarian State in China: *Cambridge University Press*; Schwartz, Jonathan. 2004. "Environmental NGOs in China: roles and limits." *Pacific Affairs*, pp. 28–49; Ashley, Jillian S, and Pengyu He. (2008). "Opening One Eye and Closing the Other: The Legal and Regulatory Environment for Grassroots NGOs in China Today." Boston University International Law Journal, vol.26, no.29, pp. 29–96.

13 For more information about China Youth Climate Action Network www.chinacsrmap.org/Org_Show_EN.asp?ID=1573.

14 GONGOs are government-initiated organizations who have strong institutional ties to government bodies. These organizations or groups were created by the state at different administrative levels to serve as support mechanisms. An important distinction between GONGOs and the state apparatus is that GONGOs do not implement projects directly through formal administrative systems (Wu 2003).

15 One foundation was established by movie star Li Lianjie in 2007. It mainly works on disaster rescue, children's welfare, and public participation.

16 The Amity Foundation was established in 1985. At first, it was initiated by Chinese Christians. It aims to alleviate poverty and offer assistance for elderly and disabled people, and orphans.

17 China Social Welfare Foundation was established by the Ministry of Civil Affairs in 2005, it focuses on poverty alleviation, disaster rescue, and assistance for elderly and disabled people.

18 Blue Sky Rescue Team is an independent, civil public interest institution that provides emergency rescue operations. It was founded in 2007 and has branches in over 31 provinces in China. Since establishment, it has participated in rescue operations in all the great disasters in China, and worked with the emergency rescue operation in the 2015 Nepal earthquake.

19 See more at www.cfpd.org.cn/detail.aspx?newsId=2053&TId=524

20 Project Hope is a public welfare project initiated by the central committee of the Youth League and China Youth Development Foundation to help out-of-school children in less developed areas. Building primary schools and subsidizing students from poor families are the main tasks of Project Hope.

21 See more at www.cydf.org.cn/xwgczjfz/

22 Data Source: *The Bulletin of Statistics on the Development of Social Services (2017)*. Retrieved from: www.mca.gov.cn/article/sj/tjgb/

23 See more at https://paungkumyanmar.org/2019/03/07/myitsone-a-case-study/

24 See more at www.greentimes.com/green/econo/shachanye/cyzx/content/2019-07/03/content_426101.htm

25 Ecological Civilization is a political phrase first raised at the 17th National Congress of the Communist Party of China, addressing the importance of saving energy and protecting environment and ecological system.

26 Guiding Opinion on Promoting Construction of a Green "One Belt One Road," 2017.

27 Guiding Opinion on Promoting Construction of a Green "One Belt One Road," 2017.

28 National Development and Reform Commission (NRDC), is a Chinese Department in charge of economic development and prices of commercial products.

29 See more at https://baijiahao.baidu.com/s?id=15989903351523718998&wfr=spider &for=pc

30 China's BRI challenge: The greening of the belt and Road, HSBC Global Research, 2018.

31 See more at https://news.mongabay.com/2018/04/chinas-belt-and-road-poised-to-transform-the-earth-but-at-what-cost/

32 These environmental NGOs include All-china Environmental Federation, China Ecological Civilization Research and Promotion Association, Chinese Society for Sustainable Development, Chongqing Environmental Protection Industry Association, Hebei Environmental Protection Industry Association, Hebei Environmental Protection Bureau.

33 See detailed report at http://sironet.cnie.org.cn/cnie_en/Documents_224/ 201712/t20171218_94520.html

34 See more at http://sironet.cnie.org.cn/cnie_en/AU_219/201711/t20171102_93033.html

35 The members of the Partnership include: All-China Environmental Federation, China Green Carbon Foundation, Chinadialogue, Energy Foundation, Global Environmental Institute, Innovative green development program, Oxfam, Greenpeace, Heinrich Boll Stiftung, Natural Resource Defence Council, the Paradise, Qiaonv Foundation, World Resources Institute, World Wildlife Foundation, The Nature Conservancy, SEE Foundation, Top10.cn, Institute for transportation and Development Policy, Carbon Disclosure Project, Chongqing Renewable Energy Society, Carbon Trust, Biodiversity Conservation and Green Development Foundation, China Ecological Civilization Research and Promotion Association, Innovation Center for Energy and Transportation, Global Connectivity Research Center of Peking University.

36 Greenovation Hub is an environmental Think-Do organization with a global outlook. They aim to promote the development and implementation of sound climate and environmental friendly policies through conducting in-depth analysis and research, and fostering dialogues among stakeholders, in order to drive China's green transition towards a sustainable, equitable, and climate resilient future, contributing to the reduction of global ecological footprint.

37 Myitsone Dam encountered stiff opposition from both Kachin and Burmese, because the dam threatened to inundate the ancestral birthplace of the ethnic Kachin people and put negative pressure on Myanmar's agriculture and fisheries.

38 See more at www.globalchinahouse.org/.

39 To see more works that have been carried out by the Paradise Foundation in Africa: www.pfi.org.cn/en/international-projects/.

References

Alagappa, M 2004, 'Civil Society and Political Change: An analytical framework', in M. Alagappa (ed), *Civil Society and Political Change in Asia: Expanding and Contracting Democratic Space*, pp. 25–57. Stanford University Press.

All China Environmental Federation 2008, *Report on the development of China's eNGOs*. Available from: https://max.book118.com/html/2017/0502/103854870.shtm.

Ashley, JS & He, P 2008, 'Opening one Eye and Closing the Other: The Legal and Regulatory Environment for "Grassroots" NGOs in China Today', *Boston University International Law Journal*, vol. 26, no. 29, pp. 29–96

Brautigam, D & Xiaoyang, T 2012, 'Economic statecraft in China's new overseas special economic zones: soft power, business or resource security?' *International Affairs*, vol. 88, no. 4, pp. 799–816.

Brook, T & Frolic, M 1997, 'The Ambiguous Challenge of Civil Society', in T Brook and M Frolic (eds), *Civil Society in China*. ME Sharpe, Armonk.

China's BRI negatively impacting the environment 2019, December 24. *The ASEAN Post*. Available from: https://theaseanpost.com/article/chinas-bri-negatively-impacting-environment.

China's Implementation of the Overseas NGO Management Law 2017, *China Development Brief*. Available from: http://www.chinadevelopmentbrief.cn/articles/chinas-implementation-of-the-overseas-ngo-management-law/.

China Development Brief, 2017, *Defining Chinese 'Charity'–Comparative Perspectives and Suggestions*. Available from: www.chinadevelopmentbrief.cn/articles/defining-chinese-charity-%EF%BC%8D-comparative-perspectives-and-suggestions-for-development/.

Economy, E 2004, The River Runs Black: The Environmental Challenge to China's Future. *Ithaca: Cornell University Press*.

Economy, E 2005, China's Environmental Movement Testimony before the Congressional Executive Commission on China Roundtable on Environmental NGOs in China: Encouraging Action and Addressing Public Grievances. edited by www.cfr.org/publication/7770/.

Enserink, B & Koppenjan, J 2007, 'Public Participation in China: Sustainable Urbanization and Governance', *Management of Environmental Quality: An International Journal*, vol. 18, no. 4, pp. 459–474

Fei, S 2016, 'Environmental non-government organizations in China since the 1970s.' In *Environment, Modernization and Development in East Asia* (pp. 203–222). Palgrave Macmillan, London.

Frolic, M 1997, State-Led Civil Society, in T Brook and M Frolic (eds), *Civil Society in China*. M. E. Sharpe, Armonk.

Fürst, K & Holdaway, J 2015, 'Environment and Health: the role on environmental NGOs in Policy Innovation.' In A Fulda (ed), *Civil Society Contributions to Policy Innovation in the PR China*: Palgrave Macmillan.

Cao, B 2010, Stories of China's Environmental NGOs. *Beijing Foreign Languages Press*.

Gallagher, M 2004, 'The limits of civil society in a late Leninist state.' *Civil society and political change in Asia: expanding and contracting democratic space*, pp. 419–452.

Gleiss, MS 2014, (Re)making political space: Labor NGOs and migrant workers in China. Faculty of Social Sciences, *Department of Sociology and Human Geography, University of Oslo*.

Gong, J 2009, *A Report on the Development of Environmental NGOs in China. INSAM*. Available from: www.agrometeorology.org/topics/environment-and-sustainability/a-report-on-the-development-of-environmental-ngos-in-china.

Han, S & Zhang, L 2006, 'China's environmental governance of rapid industrialisation.' *Environmental Politics*, vol. 15, no. 2, pp. 271–292.

Ho, P 2001, 'Greening without conflict? Environmentalism, NGOs and civil society in China.' *Development and Change*, vol. 32, no. 5, pp. 893–921.

Hou, X 2016, *"Mekong Bright Action" brings brightness to poor cataract patients in Laos.* Available from: www.chinadevelopmentbrief.cn/news/mekong-bright-action-brings-brightness-to-poor-cataract-patients-in-laos/.

Hsu, C 2010, 'Beyond Civil Society: An Organizational Perspective on State–NGO Relations in the People's Republic of China.' *Journal of Civil Society,* vol. 6, no. 3, pp. 259–277.

Hsu, Jennifer YJ, Timothy Hildebrandt, and Reza Hasmath. ' "Going out" or staying in? The expansion of Chinese NGOs in Africa.' *Development Policy Review* 34, no. 3 (2016): 423–439.

Lin J & Zhang, J 2016, Chinese NGOs "Going Global": Current Situation, Challenges and Policy Recommendations, Global Environmental Institute.

Jia, Xijin, 2004, Minjianzuzhi de dingyi yu fenlei (Definition and Classification of Nongovernmental Organizations), in M Wang and P Liu (eds), *Minjian zuzhi tonglun (General Introduction to Nongovernmental Organizations).* Beijing: Shishi chubanshe, pp. 3–24.

Kang, X & Feng, L 2006, NGO Governance in China: Achievements and Dilemmas, in L Jordan & P vab Tuijl (eds), *NGO Accountability, Politics, Principles and Innovations.* London: Earthscan.

Knup, E 1997, 'Environmental NGOs in China: An Overview.' *China Environment Series:* 9–15.

Larson, C 2010, 'Liang Conjie: The Godfather of China's Green Movement.' *The Atlantic* 30.

Li, X, 2019, Interview: BRI's green commitment significant to global development – NPO leader, Xinhua Net. www.xinhuanet.com/english/2019-04/26/c_138012531.htm

Liu, C 2006, The Impact of Transnational Environmental NGOs on Local NGOs' Agenda-setting Power in China. *SA Annual Convention 2006.*

Liu, X, Dong, Y, Wang, C & Shishime, T 2011, 'Citizen Complaints about Environmental Pollution: A Survey Study in Suzhou.' *Journal of Current Chinese Affairs* vol. 40, no. 3, pp. 193–219.

Lu, Y 2007, 'Environmental Civil Society and Governance in China.' *International Journal of Environmental Studies,* vol. 64, no. 1, pp. 59–69.

Ma, Q 2006, *Non-Governmental Organizations in Contemporary China: Paving the Way for Civil Society?.* London: Routledge.

Martens, S 2006, 'Public Participation with Chinese Characteristics: Citizen Consumers in China's Environmental Management,' *Environmental Politics,* vol. 15, no. 3, pp. 211–230.

Myitsone: A Case Study 2019, March 7, *Paung Ku.* Available from: https:// paungkumyanmar.org/2019/03/07/myitsone-a-case-study/.

Norris, W 2016, *Chinese Economic Statecraft: Commercial Actors, Grand Strategy, and State Control.* Ithaca, NY, and London: Cornell University Press.

Qiao, L & Peng, W 2005, ' "The 26 Degrees Campaign": Saving Energy', in C Liang & D Yang (eds), *The China Environment Yearbook (2005): Crisis and Breakthrough of China's Environment.* Beijing: Social Sciences Academic Press.

Saich, T 2000. 'Negotiating the state: The development of social organizations in China.' *The China Quarterly* vol. 161, no. 3, pp. 124–141.

Salamon, Lester, and Helmut K. Anheier, 1997, *Defining the Nonprofit Sector.* Manchester: Manchester University Press.

Schwartz, J 2004, 'Environmental NGOs in China: roles and limits.' *Pacific Affairs:* pp. 28–49.

Schwartz, Jonathan, and Shawn Shieh, eds., 2009, *State and society responses to social welfare needs in China: Serving the people*. Routledge.

Shen, W 2013, EU-China Relations on Human Rights in Competing Paradigms: Continuity and Change, in TE Kirchner, TK Christiansen & PBM Jørgensen (eds), *The Palgrave Handbook of EU-Asia Relations*, pp. 165–180. Palgrave Macmillan, London.

Spires, AJ 2011, 'Contingent symbiosis and civil society in an authoritarian state: Understanding the survival of China's grassroots NGOs.' *American Journal of Sociology*, vol. 117, no. 1, pp. 1–45.

Tang, SY & Zhan, X 2008, 'Civic environmental NGOs, civil society, and democratisation in China.' *The Journal of Development Studies*, vol. 44, no. 3, pp. 425–448.

The BRI's environmental challenges 2019, February 14, *OBOReurope*. Available from: www.oboreurope.com/en/the-bri-environmental-challenges/.

Thousands of Downstream Villagers Protest Against Myitsone Dam 2019, April 22, *The Irrawaddy*. Available from: www.irrawaddy.com/news/burma/thousands-downstream-villagers-protest-myitsone-dam.html.

Turner, J 2003, The growing role of Chinese green NGOs and Environmental journalists in China. Woodrow Wilson Center. Available from: www.cecc.gov/sites/chinacommission.house.gov/files/documents/roundtables/2003/CECC%20Roundtable%20Testimony%20-%20Jennifer%20Turner%20-%201.27.03.pdf.

Unger, Jonathan, and Anita Chan. 'China, corporatism, and the East Asian model.' *The Australian Journal of Chinese Affairs* 33 (1995): 29–53.

Wang, S & He, J 2004, 'Associational revolution in China: Mapping the landscape.' *Korea Observer*, vol. 35, no. 3, pp. 485–532.

Wexler, R, Ying, X & Nick, Y 2006, September, NGO Advocacy in China. *China Development Brief Special Report*.

Wu, Fengshi 2003, 'Environmental GONGO autonomy: Unintended consequences of state strategies in China.' *The Good Society* 12, no. 1, pp. 35–45.

Wu, Fengshi 2013, 'Environmental activism in provincial China.' *Journal of Environmental Policy & Planning* 15, no. 1 (2013): 89–108.

Wu, Joshua Su-Ya. 2009, 'The state of China's environmental governance after the 17th Party Congress.' *East Asia* 26, no. 4, p. 265.

Xie, L 2011, 'China's Environmental Activism in the Age of Globalization.' *Asian Politics & Policy*, vol. 3, no. 2, pp. 207–224.

Xu, Y & Zhao, L 2010, China's Rapidly growing NGOs. *EAI Background Brief No. 514* Available from: www.eai.nus.edu.sg/BB514.pdf.

Yang, Guobin 2005. 'Environmental NGOs and institutional dynamics in China.' *The China Quarterly* vol. 181, pp. 46–66.

Zhang, D & Smith, G 2017, 'China's foreign aid system: structure, agencies, and identities.' *Third World Quarterly*. Doi: 10.1080/01436597.2017.1333419.

Zhao, X 1993, Fazhanzhong de Huanjing Baohu Shehui Tuanti (Environmental Social Organizations in Development). MSc Thesis Tsinghua University. *Beijing NGO Research Centre*

Zhao, X 2013, Non-governmental charity organization called on decreasing the tax burdens (Mingjian Gongyi Zuzhi Huju Shuishou Jiandan). (Nanfang Zhoumu).

10 High-hanging fruits and the Belt and Road Initiative

Sustainability through entrepreneurship[1]

Gordon C.K. Cheung

Introduction

The Belt and Road Initiative (BRI) was first conceived after Xi Jinping's visits to Kazakhstan on 7 September 2013 and Indonesia on 3 October 2013. The Silk Road Economic Belt and the Maritime Silk Road are the two legs of the BRI. According to Li Yining, Justin Lin Yifu, and Zheng Yongnian, the BRI brings some new markets for China. In general, more than 65 countries and 4.4 billion people will be along the BRI. They account for 13.9% of international trade, and 6.5% of FDI. The BRI is very likely to be the third regional economic pillar after North America and Europe (Li, et al. 2015, 8–9). China's perspectives on the BRI have always focused on infrastructure, peaceful cooperation, inclusiveness and interdependence, free trade, and cultural cooperation (Feng 2015, 23). However, other academics found the BRI not necessarily a 'grand strategy' from the top down, but more like mixed interests from local and diversified interests crisscrossing and even sometimes contradicting the views of Xi Jinping (Jones and Zeng 2019, 1429). According to Yang Jiechi, the Chair of the Organizing Committee of the 2nd Belt and Road Forum for International Cooperation on 10 April 2019 in Beijing, up to March 2019, 125 countries and 29 international organizations had already signed up with China to promote the BRI, including Italy, which is one of the G7 countries, formally joined the BRI. In terms of trade, more than US$6 trillion has been involved among the BRI countries and China had already invested US$70 billion (Yang 2019, 7). Therefore, the BRI is certainly going to be a long-term development project and will raise the eyebrows from different stakeholders and touch the nerves of some established power relations in the global political economy.

In *Global Transformations: Politics, Economics, and Culture*, David Held, et al. (1999) categorized globalization in four types. Two of them are particularly useful for understanding China's BRI in the current global economic order which is still very much dominated by the west and led by the US. The first type is called *expansive globalization*, which is mainly captured by the period when the 'European empires had acquired a tentative global reach with considerable intercivilizational impacts', while the second type, *thin globalization*, refers to the 'early and luxury trade circuits connecting Europe with China and the East' (Held, et al. 1999, 22). They particularly criticized that the post World War II economic infrastructure, such as the Bretton Woods System (BRS) was not inclusive enough, deliberately excluding the communist countries from the structure (ibid., 200). For one thing, the European empire has gone and some of the previous colonies had made remarkable economic achievements, Singapore being one example. After World War II, the decolonization process demonstrated a retrenching effect of the expansive globalization and the solidarity movement among the developing economies. The Bandung Conference, which took place in 1955 in Indonesia, signified such a movement. Yet, it was short-lived and countries dissipated and began to search their own economic way out, partly due to the Containment policy from the US. Increasingly, the market potential of the countries along the BRI and the increasing numbers of Chinese middle-class consumers China have witnessed the change, and the BRI can be interpreted as reconnecting the previously neglected economic actors and countries who were considered to be not economically viable.

In East Asia, the Korean War in the early 1950s again redefined the geopolitical relations and also began the way of the US-led Cold War economic leadership in East Asia. We have witnessed the rise of Japan and the economic miracle of the Asian tiger economies. In terms of economic infrastructure, the General Agreement on Tariffs and Trade (GATT) and the International Monetary Fund (IMF) were created to regulate international trade as well as international finance. Yet, one of their major drawbacks was that such global economic infrastructure "neglected" a majority of the countries that did not follow the US tutorage. Some of them followed socialism and somehow relied on different economic principles and political systems. Many others were plunged into domestic political chaos resulting in military dictatorships. Thailand and Indonesia are typical examples. China, interestingly, both did not follow the US economic tutorage after 1949 and also was dragged into domestic chaos and political struggle, highlighted by the Cultural Revolution between 1966 and 1976.

The fundamental weakness of the blueprint for the global economic infrastructure after World War II has continued, and the voice of many countries has not been heard in the construction of global economic infrastructure, even nowadays. One of the most vocal countries has always been China. Not only is that China the second largest economy in the world but it has comprehensive power and regional and even some areas of global influence, which is tremendously significant. Fareed Zakaria, the host of *Fareed Zakaria GPS* on CNN, criticized the fact that "The old order – in which small European countries act as global heavyweights while behemoths such as China and India are excluded from the first ranks of global institutions – cannot be sustained" (Zakaria 2020, 62). The reason why a quote from Fareed Zakaria is important is that he did extensive research when he wrote the book *From Wealth to Power: the Unusual Origins of America's World Role* (Zakaria 1998). He coined the term "state centred realism" to refer to those "*nations try to expand their political interests abroad when central decision-makers perceive a relative increase in state power*" [italic in original] to try to explain the American expansionism from 1865 to 1908 (ibid., 38). It appeared that the current economic rise of China could feature some of the characteristics behind his understanding of the previous US expansion approach and therefore more inclusive of China in the current global economic order may pose some effective foreign policy from the US interest too!

It is in this direction that China's BRI should be taken into serious consideration, especially when we are talking about of sustaining the global economic order by reconnecting with the former neglected economies and developing countries through many infrastructure projects and development of growth from below – for the thickening of the future globalization process. The scale and scope of the BRI is unprecedented. From geo-economic points of view, the BRI connects China with the world economy with profound political and economic impact. Instead of overturning the global political and economic infrastructure, the BRI generates a new drive/direction of growth and development connecting flows of people and goods by tapping into some less explored regions and countries, which may help put back the jigsaw pieces missing from the established global economic structure, which requires the entrepreneurial spirit of Chinese global economic integration.

This chapter is divided into four sections. The first section tries to understand the competitive nature and the dynamic of views on development between the west and China. The hegemonic stability theory in understanding the US post-WWII role in East Asian economic development was tested particularly after the 1997 Asian Financial Crisis. Also, the neo-liberal view on the market forces and the small government principles were further challenged in the 2008 global financial crisis. Yet, China's competitive view on economic development by following the peaceful rise, state-centric approach, development and soft power somehow prepares the foundation of the nature of the BRI along growth and development.

The second section tries to understand the connection between the BRI and China's 'go-out' or 'go global' strategy. Very different from the Manifest Destiny of American expansionism, China's foreign investment follows some solution from China's own economic development experiences, for example the new normal and the shifting to a qualitative and innovative growth pattern. New economic growth strategies need to coincide with regional economic affairs because China is bounded by the less known areas among those new investment destinies.

Section three tentatively examines between the *renminbi* (yuan) and the building of evidence-based trust, which should be interesting in working with the trading and globalization of China's potential outlets of the yuan.

The final section examines technological change and the protection of innovation through intellectual property rights (IPRs). We will discuss further the notion of shared economy and the *Shanzhai* culture. BRI has been connecting the previous 'underdogs' in terms of economic development. Yet once you have been able to share the IPRs, that may counteract the established economic structure derived by the advanced economies.

Competitive nature and dynamics of views on development between the west and China

China's economic foreign policy strategies are very different from the established theories on power relations or pure national interest based on foreign policy objectives. As far as the BRI is concerned, China's economic foreign policy involves many elements that have to be studied in detail before realising the characteristics behind China's plan. When Charles Kindleberger (1973) questioned the US role in the 1929 financial crisis, his assessment led to what was later known as the beginning of the hegemonic stability of the US. In the UK, Michael Cox,[2] a former professor from the London School of Economics and Political Science, argued that we should not judge the US long-term future by one president or someone who is in the inner circle of the leadership (Cox 2007, 8). However, US hegemony has been challenged by small economies as being too pushy or simply just making it too difficult to abide by demanding US policies. (Sardar and Davies 2002: 195) In witnessing China's application to be the member of the World Trade Organization (WTO) in 1999 (two years before China was actually accepted to be a member in 2001), according to Joseph Stiglitz, former Chief Economist at the World Bank and Professor of Finance and Economics at Columbia University, the 'US Treasury insisted on a rapid opening up of China's financial markets, allowing, for instance, short-term speculative capital to flow in and American banks to sell their risky derivatives' (Stiglitz 2003, 214). Obviously, even the United States Trade Representative (USTR) realized that the US was asking too much, the pressure on China was basically to serve America's short-term financial interest (ibid.). These cases demonstrated that the US was getting less and less willing to shoulder the global hegemonic roles. Instead, it is highly likely to capitalize on the vulnerability of those developing economies.

The question is why the world still relies on US leadership. When studying the post-WWII US hegemonic role in global mass production, Mark Rupert contended that "In the postwar years, the USA provided the framework of ideological, political and economic stability necessary for growth to resume on a liberal capitalist basis and for existing welfare-nationalist states to be reconstructed in neoliberal form, in the context of an open, interdependent, American-led world order" (Jordan, et al.1995, 54). The point is that the world has been relying on US global economic leadership for a very long time, during which things have been doing fine, and countries took it for granted.

Thinking again of the context of the global economic system, its operation has not necessarily been due to the strength of the US economic policy but because of the dependence of the rest of the world on US global leadership. In Carla Norrlof's study of the hegemonic power of the US, she pointed out that the US is increasingly gaining more than giving to the world.[3] But the system is still working. The reason that the system is still working is because other states are "too dependent on America" (Norrlof 2010, 251). But she explicitly stated that, if this is the case, then "China does not want to be just another Great Power on the block. It has its eyes set on superpower status" and her suggestion is that "If other Great Powers become serious about closing the American era, they will not be able to continue to depend on the American system for their economic well-being and basic security" (ibid., 250–251).

I think this is a fair point. Clearly, countries should no longer be freeriding on US security and economic support if they want to challenge US leadership! If war is not the resolution to challenge the US (hegemonic succession theoretically is highly likely to be followed by wars which help define more clearly who is a real leader), China should at least follow a more independent economic policy, and the BRI appears to be a potential experiment to launch a more inclusive foreign policy, which naturally will test China's entrepreneurship. The previous high growth and production-cum-export policy has been following the developmental approach – freeriding on US global and regional economic structure while following the economic growth of many East Asian economies.

Apparently, since Donald Trump took office in 2016, the US has witnessed a sharp retraction from some global leadership, such as the withdrawal from the Paris Agreement and pulling back from the Transpacific Partnership (TPP). Neoliberalist economic thinking, despite having dominated the US economic policy for decades, is increasingly finding its limitations, especially when inequality has become the day-to-day experience among much of the American general public. The CNN 2019 reported that, according to the review from the Federal Reserve, over the past 30 years the US has become extremely unequal.[4] Turning to the previous discussion on the US leadership, it means the leader has been experiencing a much deeper economic difficulties and will need more supporting/sharing in matters relating to global public goods.

In East Asian region, the Asian financial crisis in 1997 witnessed the extent of the neo-liberalist policy from the IMF toward the bailing out of the countries in East Asia, leading up to some went deep trouble (South Korea) and some even experienced the "regime change." Indonesia became democratized when Suharto stepped down in 1998 after Indonesia required the bailing from the IMF of which discovered the crony capitalists or the patron-and-client relations between the leader and his relatives and friends. Asian economies began to search for their own economic identity and became more sceptical toward the US. In a recent article from the *Foreign Affairs*, Miatta Fahnbulleh, the Chief Executive of the New Economics Foundation, called the neoliberal collapse and demonstrated that "Economists, policymakers, and ordinary people have increasingly come to see that neoliberalism–a creed built on faith in free markets, deregulation, and small government, and that has dominated societies for the last 40 years–has reached its limit" (Fahnbulleh 2020, 38). I am more incline to say that the reason that it has reached its limit is because it is natural for the US to become more 'normal' in order to consider its own welfare and the livelihood of its own people rather than overstretching too much to providing too many global public goods which increasingly can be shouldered, and very often much cheaper or more effectively, by other emerging economies, where China is somehow showing genuine economic and political interest to perform more roles and handle more responsibilities.[5]

The peaceful rise (*heping jueqi*) of China has long been adopted as an alternative of the hegemonic stability, particularly after Hu Jintao – China's former leader before Xi Jinping – first used the term in autumn 2003. Later, Zheng Bijian, Vice-President of the Central Committee's Central Party School, in an article published in *Foreign Affairs* (Zheng 2005) very clearly indicated the perpetuation of economic reform and the search for resolution from the cultural rise (or soft power in many cases) of China, rather than military expansionism. On the economic front, the manifestation of China's economic rise is very much induced by the state-driven growth and reform process, especially through the "go out" strategies, first initiated by Jiang Zemin in the early to mid 1990s. The reform period and the growth in China after 1978 and especially after the Southern Tour of Deng Xiaoping in 1992 set the tone of economic development as permanent. Before the Southern Tour, China's reform pathway could have been retracted.

Although it was Joseph Nye who first coined the term soft power in *Bound to Lead* (Nye 1991), his introduction of soft power was aiming to help US to use a more effective power resource rather than the costly military power. The BRI is still in the process of providing alternative economic models, by bringing regionally and economically viable countries together, instead of purely relying on their ideology or political interest. China's drive to grow through qualitative development and innovation unavoidably require natural resources, and neighbouring countries of the BRI help to facilitate that. On the other hand, China's method of investing in infrastructure through the BRI projects creates win-win economic benefits.

Go-out strategies, the China model and the BRI

The 'go-out' strategy 1.0 was initiated by then President Jiang Zemin in 1999. He encouraged Chinese business to promote Chinese investment abroad. Technical innovation and the promotion of independent technology gained currency, and a number of big businesses such as Baidu, Lenovo, Huawei, Xiaomi, and Alibaba have become global household names. "After more than a decade," according to the *Policy Review* in 2005, "the 'go out' strategies have been changed and modified to include the provision of natural resources, the promotion of exports of goods and services, the rebranding of Chinese MNCs, the enhancement of host countries' economic development and employment and trade conflicts reduction" (Cheung 2018, 136).

As can be seen from Table 10.1, the go-out strategies, nevertheless, coincided with Chinese leaders' perspective on globalization. Hu Jintao tried to bring China and Asian economies together to better harness globalization. Xi Jinping encouraged China to be more integrated with the global economy and to make the best use of the global market. BRI, at this stage, can be considered as extending China's economic reach to the Middle Eastern, Southeast Asian as well as central Asian economies.

However, in 2015, Chinese Premier Li Keqiang contended that China could not just export toys, apparel, and shoes. China needed to raise the bar and to

Table 10.1 Chinese leaders' views on globalization and adaptation

China's leaders	Viewpoint of the speech	Event
Jiang Zemin	Opening to the outside world is a long-term basic state policy. Confronted with the globalization trend in economic, scientific, and technological development, we should take an even more active stance in the world by improving the pattern of opening up in all direction, at all levels and in a wide range, developing an open economy, enhancing our international competitiveness, optimizing our economic structure, and improving the quality of our national economy.	1997, 15th Party Congress
Hu Jintao	It also shows that with surging economic globalization, China and Asia are quickly becoming a new growth engine for the world, while the global boom is also generating more important opportunities for China and Asia.	2005, Fortune Global Forum
Xi Jinping	The point I want to make is that many of the problems troubling the world are not caused by economic globalization... It is war, conflict and regional turbulence that have created this problem, and its solution lies in making peace, promoting reconciliation and restoring stability. The international financial crisis is another example. It is not an inevitable outcome of economic globalization; rather, it is the consequence of excessive chase of profit by financial capital and grave failure of financial regulation. Just blaming economic globalization for the world's problems is inconsistent with reality, and it will not help solve the problems.	2017, Davos World Economic Forum

Source: (Moore 1999, 65–66), CNN [http://edition.cnn.com/2005/WORLD/asiapcf/05/16/eyeonchina.hujintao.fulltext/] (accessed 14 January 2020) and The State Council [http://www.china.org.cn/node_7247529/content_40569136.htm] (accessed 14 January 2020)

produce equipment that was globally competitive. In other words, Li wanted to create some national champions of businesses such as high speed rail, electric cars, and aircraft. We could call it the go-out strategy 2.0 (*China Policy* 2017). To put the go-out strategies in a very clear manner, Wang Hongying, Senior Fellow of the Centre for International Governance Innovation (CIGI) in Canada came up with the following summary.

To summarize, China's going out policy is driven and shaped by complex domestic and international factors. It is important to consider both sets of dynamics in trying to understand the trajectory of its course. There is a tendency to underestimate the obstacles for China's OBOR initiative both inside and outside of China, which has led to excessive optimism on the part of its supporters and exaggerated concern on the part of those fearing a more powerful China.

(Wang 2016, 3)

Her concern is that there is no plain sailing for China in nurturing the BRI. Domestically, China is facing the new normal with slower growth rate. Externally, the trade war (starting from March 2018) between the US and China also hindered China's ambition to go out and shake the confidence of many countries who are still not entirely sure about the BRI. The signing of the phase one trade deal between Donald Trump and Liu He on 15 January 2020 was still not totally conclusive, nevertheless. China's productivity and the rising cost of production means that it is gradually losing its competitive edge compared with developing countries, such as Cambodia, Vietnam, or even Myanmar or Laos. However, it would be considered as a threat to the East Asian less developed economies if China kept producing lower-end products (Lall and Albaladejo 2004, 1458). Domestically, China's economic reform faces a bottleneck, which can be seen from its social problems and conflict. Whether China can harness the reform energy will be the linchpin of the sustainability of China's economic development and this is 'life or death' and is extremely significant (Wu 2013, 46). To achieve the transition from a production- to a consumption-based economy, China also faces a habitually weak internal demand.

China's position in the global value chain is still on the very lowest rung. China's industrial value-added is about 26–30%, US and Germany is over 40% (Yu et al. 2015, p. 2082). The new normal "requires China to build a strategic ecosystem for industrial transformation and upgrade" (ibid., 2088). At the other end of the spectrum, China is directly competing with developed countries on high-end industrial products. The current trade war with the US is, on the surface, about the US trade deficit. However, beneath the surface, the west, especially the US, is worried about competition from China. For instance, *Made in China 2025* has been a bone of contention with the US, among those industries that China is trying to lead by 2025.

To use China's investment in African countries as an illustration, one perspective is that Chinese–African relations are economically oriented, and the enormous natural resources of Africa can feed China's manufacturing as well as to enable it to continue its growth and development (Power et al. 2012). Yet, based on extensive research and interviews in many African countries between 2007 to 2009, Brautigam and Tang (2011) argued that African countries' hosting of many Chinese Special Economic Zones (SEZs) 'form a unique, experimental model of development cooperation in Africa: market-based decisions and investment by Chinese companies are combined with support and subsidies from an Asian "developmental state"' (Brautigam and Tang 2011, 27). Although even they were not totally sanguine about the SEZs and the cooperation between China, Africa, and the investors, the understanding being that there should be some successful cases and therefore some economic synergy generated between China and Africa.

The Second African Policy Paper was released in 2015 (the first one was released in 2006). According to the Policy Paper, China and African will create a more comprehensive and strategic cooperation because the compatibility between them and the external environment somehow pushes China and Africa together (*China Daily*, 5 December 2015). According to the Ministry of Foreign Affairs, China should "unswervingly carry forward the tradition of China-Africa friendship, and, proceeding from the fundamental interests of both the Chinese and African peoples, establish and develop a new type of strategic partnership with Africa, featuring political equality and mutual trust, economic win-win cooperation and cultural exchange."[6] Technological transfer through Chinese investment, for example in a number of Nigerian cities did suggest some positive effect (Chen et al. 2017). In stark contrast to Donald Trump's insults to African countries, and calling Haiti, El Salvador, and African nations "shithole countries," whose people were not welcome in the US, China's economic model at least appeals financially to many African countries (*The Guardian*, 12 January 2018).

Speaking of SEZs in China, it was one of the most significant policies of Deng Xiaoping's economic reform after 1978. While the four early SEZs (Shenzhen, Zhuhai, Shantou, and Xiamen) created in the 1979 are still running strongly, the fact is that Shenzhen (already an innovative city) will be given further support by the State Council of China to be a model city in China and the world in innovation, public service, and environmental protection by 2025 (*South China Morning Post*, 18 August 2019). Shenzhen's future development is likely to alter the dynamic, if not outperform the previous "inter-city competition and cooperation" (Shen 2009, 187) model with Hong Kong. Alas, Hong Kong's economic growth is increasingly being slowed, both politically and economically, by the continuous protests that started in June 2019. Apart from the African economies, does the China model appeal to the BRI countries? What would be the foundation and the current evolvement of the China model? When Joshua Cooper Ramo wrote *The Beijing Consensus* in 2004 for the Foreign Policy Centre, a thinktank in London, he already clearly indicated that the model that China has been using was not just for China but to 'remake the whole landscape of international development, economics, society and, by extension, politics' (Ramo, et al. 2004, 3). As we have pointed out, the 1997 Asian financial crisis became the watershed which gradually allowed more Asian economies to turn away from the US because they felt they were let down and somehow the US left them to rot through the globalization of finance![7] China's economic development is certainly attractive. The infrastructure again provides further impetus for developing economies to emulate China's success, which fundamentally changed China from a poor economy to the second largest economic power in the world.

Among the characteristics of the China model, are many features including rapid economic growth, incremental economic reform rather that 'shock therapy', a single party, big market, the significance of the state sector (together with the private sector), and continuous Chinese investment. Yet, the significance of the China model is to facilitate economic development, demonstrate an alternative to the current development model of the US, showcase the peaceful rise of China, and, very importantly according to Zheng Yongnian, the former Director of East Asian Institute at the National University of Singapore, to come up with a 'Grand Bargaining' between the west and the rest (Zheng 2010, 100). Increasingly, the rest of the world, mostly developing economies, is urgently looking for some alternative pathway of economic growth and a more proactive direction to achieve that. In *China's Many Dreams*, Kerr regarded the debate of the China model as best being framed "as a Chinese form of modernization theory" (Kerr 2016, 63). The China model, if looked at from the political economic perspective, is more on national and international development (Breslin 2011). But Zhao (2010) regarded the China model as political development in order to answer the question of modernity or of the changing relations between states and the public.

To improve the assessment of the China model, Chen and Naughton further illustrated that there is no single China model, "but rather successive generations of equilibrium among economic and political forces" (2017, 23). Going back to an understanding of economic development, this means that countries who want to follow in China's economic footsteps can still derive something closer to their open characteristics of the political economy as long as a balance can be reached. The BRI is a clear orientation towards the potential application of the China model, although Chinese leaders have always denied that China is exporting this idea. But, the very nature and extent of the geographical diversities and the cultural differences between the countries may in fact prove that there is no single model and the continuous searching and combination should happen alongside the economic and social and even cultural characteristics of the individual economies.

Renminbi and the building of evidence-based trust for the BRI

In this section, we are going to use the internationalization of the Chinese currency to shed some light on the potential of the RMB among the BRI economies. Understandably it is still too early to say anything concrete about how it might go. However, financial globalization and the strength of the RMB and the trust that China is hoping to generate, allow some imagination to be siphoned into seeking the potential as well as the obstacles behind the use of the RMB across the BRI. China won enormous regional support by not devaluating the RMB after the Asian financial crisis in 1997. A decade later, when the 2008 global financial crisis hit the US heartland, New York, China quickly reacted by injecting a huge stimulus package of four trillion yuan (around US$570 billion) in the following two years to many areas, such as infrastructure, housing, environment, and technological innovation, in order to keep the economic engine running.[8] Originally, the stimulus package was to restore confidence domestically. However, the world economy was also thankful for that. RMB received strong support from those East Asian economies that had significant trade relationships with China. But the global acceptance remained weak. Nevertheless, in November 2015, the RMB was included in the official reserve currency of the Special Drawing Rights

(SDRs) under the IMF. It was a triumphant moment for the Chinese government because the announcement was a symbol of recognition that the global financial institution took RMB seriously. It could be compared with 2001, when China was accepted as the member of the WTO, which recognized China's role in global trade and production.

Coupled with the experiences from two financial crises, China has become more proactive in pushing the internationalization process of the RMB. In *2008 China Capital Market Study* written by Wu Xiaoqiu, Director of Finance and Securities Institute of Renmin University of China, he suggested that "the policy focus of China's capital market should be to increase supply, optimize structure" because "Capital market has become the platform of financial games of economic powers in the twenty-first century" (Wu 2008, 8). The *13 Five Year Plan (2016–2020)* stated that "We will take systematic steps to realize RMB capital account convertibility, making the RMB more convertible and freely useable, so as to steadily promote RMB internationalization and see RMB capital go global" (2016, 206–07). By RMB internationalization, the most important significance for China is capital account convertibility. Zhou Xiaochuan, former chairman of the People's Bank of China, kept saying that step-by-step realization of China's account convertibility is the future determination of China. He argued that there is no definition of a country's currency convertibility, not even from the International Monetary Fund (IMF) (Zhou 2013, 239). In other words, China can follow fully its pace and demand capital account convertibility for the RMB. Providing more channels for cross-border investment for individuals, relaxing foreign exchange control allowing more overseas investors to get access to China's capital market are all facilitating the internationalization of Chinese currency.

Paola Subacchi's *How China is Building a Global Currency: The People's Money* (2017) asked some big questions. For example, should a great economy have a great currency? China has become the second largest economy in the world and yet the RMB is much less internationalized than it should be. Nevertheless, across East and South East Asian countries (Laos, Indonesia, Malaysia, the Philippines, Singapore, Thailand, South Korea, etc.), they care more about the RMB than the US dollar. She pointed out:

> To absorb and use this pool of *renminbi*, informal *renminbi* exchange markets were established in neighbouring countries. Many of these were dominated by money changers that were generally subject to less stringent supervision that bank. ... limitations as an international currency, the RMB was widely used in Mongolia, Cambodia, Vietnam, Burma/Myanmar, and Laos... Called "small dollars" in Laos.
>
> (Subacchi 2017, 109–110)

Subacchi also asked why does it not matter whether you trust US dollars, British pounds or Japanese yen? Very often it is just an old habit! In addition, she clearly pointed out that she does not want to make Chinese currency a direct challenger to the US dollar (ibid., viii).

Simply put it is about trust when we talk about global currency.[9] We trust other international currencies such as British pounds and US dollars because these currencies are based on history and habit. British pounds are based on her industrial and colonial empire, trade and investment etc. for more than 200 years. We trust US dollars because the US came up with the BRS after WWII (but we have already mentioned that the IMF neglected many developing economies in the first stage of its creation!), together with trade, multinational corporations (MNCs), and financial management, etc. These historical experiences generate habitual trust, but the trust in China's currency is more complicated. It is more like evidence-based trust. There is no habitual trust and reliance on RMB because it had not appeared in the international arena, only gradually being accepted by a handful of trading partners. There is none of the history that we need to rely on for the currency and no track record. However, we need to derive some evidence-based trust in order to take into consideration the Chinese currency. That evidence could be things like: China's trade volumes, production as a share of global GDP, Chinese foreign reserves, financial regulation, pace and rate of outward FDI, or transparency of financial recording.

To put it in a more situational context of the BRI, as we have pointed out earlier, the regional identity after the 1997 Asian financial crisis has changed, especially in questioning the US hegemonic role in global finance. From the regional perspective, countries – especially those that are less developed – demanded some alternative currency to the US dollar. Chinese currency, if evidence-based trust can be sustained, will certainly help generate support from the BRI neighbours to strive for further economic cooperation. Once transactions in the RMB have become habitual, more countries will follow and rely on Chinese currency. To use the repeated games research done by Robert Axelrod (1984) to illustrate this, countries will eventually cooperate when more and repeated interaction have taken place. At the end of the day, Kenneth Arrow, a former Nobel Laureate in Economics strongly argued that "Virtually, every commercial transaction has within itself an element of trust" (Arrow 1972, 357). This helps us understand both more about the internationalization of Chinese currency and about the relations between the BRI economies and trading partners with an eye to their investment destinies.

According to *The Future is Asian*, Parag Khanna argued that

> Instead of underwriting the US dollar, Asians are gaining confidence in investing in their own debt and capital markets. … In that area, China accounts for about half of Asia's debt issuance. Foreigners own only about 2 percent of China's sovereign debt, but China has indicated that it would be comfortable with about 15 percent foreign holdings and has given the green light to offshore renminbi "panda bonds" being issued by banks such as the United Kingdom's Standard Chartered. This could mean an additional $3 trillion in liquidity by 2025 to support China's continuing investments at home and abroad.

> (Khanna 2019, 165)

We need to build up a new kind of trust on Chinese currency if that currency is to be used more normally together with other currencies among the BRI economies for some basic functions such as medium of exchange, store of value, and standard for defer payment. Like any other projects these days, financial sustainability is the linchpin to success. Goh Sui Noi, the China bureau chief of *The Straits Times* in Singapore pointed out that "At the World Economic Forum in Davos in January 2018, Mr Jin Liqun, president of the China-led AIIB, which is one of the institutions funding BRI projects, said financial sustainability was key to the long-term success of the initiative" (Goh 2018, 6).

Some people regard the BRI as China's new move to global dominance, but James Kynge from the *Financial Times* argued that yes, the two largest policy bank in China: China Development Bank and the Export-Import Bank of China

> ... disburse more in loans each year than the world's six largest multinational lending institutions put together ... But, China's investments and diplomatic alliances are overwhelmingly in the developing world. In this sense, its vision is not global but sub-global; it is aiming to influence those countries where it can make a difference, reap the rewards and remain insulated from western demands to liberalise its political system and inculcate democratic values.
>
> (Kynge 2017, 9)

The BRI is grounded in infrastructure and extended across many neglected developing economies. According to the report of the *Global Times* in 2017, "China's yuan reform will be finished over the next five years. By then, the Chinese currency is expected to be fully convertible, laying the groundwork for the yuan's growing role as an international reserve currency."[10] Similar reports have also appeared in the mainstream newspapers; for instance, *The Telegraph* (15 May 2018) reported that the internationalization of the RMB is likely to continue because 60 countries have used RMB as their reserve currency and more than a quarter of cross-border trade was settled in RMB in 2017.[11]

Can RMB be the linchpin of the core currency to be used in the BRI? As I have mentioned earlier, the BRI is less mature because it has only seven years of history. More empirical support is needed to authenticate such movement. But David Kang clearly pointed out that, especially going back to the history of China with the neighbouring economies in East Asia, countries have tended to bandwagon with China rather than balance China out when China became strong and stable (Kang 2003, 66). The BRI is about development, and China has shown, with flying colours, how economic development can look like even as a very latecomer. To bandwagon with China allows investment to take place, and more infrastructure to be built, and that is not unthinkable if one takes the clock back to the cultural and the historical relations between China and neighbouring economies.

Technological change and the protection of innovation through intellectual property rights, sharing or *Shanzhai* culture

This section aims to stretch further the notion of entrepreneurial spirit of the Chinese development path to connect technological change and IPR with a view of looking at the potential of the sharing society. We also examine the *Shanzhai* culture in order to argue for a different economic pathway for the BRI. We try to bring China's experience back to the front to demonstrate how China might act as far as BRI is concerned.

From the developing countries' points of view (there are enormous developing economies across the BRI), the day-to-day law suits filed between the big global firms such as Apple and Samsung are not economically viable for developing economies. They want development and technology as well as to realize their economic potential. A more flexible management of IPRs – for instance, a low cost or even public repository of intellectual property (IP) products – could help them to carry out their daily work at high quality but not necessarily with extremely high-tech products. While the World Intellectual Property organization (WIPO) is paying more attention to the realization of the commercial aspects of IPR protection, such as patents, copyright and trademark applications, the WTO is more about inclusiveness and technological transfer among member economies. Under the Agreement on Trade Related Aspects of Intellectual Property Rights (TRIPS), Article 7, the protection of 'technological innovation' and the 'transfer and dissemination' of technology are both considered (Correa 2000: 6). Under TRIPS, developing countries are allowed to be given more time in order to follow IPRs standards and protection. Developing countries can 'use bargaining power and secure trade-offs in negotiating favourable terms' under the TRIPS in the WTO (Adede 2003, 26). The Dispute Settlement Understanding (DSU) under the WTO gives developing countries a more impartial body rather than the developed countries' own policy coercion.

IPRs are designed to protect the commercial interest of innovation and creativity. In *Piracy and the State: The Politics of Intellectual Property Rights in China*, Dimitrov (2009) painstakingly elaborated the politics of IPRs in China by recognizing the legal protection of the IPRs but questioning the enforcement of IPRs, especially the existing campaign-style enforcement methods. After China signing the Sino–American Memorandum of Understanding on the Protection of Intellectual Property with the US in 1992, the pressure from the US became clear and present. Between June 1993 and February 1995, the US held 12 negotiation sessions with China on IPR protection or its infringement. The Joint Commission on Commerce and Trade (JCCT) between the US and China also acted as another policy push for China on IPR protection. When Hu Jintao, former President of China, was invited to Seattle as a guest in the house of Bill Gates, the co-founder of Microsoft, Hu inevitably mentioned that protecting IPRs was 'essential' for China. The annual *Special 301 Report* of the USTR continued to place China on, mostly, the top of the priority watch list. Yet, since the *Outline of the National Intellectual Property Strategy* was launched by the Chinese government in 2008,

Table 10.2 Applications of patents in China, domestic and international (April 1985 to December 2016)

	Year	Total	Invention	Application	Industrial Design
Total	1985–2009	5,810,195	1,932,317	2,001,940	1,875,938
	2010	1,222,286	391,177	409,836	421,273
	2011	1,633,347	526,412	585,467	521,468
	2012	2,050,649	652,777	740,290	657,582
	2013	2,377,061	825,136	892,362	659,563
	2014	2,361,243	928,177	868,511	564,555
	2015	2,798,500	1,101,864	1,127,577	569,059
	2016	3,464,824	1,338,503	1,475,977	650,344
Domestic	1985–2009	4,885,939	1,135,064	1,987,737	1,763,138
	2010	1,109,428	293,066	407,238	409,124
	2011	1,504,670	415,829	581,303	507,538
	2012	1,912,151	535,313	734,437	642,401
	2013	2,234,560	704,936	885,226	644,398
	2014	2,210,616	801,135	861,053	548,428
	2015	2,639,446	968,251	1,119,714	551,481
	2016	3,305,225	1,204,981	1,468,295	631,949
International	1985–2009	924,256	797,253	14,203	112,800
	2010	112,858	98,111	2,598	12,149
	2011	128,677	110,583	4,164	13,930
	2012	138,498	117,464	5,853	15,181
	2013	142,501	120,200	7,136	15,181
	2014	150,627	127,042	7,458	16,127
	2015	159,054	133,613	7,863	17,578
	2016	159,599	133,522	7,682	18,395

Sources: (*Zhongguo Zhishichanquan Nianjian* 2015 2015, 384 and *Zhongguo Zhishichanquan Nianjian* 2017 2017, 424)

IPR protection has become a 'national strategy' (Cheung 2018, 90). In the same year, the Summer Olympics was held in Beijing and, two years later, the Expo was held in Shanghai. These mega-global events provided additional reasons for China to become more compliant to IPR protection because they know that global attention will be following them every step of the way.

As can be seen from Table 10.2, the application for patents in China has shown the trend of the domestic applications significantly outnumbering the international applications. For instance, from 1985 to 2009, the total number of patent applications (invention, application, and industrial design) reached 5,810,195, of which domestic applications accounted for 4,885,939. Yet, in 2016 alone, the total number of applications was 3,464,824 (3,305,225 were domestic and only 159,599 were international).

In 2016, Beijing, Jiangsu, Zhejiang, and Guangdong had the most patent applications among the various Chinese cities and provinces (Table 10.3). These cities and provinces were those areas that first opened up after Deng Xiaoping's

Table 10.3 China domestic patents application (selected provinces/cities) (2016)

Area	Invention	Application	Industrial design
Total	1,204,981	1,468,295	631,949
Beijing	104,643	64,496	19,990
Tianjin	38,153	63,589	4,772
Shanghai	54,339	51,836	13,762
Jiangsu	184,632	192,636	135,161
Zhejiang	93,254	199,244	100,649
Shandong	88,359	106,100	18,452
Shenzhen	56,326	56,881	32,106
Qingdao	34,953	21,009	3,566
Guangdong	155,581	203,609	146,477

Sources: (*Zhongguo Zhishichanquan Nianjian* 2017 2017, 424–426)

Table 10.4 International application for Chinese patents (selected countries) (2016)

Area	Invention	Application	Industrial design
Total	133,522	7,682	18,395
Swiss	3,453	212	785
Germany	14,158	757	1,726
France	4,631	301	843
UK	2,372	131	610
Italy	1,610	145	675
Japan	39,207	2,134	3,810
Netherlands	3,155	92	304
USA	35,895	2,070	3,771
Korea	13,764	814	2,982

Sources: (*Zhongguo Zhishichanquan Nianjian* 2017 2017, 426–430).

economic reforms in 1978, and they are the most proactive cities and provinces in using IPRs to harness innovation and technological development.

Using the same 2016 year to illustrate (see Table 10.4), among the other countries that applied for Chinese patents, Germany, Japan, the US, and Korea took the lion's share. To a large extent, those are the most advanced economies and they have already tried to tap into the potential of the Chinese market as well as to keep up with the innovation, technological change, and basically the next step of Chinese economic development. As far as the BRI economies are concerned, China's road from being one of the biggest counterfeiters to IPR protection, was as a response to global pressure (the US in particular), and this will certainly inspire other developing economies who are also looking for economic growth, technological advancement, and development.

Chinese campaign-style IPR protection may need some reform and modification. However, Table 10.5 indicates that in terms of customs confiscation,

Table 10.5 China customs counterfeit confiscation in 2016 (by products)

Categories	Numbers	Percentage
Tobacco	13,768,890	32.74
Food and beverage	316,706	0.75
Light industrial goods	808,257	1.92
Machinery	3,004,736	7.14
Cosmetic/personal health	6,919,410	16.45
Clothes	1,063,097	2.53
Shoes	655,616	1.56
Other machinery and electronic goods	2,025,256	4.82
Hats	87,955	0.21
Cars, motor	109,078	0.26
Leather goods	169,370	0.40
Telecommunication	287,783	0.68
Watches	54,754	0.13
Toys/games	234,824	0.56
Pharma products	1,392,446	3.31
Storage medium	199,524	0.47
Sports facilities	112,915	0.27
Jewelries	7,926	0.02
Medical instruments	20	0.00
Others	10,839,653	25.77

Sources: *(Zhongguo Zhishichanquan Nianjian* 2017 2017, 491–492).

tobacco (32%), machinery (7.14%) and cosmetic/personal health (16.45%) were the main targets. In other words, IPR protection is underway and the "high hanging fruits" would not be obtained if the government was not moving forward with confiscation and combatting counterfeiting. Table 10.5 also shows that the potential investors in the global economy will be relying on how IPR protection will be implemented before placing their investment in China, especially in high-tech industries.

Starting from March 2018, the US and China have been engaging in a trade war, and Huawei, the world's largest telecommunication company, was mentioned repeatedly by the US as allegedly threatening the US by "spying" through their 5G technological leadership as well as the company's connection with the Chinese government. However, in terms of IPR protection, Huawei has gone above and beyond. On 5 November 2019, Ren Zhenfei, the Chairman of Huawei was interviewed by Matt Murray, the Chief Editor of the *Wall Street Journal* in the Headquarters of Huawei in Shenzhen. Ren replied that Huawei so far received about US$1.4 billion royalties from IPRs but it paid out more – about US$6 billion in total. Every year, Huawei spent between US$15 to US$20 billion on research and development (R&D). Huawei has 80,000 to 90,000 researchers and, according to Ren, you cannot be the leader in global technology by counterfeiting alone.[12] In another example, Cloudary (under Tencent) is China's largest internet digital literature platform, which occupies 72% of China's original literature market. Their economic model is to recruit internet authors to create original novels, using Cloudary as a platform for subscribers to pay to read the novel online. Apart from being a new model of IPR protection, the externality is that many Chinese internet novels have become exportable to overseas, which also enhances China's soft power abroad (Gao, et al. 2014, 116–117).

The late MIT professor, Lester Thurow (1997), argued that the one-size-fits-all legal system for IPR protection is not working. There should be a clear balance between production and distribution of new ideas. Developing countries have learnt that every country that has 'caught up' has done so by copying. In fact, by using Xiaomi (a very famous mobile phone brand in China), Raustiala and Sprigman argued that imitation and innovation co-exist and the fact is that the designing process of Xiaomi's mobile phone is more democratic than I-phone (Raustiala and Sprigman 2013, 26–27). No system of protecting IPRs can work unless most of the governments of the world agree to enforce it. The BRI comprises mostly developing countries which were deliberately "neglected" by the world economic infrastructure after World War II. If they were neglected in the first place, why should they be fully bounded by the same principle that governed the capitalist west for so long? If they want to harness technological development and growth by innovation and creativity, they should be given some leeway. Chang Ha-Joon, a development economist from Cambridge University argued in *Bad Samaritans* that "The other industrializing countries in Europe, and the US, had to violate those laws [in the 19th century] in order to acquire superior British technologies," and he continued "Developing countries should be allowed to grant weaker IPRs, shorter patent life, lower licensing royalty rates (probably graduated according to their abilities to pay)" (Chang 2008, 128 and 143). By giving concession, nevertheless, creativities may not be undermined but instead will be enhanced.

In studying China's domestic copyright development of the film and music industries, Lucy Montgomery and Jason Potts concluded that "In consequence, IP law does not really matter; yet for a given IP law, what matters is who is most adapted to its weakest versions. And that has been with the central lesson of our case study of China's creative industries. Strong competitive advantage thus flows from weak, not strong, IP environments" (2008, 256). In the economic context of China, the new normal, and slowing economic growth have been pushing China to adapt to compete through quality and innovation. The other potential consequence is the search for countries that are more in common, especially in terms of economic development and the BRI, is likely to be the modus operandi of a significant numbers of economic "underdogs" to search for common development opportunities in a non-institutionalized manner.

Their "underdog" nature unavoidably allows one to explore the potential of *Shanzhai* culture in IPRs studies in China. Jessica Chubb provided a vivid explanation:

> China's shanzhai culture as a result of processes of hybridization of China's economic life and cultural consciousness, highlight[ed] the interplay between

local purposes and desires, and global and national economic and cultural authorities. Those who produce and consume China's shanzhai culture are influencing the development of the emergent global industrial and cultural economy, even as their own encounters with its local variant, capitalism with Chinese characteristics have redefined their practices, needs and desires.

(Chubb 2015, 261)

In the Chinese case, *Shanzhai* reminds them of the rebellious nature of people who are suppressed by a big power and particularly the MNCs. But, in the case of IPRs, it is not destructive, but more like hybridization, a constant reform and modification to suit domestic needs and the broader community. Rather than a purely "creative destruction" which embodies the gist of the capitalist spirit, *Shanzhai* is certainly disruptive. But it is constantly modernizing with inclusiveness in mind because the individuals or actors are somewhat connected with the common understanding that *changing is everything*. In *The End of Copycat China*, Shaun Rein reminded the audiences that *Shanzhai* was the early move for many Chinese companies. But innovation and creativity come later, when the companies started thinking about the Chinese domestic market (Rein 2013, 91). *Shanzhai* is transformative as well as disruptive in the Chinese context.

In showing the significance of the network power, Grewal used free software to illustrate the sharing and the usefulness of open source. He concluded that "globalization is best understood as the emergence and consolidation of transnational and international networks that link people – or groups of people, including entire countries – through the use of shared coordinating standards" (Grewal 2008, 292). The common denominator of the BRI economies is economic development and the cornerstone is infrastructure. China has demonstrated, loud and clear, that state intervention of the special economic zones helps China move to a technology- and innovation-driven economy. Countries along the BRI are a testing ground to emulate China's economic growth experience rather than US hegemonic control.

Conclusion

China's economic growth became connected more closely with the world economy through joining the WTO in 2001, securing the position of second largest economy in 2010, and including RMB in the SDRs of the IMF in 2015. But the new normal also structurally changes the political economy and pushes China to move up the technological ladder to be more innovative and creative before harnessing the next phase of economic growth. Many have already discussed the negative externalities of economic reform such as the inequality between coastal and inner cities, environmental pollution, corruption, and industrial relations, yet, Randall Peerenboom, professor of the Law School at UCLA and Director of China programmes for the Oxford Foundation of Law, Justice and Society, concluded that "Despite a variety of problems. China does well relative to its level of development on most measures of human rights and well-being" (Peerenboom

2007, 162). The main point is that he rightly points to "relative to its level of development." The BRI is trying to connect the economies having relatively (some more advanced and some less) equal levels of economic development with that of China. China's economic model and growth experiences will certainly be useful for them, although it may not be totally transferrable. More importantly, as I have demonstrated earlier, most of the economies along the BRI were "neglected" by the global economic infrastructure for more than half a century. The economic rise (some may say resurgence) of China invited lots of criticisms in academic circles, but when tested by and compared with other studies, the BRI shows a platform in which economic growth and development can be inclusive too. Many established economies, however, will be unhappy. The trade war (from March 2018 to January 2020 after the first phase of agreement was signed) between China and the US is certainly not helping. But, on a practical level, we have seen the recognition of China's BRI some significant supporters, including Italy, a G7 economy. The BRI is more like a bottom-up economic development experiment, so it may take some time before the academics and development theorists can formulate more mature academic perspectives.

China is moving to a more consumption-based economy and its increasing imports are expected to become a new long-term driver for China's growth. The first China International Import Expo (CIIE) was held 5–10 October 2018 in Shanghai (Xu et al. 2018, 19). It will open up further the consumer-driven sectors of China's market. The go-out strategies, the China model, the internationalization of the RMB, and IPR protection are testing and seemingly providing a reasonable trajectory for the way forward for China's economic interaction with the world economy. Yet, nothing is perfect and the challenge from the outside world is unstoppable. This does require the mentality of the Chinese government of moving away from developmental learning and copying the existing successes, but becoming more entrepreneurial in many aspects. Risk, courage, and cooperation are all essential factors to determine the pathway of China's economic development.

Notes

1 I would like to thank Victor Zheng for his invitation to contribute this book chapter, and Guo Hua's managing of the entire submission process. The invitation came at the time when I was very busy with other research and university engagement. I very much appreciate their patience and support. I would also like to thank the Universities Service Centre for China Studies at the Chinese University of Hong Kong for their archival and library support for some of the research of this chapter. In some areas of this chapter, I have added and taken some points from Biswajit Dhar, the reviewer of my book, *China in the Global Political Economy: From Developmental to Entrepreneurial* in the *China Report*. I'm grateful for those useful comments.

2 He was also the Academic Director of the LSE-PKU Summer School.

3 See also (Gilpin 1981, 156). He very clearly provided the argument that the hegemonic stability will cease to exist if the marginal cost of keeping the hegemony is greater than the marginal benefit of having the hegemony.

4 CNN [https://edition.cnn.com/interactive/2019/09/politics/inequality-in-america/index.html] (accessed 20 December 2019).
5 For example, China already provided 10.25% of the UN peace-keeping budget and providing more than 8,000 personel for the global peace-keeping force. *The Diplomat* [https://thediplomat.com/2018/04/china-takes-the-lead-in-un-peacekeeping/] (accessed 24 December 2019).
6 Ministry of Foreign Affairs, China [www.fmprc.gov.cn/zflt/eng/zgdfzzc/t463748.htm] (accessed 29 December 2019).
7 From the summer to the end of 1997, the US did not fully recognize the crisis and kept saying it was regional. But in 1998, when Clinton addressed the UN General Assembly, he started recognizing the crisis was in fact global!
8 Los Angeles Times [https://www.latimes.com/archives/la-xpm-2008-nov-10-fi-china10-story.html] (accessed 10 October 2020).
9 I was invited to give a talk in Chatham House, London in a panel entitled 'The Renminbi: A New Global Currency?' on 23 February 2017. I talked about the significance of trust in the RMB. Other panel members were Dr Paola Subacchi, Research Director, International Economics, Chatham House and Dr Gao Haihong, Professor and Director, Research Centre for International Finance, China Academy of Social Sciences. It was chaired by Dr Linda Yueh, Fellow in Economics, St Edmund Hall, Oxford University and Adjunct Professor of Economics, London Business School. The link for the event is: www.chathamhouse.org/event/renminbi-new-global-currency
10 *The Global Times* [www.globaltimes.cn/content/1073339.shtml] (accessed 5 January 2020).
11 *The Telegraph* [www.telegraph.co.uk/china-watch/business/rise-of-chinese-yuan/] (accessed 5 January 2019).
12 (https://mp.weixin.qq.com/s/cJcYQTQe9M_StrddPfl_pQ) (accessed 31 December 2019).

References

13th Five-year Plan for Economic and Social Development of the People's Republic of China (2016–2020). 2016. Beijing: Central Compilation & Translation Press.

Adede, Adronico O. 2003. 'Origins and History of the TRIPS Negotiations.' In *Trading in Knowledge: Development Perspectives on TRIPS, Trade and Sustainability*, edited by Christophe Bellmann, Graham Dutfield and Ricardo Melendez-Ortiz, 23–35. London: Earthscan.

Arrow, Kenneth. 1972. 'Gifts and Exchanges.' *Philosophy and Public Affairs* 1(4): 343–362.

Axelrod, Robert. 1984. *The Evolution of Cooperation*. New York: Basic Books.

Brautigam, Deborah and Tang, Xiaoyang. 2011. 'African Shenzhen: China's Special Economic Zones in Africa.' *Journal of Modern African Studies* 49(1): 27–54.

Breslin, Shaun. 2011. 'The "China Model" and the Global Crisis; from Friedrich List to a Chinese Mode of Governance?' *International Affairs* 87(6): 1323–1343.

Chang, Ha-Joon. 2008. *Bad Samaritans: The Myth of Free Trade and the Secret History of Capitalism*. London: Bloomsbury.

Chen, Ling and Barry Naughton. 2017. 'A Dynamic China Model: The Co-Evolution of Economics and Politics in China.' *Journal of Contemporary China* 26(103): 18–34.

Chen, Yunnan, Irene Yuan Sun, Rex Uzonna Ukaejiofo, Xiaoyang Tang and Deborah Brautigam. 2016. 'Learning from China? Manufacturing, Investment, and Technological Transfer in Nigeria.' *SAIS China Africa Research Initiative Working Paper* 2: 1–27.

Cheung, Gordon C. K. 2018. *China in the Global Political Economy: From Developmental to Entrepreneurial.* Cheltenham: Edward Elgar Publishing Inc.

China Policy. 2017. 'China Going Global between Ambition and Capacity.' Beijing: China Policy, 1–11.

Chubb, Andrew. 2015. 'China's Shanzhai Culture: "Grabism" and the politics of hybridity.' *Journal of Contemporary China* 24(92): 260–279.

Correa, Carlos M. 2000. *Intellectual Property Rights, the WTO and Developing Countries: The TRIPS Agreement and Policy Options.* London: Zed Books.

Cox, Michael. 2007. 'Still the American Empire.' *Political Studies Review* 5: 1–10.

Dimitrov, Martin K. 2009. *Piracy and the State: The Politics of Intellectual Property Rights in China.* Cambridge: Cambridge University Press.

Fahnbulleh, Miatta. 2020. 'The Neoliberal Collapse: Markets Are not the Answer.' *Foreign Affairs* 99(1): 38–43.

Feng, Bing. 2015. *Yidai, yilu' quanqiu fazhan de Zhonggouluoji* [One Belt, One Road: The Chinese Logic for Global Development]. Beijing: Zhongguo minzhu fazhi chubanshe.

Gao, Xianmin and Kaihua Zhang. 2014. *Zhongguo Kongzi: Zhiba shijie de liuda guanjianzi* [*China "Control": Six Keywords of Conquering the World*]. Taipei: Shangqi Zixun.

Gilpin, Robert. 1981. *War and Change in World Politics.* Cambridge: Cambridge University Press.

Goh, Sui Noi. 2018. 'China's Belt and Road Initiative: An Overview of Developments.' *China and the World-Ancient and Modern Silk Road: An International Journal* 1(2): 1–11.

Grewal, David Singh, 2008. *Network Power: The Social Dynamics of Globalization.* New Haven & London: Yale University Press.

Held, David et al. 1999. *Global Transformations: Politics, Economics, and Culture* Stanford, CA: Stanford University Press.

Jones, Lee and Jinghan Zeng. 2019. 'Understanding China's "Belt and Road Initiative": Beyond 'Grand Strategy' to a State Transformation Analysis.' *Third World Quarterly* 40(8): 1415–1439.

Jordan, Amos, A. and Jane Khanna 1995. 'Economic Interdependence and Challenges to the Nation-State: The Emergence of Natural Economic Territories in the Asian Pacific.' *Journal of International Affairs* 48(2): 433–462.

Kang, David C. 2003. 'Getting Asia Wrong: The Need for New Analytical Frameworks.' *International Security* 27(4): 57–85.

Kerr, David, ed. 2016. *China's Many Dreams: Comparative Perspectives on China's Search for National Rejuvenation.* Basingstoke: Palgrave.

Khanna, Parag. 2019. *The Future is Asian: Global Order in the Twenty-First Century.* London: Weidenfeld & Nicolson.

Kindleberger, Charles. P. 1973. *The World in Depression, 1929–1939.* Berkeley: University of California Press.

Kynge, James. 2017. 'China Coverts Regional Primacy Rather Than World Domination.' *Financial Times,* 28–29 January, 9.

Lall, Sanjaya and Albaladejo, Manuel. 2004. 'China's Competitive Performance: A Threat to East Asian Manufactured Exports?' *World Development* 32(9): 1441–1466.

Li, Yining, Justin Yifu Lin and, Yongnian Zheng. 2015. *Doudong yidai yilu: Guojia zhiku dingji xuezhe qianzhan zhongguo xinsilu* [Understanding One Belt, One Road: Future Prospects of China's New Silk Road from Top Scholars of the National Think Tank]. Beijing: Zhongxin chubanshe.

Montgomery, Lucy and Jason Potts. 2008. 'Does Weaker Copyright Mean Stronger Creative Industries? Some Lessons from China.' *Creative Industries Journal* 1(3): 245–261.

Moore, Thomas G. 1999. 'China and Globalization.' *Asian Perspective* 23(4): 65–95.

Norrlof, Carla. 2010. *America's Global Advantage: US Hegemony and International Cooperation.* Cambridge: Cambridge University Press.

Nye, Joseph. 1991. *Bound To Lead: The Changing Nature of American Power.* New York: Basic Books.

Peerenboom, Randall 2007 *China Modernizes: Threat to the West or Model for the Rest!* Oxford: Oxford University Press.

Power, Marcus, Giles Mohan and May Tan-Mullins. 2012. *China's Resource Diplomacy in Africa: Powering Developing?* Basingstoke: Palgrave.

Ramo, Joshua Cooper. 2004. *The Beijing Consensus.* London: The Foreign Policy Centre.

Raustiala, Kal and Christopher Sprigman. 2013. 'Fake It Till You Make It: The Good News About China's Knockoff Economy.' *Foreign Affairs* 92(4): 25–30.

Rein, Shaun. 2013. *Shanzhai Zhongguo de zhongjie: chuangzaoli, chuangxinli yu gerenzhuyi zai yazhou de jueqi* [*The End of copycat Chin: The Rise of Creativity, Innovation, and Individualism in Asia*]. Translated by Yaoyi Wu. Shanghai: Shanghai Yiwen chubanshe.

Sardar, Ziauddin and Merryl Wyn Davies. 2002. *Why Do People Hate America?* Cambridge: Icon Books.

Scalapino, Robert A. 1991–92. 'The United States and Asia: Future Prospects.' *Foreign Affair* 70(5): 19–40.

Shen, Jianfa. 2009. 'Inter-City Cooperation and Competition between Hong Kong and Shenzhen: Institutional Constraints and Asymmetric Urban Governance.' In *The Strategic Choices for Asian Cities under Globalization* [*Quanqiuhua beijingxia yazhou chengshi de zhanluexing xuanze*] edited by Guixin Wang and Ruwan Yang, 169–192. Shanghai: Renmin chubanshe.

Stiglitz, Joseph. 2003. *The Roaring Nineties: Why We're Paying the Price for the Greediest Decade in History.* London: Penguin.

Subacchi, Paola. 2017. *How China is Building a Global Currency: The People's Money.* New York: Columbia University Press.

Thurow, Lester C. 1997. 'Needed: a New System of Intellectual Property Rights.' *Harvard Business Review* 75(5): 94–103.

Wang, Hongying. 2016. 'A Deeper Look at China's 'Going Out' Policy.' *Commentary.* Waterloo: Centre for International Governance Innovation (CIGI), March, 1–3.

Wu, Jinglian. 2013. 'Zhongguo gaige zaichufa' [Re-launch of China's Reform]. In *Gaige shi Zhongguo zuida de hongli* [*Reform: China's Largest Dividend*]. edited by Shangquan Gao. Hong Kong: Joint Publishing Co. Ltd, 42–52.

Wu, Xiaoqiu. 2008. *Zhongguo zhiben shichang yanjiu baogao* [*2008 China Capital Market Study*]. Beijing: Renmin daxue chubanshe.

Xu, Ming and Jia Li. 2018. 'Matters of Import.' *China Report* 67: 18–25.

Yang, Jiechi. 2019. *Belt and Road Cooperation: For A Better World*, Report on the Findings and Recommendations from the First Meeting of the Advisory Council of the Belt and Road Forum for International Cooperation (10 April), Beijing, China.

Yu, Dianfan and Yajun Zhang. 2015. 'China's Industrial Transformation and the "New Normal".' *Third World Quarterly* 36(11): 2075–2097.

Zakaria, Fareed. 1998. *From Wealth to Power: The Unusual Origins of America's World Role.* Princeton: Princeton University Press.

Zakaria, Fareed. 2020. 'The New China Scare: Why America Shouldn't Panic About Its Latest Challenger.' *Foreign Affairs* 99(1): 52–69.

Zhao, Suisheng. 2010. 'The China Model: Can It Replace the Western Model of Modernization?' *Journal of Contemporary China* 19(65): 419–36.

Zheng, Bijian. 2005. 'China's "Peaceful Rise" to Great Power Status.' *Foreign Affairs* 84(5): 18–24.

Zheng, Yongnian. 2010. *Zhongguo Moshi: Jingyan yu Kunju* [*China Model: Experience and Difficulties*]. Zhejiang: Zhejiang People's Publishing House.

Zhongguo Zhishichanquan Nianjian 2015. 2015. *Yearbook of China's Intellectual Property Rights 2015* Beijing: Zhishichanquan chubanshi.

Zhongguo Zhishichanquan Nianjian 2017. 2017. *Yearbook of China's Intellectual Property Rights 2017.* Beijing: Zhishichanquan chubanshi.

Zhou, Xiaochuan. 2013. 'Zhubu shixian renminbi ziben xiangmu ke duihuan (Gradually realising renminbi capital account convertability).' In *Gaige shi Zhongguo zuida de hongli* (*Reform: China's Largest Dividend*), edited by Shangquan Gao. Hong Kong: Joint Publishing Co. Ltd, 230–248.

11 An integrated approach to sustainable infrastructure standards for the Belt and Road Initiative

Stephen Y.S. Wong, Johnson C.S. Kong, Gloria W.T. Luo, and Natalie H.T. Lau

11.1 Introduction

The China-led Belt and Road Initiative (BRI) was first raised by President Xi Jinping in 2013, with a vision of connecting China with the rest of Asia, Europe, and Africa through financing infrastructure development and achieving "peace, development, cooperation and mutual benefit" in the 21st century (NDRC 2015). By April 2019, 126 countries had signed up to the BRI, representing around 23% of global gross domestic product (GDP) (Ma and Zadek 2019). Alongside the BRI's potential economic influence, one recent estimate suggests that in 2015 the electricity generation of the BRI participating countries was responsible for 34.45% of global carbon emissions from electricity generation (Zhang et al. 2019).

This is where the discussion around infrastructure comes into focus. Ranging from coal mines in Pakistan to seaports in Azerbaijan, the promise of the BRI encompasses all sorts of infrastructure development, which has long been associated with rapid industrialization, urbanization, and wealth accumulation. A 2019 World Bank report estimated the full implementation of the BRI's transport infrastructure projects alone could add 1.7–6.2% to global trade and 0.7–2.9% to global real income (World Bank 2019). In contrast to understanding the economic impact of the BRI, however, we are still at a nascent stage of fully understanding its costs and implications for the environment and society. As the climate crisis looms large, increased global attention has been placed onto the sustainability implications of the BRI.

The rising worldwide concern relates to the decade-long, heated debate on the impact of infrastructure development on environmental sustainability, especially when it comes to the developing world. While infrastructure development still carries the stigma associated with the practices of the past decades, that have all the earmarks of negative consequences such as pollution, resource depletion, and labour abuses, infrastructure remains crucial to achieving systematic and meaningful change for global sustainable development. The central role of infrastructure in supporting the delivery of the 17 United Nations

Sustainable Development Goals (SDGs) has started to gain international recognition (Thacker et al. 2018). For instance, infrastructure systems for energy and buildings can help attain SDGs 1, 7, 8, and 9. Achieving social inclusiveness represented by SDGs 4, 5, and 10 would rely on transport and telecommunication systems. Enhancing human health and wellbeing in accordance with SDGs 2, 3, and 6 calls for access to clean water and food (Hastings 2019).

As infrastructure can be a double-edged sword for sustainability, a constructive dialogue on what constitutes "sustainable infrastructure" is crucial. Serebrisky et al. (2018) from the Inter-American Development Bank (IDB) Group, after examining existing definitions, frameworks, and principles, synthesized four prongs of sustainable infrastructure:

(i)   *Environmental sustainability*: infrastructure that preserves, restores, and integrates the natural environment, including biodiversity and ecosystems;
(ii) *Social sustainability*: infrastructure that is inclusive, broadly supported by the affected communities, and contributing to enhanced livelihoods and social well-being;
(iii) *Economic and financial sustainability*: infrastructure that generates a positive net economic return and an adequate risk-adjusted rate of return for project investors;
(iv) *Institutional sustainability*: infrastructure that is aligned with national and international commitments and based on transparent and consistent governance systems.

To make infrastructure development sustainable, it is widely agreed that early consideration of sustainability is crucial (Serebrisky et al. 2018; UNEP 2019). The cost of inserting sustainability elements is relatively low in the project preparation and design stage. Upstream planning of infrastructure development at local, regional, national, and transnational levels is also crucial for capturing systemic opportunities for sustainability such as proper siting and synergies between infrastructure projects. Generally speaking, most opportunities for promoting sustainability lie in the pre-construction stages, namely the upstream planning, preparation and design, and financing stages – sustainability should be considered in these stages, and the sooner the better.

Unfortunately, as this chapter will argue, the heterogeneity of sustainability standards could make communication between project participants difficult and could undermine early consideration of sustainability in infrastructure development. Existing sustainability standards have limited coverage for upstream planning, leaving some sustainability opportunities in the earliest stage of development uncaptured. We observe that a lot of development finance institutions (DFIs) tend to get into these projects at a later stage. In order to remove the barriers for them to get involved earlier, it is important to have an integrated approach related to sustainability standards across all stages. Specifically, it is important to, firstly, harmonize existing standards across stages of project development, and secondly, consolidate upstream planning standards to provide a set of best practices as the basis for further development.

In this chapter, Section 11.2 elucidates the current situation of sustainable development in the BRI context. It will start by detailing the significance of sustainable infrastructure development, move on to depict the policy landscape of China's commitments to "greening" Belt and Road infrastructure, and then contrast the policy vision with key challenges of sustainable development when rolling out BRI projects. Section 11.3 narrows the discussion to sustainability infrastructure standards as a key tool to operationalize sustainability. An analysis based on a literature review will be presented to delve into the role of standards, the state of play, and the issues of existing sustainable infrastructure standards. Section 11.4 will summarize earlier findings and discuss an integrated approach to developing sustainable infrastructure standards for the BRI. Recommendations will be made in terms of the strategic directions for integration as well as the role of Hong Kong in facilitating the process of integration. This chapter will then conclude with the limitations, and highlight future research areas for attention.

11.2 Sustainable development in the Belt-and-Road Initiative

Economic development today is full of sustainability challenges, and the BRI is no exception. Among the global challenges represented by the 17 SDGs, climate change is considered to be the biggest challenge to global sustainability and requires immediate attention on all fronts. According to the Intergovernmental Panel on Climate Change, an intergovernmental body under the United Nations, human-induced warming reached approximately 1°C above pre-industrial levels in 2017 (IPCC 2018). A 1.5°C to 2°C increase in average global temperature, which seems unavoidable in the absence of large-scale actions and systematic changes, would have devastating impacts on the ecosystem and, very likely, human civilization survival, constituting an imminent risk that makes aggressive climate strategies absolutely essential (IPCC 2018).

Moreover, the perspective of climate justice adds another layer of complexity to the fight against climate change. Whether economic development and sustainability are mutually exclusive has long been a topic of debate. One school of thought has suggested that posing restrictions on economic activity is necessary to stop environmental damage and resource depletion. Nonetheless, some climate justice advocates highlight the state of development in poor countries, where infrastructure development is most needed and their contribution to the historical global carbon emissions is minimal. It would be unfair for these developing regions to sacrifice growth for saving the planet. A sensible and practical alternative is to inject sustainability as much as possible into the economic development of these countries to minimize costs to the environment and to society.

The need to uphold climate justice for developing countries is particularly relevant in the BRI context. In light of the threats posed by climate change, the compatibility of the BRI with the global climate agenda and the associated sustainability considerations has thus been in the international spotlight, and developing sustainable infrastructure could offer a solution. The following section will unravel why infrastructure development should be sustainable, review the policies regarding "greening" the BRI, and introduce some challenges of sustainable development along the Belt and Road.

11.2.1 The significance of sustainable infrastructure

Promoting the development of sustainable infrastructure along the Belt and Road could exert significant social impacts beyond economic development. For instance, infrastructure that provides integrated services in telecommunications, electricity, transport, clean water and sanitation, etc. is essential not only for promoting economic development, but also for increasing employment opportunities for the poor and expanding their access to relevant facilities and public services, thereby alleviating deprivation of education, personal security, and well-being (Bhattacharya et al. 2016). On the other hand, involuntary resettlement and land acquisition may be involved under some infrastructure projects, which could have significant negative impacts on the local community and require thoughtful planning and mitigation strategies.

The long-lasting impacts of infrastructure development on the environment has also made the role of sustainable infrastructure especially important. If unsustainable technologies and practices have been locked in the initial stage of infrastructure development, the detrimental effects of these assets built today and in the near future will last for decades. The infrastructure sector today has already contributed to an estimated 70% of the global greenhouse gas emissions (Saha and Modi 2017). This consideration leaves us no choice but to act now and plan, design, build, and operate infrastructure sustainably and fit for a low-carbon future.

While the sheer scale and irreversibility of the climate challenge is intimidating, the imminent need to take infrastructure development in a sustainable direction does shed light on new areas to which to channel investment capital. Globally speaking, to realize a scenario that has a 66% chance of a temperature increase limited to two degrees Celsius, an estimated USD 6.9 trillion annual infrastructure investment would be required (Mirabile, Marchal, and Baron 2017). Meanwhile in the BRI context with 126 Belt and Road countries, an estimated annual investment scale of USD 785 billion in four key sectors (power, transport, manufacturing, and building) is needed by 2030 to reach the two degrees Celsius scenario (Ma and Zadek 2019). These gaps can be translated into unprecedented yet promising investment opportunities for investors to reap.

It is estimated that as much as 75% of the infrastructure that will exist in 2050 has yet to be built (Egler and Frazao 2016). If the BRI could be leveraged to fill the infrastructure gap in a sustainable way, it would represent a tremendous opportunity to contribute to the global sustainability agenda while promoting shared economic prosperity. That is also why sustainable infrastructure has been moving up the global sustainability agenda. The next section will further examine how greening the BRI has gained policy attention in China.

11.2.2 Greening the Belt and Road Initiative

The development of sustainable infrastructure is closely aligned with the strategic direction of the BRI. The importance of promoting green and sustainable growth in the BRI was reiterated in the second Belt and Road Forum for International Cooperation in April 2019:

> *Efforts are called for to build high-quality, reliable, resilient and sustainable, including environmentally sustainable infrastructure, and ensure that such infrastructure is affordable, accessible, inclusive and broadly beneficial.*
>
> (BRF Advisory Council 2019, 27)

This statement sends strong policy signals and demonstrates China's commitment to the global sustainability agenda.

Since the announcement of the BRI in 2013, China has published relevant plans, guidance, and principles to set the tone for "greening" the Belt and Road infrastructure, for example:

- In 2017, the Ministry of Foreign Affairs, the National Reform and Development Commission, and the Ministry of Commerce published the *Guidance on Promoting Green Belt and Road*. This offered high-level direction to establish an environmental cooperation and exchange system between BRI countries and develop and implement a series of eco-environmental risk prevention policies and measures in three to five years, and to set up a comprehensive eco-environmental service, support, and guarantee system in five to ten years (Belt and Road Portal 2017a).
- In 2017, the Ministry of Environmental Protection published the *Belt and Road Ecological and Environmental Cooperation Plan*, where eco-friendly infrastructure construction was emphasized and the participation of the private sector in environmental governance was advocated (Belt and Road Portal 2017b). Moreover, the Ministry has committed itself to strictly enforcing environmental standards and practices in sectors such as transportation, real estate, and energy, as one of the focal points to promote low-carbon constructions and operations (Belt and Road Portal 2017b).
- While the above two official documents serve more as high-level guidance, there are two other documents providing practical implementation advice to practitioners. The first one is the *Green Investment Principles for the Belt and Road*, issued by the Green Finance Committee of China Society for Finance and Banking in 2018, which aims to orient and leverage a larger scale of capital into sustainable investments (GFC and GFI 2018). The other is the *Guidelines of Sustainable Infrastructure for Chinese International Contractors*, issued by the China International Contractors Association in

2017, which clarifies guidelines for environmental and social sustainability, as well as sustainability governance rules (CICA 2017).

It is shown above that great strides have been made towards injecting the vision of a sustainable BRI into China's high-level policy design, and the integration has been seen in multiple fields related to environmental protection, economic development, and the investment and construction industries, reflecting the cross-sectoral nature of sustainability issues. Nonetheless, observations can be made and should not be disregarded that these plans, guidance, and principles have remained conceptual blueprints. Moreover, a higher priority seems to be assigned to environmental sustainability than the other dimensions of sustainability such as social sustainability.

The next phase of policy development for the BRI, therefore, should provide granularity in goal setting, comprehensive and operational contents, and actionability to enable mainstream adoption of sustainable infrastructure practices. The next section will briefly review the sustainability challenges of BRI projects to better understand the landscape and the need for sustainable infrastructure development in BRI countries.

11.2.3 Sustainability challenges in the Belt and Road Initiative

Realizing the vision of a sustainable BRI is challenging because many of the BRI countries have poor sustainability performance in general terms. Here, we present a detailed review of some sustainability challenges in the BRI. The literature in this regard is largely dominated by environmental studies, with some scholars attempting to develop typologies of environmental impacts of infrastructure development under the BRI (Teo et al. 2019), while some assess the actual environmental impacts of specific projects. It will be shown that these challenges of greening the BRI, at the same time, imply significant opportunities for impactful sustainable investments.

11.2.3.1 Environmental management

The most common concern stems from the poor environmental management of economic activities in BRI countries. Issues emerge as these are mostly emerging countries with a poor carbon emission track record and insufficient governance and regulatory structure over environmental sustainability. Rauf et al. (2018) analyzed the relationship between economic development and environmental sustainability of 47 BRI economies between 1980 and 2016. The panel data over 30 years shows that most economic indicators, including GDP growth, urbanization, capital formation, and financial development, except for trade openness, are significantly and positively correlated with carbon emissions. For example, every 1% of economic growth leads to a 0.04% increase in carbon emissions (Rauf et al. 2018). A similar study was conducted by Hafeez et al. (2018) on 52 BRI countries, which found that the long-run impact of foreign direct investment on environmental degradation varies across BRI countries. A positive relationship between finance and environmental degradation was found in 36 cases out of the total 52, in contrast to only ten cases with negative relationships, and the remaining six where no impact was identified (Hafeez et al. 2018). These studies justify the worries that, without properly taking sustainability into account, the infrastructure investment and economic development catalysed by the BRI could entail a devastating impact on the environment.

11.2.3.2 Biodiversity

Biodiversity is another commonly discussed sustainability challenge in the BRI. Through performing a geo-spatial analysis of the investment projects along the six proposed BRI economic corridors,[1] Liu et al. (2019) identified 14 spots that run a high risk of alien species invasion, which is a primary anthropogenic threat to global biodiversity. With the BRI countries overlapping 27 out of the 35 global biodiversity hotspots, infrastructure construction projects need strict surveillance of alien species to ensure sustainable development (Liu et al. 2019). In another study using topographic data, it is found that as much as 15% of the Key Biodiversity Areas (KBAs) are within one kilometre of railways proposed through the BRI. This poses a significant risk to biodiversity given that a majority of KBAs remain unprotected, calling for necessary planning and mitigation strategies alongside BRI development (Hughes 2019).

11.2.3.3 Water stress

As yet another example, the impact of infrastructure projects on water stress in the BRI has drawn attention from scholars. Alkon et al. (2019) assessed the impacts on water stress of seven coal-fired power plants in Pakistan backed by Chinese funding. By simulating water withdrawal and total availability of water, it is estimated that the increase of water stress in Pakistan by 2055 would range from 36% to 92% in comparison with the baseline level in the 2010s. It is suggested that these investment projects, which add significantly to the water demand, would threaten the agriculture sector and food security of an already water-scarce country and adversely impact the poorest and most vulnerable households (Alkon et al. 2019).

11.2.3.4 Turning challenges into opportunities

The sustainability challenges of the BRI entail great potential for sustainability improvement in different areas, such as energy efficiency. Zhang, Jin, and Shen (2018) conducted a quantitative assessment on the potential of 56 BRI countries to save energy and reduce carbon dioxide (CO_2) emissions between 1995 and 2015. The potential energy saving from these BRI countries was estimated to be 9.95 billion metric tons of oil equivalent, while the potential reduction of carbon emissions could reach 50.87 billion metric tons over the 20-year period (Zhang, Jin, and Shen 2018).

In another BRI case study on China's infrastructure investment in Azerbaijan-based Port Baku, a strategic trade spot with strong growth potential, Yang and Yang (2019) compared the future energy consumption of the port in two scenarios: the business-as-usual scenario, with power generation based on fossil fuel, and a port-greening scenario, where wind energy is used. It was found that with an additional 5% of total investment to green the port, each additional dollar invested can reduce 424 kg of CO_2 emissions. Based on the analysis, the authors suggested that if the case is applicable to 10% of BRI's total infrastructure investments, an additional investment of $20 billion can lead to a total of 8.48 billion tons of CO_2 reduction (Yang and Yang 2019).

The case above demonstrates the need for investment in sustainable infrastructure projects in order to realize the vision of a sustainable BRI. A question that naturally follows is: how could we operationalize the concept of sustainable infrastructure, thereby channelling capital to finance more sustainable infrastructure projects? That is where sustainability standards, the focus of this chapter, come in.

11.3 Unpacking standards for sustainable infrastructure

The sustainable concepts above translate into real-life projects by following various standards and assessment tools of sustainable infrastructure.

The following section will discuss the pre-construction stages of sustainable infrastructure development, the critical role of standards in operationalizing the concept of sustainability, and the state of play with an attempt to give a glimpse of the landscape of the application of sustainability standards in the BRI. The section will be concluded with a discussion of two issues of existing standards that are barriers to considering sustainability in the early stages.

11.3.1 Pre-construction stages and the role of financial institutions

Sustainable infrastructure, as discussed earlier, is a multi-faceted and complex concept with multiple development stages from upstream planning to demolition as outlined in Figure 11.1. Operationalizing the four prongs of sustainability is especially important in the pre-construction stages to ensure that the

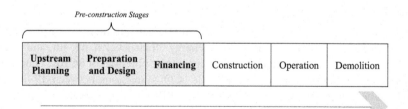

Figure 11.1 Life cycle of an infrastructure project

infrastructure is developed in a sustainable manner. The three pre-construction stages are (OECD, The World Bank, and UNEP 2018; Serebrisky et al. 2018):

(i) *The upstream planning stage* refers to the high-level development plans which include the policies, legislation, laws, and regulations that encourage and enable projects to consider sustainability aspects in later stages. This is where optimal opportunities to drive sustainability results lie, because early planning for sustainability can capture systematic opportunities including proper siting and inter-project synergies, and minimize the needs for substantial modifications in later stages that would incur significant costs.

(ii) *The preparation and design stage* is where infrastructure owners, together with design, construction, and project management practitioners, develop practices for implementation in line with the planning stage objectives. While systematic opportunities may be missed, there remains ample opportunities for designers to improve sustainability outcomes at the project design level.

(iii) *The financing stage* concerns investment or financing decisions in relation to sustainable infrastructure projects. Opportunities to improve sustainability outcomes become scarce and the cost of changes increases in this stage. Substantial modification in terms of project design may incur unavoidable project delays.

In general, most opportunities for promoting sustainability lie in the three pre-construction stages, with diminishing opportunities and rising costs. Therefore, sustainability should be considered in these stages, as early as possible. In practice, this must be driven by certain players in the process rather than naturally occur. Notably, financial institutions, especially DFIs, can play a significant role as the main driver for early-stage consideration of sustainability. Some DFIs engage and provide technical assistance to countries that have inadequate capabilities in terms of development and project planning. Some adopt a more hands-on approach and intervene early in the preparation and design stage to ensure that projects meet their standards in the financing stage (WWF and AECOM 2017; UNDP and CDB 2019). These existing practices place DFIs in a favourable position to drive early consideration of sustainability in the process of infrastructure development, although their full involvement in the early stages seems to be far from being the norm (WWF and AECOM 2017).

11.3.2 *The role of standards*

To put the concept of sustainability into practice, standards set minimum requirements to define sustainable infrastructure and operationalize its implementation (Egler and Frazao 2016). In contrast to the mandatory approach of laws and regulations, standards are rule-based for common and voluntary use, clarifying technical, non-technical, process, or outcome criteria (Brunsson et al. 2012). The approach has been widely adopted in many areas of different societies as a ubiquitous tool to govern individual or collective behaviour towards achieving certain objectives, such as environmental or social management (Brunsson et al. 2012).

To organize societies towards achieving the four-pronged objectives of sustainability, it is essential to develop standards on the "how-to" of sustainable infrastructure development, so that they can inform decision-making at all levels. Research and academic exploration into the best approach of sustainability assessment regarding the suitable criteria, indicators, or methodologies has been extensive (Patil et al. 2016). While the literature to date has not yet reached a conclusive set of standards for sustainable infrastructure, existing standards are abundant, varying with their purpose, scope, and characteristics.

11.3.3 State of play of existing standards

Since the concept of sustainability was introduced in the Brundtland Report of 1987, a wide array and plethora of general sustainability standards and certificates have emerged, whose number could go as high as 500 according to a UNEP estimate in 2016 (Egler and Frazao 2016). When it comes to the infrastructure sector, current literature carrying out comparative reviews on existing standards has focused on examining two categories of standards, which are not exhaustive, but influential and prominent:

11.3.3.1 Sustainability rating systems

Establishing a rating system and grading the performance against set indicators is an important approach to sustainability assessment, which is commonly applied in the construction sector (Bueno et al. 2015). The development of this category of sustainability standards started as early as the 1990s, when the construction sector established green building rating systems, and has now expanded to the civil infrastructure arena with the emergence of *CEEQUAL* (mostly adopted in the UK, Ireland, and Hong Kong), *SuRe* (globally applicable), *Envision* (United States), and *IS Rating* (Australia) since the 2000s (Griffiths et al. 2015). The International Federation of Consulting Engineers has consolidated a total of 30 major sustainability rating and certification tools available across the world. Among those, only four apply to general civil infrastructure projects, five are designed only for transport or hydropower sectors, and the remaining bulk are applied to buildings (IFCE, "Rating", n.d.).

11.3.3.2 Assessment tools of development finance institutions

DFIs have developed multilateral efforts in promoting sustainable infrastructure, particularly in the developing world, playing a dual role in supporting local governments to create an enabling environment for sustainable infrastructure, as well as offering innovative financial instruments to attract private sector participation (Wright et al. 2018). During the process, DFIs such as International Finance Corporation (IFC) and the Asian Infrastructure Investment Bank (AIIB), adopt internal environmental and social (E&S) safeguards, performance standards, or other tools to assist project appraisal, screening, and financing decision-making (WWF and AECOM 2017). These standards are usually applied to investments beyond infrastructure projects (WWF and AECOM 2017). Although these standards are meant for internal use and specific objectives, they are exerting a broader influence on the development of sustainable infrastructure and have attracted scholarly attention. For instance, between 2006 and 2016, the emerging markets saw an estimated investment amount of $4.5 trillion adhering to IFC's Environmental and Social Performance Standards, or principles inspired by them (IFC 2016). The assessment process of DFIs therefore serves as an important way of integrating sustainability considerations into infrastructure projects through finance and investment.

11.3.4 Application of sustainability standards in the Belt and Road Initiative

Before moving on to a discussion of problems and solutions related to sustainability standards, it would be beneficial to map the landscape of the application of sustainability standards to BRI projects. Unfortunately, the literature remains scant, calling for future research on this topic. Nonetheless, a preliminary study conducted by Qin, Peng, and Dong (2019) on the adoption of general engineering standards among the 569 foreign BRI projects involving Chinese enterprises reveals that 35% of these projects adopted Chinese standards for construction, 24% adopted local standards, and the rest adopted other standards including American, British, or French. Moreover, the adoption of engineering standards can be associated with investor types. For instance, China's foreign aid projects and those financed by Chinese policy banks and commercial banks tended to adopt Chinese standards, while the adoption rate of Chinese standards is relatively low for global public tenders from development banks such as World Bank Group (WBG) and Asian Development Bank (ADB), or projects funded locally (Qin et al. 2019). Although this study only discusses general engineering standards without specification of the sustainability components, it sheds light on two possible driving forces of standard adoption in the BRI context to be further examined: the Chinese construction standards, and the Chinese-backed financiers and investors.

Existing Chinese construction standards are far from adequate in assessing and addressing sustainability issues. Regarding the development of sustainability rating systems, China established its own national Evaluation Standard for Green Building in 2006 (IFCE, "Sustainable", n.d.), but its use is limited to building projects only, not for other types of infrastructure such as transportation. Local general construction standards that are applied to all types of infrastructure projects mainly cover specific issues of construction safety inspection, operation and maintenance of building-mounted photovoltaic systems, energy-efficient building design, or construction and demolition waste treatment (Chang et al. 2016). The other environmental or social aspects of sustainability have received much less attention.

An engagement report by the Embassy of Sweden in Beijing (2018) pointed out that China, as it is developing its own international standards under the BRI, mainly focuses on exporting and marketing economic development models, such as high-speed railway development. It remains unclear how these Chinese standards under development would adhere to international standards that govern sustainable infrastructure development with a growing emphasis on environmental and social aspects (Embassy of Sweden in Beijing 2018).

Another key driver worth examining is the Chinese-backed financiers and investors. Major participating institutions in BRI financing include Chinese financial institutions, such as the Silk Road Fund, policy and commercial banks, as well as international financial institutions including the DFIs. An analysis conducted by Quek and Huleatt (2018) shows that two Chinese policy banks, the China Development Bank and the Export-Import Bank of China, lag behind DFIs such as AIIB and IFC in the areas of setting published detailed standards for sustainability, ensuring transparency in information disclosure and grievance handling, despite being the largest funders of global carbon-intensive infrastructure.

Moreover, while the AIIB has been making substantial investments, the application of their sustainability standards remains a concern. Even though AIIB has established an E&S policy that shares a similar policy and compliance approach to social and environmental standards as its DFI peers (AIIB 2016), as the case study reveals, AIIB may be less stringent than other DFIs when it comes to the environmental and social impact analysis conducted and submitted by the investee.

Case study

In 2017, AIIB financed a 'Coal-to-Gas' Pipeline project in China where local gas companies would substitute pipelined natural gas for coal. The investee developed a comprehensive risk mitigation plan to address environmental impacts across the design, construction, and operation phases, and well-defined responsibilities of relevant entities.

In the same year, the WBG and AIIB also co-financed a hydro power plant extension project in Pakistan. The project aimed to develop the existing tunnel at the Tarbela Dam into a power generation source to provide an affordable and clean energy option in a relatively short period of time. As the investment is distributed as a form of additional financing for an investment project that was originally constructed in the 1970s, the investee only included socio-environmental risks at the construction and operation level (Pakistan Water and Power Development Authority 2016).

The hydro power plant project was required to comply with WBG's safeguard policies and requirements with the comprehensive submission of (i) a detailed stakeholder engagement plan, (ii) baseline socio-environmental condition of the project location, (iii) an E&S assessment, (iv) an alternative analysis, and (v) a risk mitigation plan (Pakistan Water and Power

Development Authority 2016). In contrast, the coal-to-gas project was approved without the documents and analysis related to (ii) and (iv) above to the AIIB (AIIB 2017; Beijing Gas Group 2017). Furthermore, the E&S assessment, alternative analysis, and risk mitigation plan of the hydro power plant project are not only led by a team of scholars with prior experience on impact assessment of infrastructure projects, but the methodology and analysis were much more detailed and robust than that of the AIIB. For example, the risk mitigation plan of the Pakistani project lays out specific policies and action plans against every single source of environmental impact, ranging from solid waste to a chemical spill, while the AIIB counterpart only shows a broad set of mitigation directions (Pakistan Water and Power Development Authority 2016).

Through this project comparison, it is interesting to see that investees may adopt the sustainability policy or framework of the largest financier based on the share of investment. This has an observable impact on the application of E&S standards, as different DFIs may have varying levels of stringency.

Despite the lack of a systematic review of standards in BRI projects, it seems sustainability standards are far from the norm that are fully embedded in BRI infrastructure development.

11.3.5 Limitations of standards – barriers for early-stage involvements of DFIs

As illustrated in Section 11.3.1, early consideration of sustainability is crucial for enhancing the sustainability outcomes of infrastructure development, and financial institutions, especially DFIs, are in a favourable position to drive early consideration of sustainability.

However, as we discuss here, there are two issues in the current landscape of sustainable infrastructure standards that could potentially be barriers for DFIs to get involved earlier, namely the heterogeneity of standards and the lack of coverage for upstream planning.

11.3.5.1 Heterogeneity of standards

The heterogeneity of existing sustainable infrastructure standards could make communication between project participants difficult and can undermine early consideration of sustainability in infrastructure development. A lack of coordination among actors inevitably results in the absence of a common standard that allows different parties, such as project owners, financiers, investors, and civil society to communicate effectively when identifying sustainable infrastructure projects or benchmarking sustainable performance on a comparable basis.

As discussed in Section 11.3.3, sustainability rating systems differ in both nature and purpose from the assessment tools of DFIs, with the former mainly catering for the need to inform project design for sustainability during the preparation and design stage, while the latter are mostly customized for orienting capital into sustainable infrastructure investments during the financing stage. Even within standards of the same category, such as sustainability rating systems, their requirements and criteria can vary significantly in addressing the same issue. Carbon emission, for instance, is an important issue that drives the development of low-carbon infrastructure, but has been assessed differently across standards, as shown in Table 11.1.

With reference to only carbon emission, the above comparisons demonstrate the heterogeneity of the standards. The rating systems categorize carbon emissions into different levels, and the DFIs' tools focus on disclosures and potential risk mitigations. As a result, each standard differs from the others, rewarding different mitigation practices and performances (Griffiths et al. 2019). These

Table 11.1 Assessment criteria for carbon emission in different standards

Standards		Sustainability Issue (carbon emission)
Category	Name	Assessment Criteria
Rating systems	CEEQUAL	- Questions about carbon-related management practices, e.g. lifecycle assessments for construction and materials - Points awarded for carbon reduction in project life cycle
	SuRe	- Different performance levels: (1) reduction of Scope 1&2 emissions; (2) zero net carbon emissions of Scope 1&2; (3) zero net carbon emissions including Scope 3
	Envision	- Points awarded for: (1) life-cycle carbon assessment done; (2) carbon reduction; (3) carbon neutral or carbon negative
	IS Rating	- Points awarded for: (1) life-cycle carbon assessment done; (2) demonstrate carbon reduction
DFIs' tools	IFC's Performance Standards	- Consider carbon reduction measures on resource efficiency and feasible, cost-effective design & operational alternatives - Conduct annual quantification of direct and indirect emissions for projects > 25,000 tons of carbon emissions
	AIIB's E&S Framework	- Due diligence, assessment, and management plan of project E&S risks and impacts in general, without specific requirement to quantify project carbon emissions

Source: Compiled by the authors from various sources (Bennon and Sharma 2019; IFC 2012; WWF and AECOM 2017; AIIB 2016)

varying criteria could be the result of different objectives and standard-setting methodologies, but it is usually unclear how criteria are selected and weighted in rating systems or DFIs' investment decisions, as there is a lack of transparency and objectivity in terms of methodologies (Bueno et al. 2015).

Some are worried that the heterogeneity of standards may hinder investors from fully understanding the sustainability performance of infrastructure projects in a consistent way (Kirchherr et al. 2018; African Development Bank et al. 2019), making their early consideration of sustainability more difficult. In a nutshell, the heterogeneity of sustainable infrastructure standards across the design and financing stages could undermine their original function of setting norms and criteria that enable communication between project participants, which is unfavourable for enabling financial institutions, especially the DFIs, to play a more significant role in driving early consideration of sustainability.

11.3.5.2 Lack of coverage for upstream planning

Existing sustainable infrastructure standards are mostly developed for the preparation and design stage and the financing stage, with minimal coverage for the upstream planning stage, where national, sub-national, and sector entities set up policies, laws, and regulations to facilitate the sustainable development of infrastructure. Serebrisky et al. (2018) at IDB Group conducted a comprehensive review of ten sustainability standards, among which four are rating systems used for general infrastructure development, three are sector-specific rating systems, and the rest are assessment tools of DFIs, including IDB, IFC, and WBG. The study benchmarked these standards against a proposed overarching framework with criteria falling under economic and financial, environmental, social, and institutional sustainability across three key infrastructure stages (upstream planning, preparation and design, and financing). The analysis indicated that most of the standards have minimal sustainability aspects in the upstream planning stage, despite its significance in influencing sustainability results (Serebrisky et al. 2018).

Upstream planning is important for maximizing the sustainability performance of infrastructure. When sustainability comes as an afterthought in later stages, systematic opportunities may already be missed and substantial modifications that delay projects and incur costs may be needed (Serebrisky et al. 2018). Especially when different pieces of infrastructure are considered as an interconnected system, such that the sustainability performance of a project could impact others, the role of upstream planning becomes more vital. For example, a sustainable energy system is crucial to enhancing the sustainability performance of infrastructure in other sectors such as transport, whereas the energy efficiency of the transport sector can influence the demand for energy and the impact of related infrastructure (UNEP 2019). According to the United Nations Environment Programme (UNEP) (2019, 25), upstream planning "can help to avoid oversupply of infrastructure, limit the footprint of impacts, avoid sensitive ecosystems, and increase resilience and safety of infrastructure through proper siting."

The lack of sustainability integration into early-stage planning processes could be explained by the concerns that incorporating such considerations would add complexity, delay decision-making, and increase costs (Kirchherr et al. 2018). It is therefore important to have a set of sustainability standards that simplifies and guides the integration of sustainability into upstream planning with demonstrated effectiveness in reducing risks and avoiding costs and delays later on. The lack of sustainability standards for upstream planning may make DFIs' engagement and technical support for infrastructure planning less effective, as it remains unclear how opportunities in the upstream planning stage could be most effectively captured without a common benchmark as a basis for evaluation and comparison.

11.4 An integrated approach to sustainable infrastructure standards

As we discussed above, a lot of DFIs tend to get into infrastructure projects at a later stage and may not be able to maximize sustainability impacts. In order to remove the barriers for them to get involved earlier, it is important to have sustainability standards integrated across all stages. The following section will suggest an integrated approach to sustainable infrastructure standards as a solution, discuss certain strategic directions for the integrated approach, and shed light on the role of Hong Kong in facilitating the integration process.

11.4.1 An integrated approach in need

To tackle the two issues raised in Section 11.3.5, an integrated approach to sustainable infrastructure standards is needed. Specifically, the integration of standards means firstly, to harmonize existing sustainability standards across stages of project development, and secondly, to consolidate upstream planning standards for further development.

A study led by Mercer and IDB (2017), based on findings from investor engagement, proposed the integration of existing sustainability infrastructure principles, frameworks, approaches, and best practices to address the lack of common definitions that confuses both companies and investors. This is echoed by the latest global development and advocacy efforts, as the UNEP launched the Sustainable Infrastructure Partnership in 2018. One of its core goals is to "develop streamlined normative and technical guidance to scale up the application and the integration of existing tools and approaches in support of different SDG priorities" (UNEP n.d.).

As part of its pledge to greening the BRI, China has proposed to integrate ecological and environmental protection standards into all stages and aspects of infrastructure development (Belt and Road Portal 2017a). This could be an opportunity for China to establish an integrated standard for sustainable infrastructure and promote it through the BRI to support sustainable infrastructure development in BRI countries. In fact, the United Nations Development Program and China Development Bank (2019) launched a joint report on the harmonization of investment and financing standards for sustainable development in the BRI. A core set of principles was developed based on an analysis of global best practice, including those of multilateral and national development banks, to provide a basis for harmonizing the standards (UNDP and CDB 2019).

The report recognizes the importance of early consideration of sustainability and, specifically, Principle 7 supports the establishment of risk management frameworks from an early stage of the project (UNDP and CDB 2019, 186). Unfortunately, only investment and financing standards are addressed, without any explicit consideration of the role of sustainability rating systems like CEEQUAL and SuRe, and other standards for upstream planning. This may undermine the effectiveness of the effort to enable financial institutions to drive early-stage consideration of sustainability in BRI projects. It is important for China to uphold the integration of sustainable infrastructure standards, particularly consideration of the role of standards in the earlier stages of infrastructure development.

11.4.2 Strategic directions for an integrated approach

To enable financial institutions to drive early consideration of sustainability, an integration of standards that harmonizes existing standards across design and financing stages of project development and consolidates standards for upstream planning is critical. Built on the above analysis, some strategic directions for the integration process will be outlined to tackle the two issues of sustainable infrastructure standards brought out in Section 11.3.4.

11.4.2.1 Harmonization of standards across stages of project development

To address the first issue of heterogeneity of existing standards, the fundamental discrepancy between engineering (represented by sustainability rating systems) and financing standards (represented by DFIs' assessment tools) needs to be reconciled so that the adoption of a common set of sustainability standards becomes more practical across stakeholder groups. In this integration process, it is a necessary step to conduct a comprehensive mapping exercise on these standards and identify international best practice that help break down silos. For instance, the SuRe Standard, whose comprehensiveness has been well recognized, is the only rating system attempting to categorize its sixty-one technical criteria into environmental, social, and governance (ESG) aspects, so that it can better be communicated with investors in line with mainstream ESG investing practice. However, SuRe so far has limited impact on bridging the fundamental gaps between standards meant for use in the design and financing stages, since quite a number of its technical indicators or details do not directly inform financing decisions in a way which investors might expect.

A harmonized standard should integrate international best practice so that effectively different standards are used to fill the gaps of each other. For instance, ADB adopts a hands-on approach to managing climate risk by participating in the project design stage to identify and select the most viable adaptation options, but the climate risk management framework is rather generic, lacking a more specified approach to climate resilience. On the other hand, the SuRe and Envision standards have set up similar, but much more detailed, criteria and processes requiring projects to assess climate risks and vulnerabilities and identify adaptation options (GIB Foundation 2018; ISI 2018), from which ADB can take reference. A harmonized standard based on the integration of international best practice could be used, on the one hand, by DFIs such as ADB to enhance the effectiveness of its early involvement, and on the other hand, by project owners to embed sustainability into their infrastructure projects with confidence that the projects will be assessed against the same standard by the DFIs.

One way to integrate and build standards that can be used across the preparation and design stage, and the financing stage, would be to develop criteria that are suitable for both sustainability evaluation and valuation purposes, so that the project-level practices and performances can be better integrated and aligned with financial analysis. A study conducted by WWF Switzerland and Cadmus Group, through investor interviews and workshops, echoes such needs for standardization, while introducing an example of alignment between Envision, the sustainability rating system, and AutoCASE, a valuation software tool for triple bottom line cost–benefit analysis tailored to buildings and infrastructure (Sloan et al. 2019). The framework of AutoCASE is modelled on that of Envision, but with the added and complementary ability to analyse projects from a value-based and risk-adjusted angle based on its calculation of "the value (net social benefit) accounting for risks" (Parker 2015). The innovative approach offers a channel to integrate and align standards for engineering and financing purposes so that performance metrics can be used to build a case for investment decisions in a consistent way and support inter-stage cooperation between different participants.

11.4.2.2 Consolidating upstream planning standards

To address the second issue, that sustainability in the upstream planning stage tends to be disregarded in existing standards, firstly, international best practice in this area should be consolidated. Although the coverage for upstream planning aspects by existing sustainability standards is limited, some provide important sector-specific references. Among the standards reviewed in the IDB study, the SE4All Regulatory Indicators for Sustainable Energy Tool (RISE) is the only one designed for direct application to upstream planning. The Infrastructure Voluntary Evaluation Sustainability Tool (INVEST), the Hydropower Sustainability Assessment Protocol (HSAP), and the Sustainable Transport Appraisal Rating (STAR) methodology also have certain elements to cover the upstream planning stage (Serebrisky et al. 2018). For example, INVEST contains two modules for system planning where criteria are set to guide planning activities such as goal setting, stakeholder engagement, system evaluation, monitoring, and reporting (FHA n.d.). Building on these standards and other references, the IDB has also developed a comprehensive framework which indicates gaps in existing standards and complementarities needed. The integration of international best practice from these existing standards would provide a basis for furthering development in standards for the upstream planning stage.

The integration of upstream planning standards should develop a holistic approach to sustainable infrastructure development. As advocated by the UNEP, an integrated approach to sustainable infrastructure is much needed to take into account the interconnectivities and interdependencies between infrastructure projects (UNEP 2019). This consideration should be made in the upstream planning stage of infrastructure development at the system level, so sustainability standards for upstream planning would be crucial for the success of an integrated approach to sustainable infrastructure. Therefore, in the integration process of existing upstream planning standards, it would be important to consider the interrelation between different infrastructure sectors in affecting their sustainability performance and to construct an approach to consider infrastructure development holistically. This may involve the development of new quantitative modelling tools for upstream planning practices (UNEP 2019), but the sustainability opportunities to be captured are promising.

In the BRI context, where infrastructure projects could be transboundary, an integrated standard for upstream planning would be especially important to enable communication and cooperation between different national and subnational agencies across national boundaries. In fact, the *Guidance on Promoting Green Belt and Road* published by the Chinese government represents an attempt to plan the development of the green BRI, with a plan to establish a system facilitating environmental cooperation between BRI countries. The integration process of upstream planning standards should produce a set of standards that facilitate transnational cooperation and coordination in planning. For example, in the processes of stakeholder consultation and public participation, which are important for upstream planning (UNEP 2019), the standard should define best practice in considering and consolidating concerns from across populations and countries in the BRI.

11.4.3 The role of Hong Kong

The above analysis highlights two key issues that might hinder financiers and investors from driving early-stage consideration of sustainability during BRI infrastructure development and suggests an integrated approach to sustainable infrastructure standards with specific strategic directions. Hong Kong, as an international financial centre and the premier offshore renminbi business hub, could play an important role in providing, structuring, and blending financing for sustainable infrastructure projects along the Belt and Road. Hong Kong not only has ready access to global capital markets, but also offers exemplary professional services, given its experience in infrastructure development and other core competencies in its legal and economic systems that enable free flow of capital, goods, information, and people (Law and Fung 2018; Pao 2019; InvestHK 2018). Therefore, Hong Kong has an advantageous position in attracting private capital and enabling public–private partnerships to realize the sustainable vision of BRI. In a time of the worsening climate crisis and increasing global awareness of sustainable development, the Hong Kong government has already been strengthening recent years' efforts in promoting green finance, poised to speed up the city's ambition to become an international centre of green finance. At the forefront of sustainable infrastructure development along the Belt and Road, Hong Kong could also take the lead in enabling and strengthening the early involvement of financers and investors to capture optimal opportunities for sustainability results and facilitating the integration of sustainable infrastructure standards based on international best practices.

For instance, the Centre for Green Finance (CGF) has been established under the Infrastructure Financing Facilitation Office of the Hong Kong Monetary Authority in order to provide technical support for the industry. The CGF could consider bringing together key cross-sectoral actors through the creation of a collaborative platform to facilitate an integrated approach to sustainable infrastructure standards, as suggested in this chapter, and promote its use across the life cycle of infrastructure projects among BRI participating financiers and investors. The CGF can also provide capacity-building training for BRI participants ranging from public sponsors, financiers, investors, project managers, designers to engineers. Adequate technical and talent support would be crucial to the actual implementation of the integrated standards for BRI infrastructure projects.

11.5 Conclusion

Sustainable infrastructure development has emerged as an immediate imperative for both the world and the BRI. The sheer scale, widespread impact, and technological lock-in of infrastructure development is urging for the right decisions to develop ports, highways, airports, roads, and dams in a sustainable manner. China, under President Xi Jinping's leadership, has placed sustainable development at the core of BRI's policy vision, where early consideration of sustainability in infrastructure development would be crucial for its success.

As this chapter has argued, sustainability standards play a key role in operationalizing the concept of sustainable infrastructure into practice, and specifically, enabling financial institutions to drive effective consideration of sustainability in the early stages of infrastructure development. Yet, the heterogeneity of sustainability standards makes communication difficult and undermines early consideration. Furthermore, existing sustainability standards have limited coverage for the upstream planning stage of infrastructure development. An integrated approach to sustainability standards is missing, yet is most needed to address these two issues. China is in a position to integrate sustainable infrastructure standards that are applicable to the BRI context as a common language. It is recommended that Hong Kong should proactively facilitate the integration process and provide various forms of support.

The limitations of this chapter are in three key areas. Firstly, this chapter is not intended to be a systematic review on all the tools available, which include standards, regulation, legislation, tax, and subsidies. We have placed standards at the centre of our discussion, but the role of other tools in promoting sustainable infrastructure is also noteworthy. Secondly, we have focused the discussion on two major types of sustainable infrastructure standards, which are the sustainability rating systems and DFIs' assessment tools. Although we believe that these standards are sufficient to support our discussion on the two issues that might undermine the effectiveness of sustainability standards, it would greatly strengthen our argument and might add new issues if an exhaustive review of the universe of standards were conducted. Last but not least, the chapter briefly discussed the potential role of Hong Kong in facilitating the integration of sustainable infrastructure standards for the BRI, but a more in-depth analysis would be needed in order to provide specific and robust policy recommendations for enhancing the role of Hong Kong in greening the BRI.

This chapter also indicates the following three areas that can be further examined in future research on sustainable infrastructure development along the Belt and Road. First, there has been a lack of systematic and comprehensive review on the sustainability performance, or the use, of sustainability standards in BRI projects, although the lack of transparency would be a major obstacle to conducting such research. In addition, empirical evidence remains sparse when it comes to assessing the impacts of adopting sustainability standards on the outcomes of infrastructure projects. Finally, the operational nuance of integrating sustainable infrastructure standards for the BRI goes beyond the ambition of this chapter, but is crucial for realizing the vision of a sustainable BRI in a practical manner.

Note

1 The six corridors refer to: (1) the New Eurasian Land Bridge; (2) the China-Central Asia-West Asia Corridor; (3) the China-Pakistan Corridor; (4) the Bangladesh-China-Myanmar Corridor; (5) the China-Mongolia-Russia Corridor; (6) the China-Indochina Peninsula Corridor.

References

Advisory Council of the Belt and Road Forum for International Cooperation (BRF Advisory Council) 2019, 'Belt and Road: For a better world – Report on the findings and recommendations from the first meeting of the advisory council of the Belt and Road Forum for International Cooperation'. Available from: www.beltandroadforum.org/NMediaFile/2019/0424/YIDAI201904240815000232827728534.pdf. [2 December 2019].

African Development Bank, Asian Development Bank, Asian Infrastructure Investment Bank, Inter-American Development Bank, International Development Finance Club, Islamic Development Bank, European Investment Bank, European Bank for Reconstruction and Development, and World Bank Group 2019, 'A framework for climate resilience metrics in financing operations – joint MDB IDFC technical paper'. Available from: www.ebrd.com/documents/climate-finance/a-framework-for-climate-resilience-metrics-in-financing-operations.pdf. [2 December 2019].

Asian Infrastructure Investment Bank (AIIB) 2016, 'Environmental and social framework'. Available from: www.aiib.org/en/policies-strategies/_download/environment-framework/Final-ESF-Mar-14-2019-Final-P.pdf. [2 December 2019].

Asian Infrastructure Investment Bank (AIIB) 2017, 'Project summary information (PSI)'. Available from: www.aiib.org/en/projects/approved/2017/_download/beijing / beijing-air-quality.pdf. [2 December 2019].

Alkon, M, He, X, Paris, AR, Liao, W, Hedson, T, Wanders, N, & Wang, Y 2019, 'Water security implications of coal-fired power plants financed through China's Belt and Road Initiative', *Energy Policy*, vol. 132, issue September, pp. 1101–1109.

Beijing Gas Group 2017, '北京市"十三五"时期农村"煤改气"工程环境及社会管理计划 [Environmental and social management plan for "coal to gas" project in rural areas during the "Thirteenth Five-Year Plan" period in Beijing]'. Available from: www.bjgas.com/Thematic.ashx?newsid=6226. [2 December 2019].

Belt and Road Portal 2017a, 'Guidance on promoting green Belt and Road'. Available from: https://eng.yidaiyilu.gov.cn/zchj/qwfb/12479.htm. [2 December 2019].

Belt and Road Portal 2017b, 'The Belt and Road ecological and environmental cooperation plan'. Available from: https://eng.yidaiyilu.gov.cn/zchj/qwfb/13392.htm. [2 December 2019].

Bennon, M & Sharma, R 2019, 'State of the practice: Sustainability standards for infrastructure investors'. *Guggenheim Partners, Stanford Global Projects Center, and World Wildlife Fund*. Available from: www.guggenheiminvestments.com/GuggenheimInvestments/media/PDF/WWF-Infrastructure-Full-Report-2018.pdf. [2 December 2019].

Bhattacharya, A, Meltzer, JP, Oppenheim, J, Qureshi, Z & Stern, N 2016, 'Delivering on sustainable infrastructure for better development and better climate', *Global Economy and Development, The Brookings Institution*. Available from: www.brookings.edu/wp-content/uploads/2016/12/global_122316_delivering-on-sustainable-infrastructure.pdf. [2 December 2019].

Brunsson, N, Rasche, A & Seidl, D 2012, 'The dynamics of standardization: Three perspectives on standards in organization studies', *Organization Studies*, vol. 33, no. 5–6, pp. 613–632.

Bueno, PC, Vassallo, JM & Cheung, K 2015, 'Sustainability assessment of transport infrastructure projects: A review of existing tools and methods'. *Transport Reviews*, vol. 35, no. 5, pp. 622–649.

Chang, R, Soebarto, V, Zhao, Z & Zillante, G 2016 'Facilitating the transition to sustainable construction: China's policies', *Journal of Cleaner Production*, vol. 131, issue September, pp. 534–544.

China International Contractors Association (CICA) 2017, 'Guidelines of sustainable infrastructure for Chinese international contractors'. Available from: www.chinca.org/CICA/info/17113010581611. [2 December 2019].

Egler, H, & Frazao, R 2016, 'Sustainable infrastructure and finance: How to contribute to a sustainable future'. *The UNEP Inquiry/ Global Infrastructure Basel Foundation*. Available from: http://unepinquiry.org/wp-content/uploads/2016/06/Sustainable_Infrastructure_and_Finance.pdf. [2 December 2019].

Embassy of Sweden in Beijing 2018, 'The Belt and Road Initiative from a sustainability perspective'. Available from: www.swedenabroad.se/globalassets/ambassader/kina-peking/documents/csr-new/the-implication-of-the-bri-from-a-sustainability-perspective_20180930_final.pdf. [2 December 2019].

Federal Highway Administration – U.S. Department of Transportation (FHA) n.d., 'Criteria: Explore all criteria within the four modules of INVEST'. Available from: www.sustainablehighways.org/664/browse.html. [2 December 2019].

Global Infrastructure Basel Foundation (GIB Foundation) 2018, 'SuRe® – The standard for sustainable and resilient infrastructure'. Available from: www.gib-foundation.org/content/uploads/2018/07/ST01_Normative_Standard_v1.1_clean.pdf. [2 December 2019].

Green Finance Committee of the China Society for Finance and Banking (GFC) & City of London's Green Finance Initiative (GFI) 2018, 'Green investment principles for the Belt and Road', 1 December. Available from: www.greenfinanceinstitute.co.uk/uk-china/green-finance/green-belt-and-road/text-of-the-gip/. [2 December 2019].

Griffiths, K, Boyle, C & Henning, T 2019, 'Comparison of project performance assessed by infrastructure sustainability rating tools', *Proceedings of the Institution of Civil Engineers – Engineering Sustainability*, vol. 172, no. 5, pp. 232–240.

Griffiths, K, Boyle, C & Henning, T 2015, 'Infrastructure sustainability rating tools – How they have developed and what we might expect to see in the future'. Available from: www.researchgate.net/profile/Kerry_Griffiths/publication/299366012_Infrastructure_sustainability_rating_tools_-_how_they_have_developed_and_what_we_might_expect_to_see_in_the_future/links/56fc57f008ae1b40b8064702.pdf. [2 December 2019].

Hafeez, M, Chunhui, Y, Strohmaier, D, Ahmed, M & Jie, L 2018, 'Does finance affect environmental degradation: Evidence from One Belt and One Road Initiative region?', *Environmental Science and Pollution Research*, vol. 25, no. 10, pp. 9579–9592.

Hastings, C 2019, 'Sustainable infrastructure: Protecting the planet of tomorrow requires the right decisions to be made today', *SDG Knowledge Hub*, Blog, 16 May 2019. Available from: https://sdg.iisd.org/commentary/guest-articles/sustainable-infrastructure-protecting-the-planet-of-tomorrow-requires-the-right-decisions-to-be-made-today/. [2 December 2019].

Hughes, AC 2019, 'Understanding and minimizing environmental impacts of the Belt and Road Initiative', *Conservation Biology*, vol. 33, no. 4, pp. 883–894.

International Finance Corporation (IFC) 2012, 'Performance standard 3: Resource efficiency and pollution prevention'. Available from: www.ifc.org/wps/wcm/connect/1f9c590b-a09f-42e9-968c-c050d0f00fc9/PS3_English_2012.pdf?MOD=AJPERES&CVID=jiVQIwF. [2 December 2019].

International Finance Corporation (IFC) 2016, 'Sustainability is opportunity: How IFC has changed finance', November. Available from: www.ifc.org/wps/wcm/connect/news_ext_content/ifc_external_corporate_site/news+and+events/news/impact-stories/how-ifc-has-changed-finance. [2 December 2019].

International Federation of Consulting Engineers (IFCE) n.d., 'Rating & certification tool: China green building evaluation label'. Available from: http://fidic.org/sites/default/files/R%26C%20China%20Green%20Building%20-%20final.pdf. [2 December 2019].

International Federation of Consulting Engineers (IFCE) n.d., 'Sustainable infrastructure: rating and certification tools'. Available from: http://fidic.org/node/5943. [2 December 2019].

Invest Hong Kong (InvestHK) 2018, 'Hong Kong: A key link for the belt and road'. Available from: www.investhk.gov.hk/sites/default/files/2019.01_BnR%20Booklet_EN.pdf. [2 December 2019].

Intergovernmental Panel on Climate Change (IPCC) 2018, 'Global warming of 1.5°C. An IPCC special report on the impacts of global warming of 1.5°C above pre-industrial levels and related global greenhouse gas emission pathways, in the context of strengthening the global response to the threat of climate change, sustainable development, and efforts to eradicate poverty'. Available from: www.ipcc.ch/site/assets/uploads/sites/2/2019/06/SR15_Full_Report_Low_Res.pdf. [4 December 2019].

Institute for Sustainable Infrastructure (ISI) 2018, 'Envision: Sustainable infrastructure framework (version 3)', *Institute for Sustainable Infrastructure*. Available from: https://sustainableinfrastructure.org/wp-content/uploads/EnvisionV3.9.7.2018.pdf.   [2 December 2019].

Kirchherr, JW, Repp, L, Santen, R, Verweij, PA, Hu, X & Hall, J 2018, 'Greening the Belt and Road Initiative: WWF's recommendations for the finance sector', *World Wildlife Fund* (WWF). Available from: https://dspace.library.uu.nl/handle/1874/362894. [2 December 2019].

Law, C, & Fung, K 2018, 'Hong Kong under "Belt and Road Initiative": Challenges in infrastructure investment in Asia', *The Twenty-First Century Review*, no. 168, issue August, pp. 27–42.

Liu, X, Blackburn, TM, Song, T, Li, X, Huang, C & Li, Y 2019, 'Risks of biological invasion on the Belt and Road'. *Current Biology*, no. 29, vol. 3, pp. 499–505.

Ma, J & Zadek, S 2019, 'Decarbonizing the Belt and Road: A green finance roadmap'. Available from: www.climateworks.org/wp-content/uploads/2019/09/Decarbonizing-the-Belt-and-Road_report_final_lo-res.pdf. [2 December 2019].

Mercer & InterAmerican Development Bank (IDB) 2017, 'Crossing the bridge to sustainable infrastructure investing: Exploring ways to make it across'. Available from: https://publications.iadb.org/en/crossing-bridge-sustainable-infrastructure-investing- exploring-ways-make-it-across. [2 December 2019].

Mirabile, M, Marchal, V & Baron, R 2017, 'Technical note on estimates of infrastructure investment needs: Background note to the report, investing in climate, investing in growth', *Organisation for Economic Co-operation and Development* (OECD). Available from: www.oecd.org/env/cc/g20-climate/Technical-note-estimates-of-infrastructure-investment-needs.pdf. [2 December 2019].

National Development and Reform Commission of P R China (NDRC) 2015, 'Vision and actions on jointly building the silk road economic belt and 21st Century maritime silk road'. Available from: http://2017.beltandroadforum.org/english/n100/2017/0410/c22-45.html. [2 December 2019].

Organization for Economic Co-operation and Development (OECD), The World Bank, & United Nations Environment Programme (UNEP) 2018, 'Financing climate futures: rethinking infrastructure, *Organisation for Economic Cooperation and Development* (OECD).   Available   from: https://doi.org/10.1787/9789264308114-en.   [2 December 2019].

Pakistan Water and Power Development Authority 2016, 'Environmental and social assessment of Tarbela 5th extension hydropower project'. Available from: http://documents.worldbank.org/curated/en/787431468290411161/pdf/SFG1900-V2-EA-P157372-Box394869B-PUBLIC-Disclosed-3-3-2016.pdf. [2 December 2019]

Pao, J 2019, 'Leaders tout HK advantages at BRI summit', *Asia Times*, 12 September 2019. Available from: www.asiatimes.com/2019/09/article/leaders-tout-hk-advantages-at-bri-summit/. [2 December 2019].

Parker, J 2015, 'AutoCASE and envision', *Autocase*, Blog, 16 February 2015. Available from: https://autocase.com/autocaseenvision/. [2 December 2019].

Patil, NA, Tharun, D & Laishram, B 2016, 'Infrastructure development through PPPs in India: Criteria for sustainability assessment', *Journal of Environmental Planning and Management*, vol. 59, no. 4, pp. 708–729.

Qin, Y, Peng, F & Dong, J 2019, '我国工程建设标准在"一带一路"沿线国家的应用 [Application of Chinese engineering construction standards in countries along "The Belt and Road"]', 建筑经济 *[Construction Economy]*, vol. 2019, no. 4, pp. 11–16.

Quek, C & Huleatt, L 2018, 'Green evolution: Can China's new multilateral banks make Belt and Road more sustainable?' *Panda Paw Dragon Claw*, Blog, 16 May 2018. Available from: https://pandapawdragonclaw.blog/2018/05/16/green-evolution/. [2 December 2019].

Rauf, A, Liu, X, Amin, W, Ozturk, I, Rehman, O & Sarwar, S 2018 'Energy and ecological sustainability: Challenges and panoramas in Belt and Road Initiative countries', *Sustainability*, vol. 10, no. 8, pp. 2743–2764.

Saha, D & Modi, A 2017, 'Low-carbon infrastructure private participation in infrastructure (PPI): 2002 to H1 2017 (English)', *World Bank Group*. Available from: http://documents.worldbank.org/curated/en/197351524565842344/Low-carbon-infrastructure-private-participation-in-infrastructure-PPI-2002-to-H1-2017. [2 December 2019].

Serebrisky, T, Watkins, G, Ramirez, MC, Meller, H, Melo, R & Georgoulias, A 2018, 'IDBG framework for planning, preparing, and financing sustainable infrastructure projects: IDB sustainable infrastructure platform', *Inter-American Development Bank*. Available from: https://doi.org/10.18235/0001037.

Sloan, W, Wright, K, Crowe, J, Daudon, J & Hanson, L 2019, 'Valuing sustainability in infrastructure investments: Market status, barriers and opportunities – A landscape analysis', *World Wildlife Fund* (WWF) *Switzerland* & *The Cadmus Group*. Available from: https://d2ouvy59p0dg6k.cloudfront.net/downloads/wwf_report_3_11_19_final.pdf. [2 December 2019].

Teo, HCh, Lechner, AM, Walton, GW, Chan, FKS, Cheshmehzangi, A, Tan-Mullins, M, Chan, HK, Sternberg, T & Campos-Arceiz, A 2019, 'Environmental impacts of infrastructure development under the Belt and Road Initiative', *Environments*, vol. 6, no. 6, pp. 72–84.

Thacker, S, Adshead, D, Morgan, G, Crosskey, S, Bajpai, A, Ceppi, P, Hall, JW, & O'Regan, N 2018, 'Infrastructure: Underpinning sustainable development', United Nations Office for Project Services (UNOPS). Available from: https://content.unops.org/publications/Infrastructure_underpining_sustainable_development_EN.pdf?mtime=20181109113757. [2 December 2019].

United Nations Development Programme (UNDP) & China Development Bank (CDB) 2019, 'Harmonizing investment and financing standards towards sustainable development along the Belt and Road'. Available from: www.cn.undp.org/content/china/en/home/library/south-south-cooperation/harmonizing-investment-and-financing-standards-.html. [2 December 2019].

United Nations Environment Programme (UNEP) n.d., 'Sustainable infrastructure partnership (SIP)', *Economic and Fiscal Policy*. Available from: www.unenvironment.org/explore-topics/green-economy/what-we-do/economic-and-fiscal-policy/sustainable-infrastructure. [2 December 2019].

United Nations Environment Programme (UNEP) 2019, 'Integrated approaches to sustainable infrastructure'. Available from: www.greengrowthknowledge.org/sites/default/files/downloads/resource/Integrated_Approaches_To_Sustainable_Infrastructure_UNEP.pdf. [2 December 2019]

World Bank 2019, 'Belt and Road economics: Opportunities and risks of transport corridors'. Available from: https://doi.org/10.1596/978-1-4648-1392-4.

World Wildlife Fund (WWF) & AECOM 2017, 'Review of screening tools to assess sustainability and climate resilience of infrastructure development'. Available from: www.transparency-partnership.net/system/files/document/WWF_AECOM_2017_Review%20of%20screening%20tools%20to%20assess%20sustainability%20of%20CR%20and%20infrastr%20developm.pdf. [2 December 2019].

Wright, H, Dimsdale, T, Healy, C, Orozco, D, Mabey, N & Williamson, S 2018, 'Sustainable infrastructure and the multilateral development banks: Changing the narrative', *E3G*. Available from: www.e3g.org/docs/E3G-Briefing-Sustainable-Infrastructure.pdf. [2 December 2019].

Yang, F & Yang, M 2019, 'Greening the One Belt and One Road Initiative', *Mitigation and Adaptation Strategies for Global Change*, vol. 24, no. 5, pp. 735–748.

Zhang, X, Zhang, H, Zhao, C & Yuan, J 2019, 'Carbon emission intensity of electricity generation in Belt and Road Initiative countries: A benchmarking analysis', *Environmental Science and Pollution Research*, vol. 26, no. 15, pp. 15057–1568.

Zhang, Y, Jin, Y & Shen, B 2018, 'Measuring the energy saving and CO2 emissions reduction potential under China's Belt and Road Initiative', *Computational Economics*, August, https://doi.org/10.1007/s10614-018-9839-0.

Index

Printed in the United States
By Bookmasters